"David Capes shows how the Old Testan[t] scaffolding for the gospel of Matthew. Indeed, [...] Sermon on the Mount, all the way through to the Great Commission, Capes carefully and convincingly shows how the entire story is suffused with the fulfilment of Scripture. An informative read and a necessary tool for teachers and preachers of Matthew's gospel."

—Michael F. Bird,
Academic Dean,
Ridley College, Melbourne, Australia

"As one more incredibly beneficial contribution to a wonderful series, *Matthew Through Old Testament Eyes* offers readers a thorough, yet not dense, treatment of the first gospel. It lives up to its promise. Even in passages I have studied for years, Capes's approach presented fresh perspectives I have never considered before. With this intentional focus on the Old Testament, Capes is able to trace out many of the threads from Israel's story in each section, uncovering an intricate and beautiful cloth revealing the face of the Messiah."

—Amy Peeler,
Associate Professor of New Testament,
Wheaton College

"*Matthew Through Old Testament Eyes* is a gem for all Bible readers. I wish I had this book when I was a local church pastor who preached regularly. David Capes not only provides keen insights into Matthew's message, but also offers guidance for all interpreters—preachers, teachers, scholars, and other students of Scripture—to enhance their own exegetical work."

—Dennis R. Edwards, Seminary Dean,
North Park Theological Seminary

"David Capes applies his extensive knowledge of the Old Testament and Second Temple Judaism to reveal the world of Jesus in Matthew's gospel. *Matthew Through Old Testament Eyes* adds layers of historical and theological context to familiar verses and sheds light on puzzling passages. Capes's long-standing friendships with rabbis is evident in his careful descriptions of Jesus' interlocutors. Everyone preaching or teaching on Matthew should have this commentary ready on hand."

—Lynn Cohick,
Distinguished Professor of New Testament and Director,
Houston Theological Seminary

Through Old Testament Eyes
New Testament Commentaries
Series Editors: Andrew T. Le Peau and Seth M. Ehorn

MATTHEW

THROUGH OLD TESTAMENT EYES

David B. Capes

ANDREW T. LE PEAU AND SETH M. EHORN
SERIES EDITORS

For Becky and Mark Lanier

CONTENTS

SERIES PREFACE

The New Testament writers were Old Testament people. Their minds were populated with Old Testament stories and concepts. Their imaginative world was furnished with Old Testament images, motifs, metaphors, symbols, and literary patterns. When Jesus came and turned much of their conventional wisdom on its head, they largely had Old Testament tools to understand what was going on in order to explain Jesus to others and to themselves. So that's what they used.

For many Christians the Old Testament has, unfortunately, become a closed book. It seems long, mysterious, and boring with a confusing history full of many strange, unpronounceable names. And then there are those sometimes bizarre prophecies populated with strange creatures. Yet my consistent experience in teaching the New Testament is that when I turn the attention of students to relevant Old Testament passages, the proverbial light bulbs go on. The room is filled with "aha"s. Formerly obscure New Testament passages suddenly make new sense in light of the Old. Indeed the whole of each book of the New Testament takes on fuller, richer dimensions not seen before.

The purpose of the Through Old Testament Eyes commentaries is to give preachers, teachers, and other readers this same experience. This series opens the New Testament in greater depth to anyone who wants to see fresh ways that Scripture interconnects with Scripture.

Scholars have long known that the Old Testament influenced the New Testament (an idea known as intertextuality). In fact, more than a millennia and a half ago Augustine famously proposed that we understand the relationship of the two testaments in this way: "The new is in the old concealed; the old is in the new revealed." Yet no commentary series is as devoted as this one is to seeing the richness of Old Testament allusions, references, echoes, and background to illuminate both puzzling passages and explain others in fresh ways.

Practices like baptism, meals, fishing, and fasting; concepts like rescue, faith, sin, and glory; and terms like *wilderness*, *Sabbath*, and *Lord* are just a few of the dozens of words in each New Testament book and letter with deep Old Testament resonances. Sometimes a narrative arc or an argument is also shaped by the Old Testament. An appreciation of this background enriches our understanding and helps us appropriately apply each passage.

In these commentaries you will find four repeating features which will enrich your encounter with the Scripture.

Running Commentary

Verse-by-verse or paragraph-by-paragraph commentary will include Old Testament background as well as other key information to give readers an understanding of the text as a whole and to answer questions as they naturally arise.

Through Old Testament Eyes

Periodic summaries offer overviews of chapters or sections. These occasional pauses give the opportunity to step back from the detail to see the bigger picture of how Old Testament themes and motifs are being used by the New Testament authors.

What the Structure Means

New Testament authors often get their points across through the way they structure their material. The very organization of their writing conveys significant meaning in and of itself. How the events and teachings are linked makes a difference that, while not explicit, is an important part of the message. Again it is important to not take verses out of context as if they were timeless truths standing apart from their original settings, which affect how we understand them.

The authors of the New Testament also deliberately use, for example, repetition, contrast, hyperbole, metaphor, story, and other techniques so they can have the maximum impact on their readers. "What the Structure Means" will highlight these every so often and help us keep track of the overall flow of each book and letter so that the Old Testament background can be seen in its proper context.

Going Deeper

New Testament writers did not want merely to convey information. They wrote with the needs of the early church in mind. What should their attitude be toward family members who weren't Christians? How should they respond to challenges from Jewish or Roman authorities?

What about internal disputes within the church? These and many other issues were on their minds, and the New Testament addresses them and many more.

Through Old Testament Eyes commentaries will not only leave readers with an enriched understanding of the text but with enriched lives. In "Going Deeper" the authors will unpack the practical implications of each book and letter for Christians and churches, especially drawing from the Old Testament dimensions uncovered in the text.

As much as this series champions the importance of understanding the New Testament's use of the Old, two key points need to be mentioned. First, the Old Testament is not merely a tool for understanding the New. The Old Testament is important and valuable in its own right. It was the Bible of Jesus and the first Christians. They guided their lives by it. The Old Testament needs to be and deserves to be understood on its own terms, apart from the lens it provides for seeing the New Testament clearly. All the commentary authors in this series begin just here as they approach the text. In fact, our hope is that these commentaries will be a window into the Old Testament that will motivate many readers to look more deeply into what some have called the First Testament.

Second, the Old Testament is not the only interpretive lens we need to understand the New. Roman and Greek culture and history, for example, had a very significant influence on the New Testament era. So did the Second Temple period (from the start of rebuilding the temple about 537 BC to the destruction of the temple by Rome in AD 70). Where essential, these commentaries will reference such background material. But the emphasis will be on providing in-depth Old Testament background that readers too often overlook.

While these commentaries are grounded in solid scholarship, they are not intended primarily for an academic audience. For this reason many topics, approaches, and debates found in technical commentaries are absent. This series is for those who want to teach or preach, as well as any serious reader committed to understand Scripture.

The past is always present. The question is: Are we aware of how it affects us or not? The Old Testament was present with the New Testament writers. They knew that and treasured it. We can too.

—Andrew T. Le Peau and Seth M. Ehorn
Series Editors

INTRODUCTION

I work at an amazing place called the Lanier Theological Library in Houston, Texas. I describe it as a piece of Oxford that broke off and fell in northwest Houston.

On our campus we have a building called "The Stone Chapel." It was built according to the footprint of the ruins of a Byzantine chapel (erected about AD 500) documented by archaeologist and adventurer Gertrude Bell.

At the heart of the building is a dome that depicts a heavenly scene of Christ seated on his throne. The crucified one who now rules in power has hands and feet that still bear the marks of his rejection and execution. The chapel is filled with Byzantine symbols. In the dome there are four windows made of alabaster.

These four windows face "the four corners" of the earth—north, east, south, and west. Each window is flanked by paintings of the four gospel writers: Matthew, Mark, Luke, and John. As I look up from beneath the dome, the north-facing window has Matthew to its right and John to its left. These windows and the artwork around them remind us that the four gospel writers approach the life of Jesus—the crucified, now enthroned One—in different ways, from different perspectives. Just as the four corners of the earth are discrete "places," so the gospel writers themselves are writing their stories from different "places." Yet as this book series shows, the place of each writer is flooded by light, a light that shines through the Old Testament Scriptures. The task before us is to understand how the writer of the first canonical gospel, Matthew, saw that light illuminating the life of the most extraordinary man who had ever and will ever live.

The Church's Gospel

It is safe to say that Matthew was a favorite gospel of the second-century followers of Jesus. It is one of three New Testament gospels referred to by scholars as "synoptic" because they tell many of the same stories, in a similar order, and in sometimes (nearly) identical words. The term *synoptic* means literally to "see together" because they share these similarities on the life of Jesus, but each has its own, unique features. Alan Culpepper refers to Matthew as "a 'user friendly' handbook for the church."[1]

By about AD 100 the four canonical Gospels had been written and were being shared among a network of churches. Matthew's placement as the first gospel in our New Testament reflects its privileged status from the beginning. Canonical lists and references that go back to the first few centuries feature Matthew in the prime position.

One of the earliest attempts to compose a list of accepted books is known today as the *Muratorian fragment*. It was likely written in Greek in the mid- to late-second century, but it is badly preserved and fragmentary where it mentions the Gospels. While it is clear the unknown compiler accepts four Gospels and the last two are Luke and John, scholars deem it likely the first two were Matthew and Mark.[2]

When Eusebius (c. 260–340) quotes Irenaeus (c. 130–200) on the formation of the "sacred Gospels," he does so in the order we have them today: Matthew, Mark, Luke, John (Eusebius, *Church History* 5.8.1–4). Elsewhere Irenaeus refers to these books as "the holy tetrad of the Gospels" (Eusebius, *Church History* 3.25.1). He cites Irenaeus as saying, "Now Matthew brought out a written gospel among the Hebrews in their own dialect" (Eusebius, *Church History,* 5.8.2, author's translation). Early on, the church leaders recognized the gospel of Matthew as written to and for the Hebrews. This is still recognized today as most regard it as the most Jewish gospel. We cannot be certain what Irenaeus meant about how Matthew's gospel is composed.

We should note that more early copies of Matthew and John are extant than copies of Mark and Luke. The more a gospel was used, the more it was copied. Since copying a manuscript as extensive as any gospel took a lot of time and expense, it is understandable that demand for copies at that time could correspond to the number of copies made and available for later discovery. Consider this: If in Matthew you have about 90 percent of Mark's gospel (depending on how correspondence is figured), then why go to the time and expense to copy Mark if you already have Matthew? Correlated to that is the fact that fewer copies of Mark from the first few centuries have been discovered than the other three gospels. An occasional manuscript discovery may be accidental, but a pattern of discoveries likely points to the gospel's standing one way or another.[3]

Probably the most compelling fact suggesting Matthew's favored status among early Jesus followers has to do with the frequency with which early writers quoted from or alluded to Matthew in their letters, essays, church orders, and the like. Let me draw on a modern analogy. A friend and colleague of mine saw the Broadway musical *Hamilton: An American Musical* not long after it premiered in 2015. When we last discussed it, he had seen live performances three times in cities around the country. As this man showered in the morning, he did so to the soundtrack of the musical. When you went into his office, he would be playing it. He often rapped its lines and quoted from it in meetings and in casual conversation. He knew, and still knows to this day, every word of it. On one occasion, he stated without equivocation that it was his favorite musical and "the best ever." While musical theater has been a fixture in American entertainment for decades, I never heard him sing songs or quote dialogue from *The Lion King, The Phantom of the Opera,* or *Wicked.* Needless to say, my friend was not alone in his praise of *Hamilton,* for millions have seen and loved the musical.[4] My point is that frequent quotation reflects deep appreciation for any text, whether it is the text of Matthew or the lyrics of *Hamilton.*

We also need to consider the evidence we have from early Christian texts contained in *The Apostolic Fathers.* This collection received its title in the seventeenth century and refers to books from the generations after the New Testament era.[5] Time and space do not allow a full accounting of how Matthew figures in these texts, but we can give two examples. First, the *Epistle of Barnabas* was likely written in the last decades of the first century or early decades of the second. Most quotations and echoes in this book are from the Old Testament indicating that the unknown writer is immersed in the Jewish Scriptures and that he considers the teaching of the Old consistent completely with the New. But, we should add, the letter is a sustained attack on the blindness of the Jews to the true meaning of the Scriptures. In this short letter, I find four references to Matthew and perhaps one to John, but none that I can see to Mark or Luke.[6] Of the Gospels, Matthew appears to be Barnabas's favorite.

Then, there is the early church manual known as "The Teaching of the Apostles" (*Didache*). The manual is composed of two parts: (a) a moral teaching referred to as the "the two ways" (chs. 1–6); and (b) directions for certain practices in the church such as baptism, eucharist, the love feast, fasting, and the treatment of leaders (chs. 7–16). The former is heavily influenced by the Old Testament and Jewish moral teaching, so we will pay attention to the latter since it is the part most distinctively Christian. *Didache* 7:1 instructs the church to "baptize in the name of the Father and the Son and the Holy Spirit in living water," a formula derived from Matthew 28:19. When the *Didache* instructs regarding prayer, it uses the Lord's Prayer in the form it is found in Matthew (*Did* 8.2–3/Mt 6:9–13). In the final chapters, there are multiple references to Matthew and only one or two possible allusions to Mark and Luke.[7] I am not aware of a single quotation or allusion to the gospel of John. After an extensive investigation, Christopher Tuckett concludes that "apart from *Did* 1:3–2:1, almost all the echoes of the synoptic tradition which appear in the *Didache* can be explained as deriving from Matthew."[8] So once again, for the unknown compiler/writer of *Didache,* Matthew appears to be the favorite gospel. We could show this over and again in the church fathers.

Finally, it is important to remember what the church would be missing if Matthew were not part of the canon. We would have never heard the Beatitudes or the Sermon on the Mount (chs. 5–7). We would not have the Lord's Prayer in the way it is still commonly recited (Mt 6:9–13).[9] Christmas creches would be without the visit of the wise men (Mt 2:1–12). We would not know of the connection between Jesus' birth and the Immanuel prophecy (Mt 1:23). We would be missing many overt connections to Jesus' life and the fulfillment of prophecy (e.g., Mt 2:5–6; 27:8–10). As we will see throughout this book, there would be many discipleship sayings that would be lost. Even the word *church* itself would be absent from the Gospels. And let us not forget that we would have never been stirred to action by the Great Commission without Matthew.

For these and other reasons, we recognize that Matthew was a preferred gospel among the early circles of Jesus. In part, that had to do with the ways in which Matthew creatively and consistently engages with the Old Testament.

Structure in Matthew's Gospel

When we consider the structure of Matthew's gospel, we must begin with the beginning, that is, the genealogy that itself is structured and based on the genealogical records of the Old Testament. Beginning with Abraham, Matthew crafts his genealogy into three sets of fourteen names: Abraham to David; David to exile; exile to Jesus. These structures are not accidental; they are an intentional nod to Jewish origins and *gematria*, a type of Jewish numerology that has been used as a way of interpreting Torah and deriving explanation of texts by appeal to the numerical value of numbers.[10]

Beyond the beginning, we see another significant structure in the five sermons Jesus teaches throughout the gospel. (See Table 0.1.) Each of these sections concludes with a phrase like, "When Jesus finished saying all these things . . ." (Mt 7:28–29; 11:1; 13:53; 19:1; 26:1). Scholars often point out that the five sermons/teachings of Jesus correspond roughly to the five books of Moses, and thus deepen Matthew's presentation of Jesus as a new Moses. As we will see in later chapters, there are several points of correlation between Jesus and Moses. We should, however, be cautious about drawing too close a connection between them. The Sermon on the Mount is not equivalent to Genesis. The instructions to the Twelve are not comparable to the codes of Exodus. Matthew would have us ponder this in the broader sense. When the evangelist wrote his account of Jesus' life, he wanted his Jewish readers to contemplate the mystery, the correspondence between the prophesied prophet like Moses (Dt 18:18) and Moses himself.

Table 0.1. Jesus' Five Sermons

Matthew 5–7	The Sermon on the Mount
Matthew 10	Instructions to "the Twelve"
Matthew 13	The Parables of the Kingdom
Matthew 18	Teachings on Discipleship
Matthew 24–25	The Destruction of the Temple and Lessons Regarding the End

We find other macro-structures in the gospel. Consider the early reference to the virgin birth and Jesus' prophetic name from Isaiah, Immanuel ("God with us"; Isa 7:14). It forms a bookend, as it were, at the front of the gospel (Mt 1:23). The back bookend is found in Matthew 28 with Jesus on a mountain in Galilee, worshiped by some and still doubted by others. The one who is granted all authority commissions the eleven to make disciples of the nations, baptize them, and teach them all his teachings with the assurance like that of Isaiah 7:14: "I am with you always" (Mt 28:20). When the evangelist crafted his grand narrative of Jesus' life, he insisted his Jewish readers contemplate the mystery that Jesus of Nazareth is more than a prophet and reminder of God's presence; he is the God-with-us-One, and his abiding presence rests with the church to the end of the age. The entire gospel should be read inside that frame.[11]

Fulfillment of Scripture

One feature of Matthew's gospel that stands out is that it sees the life of Jesus "according to Scripture" (cf. 1 Co 15:3–8). The opening line of the gospel links Jesus' origin subtly back to the story of Genesis: "the book of the origin (*geneseos*) of Jesus Christ, son of David, son of Abraham" (Mt 1:1, author's translation). By connecting Jesus to David and Abraham, the evangelist recalls their key roles in fathering the people of God and laying the groundwork for a unique covenantal relationship with God's people. The genealogy that follows borrows from and is intended to resemble the genealogies of the Old Testament. Like his namesake, Joseph, Mary's husband is guided by dreams to become Jesus' earthly father and protect his family from a tyrant.

The frequency with which Matthew employs the fulfillment formula and biblical quotations is another unique feature of this gospel. To cite just a few examples:

- The escape to Egypt (Mt 2:13–15)
  "And so was fulfilled what the Lord had said through the prophet:
    'Out of Egypt I called my son.'"

- The return to Nazareth (Mt 2:19–23)
  "So was fulfilled what was said through the prophets,
  that he would be called a Nazarene."

- Jesus begins his ministry in Galilee (Mt 4:12–16)
  "to fulfill what was said through the prophet Isaiah . . . "

- The arrest of Jesus in the garden (Mt 26:56)
  "This has all taken place that the writings of the prophets might be
  fulfilled."

We will investigate the fulfillment quotations in the commentary proper. But, as you can see, the narrative appeals sometimes to a specific prophet (e.g., Jeremiah, Isaiah); at other times it cites "the prophets" in general. These fulfillment passages are part of the landscape of Matthew's gospel.

But "fulfillment" was not a simple, one-dimensional notion in Matthew. He used it in a variety of ways and for different ends. David Gooding recognizes four usages of "fulfillment" language in the New Testament (including Matthew): (1) "fulfillment" as bringing about an Old Testament prediction in the life of Jesus or birth of the church; (2) "fulfillment" as the final, higher manifestation of a general Old Testament principle; (3) Christ's "fulfillment" of the Old Testament law; and (4) the "fulfillment" of the Old Testament law by a follower of Jesus.[12]

Matthew, for example, unlike Luke, grounds the virgin birth in Isaiah 7, and roots Jesus' divine identity in the Immanuel ("God with us") prophecy. The God who is "with us" from birth will be "with" his followers until the end (Mt 28:19–20). The evangelist does not need the word *fulfillment* to show that Jesus' life and ministry "fills full" the Old Testament. At times, the whole scheme sits quietly below the surface. It is present in both types and antitypes. First, it links Jesus with the story of Israel, even as it portrays him as a renewed Israel. Jesus is both like Israel in his call and yet unlike Israel in obedience. Second, it connects Jesus to the story of Moses, presenting him as the prophet like Moses predicted in Deuteronomy 18:18. Jesus is both like Moses in his role as teacher and unlike Moses in that he obeys God completely and writes the law on the hearts of his disciples.

In a puzzling episode, John the Baptist hesitates to baptize Jesus (Mt 3:13–17). But when Jesus insists, the upshot of the episode is that, together, John and Jesus fulfill all righteousness. It is never stated clearly what this means. Perhaps it is a reference to completing God's righteous actions through history. In contrast, Jesus calls upon his followers to fulfill righteousness (Mt 5:20), thereby calling them to a new, higher standard, less detail-oriented and more heart-oriented.

Authorship, Place, and Date

Matthew's gospel was a massive literary undertaking. Exactly when it was written, where, and by whom are questions debated by scholars. The issues are complex, so we will merely touch on them here.[13]

It is commonplace to say that the gospel of Matthew is anonymous. The reason is that, from first word to last, there is no claim to authorship made in the text as you might find in one of Paul's letters (e.g., Ro 1:1; 1 Co 1:1; Gal 1:1). But the term *anonymous* may be claiming more than is warranted. If all you mean by it is that the author does not put his name in the book, then yes, Matthew is anonymous, but if you mean that the author was unknown to those who first read or heard it, then that is claiming what is not in evidence. First, as Simon Gathercole has made clear, historians from the period did not typically append their names to the body of their compositions (e.g., Xenophon [d. 354 BC], Polybius [d. 118 BC]; Tacitus [d. AD 120]; Plutarch [d. AD 119]);[14] thus, lacking a name in a text was not a sign of anonymity. While the text of a gospel itself may not contain the name of its composer, that does not mean readers and hearers were left guessing, "Who wrote this? Where did this come from?" There were a number of ways ancient books were distinguished one from the other. On the manuscript itself, a note or title could be written somewhere on the back or front to distinguish it. In the book-roll culture, tags (*sittuboi*) were used to distinguish one book from another. Tags were attached at one end of the roll; find the tag and you found the book you wanted. So there were other ways of knowing who wrote a book in the ancient world other than an internal, upfront claim to authorship.[15] If one day you lose the cover and title page of this book (God forbid), there is a good chance no one will know who wrote it because authors seldom insinuate themselves into the pages of a book like the one you are reading.

There is a strong tradition that links the apostle Matthew to the first gospel. According to Papias (AD 60–135), an early companion to those who knew the apostles, John the elder recounted that "Matthew collected the oracles [of Jesus] in the Hebrew language, and each interpreted them as best he could" (Eusebius, *Ecclesiastical History* 3.39.16).[16] The Greek word rendered "collected" (*sunetaxato*) by Kirsopp Lake might also be translated as "composed." Alternatively, since Papias underscores that Mark's account is not "in order" (*ou mentoi taxei*), it is possible to read the verb *sunetaxato* as suggesting that Matthew brought order to the sayings (*logia*) of Jesus. It is unclear all that Papias meant by this or what Eusebius understood.[17] The immediate context had to do with Mark writing a gospel and how he had become the interpreter of Peter. Therefore, it is reasonable that Papias's statement has to do with the composition of the gospel of Matthew, not some other, lost gospel or notes used for writing what became Matthew. Furthermore, as we saw above,

Irenaeus in the second century knew of four Gospels, the first under the name of Matthew.

If these reports are reliable, then another important question is whether the gospel of Matthew has the earmarks of being an eyewitness account. Richard Bauckham makes the case that the quest for the historical Jesus would be better served if questers considered the Gospels as eyewitness testimony. Two critical features of testimony are this: the testifier asks to be trusted and claims to report accurately.[18] For the ancients, testimony served as a useful tool in reporting and reconstructing history.[19] For Bauckham, testimony is "theologically appropriate, indeed the theologically necessary way of access to the history of Jesus."[20] All the New Testament gospel writers present their accounts as having come from eyewitness testimony.

We are on good grounds to conclude that Matthew, one of the Twelve, was the initial source, inspiration, and creative energy for the gospel. Yet, writing in the ancient world was seldom a solo event. So we should not imagine Matthew sitting behind a desk for months by himself toiling away like those who write commentaries on him! There were amanuenses (secretaries) and coworkers who contributed to both small and large literary endeavors. This would not take away anything from Matthew, one of the earliest followers, initiating the project and seeing it to the end. In fact, the earliest, extant titles, "The gospel according to (kata) Matthew" and "According to (kata) Matthew," employ a common preposition in Greek, kata. It is related to an adverb, katō (long o), that means below or represents action downward. In one sense the title could be taken to mean "the gospel that has come [to us] down from Matthew."

Nothing in the book itself says when or where it is written. We are left to decipher clues in the text and to listen well to the traditions. For various reasons many scholars regard Antioch in Syria a likely birthplace for the gospel. The Jesus movement had spread there not long after Jesus' execution and made a home for itself. The city had a bustling Jewish community that spoke Greek and likely had access to the Hebrew Scriptures in Greek. Perhaps, if we take into account the Acts of the Apostles, it was also a center for the launch of the Gentile mission (Ac 11:20; 13:1–3; Gal 2:11–12), which fits the trajectory of Matthew well. Decades ago, Krister Stendahl made the case for Syria as the site of a "school" of St. Matthew which fostered a tradition of study related to linking the Jewish Scriptures with Christian teaching.[21] Again, this theory accords well with what we find in the first New Testament gospel.

Scholars wrestle with the question of when this gospel might have been written. Most say sometime between the 60s to 80s AD. Some regard it as earlier, some later. That is a broad range, but there is little in the gospel to go on and historical certainty is not possible. The key questions are these:

1. Was Matthew dependent on Mark? If so, then we have to allow time for Mark to be written and to circulate to the evangelist. Thus, the dating of Matthew depends on the dating of Mark.

2. Was Jerusalem still standing or had it already been conquered by the Romans (AD 70)? There are passages which can be interpreted to suggest the destruction of the temple and the holy city was in the past (Mt 24:1–14).

3. Was the source of the gospel a member of the Twelve and thus an eyewitness to Jesus' earthly ministry? The later you posit the date of composition, the less likely the author was an eyewitness; thus, he would have been a second-generation Christian.

4. What was the relationship between the synagogue and the church? Had a hard break occurred, or were they still orbiting one another at the time the gospel was written?

Certainty on such historical matters is hard to come by. The position taken in the chapters that follow is that Matthew is dependent on Mark, and thus later than Mark. I am uncertain whether Jerusalem still stands as the evangelist composes his gospel, mainly because the language of destruction matches the kind of prophetic oracles that often depicted the destruction of cities (e.g., Jer 6). Furthermore, having a "prophet" appear to announce the destruction of the holy city was not a one-time occurrence. Seven years prior to the destruction of Jerusalem (AD 70), another man named Jesus, this one a son of Ananias, appeared in the temple and predicted its destruction. Despite arrests, beatings, and ultimately a stone that took his life, he continued to pronounce "woe!" and the calamity to come (Josephus, *JW* 6.5.3 [300–309]). One did not have to imagine what it would be like to be a witness in a besieged city. There were stories aplenty of what it was like from Israel's past. So we might reckon a date of composition late in the 60s or early in the 70s. Fortunately, anyone wanting to read Matthew well and in context does not have to solve the question of its date.

Tensions

We conclude these introductory remarks with a feature common to all the Gospels, but that Matthew treated uniquely. All the Gospels emerged in a period we have come to regard as the turn of history. Prior to Jesus' birth, we refer to years as BC (before Christ); after his birth we designate years AD (*anno Domini*, meaning the year of the Lord's [birth]). This reworking of time itself is a development in the Christian West because believers came to understand Jesus' life, death, and resurrection as the middle of time.[22]

This was a century of great tension, pain, and suffering for the people of God. Not only did this century witness the opposition to and death of Jesus of Nazareth followed by his followers' mission against the backdrop of persecution, it also consisted of the Jewish revolt from their Roman overlords and their swift and overwhelming destruction by Roman forces (AD 70). Since many of the first followers of Jesus were Jews, stresses and strains developed internally in Judaism to deal with the ongoing question of what it meant to be God's people.

But we should also remember that this first "Christian" century was also the last century of the standing temple. We can hardly begin to understand the psychic trauma and disruption this caused the Jewish people. Not only were thousands killed or permanently maimed, homes destroyed, and cities laid waste, but the Roman legions had destroyed the center of their lives after what proved to be a militarily insignificant struggle for freedom.

From Matthew's telling, the entire story of Jesus is one of opposition and struggle, first with the tyrant, Herod, then with the devil himself and demonic forces, then with Jewish religious influencers who accused Jesus of blasphemy, violating accepted traditions, befriending sinners, and violating the Sabbath. On occasion, even Jesus' disciples find themselves in opposition to their Lord. After the confession at Caesarea Philippi (Mt 16:16–18), the Master calls Simon Peter "Satan," when he tries to disabuse Jesus of the thought he might be arrested and martyred (Mt 16:21–23). Finally, powerful people in Jerusalem—Roman and Jewish—ally themselves to put Jesus to death. The would-be Jewish king is crucified on a Roman cross under Roman charges with the assistance of highly placed Jerusalem religious leaders. The mission ahead, Jesus instructs, will be achieved only amid great persecution and tribulation (Mt 5:10–12; 24:4–28).

Tensions erupted in the gospel when some Jewish people disagreed with Jesus' claims about himself and his teaching about the kingdom. This occurred initially during Jesus' earthly ministry, but it continued into Matthew's day. The kingdom they wanted, but not Jesus. A crucified Messiah occupied no place in their hopes and aspirations. The more the gospel presses understanding about Jewish history (past, present, and future) and the claims made by Jesus, the more it records mounting anger and escalating rhetoric. The parting of the ways between the Jesus movement and what became rabbinic Judaism was underway. In this space, Matthew can be polemical and apologetic.

Jesus is often at odds with members of the sect known as the Pharisees. Among the people, they were popular religious figures and interpreters of the law, which may account for the harshness of Matthew's gospel as they are repeatedly called hypocrites (especially, Mt 23:13, 15, 16, 23, 25, 27, 29).[23] Josephus (*Ant* 13.297, 399–417) has a different take, of course: he describes them as faithful interpreters of the law, able to pivot after the destruction of the temple, reinvent themselves in Galilee, and secure the survival of their ancestral religion.[24]

Intrafamily conflict is the most emotional; with family we have the most at stake. People involved in intrafamily conflict engage in typical, often severe verbal attacks on one another. If you strip this rhetoric from its family context, you are prone to misunderstand and absolutize the language. In other words, you miss the point altogether. You walk away thinking there is abject hatred between the parties when there are actually delicate, frayed family relations. This is why some historically have misunderstood the sensitive balance between Matthew as the most Jewish gospel and Matthew as a gospel that confronts and condemns the Jewish opposition. Matthew is clear: Jesus is a Jew, his disciples are all Jews, and *not all Jews are complicit in the death of Jesus.* It is disastrous and a sign of great shame that over the centuries Christians in powerful positions used their influence to punish Jews on a misreading of Matthew (or the other gospels for that matter); it has been a great injustice to the Jewish people themselves; it has deprived the world of many gifts of the Jewish people; and it has scarred the souls of countless generations of Christians (see comments on Mt 27:24–26). In the chapters that follow, we seek to be sensitive to the balance, and we encourage others to seek it as well.[25]

COMMENTARY

MATTHEW 1

Like many people, I have started and stopped plans to read the Bible through in a year. That plan usually involved reading several chapters a day from the Old Testament, followed by reading one to two chapters from the New Testament. Inevitably, in January I came to the book of Matthew. In the past, I often skipped over Matthew 1:1–16 because it was just a list of names, most of whom I had never heard of. It is often referred to as the "begat" section because in the Authorized Version the genealogy reads "Abraham begat Isaac, Isaac begat Jacob, Jacob begat . . .". You get the idea. Modern versions have rendered the "begat" in favor of a translation like "was the father of." Still, the list of names, if you have no orientation, is formidable.

For those schooled in the Old Testament, however, the list of names and events is anything but meaningless. It is a family tree, a history full of saints and sinners. For those with Old Testament eyes, it is more akin to a family album than an ancient cast of characters.

Depending on how they are counted, there are twenty-five to thirty genealogies in the Old Testament, concentrated mainly in Genesis and 1 Chronicles. Genealogies shape the character of these books in key ways. Coming as they do from the ancient world, genealogical accounts were important ways of connecting people, establishing legitimacy, and passing history on to future generations.

What the Structure Means: Genealogies (Mt 1:1–17)

Typically, genealogies were patrilineal; that is, they listed the fathers, only occasionally mentioning the mothers despite their important role in "begetting" the children (e.g., Ge 11:29–31; Ex 6:23–25). Genealogies provided a kind of map of social location, and in some

cases made claims about land and territories owned (Nu 34:16–29).[1]
Each genealogy adds a chapter to the story of redemption. As such, the
genealogies often make theological claims documenting the progress
of God's covenant and call upon Abraham's people. Abram, as he is
known early in the story, comes from Terah's family and is destined to
found one of the greatest families in the world. Among all the families
and nations, God selected Abram and promised him that one day his
seed would become a blessing to all.[2]

That story, or perhaps it would be better to say those stories, sit on the
surface of Matthew's genealogy as he introduces Jesus to his audience. It
may be worth noting that many genealogies from the ancient Near East
were connected to royalty, so it is not insignificant that Matthew ends up
making royal claims about Jesus as the Messiah and Son of David.

1:1 *This is the genealogy of Jesus the Messiah the son of David, the son of
Abraham.* Jesus is who he is, in large part, because of the family into which he
is born. Most Westerners have a hard time understanding this because of our
cultural bent toward individualism. Family is the reason we go to therapy, not
the foundation or shaping of our identities. To grasp Jesus' significance, we
must understand his family.

- Jesus, the Messiah
- Son of David
- Son of Abraham

Matthew begins his gospel with a series of bold claims about Jesus. These
claims are affirmed and then worked out through the story Matthew tells, a
story shaped in the main by Old Testament themes and deep structures.

The Messiah. Fundamental to Matthew's portrait of Jesus is the claim
that Jesus is the Messiah, or Christ. *Christ* is not a name; it is more like a
title, the Greek translation of the Hebrew "Messiah." Scholars debate whether
"Messiah" was an established title or not, and if so what kind of title it might
be. Matthew Novenson has made a cogent case that "Christ" was not a name
or title exactly, it was an "honorific,"[3] which is usually regarded as a word
or phrase that conveys honor or respect to a person. The "Venerable" Bede,
for example, was not always "venerable." Octavian was not always "*Augustus
Caesar.*" These words became part of their mantle of honor. Over time, with
use, some do become titular. *Augustus* becomes a title that was used by Roman
emperors in subsequent generations.

There was no standing definition or expectation of "the Messiah" during Jesus' lifetime. Some thought the Messiah might be a single, royal figure. Others considered the Messiah to be two people, a priestly and a royal redeemer. Still others doubted there would be a Messiah at all. Regardless, there are still some identifiable aspects for the informed reader.

The word *Messiah* or *Christ* comes from a Hebrew root meaning "anointed" and carried strong political associations (e.g., Isa 45; *Psalms of Solomon* 17–18).[4] The Roman overlords knew well a claim to be Messiah was a royal claim, so they crucified Jesus on a Roman cross for sedition, that is, for imagining himself king of the Jews. Matthew uses this supercharged title boldly and then lets the story he tells reveal its meaning. For Matthew, "Messiah" refers to God's chosen (anointed) agent whose task is to liberate the world from disease, death, sin, and oppression in all forms. Jesus' teachings and miracles demonstrate instances when Jesus' messianic role is on full display. But during his public ministry, Jesus never said in so many words, "I am the Messiah."[5] He led his disciples inch by inch to the confession in Caesarea Philippi (Mt 16) and then immediately began to reverse their aspirations by saying he was destined to suffer, die on a cross, and be resurrected.

On the day we now know as Palm Sunday, the crowds hail him in Matthew 21:9 as "the Son of David" with the cry "hosanna" on their lips and Psalm 118:25–26 resonating in their hearts:

> Save us, we beseech you, O LORD!
> O LORD, we beseech you, give us success!
> Blessed is the one who comes in the name of the LORD.
> We bless you from the house of the LORD. (NRSV)

What Jesus had avoided during his ministry—the public declaration that he was Israel's true king—he accepted and defended on his way to Jerusalem that day. But this was to be a prelude to the end. Powerful forces would align against Jesus before the week is out.

Son of David. "Son of David" is a specialized, messianic title which reminds any competent reader or hearer of God's millennial-old covenant with David (2 Sa 7:12–16). In this pivotal scene, God makes a series of promises to King David. The king had just sworn to build YHWH, his God, a temple in Jerusalem so that the ark of the covenant could have a true home. That was David's plan, but God had a better idea.

God instructs David through his court prophet, Nathan, and assures him the temple will be built, not by David but by his son. First, God promises David that his dynasty will continue. Unlike Saul, who was a one-king dynasty (ruling family), a son of David would sit on the throne after David was buried with his fathers. Second, David's son would build YHWH a house.

Indeed, Solomon did build God a temple and dedicated it around 950 BC (1 Ki 8:22–9:9). Third, God promises to have a Father-Son relationship with David's son. He promises further to discipline him if and when he steps out of line. Note carefully: this implies that "Son of God" is first a messianic title; it may mean more than that, but it is at least that. Finally, God vows to extend the first promise; not only will David's throne continue after his death, but God guarantees David that his house and kingdom will stand forever.

Son of Abraham. This title takes the hearer/reader back even earlier in Scripture to God's covenant promises to Abraham. In calling Abraham (Ge 12:1–3), God promised to give him land and make of him and his kin a great nation. He promised to bless the nomad, provide for him, and make his name great. Finally, God promised to make Abraham and his family a universal blessing: "And all peoples on earth will be blessed through you." Abraham's kin may have become a great nation, occupied the promised land (until the exile), and enjoyed heaven's provisions and protections, but they did not become a blessing to all the nations until Jesus arrived and commissioned his followers to go into the world with the gospel (Mt 28:19–20). Many people could have claimed to be "a son of Abraham," but Jesus is "*the* Son of Abraham" whose mission extended beyond Israel to be a light to the nations (Isa 49:6). For Matthew, Jesus embodies the ideals of Israel (with Jacob, the family name of Abraham became better known as "Israel" [Ge 32:22–32]). Jesus of Nazareth was the true Jew. He was everything Israel was supposed to be in relation to God, the world, and the nations.

What the Structure Means: Chiasm (Mt 1:1–16)

Matthew introduces Jesus to his audience with a series of titles and historical claims. But he does so in an artistic, literary manner known as *chiasm.* Chiasm is a type of parallelism we see in the Hebrew Bible (e.g., Ps 118:2–4). Writers use chiasm to show balance and indicate emphasis. (See also "What the Structure Means: Questions and Answers" at Mt 19:8–9.) Perhaps it is easier to see a chiasm than to describe it. Table 1.1 shows how Matthew opens his gospel.

Table 1.1. The Chiasm of Matthew 1:1–16

Mt 1:1	**A** Jesus the Messiah
Mt 1:1	**B** Son of David
Mt 1:1	**C** Son of Abraham
Mt 1:2	**C'** Abraham
Mt 1:6	**B'** David
Mt 1:11–12	(Exile)
Mt 1:16	**A'** Jesus the Messiah

As Bruno, Compton, and McFadden point out, this is a "broken chiasm" since we have Abraham-David-*exile*-Messiah in the second half of the passage. As they say, "This literary device reflects the historical circumstances well. The history of Israel was indeed 'interrupted' by the exile. Therefore, our reading of Matthew's retelling of Israel's story in Matthew—and of the entire gospel—should be informed by this interruption."[6] The exile had a profound effect upon the people of God, and it would take a seismic shift, an act of God, for them to begin to move beyond it. We will consider the significance of the break in the chiasm when we discuss Matthew 1:17, and in "Matthew 1:17 Through Old Testament Eyes: Exile."

While aspects of Matthew's chiasm show balance, it is likely his point lies with the center of the structure (C and C').[7] If so, Matthew wants his audience to ponder how Jesus as Messiah is the final, full, definitive fulfillment of God's promise to Abraham to make his family a blessing to all the nations. This feature, of course, does not overshadow these other titles; it just temporarily foregrounds Abraham as the progenitor of the people of promise. Later on, as the story unfolds, other aspects of Jesus' significance will take center stage.

Each name in Jesus' genealogy represents a person whose story is told and sometimes retold through Scripture. Old Testament eyes will help us know the unique features of Jesus' ancestry. Now time or space doesn't allow us to retell every story, but there are others beyond David and Abraham whom we must consider to understand Jesus' family and therefore Jesus himself. It is often the details Matthew includes that gather our attention.

1:3 *Judah the father of Perez and Zerah, whose mother was Tamar.* Matthew could have simply said that Judah was the father of Perez and Zerah, but he did not. He added "whose mother was Tamar." Tamar is the first woman, the first mother mentioned, in the genealogy. What happened between Judah and Tamar is one of the most sordid chapters in all Scripture. And Matthew nudges his audience to remember. It is certainly not PG-rated.

Judah had settled his family in a village not far from Bethlehem (Ge 38). He married off his eldest son, Er, to Tamar, but his son's wickedness caught up with him and he died. Judah instructed another son, Onan, to perform his duty of levirate marriage (Dt 25:5–10). This custom required a surviving brother to take the deceased brother's wife in marriage and father a male descendent so that the deceased's name and legacy would live on. Onan selfishly refused his duty, maintaining an appearance of marriage but choosing instead coitus interruptus, guaranteeing the end of his brother's line—or so he thought. This displeased God greatly, and soon Onan died.

Afraid for the life of his next son—after all, two had already died—Judah told Tamar to go home to her own family and wait until his next son grew up. But even after reaching marriageable age, Judah did not marry his son, Shelah, to Tamar; so she took matters into her own hands. After learning that Judah was heading to Timnah to shear sheep, Tamar took off her widow's garments, put on a veil and went out to intercept Judah along the way. When he saw her, he thought she was a prostitute, so he propositioned her. As they were negotiating a price, she tricked him into giving her some personal items. Later, when he tried to pay up, he found she had disappeared without a trace.

Tamar conceived in that wretched act and went back home. She took with her the personal items Judah had given her and assumed again the mantle of widowhood. In a few months it became evident she was pregnant. Judah was furious at her infidelity and ordered her brought out to be killed; family honor was at stake. Tamar wisely brought with her the personal items Judah had given her and said it was the owner of these items who impregnated her (Ge 38:25). Judah was forced to acknowledge what he had done; in the end he confessed, "She is more in the right than I because I did not give her to my son Shelah" (38:26, author's translation). For some it may sound odd that Tamar was "more in the right," and that the true transgressor, the big sinner—in more ways than one—was Judah. As a patriarch he failed his family and violated God's teaching, to the detriment of those who were his.

This sordid tale is tucked away in the Old Testament. Many people have read it without thinking that these characters were part of Jesus' ancestry. But Matthew wants to remind his readers of what really happened as part of Jesus' family line. Without Tamar's action (which may seem dubious but which was praised by Judah), Judah would have had no grandson, and the line of the Messiah would have been broken. As we will also see, Matthew is setting his readers up to recognize something important about Jesus. He came from a line of sinners, but he came as a friend of sinners. That was vital to his mission. That was his reputation. He came to save his people—past, present, and future—from their sins (Mt 1:21; 28:18–20).

1:5 *Salmon the father of Boaz, whose mother was Rahab.* Again, Matthew wants us to notice some details. Rahab is the second woman mentioned in the genealogy, and she was not part of Abraham's family. She was a Canaanite, but she is inserted into Jesus' genealogy to foreshadow the influx of the nations into the new covenant community.

Before Joshua led the Israelites into the promised land, he sent two men to spy on the city of Jericho. As a ruse they entered the city and made their way to the house of Rahab, the prostitute. Men were always coming into the city to find pleasure with Rahab. She becomes the center of the story because she hid the spies from searchers, protected them, and provided a way of escape. Without her, their mission would surely have failed. As it was, they returned to Joshua with the intelligence he needed. Before they leave Rahab's house, Rahab makes an impassioned confession of faith, recognizing YHWH as the true God of all and the Israelites as the rightful inhabitants of the land (Jos 2:8–13). In a sense, this confession makes her part of the people of God. She is adopted into God's covenant family and forever celebrated. The author of Hebrews (11:31) goes on to name her as one of the heroes of faith: "By faith the prostitute Rahab, because she welcomed the spies, was not killed with those who were disobedient."

On their way out of the city she urges the spies to deal kindly with her and her family when the battle begins. The spies do as she asks, and her family is spared.

Rahab's story is summarized in brief in Joshua 6:25: "But Joshua spared Rahab the prostitute, with her family and all who belonged to her, because she hid the men Joshua had sent as spies to Jericho—and she lives among the Israelites to this day."

Matthew could have glossed over this episode if he had wished by saying simply, "Salmon was the father of Boaz." But by including Rahab, he reminds us of the story and its epilogue; she was a Canaanite prostitute whose confession of faith sealed her future as one with the covenant and people of Israel. She hid the spies, guaranteeing that Joshua's people would be successful in battle. The implications of her faith and fidelity as a one-time outsider will have much to say about the mission of Jesus and his followers.

Boaz the father of Obed, whose mother was Ruth. For the second time, Matthew reminds his readers of a remarkable woman whose ancestry is outside the covenant family. This time it is Ruth the Moabite. During the period when the judges rule Israel, there is a severe famine which drives Elimelech, his wife Naomi, and their sons from their home in Bethlehem to the land of Moab. The sons both marry Moabite women (Ruth and Orpah), but eventually Naomi's husband and two sons die. With the famine over, Naomi, too old to remarry and with no hope for security, decides to return to her land and her people (Ru 1).

Ruth and Orpah are determined to go with her, but Naomi urges them to stay since she has nothing to offer them. Orpah finally gives in to Naomi's wishes, but Ruth insists on going with Naomi, pledging her loyalty to her and her God. Moabite religion had its own gods and practices, which she promises to leave behind to become a full participant in Abraham's people (Ru 1:16–17). Ruth, like Rahab, becomes a famous proselyte to the faith of Israel.

Once back in Bethlehem with Naomi, Ruth meets Boaz. Boaz is related to Naomi, but he is distant enough not to be required under the law of levirate marriage (Dt 25:5–10) to marry Ruth and take care of her. Boaz does so nonetheless, pledging to redeem the land owned by Naomi and her deceased family as well as to take Ruth as his wife and to perpetuate her former husband's family name. The book of Ruth ends with a brief genealogy that may have served as Matthew's source for this part of the family tree (Ru 4:18–22): "This, then, is the family line of Perez: Perez was the father of Hezron, Hezron the father of Ram, Ram the father of Amminadab, Amminadab the father of Nashon, Nashon the father of Salmon, Salmon the father of Boaz, Boaz the father of Obed, Obed the father of Jesse, and Jesse the father of David."

The story of Ruth is a second reminder—a second witness if you will—in Jesus' genealogy that outsiders have been made insiders by the force of their confessions of faith and fidelity to the people of God. Both Rahab the Canaanite and Ruth the Moabite signal that God's purposes will not stop until the nations and families of the world are full participants in Abraham's blessing. For Matthew, Jesus is the fulfillment of that promise made centuries before. The inclusion here of non-Jews at the beginning of Matthew along with the Great Commission to "go and make disciples of all nations" at the end of the gospel (Mt 28:18–20) act as bookends (an *inclusio*; see Table 28.1). This suggests that Matthew seeks to emphasize in his gospel that through the Messiah the promise made centuries ago to Abraham (Ge 12:1–3) is fulfilled.

1:6 *David was the father of Solomon, whose mother had been Uriah's wife.* While David is one of the pillars of the genealogy of Jesus, Matthew reminds us that the celebrated king was deeply flawed: he defied God's commandments and committed an act of sexual assault,[8] treachery, and murder. For that, he and those involved paid a dear price.

David fathered Solomon through the wife of another man. It is one of best-known stories of the Old Testament; it pits the faithlessness of the king over against the faithfulness of Uriah, the Hittite. Matthew could have skimmed over the whole, sordid affair, ignored it, by saying simply, "David was the father of Solomon." But by including "whose mother had been Uriah's wife," he takes us back to one of the darkest episodes in the king's life. Just a few words and we are whisked back to the king's palace in Jerusalem (2 Sa 11).

One spring King David stayed home as his armies waged war. In the afternoon breeze, from the lofty vantage of his royal house, he looked down and saw a beautiful woman. He conspired to have her come to him. Her name was Bathsheba, and she was the wife of Uriah, the Hittite, one of David's soldiers. Bathsheba came as the king requested—after all, you don't refuse the king—and they had sexual relations.

When David learned she was "with child," he conspired to cover up his infidelity, so he sent for Uriah to come to Jerusalem and report on the progress of the war. David repeatedly tried to get him to go home before he returned to the front. But Uriah refused: How could he go home and enjoy the pleasures of his house for even one night while his fellow soldiers were camping in the fields in constant peril?

Frustrated by Uriah's solidarity with his fellow soldiers, David conspired with his general, Joab, to have Uriah killed in battle. David, the king, ordered what was effectively the murder of Uriah. Ironically, Uriah became the courier for the letter that sealed his fate. Uriah's allegiance and "righteousness" stand in stark contrast to the king's desperate and deadly actions.

When word of Uriah's death reached his wife, she lamented his passing. After an appropriate time of mourning, David sent for Bathsheba, and she became his wife and gave birth to a son. As the story goes, the entire affair displeased the Lord (2 Sa 12). In the end, the child grew sick and died. After David and Bathsheba grieved and consoled each other, when the time was right, they came together again, and she became pregnant again. This child was also male, and they named him Solomon. He would be the next king, the child of the promise, destined to build a temple and continue David's throne.

We have included here just enough to remind you of the story (2 Sa 11–12). This is a tragic episode in the life of the king and many of those closest to him. It set in motion a series of events that would lead eventually to a deep fracture in David's family. Matthew intentionally draws our attention to this tragic story. He does not write, "And David was the father of Solomon by Bathsheba." He reminds his audience that David fathered Solomon through a woman he took advantage of and whose husband he subsequently killed.

1:16 *And Jacob the father of Joseph, the husband of Mary, and Mary was the mother of Jesus who is called the Messiah.* Mary, the mother of Jesus, is the fifth woman mentioned in the genealogy. She will be "with child" under what many would consider suspicious circumstances. Matthew includes women in Jesus' genealogy on purpose; he wants to signal a new place for women in the mission and message of Jesus.

Going Deeper into the Inclusion of Women and "Sinners": Matthew 1:2–16

It is hard for us to understand the role women played or did not play in that deeply patriarchal society, but Jesus subverts normal customs and practices by welcoming women into the ranks of discipleship, traveling with them and accepting their financial assistance (Lk 8:1–3).

The inclusion of five women in the family tree of Jesus is Matthew's intentional effort to foreshadow an important aspect of Jesus' message. Where the gospel takes root, there will be no distinction between male and female (Gal 3:23–29), sons and daughters will prophesy (Ac 2:17, quoting Joel 2:28–32), and women too will be heroes of faith and effective leaders. This would have been a deeply countercultural move for its day. The churches will struggle with this reality against the old ways for years to come. Yet this new day—as Paul called it, "the new creation" (2 Co 5:17)—has been in the works all along, prefigured through strong, courageous, faith-filled women who did what was right in God's eyes. They were a sneak preview of things to come. God used them to bring into the world his Anointed. Regardless of what they had been—prostitutes, Canaanites, Moabites, the victim of the king's sexual aggression, intrigue, and murder—they have been given a place within God's people. Outsiders will become insiders because of the gospel. Those who previously were not my people will be called "my people." Notorious sin will be forgiven and atoned for in Jesus who will save his people from their sins.

Today, churches must follow Jesus and be on the cutting edge of educating and elevating women around the world. No one is second class if they are in Christ. Regardless of the vocations women are called to pursue— parenting, business, education, medicine, law, service, theology—women deserve respect and support. Too often the church appears to have trailed behind culture on these matters, but in fact, wherever Jesus is preached, women fare better than where he is not. This is not to say the church is perfect and where it should be. We are not. Thus, it is incumbent on us to assist women in making up for any social disadvantages cultures impose on half the world's population.

1:17 *Thus there were fourteen generations in all from Abraham to David, fourteen from David to the exile to Babylon, and fourteen from the exile to the Messiah.* Matthew intentionally constructs Jesus' genealogy into three groups of fourteen generations.[9] The number fourteen is significant because in the Jewish form of numerology known as *gematria*, the name "David" (daleth-vav-daleth, in Hebrew) equals the number fourteen (4+6+4). In the Hebrew language, the letters do double-duty both as phonetic and numeric values. We have two systems: Arabic numbers (1, 2, 3, . . .) and a phonetic alphabet (a, b, c, . . .). The Hebrew alphabet (or aleph-bet) carries the weight of both systems. The number fourteen is the numeric value of the name David, underscoring that Jesus is "the sSon of David": the one to rule on David's throne forever, build a temple, and have the ultimate "Father-Son" relationship with God.

Matthew 1:17 Through Old Testament Eyes: Exile

The threefold structure of Jesus' generations is built on four pillars: Abraham, David, the exile to Babylon, and the birth of the Messiah. We've already mentioned the significance of Abraham and David, but let's take a moment to think about the exile to Babylon. As we noted above at Table 1.1 (see page 349 for list), Matthew highlights this broken aspect of Israel's history with his broken chiasm. Other than the exodus from Egypt, no other event in Old Testament history is as significant. The Assyrian menace in the eighth century BC had been bad enough; it sent chills throughout the nation, but Jerusalem and the temple had escaped the carnage. David's dynasty was still intact.

A century and half later, the Babylonians repeatedly attacked and threatened David's kingdom in the south until they marched on Jerusalem, razed Solomon's temple, and carted off the chief citizens to Babylon. There were many interim steps to Israel's decline and sorrow. One of the few good kings of the era, Josiah, is injured and killed in battle with Pharaoh Necho (2 Ch 35:20–24). Thereafter, the Egyptians are overlords of the land and impose their own king, Jehoiakim (2 Ki 23:28–37), and severe taxes. However, as had many of his predecessors, Jehoiakim does what is evil in the sight of the Lord. But then Nebuchadnezzar, king of Babylon, marches south, subdues Egypt, and swallows up the territories that belonged to Israel and Judah in their glory days. At first Jehoiakim played nice with Babylon, but eventually he rebelled, and hordes of Babylonians, Moabites, and Ammonites marched against Jerusalem as Judah crumbled. Jehoiachin succeeded his father and walked in his wicked steps, until it became obvious Jerusalem was lost. He surrendered to the king of Babylon in 597 BC and saw the treasures of his own house and Solomon's temple be plundered and destroyed for the gold in them. A huge wave of talent and skill—warriors, artisans, and leaders—was taken in tow into captivity in Babylon, leaving mainly the poor and displaced to remain in the land (2 Ki 24:8–17).

The Babylonian-approved king, Zedekiah, remained loyal to Babylon for a while, but eventually he too rebelled and brought upon Jerusalem and God's temple the mother of all battles, and he was captured. Less than a month later, Nebuchadnezzar's army came to Jerusalem and burned and destroyed all the great houses of the city, including the house of YHWH. The walls that once protected the city were dismantled. Once again, the wealth of the temple and its city was pillaged and carted off to enrich the empire of Babylon (2 Ki 25:1–21). The historian puts it simply: "So Judah went into exile out of its land" (2 Ki 25:21 NRSV).

On a human level this was a tragedy of immense proportions. It would be hard for us to imagine what an event like this does to the psyche of a people. If you multiplied the horror of America's 9/11 times one thousand, you still would not have it. The death, destruction, and loss seemed total, for that was the Babylonian way when dealing with obstinate peoples.

The chronicler, however, reminds his readers that prior to this total destruction God repeatedly sent his servants, the prophets, to challenge them for their corruption. And, repeatedly, the people rejected them, mocked them, and ignored their corrections. So it was YHWH who sent Babylon to "correct" the idolatry and injustices of his covenant people (2 Ch 36:14–21).

Prophets like Jeremiah and Isaiah had warned such a day would come because Israel and Judah had cozied up to foreign gods, neglected the poor, and generally disobeyed the covenant. Bit by bit, the glory days of David and Solomon were forgotten, the temple and palace were destroyed, and the wealth of Israel was carried off to a foreign land (2 Ki 20:16–19). But all this happened under the watchful eye of the Lord (2 Ki 24:3–7).

Afterward, the malaise of the exile began to lift because seers prophesied a new day when God would reverse their fortunes, forgive their sins, and begin the steady march back to Zion (Isa 40). Habakkuk foresaw the defeat of the Babylonian menace and a complete restoration to the land (Hab 3:17–19). As a prophetic sign, Jeremiah purchased a plot of land in Anathoth even as Jerusalem was surrounded by the Babylonian armies: one day houses and lands would again be sold in the land (Jer 32). Ezekiel envisioned the new temple of God and gave witness that one day God's glory would return (Eze 40–43).

The Babylonian exile would last officially until 538 BC when Cyrus, king of Persia, became the overlord to the Babylonian lands. He allowed the exiles to go home, start over, and rebuild the temple (Ezr 1). But the return did not go as seamlessly as the people had imagined it would. A majority of exiles had made a place for themselves in Babylon, and not everyone was anxious to make the treacherous and uncertain journey back. Those with the courage to return found inhospitable neighbors and hardship at every turn. Mistakes had been made and reparations still had to be paid. At first, God's temple remained in ruins—Haggai shamed the people into rebuilding it, but only after they saw to their own houses first (Hag 1). Ultimately, the temple of YHWH was rebuilt under Zerubbabel (completed about 515 BC), but most people suspected its glory would never eclipse that of Solomon's temple.

The next few centuries saw one kingdom after another arise and make claims on Abraham's people and its land. God's promise to King David seemed remote and was all but forgotten. Daniel's four beasts (Da 7) symbolized four kingdoms, greedy for gain, often violent and rapacious. At first it was the Medes, then the Persians, then the Syrian Greeks. When Jesus was born, it was the Romans who had a firm grip on the Galilee and Judea. It was a Roman cross that would witness his last, earthly breath.

So if there had been an end to the exile, many people never noticed. Matthew does not mention it. He does mention the exile but not the restoration. The unsatisfying return of the exiles and yearning for liberation greeted the infant Jesus at his birth. By breaking his chiasm with the exile (see Table 1.1), Matthew emphasizes that it would be up to the Messiah to do something about it.

Matthew 1:1–17 Through Old Testament Eyes

Matthew's genealogy hits the high and low spots of Israel's history with its cast of characters. Saints and sinners alike make up the family tree of Joseph, Mary, and Jesus. The better we know the Old Testament, the more sensitive we are to the textures Matthew is laying out for his readers to see and hear. What seems clear is that the evangelist signals a new role for women in Jesus' movement, foreshadows the regular charge that he is a friend of sinners, and opens up the possibility that if the blood of outsiders/Gentiles runs in his family, then surely the blood of the new covenant must extend to all nations (Mt 28:19–20). Finally, the immoral sexual behavior by men and women echoed in the genealogy sets us up for the next moment in the Jesus story: Joseph's realization that his betrothed, Mary, is pregnant, and he is not the father.

1:18 *This is how the birth of Jesus the Messiah came about: His mother Mary was pledged to be married to Joseph, but before they came together, she was found to be pregnant through the Holy Spirit.* For Matthew, the birth of Jesus, the Messiah, marks the beginning of the end of the exile. While history might mark another day more than five hundred years earlier as the "official" end, the situation on the ground for most pious Jews remained stressful and uncertain. They awaited the restoration of David's monarchy, a glorious temple, and their great-nation status. They paid taxes and mumbled under their breath about how badly Roman officials and their puppet king, Herod, treated them. They longed for God to act.

Matthew now moves on from the genealogy to tell the remarkable story of how the Messiah is born. The word *birth* (*genesis*) takes us back to Matthew 1:1—"the genealogy [*genesis*] of Jesus the Messiah"—and perhaps further back to the first book of the Bible, whose name in Greek is *Genesis*. It is not a stretch to say that Matthew intentionally positions Jesus' story as a new creation, a starting-over story in the history of the world.

Matthew begins this next section (Mt 1:18–25) with the names that end the genealogy, Mary and Joseph. They are betrothed, that is, legally promised to be married. In Jewish law (e.g., Dt 22:23–29) betrothal was a binding state that could be dissolved only through divorce. The woman remained in her father's care prior to the wedding, and sexual relations were not permitted. Both Mary and Joseph honor that arrangement, but before they are wed, a discovery is made. Mary is with child "by the Holy Spirit" (1:18, 20). On the one hand, this appears to be in line with a number of women in the biblical record who credit their pregnancies and children to the Lord's gift. Regarding the birth of Cain, Eve declares, "With the help of the LORD I have brought forth a man" (Ge 4:1). A miraculous intervention, it is said, grants Hannah her prayer at Shiloh (1 Sa 1). In the third gospel, Elizabeth, despite her age, becomes pregnant with her own child of destiny: John the Baptist. "The Lord," she said, "has done this for me" (Lk 1:25). So, in one way, Mary's situation is consistent with some of the biblical records; still, what is happening to Mary and Joseph is also unique in all the world.

1:19 *Because Joseph her husband was faithful to the law, and yet did not want to expose her to public disgrace, he had in mind to divorce her quietly.* Joseph is described as "faithful to the law" (some translations, "righteous"). Once he is aware of Mary's pregnancy, he is determined to do the right thing in the right way. The right thing is prescribed by the law; that is, he must divorce her. The right way involves doing it privately so as not to shame her or her family. No public trial is required, only a certificate of divorce (Dt 24:1). He may have been "righteous" in other ways, but Matthew's point is that Joseph is ready to do what God's law prescribes. As he is sorting this out in his mind, he has a dream and encounters the mysterious angel of the Lord.

1:20 *But after he had considered this, an angel of the Lord appeared to him in a dream.* Throughout the Old Testament, significant moments are marked by dreams. Joseph's namesake was known for his dreams in the times of the patriarchs (Ge 37:1–11). In the first recorded dream he, though a young son of Jacob, reports that his dream predicts he will one day dominate his older siblings. In another he appears elevated even above his parents. Obviously, these dreams and his delight in them cause trouble with his family. But it is Joseph's remarkable ability to interpret the dreams of others that brings him his greatest successes and ultimately opens the door for him to rule in Egypt (Ge 41:1–57).

Others, too, in those days had revelatory dreams. At Bethel Joseph's father, Jacob, had a dream that the land where he slept would one day be his: the shrine at Bethel became known as the abode of God, the gateway to heaven (Ge 28:10–22). On another occasion, the angel of God appears to Jacob in a dream and instructs him to leave Laban's service and return home (Ge 31:1–13). This is not to say all dreams are revelatory; it is to say only that some notable people of the past have had revelatory dreams at precise moments when they were needed.

Our two Josephs have more in common than revelatory dreams. As Matthew's story of Jesus unfolds, the evangelist makes further connections between them. First, both Josephs have a father named Jacob. Second, both go down to Egypt because of their dreams. Third, both are subject to persecution that includes mortal threats. Fourth, both act heroically and mercifully to save their families. Finally, both Josephs are associated with Rachel. Rachel, the favored wife of Jacob, was the mother of Joseph (Ge 35:22–26); and Joseph, husband of Mary, avoids the slaughter of young boys in Bethlehem, which Matthew indicates fulfills the prophecy of Jeremiah about Rachel weeping for her children (Mt 2:18).[10]

Matthew's story of Jesus' birth taps into that stream and extends it to include his father and the magi who come to visit the child (Mt 2:1–15). In each of these dream-visions, the angel of the Lord plays a decisive role.

Matthew 1:20 Through Old Testament Eyes: The Angel of the Lord

In Matthew 1–2 Joseph has not one but a series of revelatory dreams. In each he encounters the mysterious figure described in Israel's Scripture as the angel of the Lord (YHWH). The word *angel* in both testaments means "messenger" or "special envoy." The figure known as "the angel of the Lord," however, has the role as a chief angel who moves seamlessly between heaven and earth pronouncing judgment, revealing God's will, and defending the faithful from their enemies (Ge 16:7–13; 2 Ki 19:35; Zec 3:1). Often called "the angel of God," he is God's supreme envoy, appearing sometimes in human form and often indistinguishable from God. Hagar, for example, encounters the angel of YHWH by a spring in the wilderness and is instructed to return to Abram's house and bear him a child. In this encounter, Hagar says she has seen God (Ge 16:7–13).

At the base of Mt. Sinai, the angel of YHWH appears to Moses in a flaming fire in a bush, yet it is God who speaks to Moses from the flames (Ex 3:4). Likewise, when Gideon is commissioned to fight the Midianites and bring relief to God's oppressed people, the angel of the Lord comes to sit with him under the oak at Ophrah (Jdg 6:11–27); God's messenger discusses Gideon's next steps. In the encounter Gideon is said to speak to the Lord himself.

These mysterious meetings demonstrate how close the angel of the Lord is to God. When he speaks, he speaks for God. When he acts, he acts for God. The angel's speech and actions are indistinguishable from God's. By framing Jesus' birth with his father's dream-visions, the reader who has Old Testament eyes is able to see how the God who established the covenant with Abraham and extended it through his descendants is now at work in surprising ways.

Joseph son of David, do not be afraid to take Mary home as your wife, because what is conceived in her is from the Holy Spirit. The angel of the Lord had a message for Joseph. He is not to divorce Mary; she has not been unfaithful to him. The child in her is from the Holy Spirit.

Now immediately, we must set aside any modern notions of conception, for though Matthew and his audience would have been aware of how babies were made, they were not versed fully in the biology of it. The Greek word translated "conceived" in most modern translations does not mean what moderns mean when they think scientifically regarding conception. So we must not insist that that term carry the full freight of our biological knowledge. The word simply means "to bring forth." The same word was used earlier in the chapter more than forty times to refer to how fathers bring forth children (e.g., Mt 1:2–17).

One way the ancients viewed the woman's womb was as the ground upon which the seed could be planted. Most were agricultural people whose life-images were drawn from the earth. If the seed found favorable "ground," then a child would result. If a woman's womb were "barren," then the couple remained childless.

Matthew 1:20 Through Old Testament Eyes: The Virgin Birth

Matthew does not present Mary's pregnancy as a sexual act. In fact, the way he tells the story makes it obvious that he is trying to distance his account from any notion of sexual intercourse. Perhaps that is because in his time on earth some of Jesus' opponents had charged that he was illegitimate; more likely, in my view, Matthew had a theological and apologetic purpose.

According to the first evangelist, Mary is a virgin and stays a virgin up to the time of Jesus' birth (Catholics and many other faithful believers regard her virginity as perpetual). Furthermore, the child that will come forth from her is "from the Holy Spirit" (a genitive of source governed by the Greek preposition *ek*). It is likely that Matthew knew his audience was aware of Greek myths and pagan stories of gods coming down and having sexual relations with women who gave birth to semi-divine beings (e.g., Hercules). His account of Jesus' miraculous birth is meant to distance Jesus' origins as far as possible from these pagan notions. No sexual act is committed, and Mary remains a virgin until Jesus' birth. Had Mary been violated by a god as Persephone was by Zeus, she would no longer be a virgin. From Matthew's perspective, that which is in Mary is from the Holy Spirit. Full stop. It is the work of God in her from start to finish. It is God's power at work at this crucial moment in Israel's story, as the angel of the Lord announces.

Reading Matthew's account in this way makes it possible to view Jesus as a new Adam, in line with other New Testament writers (e.g., Paul in Ro 5; 1 Co 15; and Luke in particular). The genealogy of the third gospel (Lk 3) begins with Jesus and traces his lineage all the way back to Adam. Jesus is therefore the Son of Adam, who is none other than the Son of God. The God who said, "Let there be light" and light "became" can surely say, "Let there be a child in the womb of my loyal servant, Mary," and make it so. Adam was the product of *adamah* (Hebrew for "earth") and the breath (Spirit) of God (Ge 1–3). Jesus was the product of the Holy Spirit and his holy mother, according to Matthew. What Mary did provide— by common agreement with God—was more than a nurturing place or "ground" for the Christ child to grow and develop. She provided him a body, without which the incarnation would have been impossible. From the flesh of Mary came the flesh of the Messiah. In truth, and in every conceivable way, she is the mother of Jesus.[11]

1:21 *She will give birth to a son, and you are to give him the name Jesus, because he will save his people from their sins.* The angel instructed Joseph to name the son Mary would bear, Jesus (Yehoshua), a name that means "YHWH saves." As with other Old Testament figures, his name aligns with his mission. He will save his people from their sins (Mt 1:21; 9:1–8; 20:28; 26:26–29). Now, before we jump ahead and assume we know what this means, we need to let Matthew's story speak for itself. When we think of being saved from our sins, we often imagine that Jesus' mission is to set us up for a peaceful afterlife in heaven. That may be part of the answer, but it is not the whole. Being saved from our sins is not exclusively reserved for the afterlife; it is also about how we live and experience this life. Remember God sent the children of Israel into exile because of their sins (idolatry, injustice, and neglect of the poor). Sins make us miserable in this life, injure us, and injure others in the process. They must be dealt with, not merely because they determine where we spend eternity but because they disturb God's shalom, God's peace, now in the present. Jesus' life and teaching address/undo the problem of sin and the suffering it causes.

We should also consider the Old Testament resonance of the name *Jesus*, which in Hebrew is the name "Joshua." First and foremost, Joshua was the name of the man Moses entrusted to lead Israel into the land of promise: "Now Joshua son of Nun was filled with the spirit of wisdom because Moses had laid his hands on him. So the Israelites listened to him and did what the LORD had commanded Moses" (Dt 34:9). The Torah ends with the reins of leadership handed over to Joshua. The book called "Joshua" begins with YHWH speaking to Joshua and instructing him to lead the Israelites into the land of promise (Jos 1). Joshua is a significant figure in the story of redemption, but he was no Moses nor was he the prophet like Moses God had promised (Dt 18:14–18).

1:23 *The virgin will conceive and give birth to a son.* Matthew sees the remarkable beginning to Jesus' story as the fulfillment of word of the Lord: "All this took place to fulfill what the Lord had said through the prophet" (1:22). This is the first of many fulfillment formulae that Matthew uses to announce the ways in which events surrounding Jesus' life fulfill Scripture. Now, the term *fulfill* is a complicated one. It can be taken to refer to predictions that come true. In some cases that appears to be Matthew's point (e.g., Jesus' birth in Bethlehem [Mic 5:2]). But it can also be taken in more subtle ways to connect significant people and events of the past with what is happening in and around Jesus' life. The current quotation is a good case in point.

Centuries of debate have swirled around this quotation. Is Matthew playing fast and loose with his Bible, making it mean only what he wants it to mean? Or is something more significant, more interesting, going on within his account of the good news? Is Matthew's reading of Isaiah and his context "according to Scripture" or contrary to it?

Matthew asserts (in 1:23) that the miraculous conception and birth of Jesus fulfills Isaiah's prophecy spoken in the eighth century BC, quoting Isaiah 7:14: "The virgin will conceive and give birth to a son, and will call him Immanuel."

The Greek version Matthew follows translates the Hebrew word *'almah* ("a young woman of marriageable age" [e.g., Ge 24:43; Ps 68:25; Song 1:3]) with *parthenos* (most often translated "virgin," however, see Ge 34:3, LXX). Matthew finds the miracle of Jesus' birth by Mary a fitting companion to Isaiah's prophecy.

To understand how Matthew considers Jesus' special birth the fulfillment of prophecy, we need to know more about the prophecy uttered by Isaiah about seven hundred years earlier (Isa 7:1–25).

When Ahaz was king of Judah (735–715 BC), two nations to Judah's north, Syria and Israel, formed an alliance and conspired to attack Jerusalem. They wanted to force Judah and its people into a coalition to resist Assyrian expansion. To do so, they planned to install their own king, someone not part of King David's royal line, the son of Tabeel. Yet King Ahaz had pinned his political hopes on the intervention of the Assyrians and their king, Tiglath-Pilezer III. He paid a handsome sum—gold and silver from the temple treasury—to keep out of the fray (2 Ki 16:5–16). The situation was dire; little Judah, left on her own, would surely be brought to her knees. The kingdom was in jeopardy. Even the hearts of all the people trembled (Isa 7:2).

The Lord instructed Isaiah to go out and meet Ahaz and give him a message. He is to take along his son, Shear-Jashub. His son's name means "a remnant will return." It is important to this story—and others like it—that Isaiah dramatically enacted his message by the names he gave his children. Their presence was a constant reminder of God's message to the nation through the prophet. Shear-Jashub's name was meant to be a message of hope—"a remnant will return"—God will make sure Judah survives and her people live in this land. Isaiah is not alone; other prophets enacted their messages through the way they named their children (see Hosea).

At this grim moment, Isaiah speaks directly to the king, telling him to stay calm and not worry about the threats coming from their northern neighbors. Through the prophet the Lord says nothing will come of this threat, and the two nations who bully Judah will be crushed and laid to waste. In the meantime, Ahaz must resolve to trust in the Lord alone (Isa 7:9). The Lord gives him a sign: "The virgin will conceive and give birth to a son, and will call him Immanuel" (Isa 7:14). Many people stop reading there, but the oracle continues. That child will grow up eating curds and honey, and before he reaches the age when he can discern good from bad, the land of these nations that threatened Judah will have become a wasteland. Now, the word of the prophet came true. The immediate threat from the Syria-Israel alliance came to nothing in just a few years.

This may seem to modern readers like a small event. But if you were the king of Judah, your life and the lives of your people hung in the balance; it would have been the end of the world and in many ways the end of the covenant. Yet it was not, for God stepped in and kept Judah's enemies at bay. God, in a word, saved and prolonged the life of the nation despite the king's infidelities. In Old Testament history, this was a saving event of epic proportions. In a concrete sense, the prophecy of Isaiah was fulfilled in his lifetime and in lifetime of Judah's king.

We do not know who the young woman was that the prophet referred to. Some identify her as the mother of the future king, Hezekiah (a descendant of David). Others think Isaiah may have been referring to his own wife. Isaiah did give his second son the name Maher-Shalal-Hash-Baz ("spoil speeds, prey hastens") to signify that Judah's threatening neighbors, Syria and Israel, would be conquered by Assyria (Isa 8:1–4). In the end, we cannot be certain who the young woman was. What is certain is that within a decade, roughly the period of a young child's life prior to coming of age, the two nations—Syria and Israel—have been soundly defeated by the Assyrians (c. 722 BC). Whatever we make of that history, Isaiah and Ahaz lived long enough to see the northern alliance come to nothing. Again, they lived long enough to see the prophecy "fulfilled."

So, when Matthew says that the virgin birth of Yehoshua/Jesus fulfills the prophecy, what does he mean? Matthew is linking two of God's saving acts in a strategy known as "typology."[12] The evangelist, in a sense, learned this from reading his Bible, the Hebrew Scriptures, because typology is a common strategy employed in it to recall redemptive acts of God in the past and anticipate new acts in the future: creation and new creation, exodus and new exodus, and covenant and new covenant are memorable themes from the prophets that seek "fulfillment" in God's future actions. So the way God entered the picture and "saved" Judah in Isaiah's day, despite the infidelity of her "shepherd," is connected with how God entered the world through the miraculous conception and birth of Mary's son. These two events are brought together into intertextual play to interpret one another. But typology is based on a linear view of history in which events intensify or escalate as the end (the *eschaton*) draws near. This is why Matthew is completely at ease with the LXX rendering that a *parthenos* (virgin) will be with child and bear a son whose name is Immanuel.

Matthew 1:23 Through Old Testament Eyes: Immanuel

In the history of interpretation, the emphasis has often been on the virgin birth, but for Matthew the weight should be placed on how the quotation ends: for "they will call him Immanuel." Why? Because Matthew makes nothing more of the virgin birth in his account, but he makes much of the idea that Jesus is God with us. In fact, he interprets the Hebrew *Immanuel* for his audience by calling upon Isaiah again (8:8, 10) to translate what it means: his name is "God with us." He is the God-with-us son of Mary, miraculously conceived, enfleshed, and born. How else would God enter the world? He is the ultimate "fulfillment" of Isaiah's prophecy, transcending God's rescue of Judah in the eighth century BC to now include all nations (Mt 28:19–20). Richard Hays refers to this as "the most distinctive feature of Matthew's narrative Christology: its bold identification of Jesus as Immanuel, 'God with us.'"[13] This audacious claim frames the entire gospel, for the story ends with Jesus and his eleven disciples on a mountain in Galilee—some doubting, some worshiping— as Jesus commissions them and promises: "Behold, I AM with you each day until the consummation of the age" (Mt 28:20, author's translation and emphasis). The frame around Matthew's gospel identifies Jesus with God, the I AM, with us. Everything inside the gospel should be read in light of this declaration, this promise. Who else but the God-with-us one could claim to be in the midst of two or three whenever they gather in his name (Mt 18:20)?

But as Matthew's story unfolds, it is clear that the God-with-us one wields a double-edged sword. For some, Jesus' presence means rescue; for others, judgment, just as it had in the days of Ahaz and Judah. Immanuel in Isaiah's day brought only a temporary respite from aggression and violence. Ultimately, destruction did come upon Judah; the power Ahaz trusted—not YHWH but the Assyrians—ultimately ran over little Judea. Salvation by the hand of the God-with-us one, Jesus, is not unilateral either. Even though Jesus did come to save his people from their sins, he declared the temple would be razed and Jerusalem destroyed by the Romans. God's presence in and by Jesus would mean woe to some and blessings to others. When the final assize comes, the sheep would be on the right hand, the goats on the left (Mt 25:31–46). Failure to believe in and follow Jesus would mean judgment, not salvation.

As we will see, many of Matthew's fulfillment quotations will fall within a figural (typological) range of interpretation. Richard Hays captures the "spirit" of figural reading aided by the important work of Erich Auerbach, who writes:

> Figural interpretation establishes a connection between two events or persons in such a way that the first signifies not only itself but also the second, while the second involves or fulfills the first. The two poles of a figure are separated in time, but both, being real events or persons, are within temporality. They are both contained in the flowing stream which is historical life, and only the comprehension, the *intellectus spiritualis,* of their interdependence is a spiritual act.[14]

"Figural interpretation" involves "reading backwards," a strategy that comes temporally after both poles, whether persons or events. Hays describes it primarily as a phenomenon of intertextuality that emphasizes how a later reader or writer receives the earlier texts. For him it is a strategy of "retrospective recognition" that when grasped is capable of assigning deeper meaning to both earlier and later figures.[15] Throughout our study of Matthew, we will have need to draw on how the evangelist deploys this strategy.

Some will be easier to square than others, depending on how well-versed we are in Old Testament themes and history. We will need to resist the temptation to think of prophecy merely as predictions launched hundreds of years into the future. In some cases, such "predictions" are capable of more than one fulfillment. But prophets did more that foretell the future; they served as interpreters of their current times from God's perspective: "thus says the LORD." They were God's mouthpiece. Often, they interceded for Israel and negotiated with God for mercy and better terms. They were Israel's teachers of the law when God's good teaching was all but forgotten. And they were the conscience of the nation when the people thought God wanted rituals, not a life constituted in holiness. So to be good interpreters, we need a broad and generous view of prophecy.

1:24–25 *He did what the angel of the Lord had commanded him.* So what does Joseph the righteous do? He does as the angel of the Lord directs, not as many interpreted the law to allow. He takes Mary to be his wife and, after she gives birth, names the boy "Jesus."

MATTHEW 2

2:1 *Jesus was born in Bethlehem in Judea, during the time of King Herod.* Jesus is born in time and in space. In time it was during the reign of King Herod. In space it was in the city of King David, Bethlehem. Matthew seeks to contrast the two kingdoms. As Son of David, Jesus would be a rightful king, a fulfiller of prophecy, the climax of the covenant, one who would lobby for a greater righteousness. Herod, on the other hand, was an Idumean, a violent man, an illegitimate king. Rome installed him to rule in their interests, not those of the people. Herod's cruel reign (37–4 BC) typified how the exile had continued even while many of the children of Abraham lived in the promised land. The murder of the innocent babies in and around Bethlehem (Mt 2:16–18) was a malevolent act completely in character with other acts perpetrated by the paranoid king.

Magi from the east came to Jerusalem. In Matthew's story the first to visit the Christ child were the *magoi* (magi). Although some English translations render the word "wise men," it is not clear that Christ followers would have considered them wise. They were likely Persian astrologers, people of means and schooled in magical arts.[1] Extensive travel was a luxury only for the wealthy or people with generous benefactors. The magi may have had knowledge of the Hebrew Scriptures, for they knew something of prophecies about a coming messiah-king. Since the sixth century BC, there had been a large and intellectually curious Jewish population "in the east." We cannot say for certain, but Jewish traditions and aspirations could have leaked into the surrounding cultures and fueled the imaginations of the magi. Thanks to the star, they headed for Jerusalem. Providentially, the prophets had predicted that one day people would come from north, south, east, and west to Jerusalem to worship (Isa 60:1–9; Jer 3:17; Mic 4:2; Zec 2:10–11; 8:22–23; 14:16; Mal 1:11). The magi are the first ripples of that great wave. Their visit foreshadows the commission that would take the disciples of Jesus to the ends of the earth. Thus, the words of the prophets are fulfilled, not by the nations coming to the center of worship at the holy mountain of Zion (e.g., Mic 4:1–2), but by them coming to Christ. For he is the new center, the new temple, the one who embodies the very presence of God.

2:3–8 *When he had called together all the people's chief priests and teachers of the law, he asked them where the Messiah was to be born.* Herod was less informed than the pagans, for when the question was asked, he had to gather his religious advisors and ask them where the prophecies said the future king would be born. There seemed to be no debate on the matter; they chimed in that the king would be born in Bethlehem of Judea as the prophet Micah had said (Mic 5:2–4). Bethlehem was located about six miles south of Jerusalem, roughly half a day's journey from where the magi had stopped. Ephrathah was a small clan of the Judahites, and Bethlehem was one of its villages.

Matthew's quotation (2:5–6) does not follow his typical fulfillment protocol because he quotes the religious leaders quoting Micah. But for any pious Jew the words of the prophet stand as written. The poem in its entirety reads this way (Mic 5:2–4):

> "But you, Bethlehem Ephrathah,
>   though you are small among the clans of Judah,
> out of you will come for me
>   one who will be ruler over Israel,
> whose origins are from of old,
>   from ancient times."
>
> Therefore Israel will be abandoned
>   until the time when she who is in labor bears a son,
> and the rest of his brothers return
>   to join the Israelites.
>
> He will stand and shepherd his flock
>   in the strength of the LORD,
>   in the majesty of the name of the LORD his God.
> And they will live securely, for then his greatness
>   will reach to the ends of the earth.

The poem has a number of features relevant to Matthew's story: (1) the ideal, messianic king will be born in Bethlehem despite its insignificant status; (2) he comes to rule in Israel; (3) his origin lies deep in the past, in "ancient times"; (4) the people remain in "exile" until the king's mother gives birth; (5) then they will return to rejoin the people of Israel; (6) the king will perform his shepherd's role well "in the strength of the LORD," thus ending the stream of bad shepherd-kings; (7) the people he rules will live in peace and security; and (8) the king will be a man of peace and his name celebrated throughout the earth. As Matthew develops his story of Jesus, he draws implicitly upon these elements, but within his account of the *magoi* those mentioned explicitly in the paraphrase of Micah 5:2–4 are (1), (2), and (6).

The sages' answer draws together relevant lines of Micah's messianic poem that highlight the distinction between the sorry shepherd, Herod, and the ideal shepherd, the messianic Son of David. David, of course, had been a shepherd of sheep before he shepherded Israel (1 Sa 17:20; 2 Sa 24:17; Ps 78:72; Eze 34:23). Bethlehem of Roman Judea had been small and insignificant in Micah's day, but by Matthew's it was celebrated as the birthplace of the Messiah by Jesus followers. In a few years pilgrims would make their way to Jerusalem's sister village in acts of devotion and piety.

Going Deeper into Micah's Bad Shepherds: Matthew 2:5–6

More than most prophets, Micah puts the blame for the sorry state of Israel squarely on the shoulders of the leaders. In his day they abhorred justice, took bribes, and courted violence; it was because of them that one day Jerusalem would become a heap of ruins (Mic 3:9–12). So when Micah announces the birth of a new king, a new shepherd, that person is destined to undo all the sadness and wrong brought by Judah's bad leaders. Matthew is clearly acquainted with this theme as he contrasts the child Jesus with the illegitimate king, Herod. Herod is the epitome of the bad shepherds.

Herod was not the last of the bad shepherds. Their ilk continue today in politics and, tragically, in the church itself. How many nations are in ruins today because of failed leadership? How many churches are reeling from pastors who fall into sin and immorality? In the West millions of people no longer affiliate with churches because of leadership fiascoes. No one should choose to be a leader lightly. Likewise, no one should avoid it when called. But Matthew would have every leader model their lives on the man from Nazareth. Jesus did not lead by secrecy, power grabs, bullying, and lording over others. He led simply through teaching and service. If leaders today would serve rather than seek to be served, we would all be in a better place.

2:9 *After they had heard the king, they went on their way, and the star they had seen when it rose went ahead of them until it stopped over the place where the child was.* The magi's journey began when they were in the east and observed a star. In popular imagination, the star must have been some kind of supernova, the brightest object in the night's sky. That may be the wrong way to think of it. As experts in the night sky, the magi would have been aware of the slightest change in the stars or their movements, not unlike the neurosurgeon who can expertly read an MRI. The average person may not have picked up on a subtle change to the twinkling lights, which may be why others at the time do not report any strange astronomical phenomena.

The star may well take the first hearers of this gospel back to the fourth oracle of Balaam (Nu 24:17):

> I see him, but not now;
> > I behold him, but not near.
> A star will come out of Jacob;
> > a scepter will rise out of Israel.
> He will crush the foreheads of Moab,
> > the skulls of all the people of Sheth.

Despite some ambiguity, this future oracle describes the ascendency of God's people Israel over her enemies through the images of star and scepter.[2] In his day, the prophet could see "him," but he is not ready to appear. The prophet could behold him, but he remained distant. The scepter is clearly a royal image. It appears to hearken back to Genesis 49:10, thus an intertextual echo within the Pentateuch itself:

> The scepter will not depart from Judah,
> > nor the ruler's staff from between his feet,
> until he to whom it belongs shall come
> > and the obedience of the nations shall be his.

These are Jacob's final words to his sons before his death. While most of his sons receive only a few lines, Judah's blessing rivals that of Joseph's for length. Judah will become known as the ancestor to the mightiest and most significant kings of God's people. Jesus is part of that royal line, of course, linked to Judah via King David. Together the star and scepter become symbols of the royal line that will one day rule God's covenant people, and the king—especially the idealized messianic king—embodies and represents his people. The connection between star and Messiah (Mt 2:2) was clear enough even for the magi to grasp. When Herod heard of it, he and all Jerusalem were deeply troubled. On a ruse, the Idumean promised to pay the child king homage when he learned the Messiah's true identity. Fortunately for Joseph and his family, they would escape to Egypt. Unfortunately for the parents of young boys in and around Bethlehem, they would face Herod's paranoid vengeance.

2:10–11 *When they saw the star, they were overjoyed. On coming to the house, they saw the child with his mother Mary, and they bowed down and worshiped him. Then they opened their treasures and presented him with gifts of gold, frankincense and myrrh.* The star, it seemed, had a mind of its own, for it stopped over the place where Mary, Joseph, and the young Jesus were staying in Bethlehem. The ancients would have been prepared to think of it as an angel or other celestial being.

When the magi found the child, they bowed down before him. How did Matthew and his audience think of their bowed heads and bent knees (2:11)? This was the posture one would assume before a superior or a king (2 Ki 1:13; Est 3:2, 5), but it certainly portended something greater, a time when the nations themselves would bow the head, bend the knee, and declare him "Lord" to the glory of God the Father (Php 2:9–11). Whether the magi that celebrated day bowed in "worship" before the child is a matter of debate. Some reckon the humble homage only as what would be appropriate before a king; others take it as a sign of things to come when the nations bow before the risen and enthroned Lord (Php 2:9–11; Rev 5).

Nearly a millennium earlier, another son of David received a prominent guest bearing gifts. The fame of Solomon, the wise king of Jerusalem, had reached the attentive ears of the Queen of Sheba. She came with a retinue and camels weighed down with spices, gold, and precious stones (1 Ki 10:1–10). Exactly where Sheba was located, we cannot be sure. Traditionally, it was thought she made the journey from Ethiopia, but some scholars today think she may have come from the Arab peninsula. Regardless, she observed the wealth of Solomon's wisdom, the riches of his hospitality, and the fidelity of his worship to YHWH in the temple. Thereafter she blessed the God of Solomon by name for his wondrous works in making such a wise man king. She is remembered for the lavish gifts of gold, spices, and precious stones just as the magi are remembered for bringing to the Christ child gifts of gold, frankincense, and myrrh.

2:13–15 *An angel of the Lord appeared to Joseph in a dream. "Get up," he said, "take the child and his mother and escape to Egypt."* After the magi left—without reporting to Herod—the angel of the Lord appeared to Joseph again in a dream, telling him to take the child and his mother to Egypt. We should likely see here what Matthew's audience saw first, that Jesus and his family are retracing the steps of his ancient ancestors when they left the land of Canaan to find food, safety, and security in the lands of Egypt (Ge 46–50). The Joseph narratives (Ge 37–50) describe how God used the hatred and evil schemes of his brothers to prepare the way so that Jacob and his kin would have a future; otherwise, they may have perished from the pages of history. Jacob brings his whole family to Egypt to escape starvation when he learns his son is second-in-command in Egypt. But over time the land of refuge for Israel became a snare of slavery (Ex 1–2). Joseph, Mary, and Jesus (in Matthew's portrayal) track with the children of Israel; they too will find refuge in the land of the Nile. Joseph the righteous obeyed the angel and took the family by night down roads to the south and west. They escaped Herod's campaign to rid the earth of the innocent boys in and around Bethlehem and remained in Egypt until after the wicked king died.

And so was fulfilled what the Lord had said through the prophet: "Out of Egypt I called my son." Matthew fashions for his readers another link to the Scriptures; this time it is to a prophet. The flight and return of the holy family to Egypt fulfills a prophecy spoken by the Lord through the prophet Hosea (11:1): "Out of Egypt I called my son." In context, Hosea's prophecy looks back to the exodus from Egypt (Hos 11:1–4):

> When Israel was a child, I loved him,
>   and out of Egypt I called my son.
> But the more they were called,
>   the more they went away from me.
> They sacrificed to the Baals
>   and they burned incense to images.
> It was I who taught Ephraim to walk,
>   taking them by the arms;
> but they did not realize
>   it was I who healed them.
> I led them with cords of human kindness,
>   with ties of love.
> To them I was like one who lifts
>   a little child to the cheek,
>   and I bent down to feed them.

Embedded deep within the Moses narratives is God's instruction for him to say to Pharaoh, "Israel is my firstborn son" (Ex 4:22). The language of sonship related to Israel is key to understanding Matthew's story. Jesus is connected deeply to God's people, Israel. For Hosea, Israel is "my son" whom God loved and called out of slavery in Egypt. This refers back in time to the exodus, the central event of redemption in the Hebrew Scriptures. And Matthew brings Jesus into connection with that saving event. Yet as Hosea tells the rest of the story, even though God loved and called Israel, his firstborn, the people rebelled against him, sacrificed to idols, and refused to follow his sensible teachings.

The return of Joseph, Mary, and Jesus to the land of Abraham causes Matthew to think of the rescue of God's people from its first exile, as slaves in Egypt. He thus introduces a new Old Testament feature to his gospel. Like Moses, when Jesus grows up, he will rescue his people. Unlike Israel, he is God's Son who returns from exile in Egypt not to disappoint his Father but to do his will. The saving event known in the Hebrew Scriptures as the exodus is now refracted through a new lens: the birth, life, teaching, death, and resurrection of Jesus.

Matthew 2:15 Through Old Testament Eyes: Israel and Jesus as God's Son

It would be best to read all of Hosea 11 to capture the struggle within God; it is the struggle of every loving parent who has a disloyal daughter or son. On the one hand, God threatens to punish his rebellious people by burying them deep in Egypt once again. At the same time, his compassion grows warm and tender, and he cannot—for now—bring himself to hand them over to their enemies (Hos 11:8–9).

Matthew takes Hosea's backward glance to the exodus and pulls it forward to address another "son" who does not fall into temptation, go after other gods, and refuse to honor God's teachings. As God's son, Israel had disappointed his grieving Father, and God threatens to bury his people in Egypt once again (Hos 11:5). This new Son, this new Israel, would be everything Israel was supposed to be but was not. Jesus is Israel as God had always intended. He embodies within himself the ideal for which Israel strived but never achieved. As such, it was appropriate to call him God's Son, even God's firstborn (Col 1:15).

2:16–18 *A voice is heard in Ramah, weeping and great mourning, Rachel weeping for her children.* We don't know when Herod figured out that he had been duped by the magi. When he did, he flew into a rage and sent his soldiers to slaughter all the male children in Bethlehem two and under. This may give us a hint of how much time had passed since the baby Jesus was born. At this point, he is probably no longer an infant. We will never know how many children were slaughtered out of Herod's rage. If Matthew knew, he does not record it. What he does do for his readers, however, is to link this human-caused tragedy to another event prophesied by Jeremiah (31:15):

Then what was said through the prophet Jeremiah was fulfilled:

> "A voice is heard in Ramah,
>   weeping and great mourning,
> Rachel weeping for her children
>   and refusing to be comforted,
>   because they are no more." (Mt 2:17–18)

The fulfillment formula is now familiar. What Matthew adds here is the name of the prophet who uttered these words, Jeremiah. Although it is hard to see in this quotation, the oracle itself is filled with hope that God's people will be rescued and come home. The context preserves a part of that promising word (Jer 31:15–17):

This is what the LORD says:

> "A voice is heard in Ramah,
>   mourning and great weeping,
> Rachel weeping for her children
>   and refusing to be comforted,
>   because they are no more."

This is what the LORD says:

> "Restrain your voice from weeping
>   and your eyes from tears,
> for *your work will be rewarded*,"
>   declares the LORD.
>   "*They will return from the land of the enemy.*
> *So there is hope for your descendants*,"
>   *declares the* LORD.
>   "*Your children will return to their own land.*" (italics added)

Rachel was the mother of Joseph and Benjamin (Ge 30:22; 35:16–20). She was buried on the way to Ephrath, that is, Bethlehem, the city she now prophetically weeps over because of Herod's treachery (Ge 35:19). For Jeremiah, she represents every mother who lost children through death or deportation at the hands of the Babylonian soldiers. Parental grief resonates in this passage; no mother or father should lose a child to death, disease, or deportation. It is not natural; it is not the way things are supposed to be. Yet it was so for thousands in Israel in the opening decades of the sixth century BC.

Ramah was the staging ground from which the exiles were sent on their perilous journey to Babylon. Those carried away in that day never returned to the land of promise, but some of their children's children did. That was what the Lord said through the prophet (4x "says the LORD"). So while the prophecy was "fulfilled" half a century later, there was a waiting, brooding expectation of a future that would be far more glorious when the exile was truly over. Matthew taps into that hope as he tells how the toddler Jesus and his parents fled to Egypt only to return a few years later.

The oracle quoted (Jer 31) was a favorite of early Christians because it prophesied that days were coming when God would make a "new covenant" with his people (Jer 31:31). That language is picked up and made a regular feature of the eucharistic words of Jesus (e.g., 1 Co 11:25; Lk 22:20); perhaps the author of Hebrews interprets it most completely in the New Testament (8:8–12; 10:16).

There is yet another connection to Old Testament Scripture in this tragedy. The slaughter of the innocents in Bethlehem takes us back even further to Exodus 1:15–22 and the decision of the Pharaoh to try and control the population of the Jewish slaves. He instructed the Hebrew midwives to kill any boy as he is being born "on the delivery stool." If the baby was a girl, however, they should let her live. The plan did not work because the midwives "feared God" and hid the boys. Then Pharaoh instructed his people, the Egyptians, to cast every boy born to the Hebrew slaves into the Nile. In the midst of this pogrom, a son was born to a Levite family. His name was Moses, the one destined to rescue the slaves from Egypt and bring them back to their inheritance. Despite the Pharaoh's best efforts, Moses was raised under his nose and later had unprecedented access to power. Likewise, despite Herod's best efforts, Jesus and his family fled to Egypt until the Idumean no longer posed a threat.

2:19-20 *An angel of the Lord . . . said, "Get up, take the child . . . to the land of Israel."* After Herod's death, Joseph had another revelatory dream. The time frame is unclear, but Joseph and his family were safe in Egypt. In this dream the angel of the Lord instructed him to take his wife and child and go back to the land of Israel (Mt 2:19–21). Their exile in Egypt was at an end. If Jesus was destined to be God's agent to bring the exiles home, it makes perfect sense that he too would have been a refugee who makes it home.

We may detect here a faint echo of yet another moment in Moses's life. But now Moses moves in an opposite direction, going back to Egypt after taking refuge in Midian. Like Joseph and his family, Moses left his homeland for Midian because people were out to kill him. When that threat was over, he was able to go back and do what God ordained him to do. Moses had been prepared and commissioned by God in the wilderness and lands beyond Sinai (Ex 4:18–20). Now he had a task, to rescue the Hebrew slaves whose blood ran through his veins. We do not know how old Jesus was when Joseph took him and his mother back to the land of Israel, but he, too, returns for his own commission, to take up his saving work in a few years.

2:23 *So was fulfilled what was said through the prophets, that he would be called a Nazarene.* Instead of returning to Bethlehem where he and his family started, Joseph decided to go north to the district of Galilee; again, after being warned in a dream (Mt 2:22). He settled in Nazareth, a small village not far from the larger city of Sepphoris. In Matthew's typical fashion he sees this act in some way prefigured ("fulfilled") in the prophets (2:23). We should notice that it is not a prophet but "prophets" who spoke this. But if we look throughout the Hebrew Scriptures, we will not find that statement made so directly. So what is going on? What is Matthew up to? Is he making up prophecies out of nothing? No. Not at all. He is doing what rabbis did and do all the time. He finds in the Hebrew root *nzr* key words in Scripture that hint of what is to come. The words *Nazareth* and *Nazarene* are built from that root. *Nazarene* could mean no more than "one from Nazareth," but for Matthew it means more because of its association to other key words in Scripture.

The first comes to us from Judges 13. In the Hebrew Bible, Joshua and Judges are considered among "the former prophets." The angel of the Lord appears to the wife of Manoah, a Danite, after the Lord had handed Israel over to the Philistines. The sea-people caused the children of Israel grief for years. The formerly barren wife of Manoah would give birth to a son, Samson, who would one day deliver Israel from the power of the Philistines. He was to be dedicated to God's service and live as a Nazarite (*nzr*; see Nu 6:1–21). The announcement of his birth to the wife of Manoah sounds familiar: "You shall conceive and bear a son. So then, drink no wine or strong drink and eat nothing unclean, for the boy shall be a Nazirite to God from birth to the day of his death" (Jdg 13:7 NRSV). Matthew's statement that Jesus shall be known as a "Nazarene" links him to those men and women who took the "vow" and lived distinctly as those consecrated to God's service. In Samson's case, he was dedicated to God before he was born. Even his mother had to abstain from wine during her pregnancy. Though Samson was deeply flawed, he is celebrated for his heroics as a judge and deliverer of Israel.

The second and perhaps more significant connection to Jesus for Matthew comes from Isaiah's messianic prophecy (11:1–9). The oracle begins, "A shoot will come up from the stump of Jesse; from his roots a Branch (*nzr*) will bear fruit." Jesse is, of course, David's father, so we are once again in the arena of Jesus as Messiah and Son of David. The image is of a great tree that has been cut down, but its roots and stump are still intact (cf. Da 4). After a while, a shoot comes up from the stump and a branch emerges from the roots. The life of the tree is not lost. A remnant will return. This branch, this *netzer*, arrives, and the future tree eclipses the glory and grandeur of the former. "The Spirit of the LORD" is on this Branch-king. He will judge rightly for the poor, and under his rule the meek will inherit the earth. He wears righteousness and faithfulness as his clothes, and he issues in the peaceable kingdom. Wolf and lamb dwell together in shalom and a child will lead them. Prey and predator lie down together in peace and safety. In that day the earth will be full of the knowledge of the Lord. Matthew's statement that Jesus shall be known as a "Nazarene" draws significantly from this prophecy. He is the *nzr,* the branch, who has come from God to establish an everlasting, peaceful kingdom.

In both cases, Matthew depends not on a single prophetic text. Instead he depends on the Hebrew root *nzr* to show how Jesus fulfills the prophecies. He is idealized for his unerring devotion to God (like the Nazirites), and he is celebrated as the "Branch" of David who brings about God's kingdom of peace and righteousness. Matthew is not playing fast and loose with the Scriptures; he is drinking deeply from it.

Matthew 1–2 Through Old Testament Eyes

The first two chapters of Matthew's gospel are deeply immersed in Scripture. We see this in the first phrases that claim with Jesus we have a new beginning (genesis) through the one who is the true son of Abraham, son of David, and Messiah. The genealogy, particularly the annotations, remind us of the deep flaws (sins) in humanity that must be addressed by the one who comes in bearing the names "Jesus" and "Immanuel." The arrival of the magi to the residence of the holy family foretells a future that the Hebrew prophets had already seen, that is, a day when the nations themselves would have the good news preached to them. Scripture after Scripture is "fulfilled" around Jesus. As a child he had no control over what Herod or Joseph did. He was a passive observer to those events in history. These "fulfillment" passages are not all cut from the same cloth. Some appear to be predictions from the past that came true; others link to deep structures in the Hebrew Scriptures and show how the one God is at work past, present, and future. These "figural" or "typological" readings of Scripture link Jesus to his ancestors in impressive ways, particularly to Abraham, David, Moses, and Jacob (Israel). And each of these point to Jesus as the long-awaited Messiah of Israel. But what kind of Messiah would he be? Matthew is ready to tell us.

MATTHEW 3

3:1–2 *In those days John the Baptist came, preaching in the wilderness of Judea.* Roughly three decades separates Matthew 2 from Matthew 3. You would not know it by the way the gospel writer introduces the story of John the Baptist: "in those days." Jesus is approximately thirty years old at the time of his baptism (Lk 3:23), but John's ministry likely started a few years before. Exactly how long we do not know. Enough time had to go by for his reputation to grow beyond local towns and villages.

John appeared "in the wilderness of Judea," a rugged area east of Jerusalem not far from the northern tip of the Dead Sea. Parts of the area seem as devoid of life as a lunar landscape.

John is called "the Baptist" (Mt 3:1) because of what he did, not because of any religious affiliation. *Baptist* comes from a Greek word that means to "dip" or "immerse" in water. John's identity is tied up with his actions—immersing repentant sinners in the waters of the Jordan—and his message.[1]

Matthew sums up this message in just a few words: "Repent, for the kingdom of heaven has come near" (Mt 3:2). Repentance is a consistent call of the Hebrew prophets to various generations of Israel's sons and daughters. Consider, for example, Ezekiel 18:30–32:

> Therefore, you Israelites, I will judge each of you according to your own ways, declares the Sovereign LORD. Repent! Turn away from all your offenses; then sin will not be your downfall. Rid yourselves of all the offenses you have committed, and get a new heart and a new spirit. Why will you die, people of Israel? For I take no pleasure in the death of anyone, declares the Sovereign LORD. Repent and live!

Ezekiel's message is to those in exile. Their tendency may have been to blame their ancestors for their troubled situation—don't we all!—but the prophet calls them to take responsibility and turn away from their sins and turn back to God. This is the essence of repentance. By turning away from sin, they turn to God.

John takes up and expands the prophetic message about "turning" in his own way. He calls upon his hearers to take responsibility, turn from their sins to God, and be baptized. But he relates repentance now to the approach of "the kingdom of heaven." Even the casual reader of Matthew recognizes the close connection of John's essential message and Jesus' (Mt 4:17): "From that time on [his return to Galilee] Jesus began to preach, 'Repent, for the kingdom of heaven has come near.'"

That is not the whole of Jesus' message, but that is it in a nutshell. John and Jesus connect repentance, faith, and the arrival of "the kingdom of heaven."[2]

"The kingdom of God/heaven" owes its substance again to the prophets. In particular, one could point to Zechariah 14:9: "The LORD will be the king over the whole earth. On that day there will be one LORD, and his name the only name." Zechariah's final prophecy is of a great battle that is coming one day against Jerusalem. All the nations gather for the attack, but the Lord comes with all his holy angels to defend his people and his city.

3:3 *This is he who was spoken of through the prophet Isaiah.* As is Matthew's habit, he ties John's arrival and message to prophecy: "A voice of one calling in the wilderness, 'Prepare the way for the Lord, make straight paths for him.'" Matthew identifies Isaiah as the source of this prophecy (Isa 40:3). It is essentially an oracle of comfort and hope for those in Babylon separated from their homeland. With their sins paid in full—and then some—the prophet's voice directs them to "prepare the way for the LORD." In Isaiah, the word *LORD* refers to God's personal, covenant name, YHWH. YHWH is returning to his city, his people, but the pathway through the wilderness must be prepared. That phrase "the glory of the LORD will be revealed" (Isa 40:5) refers to God's visible manifestation, God's full and unmediated presence returning back to the land of Israel.

Ezekiel has a vision of the glory of the LORD returning to the city (Eze 43:1–5). Before the temple's destruction (586 BC), Ezekiel watched as the throne-chariot bearing God's presence left the city through the east gate (Eze 10:18–19). Now he watches as the glory of Israel's God returns from exile. As "the glory" approaches, the earth shines and Ezekiel does the appropriate thing: he falls on his face. As he watches, "the glory of the LORD filled the temple."

Matthew, like Mark before him (Mk 1:1–2), draws from this glory tradition, but now he relates Isaiah's prophecy to the ministry of John the Baptist and Jesus the Nazarene. In Matthew's thought, John the Baptist is commissioned to go into the wilderness and "prepare the way." He does so by preaching the imminence of God's kingdom, calling women and men to repent, and baptizing them as they confessed their sins. Therefore, John is the voice crying out in the wilderness. And who is the Lord/LORD whose way must be prepared? For Matthew, it is Jesus the Messiah/Christ, the Nazarene. Jesus is thus identified with the divine name, YHWH. This gives strength and definition to what it means that Jesus is Immanuel, the God-with-us one. As Richard Hays has put it, for Matthew Jesus is the embodiment of the God of Israel.[3] This is a bold move made early in the gospel, an audacious claim were it not true. But Matthew is convinced that it is true, so he identifies Jesus with God's unique, unspeakable name.[4] The full implications of such a high identity will be worked out throughout the gospel.

3:4 *John's clothes were made of camel's hair, and he had a leather belt around his waist.* What are we to make of these descriptions? Are these the habits of any desert-dwelling ascetic? Are these part of John's message?

John's hairy shirt and leather belt are meant to evoke the memory of a special "man of God" in the former prophets. Elijah wore clothes like this often enough that he could be identified by them (2 Ki 1:8; Zec 13:4). Matthew, and perhaps John the Baptist, want to arouse this image and connect their ministries. John is a new Elijah, a new man of God with the habits of the old (see Mal 4:5–6).

His food was locusts and wild honey. Though locusts and honey did provide him sustenance, the prophet-like-Elijah ate them as part of his message just as Elijah lived off the supply God provided from the land (1 Ki 17:2–6). So we should not imagine John sitting behind a rock snacking on locusts and honey right before a big sermon. While most Westerners would cringe at the thought of biting into a locust, the insect is considered kosher (Lev 11:22) and would not strike a person of John's day as an odd food choice. Similarly, honey is a desirable natural sweetener.[5]

Consider also the prophetic record and what locusts represent. In Joel, an invasion of locusts is a sign of things to come when an army of the insects invades from the north and strips the land bare. Locusts are a sign of judgment. Nonetheless, if God's people will repent, turn to God, and plead with him to deliver them, then he will restore everything the locusts have stripped away (Joel 2:12–27). John dramatizes that God is on the move in ways the prophets had predicted. By eating the locusts, John enacts the destroyer being destroyed. The consumer is being consumed. And finally, the shame of their long exile is coming to an end when YHWH himself returns to his people (Joel 2:27).

Anyone who heard John in those days would have gotten the idea that the current invaders and consumers (the Roman occupiers) were going to meet their match when enough of God's people repented and submitted to John's baptism. The long day of judgment was coming to an end.

So what of the honey? Well, when enough people repented and turned from their wicked ways, when God himself intervened by destroying the destroyers and consuming the consumers, then the land would once again return to its richness for God's people. Most will recall that when the recently freed Hebrew slaves first peered into the promised land they said it was a land flowing with milk and honey (e.g., Nu 13:27).

I can imagine John lathering his hand in honey, putting it to his mouth, and savoring its sweetness as he stood in front of a group of pilgrims from Jerusalem or Judea. He proclaimed the imminence of God's kingdom in all its beauty and goodness, even as he warned his detractors of the coming judgment if they persisted in their hypocrisy.

3:5 *People went out to him from Jerusalem and all Judea and the whole region of the Jordan.* John's choice of the Jordan River as the arena of his ministry is not likely coincidence. Though it is the most obvious body of water in the region, it is also the most storied. After their forty years in the wilderness, the children of Israel finally crossed the swift waters of the Jordan into the promised land through God's intervention (Jos 3–4).

The Jordan figures prominently in other stories as well (e.g., 2 Sa 10:17; 17:22–24), but for John's narrative it is likely the Elijah-Elisha stories that matter most. After delivering a sobering message about a three-and-a-half-year drought to Ahab, Elijah the Tishbite crossed the Jordan and hid for a time by the Wadi Cherith. His time east of the Jordan and north along the coast in Zarephath formed a fitting prelude to his face-off with the prophets of Baal at Carmel (1 Ki 17–18).

Before Elijah parted from this world in a fiery chariot, he and Elisha crossed the Jordan on dry ground. Elijah had taken his mantle, struck the river, and it gave way so the two could walk together toward the east. After Elijah was taken up, Elisha returned to the river's edge with Elijah's mantle. Again, he struck the water with the prophet's garment, and the river parted so he could go back to join the company of prophets in Jericho (2 Ki 2). Such stories from the lives of these former prophets likely figured into John's sanctified imagination as he pondered the location of his own ministry. Matthew could hardly have been oblivious to the connections between John and Elijah. They figure prominently together and separately in Jesus' story in other places (Mt 11:1–15; 16:14; 17:3; cf. Lk 1:17; Jn 1:21).

3:7–10 *"You brood of vipers! Who warned you to flee from the coming wrath?"* John had a word for the Pharisees and Sadducees; it was a word of warning (3:7–10). Later in the story it was these same religious parties that gave Jesus the hardest time, and he returned the favor. They figured that they were safe from the coming wrath simply because they were children of Abraham (Ge 17:7). They were sons and daughters of the promise made nearly two millennia before; if they safeguarded that promise, should not God keep them safe? But John warns them that they too were sinners in need of repentance. They needed to change their thinking and reform their ways. They needed to produce the "fruit in keeping with repentance" (3:8). For John this meant that they too needed to confess their sins, submit to baptism, and seek acts of righteousness in keeping with God's will. In other words, they should become disciples of John and then disciples of Jesus of Nazareth, the one to whom John was pointing. Jesus had yet to make an appearance in the wilderness, but he would.

3:11 *After me comes one who is more powerful than I, whose sandals I am not worthy to carry. He will baptize you with the Holy Spirit and fire.* Matthew appears to direct these words to the Pharisees and Sadducees, but ultimately addresses them to a wider audience (cf. Lk 3:15–17). One greater than John is coming. John may immerse in water but—when "he" comes—he will immerse in the Holy Spirit and fire. The image of judgment and harvest is clear. The threshing floor will be cleared, the good grain stored, and the chaff will burn with unquenchable fire (Mt 3:12). Fire here serves two purposes: first, it burns up and consumes; second, it purifies (cf. Nu 31:21–24). The first represents judgment and destruction, the second a future and a hope. Implicitly speaking, anyone/anything immersed in the Holy Spirit and fire at the hands of the coming one is destined for the kingdom of heaven.

3:13–15 *Then Jesus came from Galilee to the Jordan to be baptized by John.* John balks at Jesus' suggestion, knowing on some level that Jesus is the coming one, the Lord whose way he is preparing. So he says, "I need to be baptized by you . . ." (3:14). In this gospel alone John voices protest against baptizing Jesus. But Jesus has a response that sounds strangely familiar for those who have been reading Matthew: "Let it be so now; it is proper for us to do this to fulfill all righteousness" (3:15). Jesus employs the language of fulfillment with respect to righteousness as Matthew has employed it with respect to Scripture. For Jesus and John to work together and cooperate in baptism is to fulfill righteousness. For Matthew, their collaboration means fulfillment in line with how Jesus' early years had lined up with Scripture.

Throughout Matthew, "righteousness" is key. In the Sermon on the Mount Jesus waxes eloquent about it (Mt 5:6, 10, 17–20; 6:1–18). In Matthew, righteousness refers to doing the right thing for the right reason, and that reason is always related to the teaching and will of God. Jesus' interpretation of the law (Mt 5:21–48) demonstrates what greater righteousness will look like in the life of a disciple. Jesus himself models righteousness by submitting to John's baptism. But if John's baptism is about the confession of sins and repentance, how does that relate to Jesus? What sins did he need to confess? Well, there is nothing in Matthew or the tradition that brands Jesus as a sinner in need of repentance. In fact, he was without sin (2 Co 5:21) even though he was tempted (Heb 4:15). So if John did not baptize Jesus for repentance's sake, he must have baptized him for righteousness' sake.

Let me suggest several reasons why Jesus went to John and insisted that the prophet dip him in the Jordan River. First, Jesus wanted to identify with John. He resonated with the Baptist's message—repentance and entry into the kingdom—and his practice of baptism. Jesus takes up both and incorporates them into his ministry. Second, Jesus wanted to identify with the women and men who were coming to John in repentance and faith. These were the "poor in spirit" Jesus would declare "blessed" in his Sermon on the Mount. Third, Jesus' baptism marks a turning point in his life. The word translated "repentance" in most Bible translations means "a change of mind" (*metanoia*). After his baptism everything changes for Jesus. He will leave behind manual labor[6] to become an itinerant preacher and healer. He will leave behind his home in Nazareth to set up his headquarters in Capernaum.

3:16–17 *At that moment heaven was opened, and he saw the Spirit of God descending like a dove and alighting on him. And a voice from heaven said, "This is my Son."* A particular image of Jesus emerges in Matthew's account of his baptism. The passage has visionary aspects that echo a number of Old Testament Scriptures. The opening of the heavens, the descent of the Spirit, and a heavenly voice's declaration of Jesus' Sonship announces God's election of him as his emissary of the coming kingdom. Scholars consider Jesus' baptism as his unique experience of God and His Spirit wrapped up in a growing awareness of his Sonship.[7]

Typically visions (what is seen) and auditions (what is heard) do not make explicit references to Scripture—"as it is written"—but by their very nature they are saturated in them.[8] For those with Old Testament sensibilities it is possible to hear and see those connections.

Matthew's account of Jesus' baptism (Mt 3:16–17) tracks closely with Mark's (Mk 1:9–11), but there are some significant differences. In particular, the heavenly voice in Mark is a personal address, "You are my Son, whom I love; with you I am well pleased." Matthew's version directs the voice to the spectators attending the baptism in the water and on the river's edge: "This is my Son, whom I love; with him I am well pleased." It is, as it were, a declaration to the world.

Matthew does share Mark's vision of Jesus as an apocalyptic seer according to the order of Ezekiel, another prophet and seer.[9] There are points of correspondence which both writers share with Ezekiel's initial vision (Eze 1). We might add another connection between Ezekiel's initial vision and Matthew's account of Jesus' baptism. Matthew adds[10] the word *behold* twice—"behold, the heavens were opened . . ." and "behold, a voice from heaven said . . ." (author's translation)—most likely to echo the frequency of the same word in Ezekiel (1:4, 15, 25). Not all translations carry the significance of this interjection. Some leave it untranslated; others translate it weakly. The point is that there may be an intertextual echo in Matthew's use of "behold" that connects Matthew's apocalyptic Jesus to Ezekiel, the apocalyptic prophet par excellence; in addition, it enlivens the story and adds spice to this extraordinary, life-altering moment for Jesus.[11] By the time Matthew writes his account of Jesus' life, Ezekiel was recognized as the prototypical seer and others attempted to imitate and formularize his visionary experience.

But Ezekiel is not the only intertextual influence on Matthew. Isaiah 63:7–64:12 may well be playing in the background too. After a psalm of praise, the prophet begins to intercede for the people, recalling God's gracious acts and deeds of mercy, steadfast love, and Israel's deliverance from bondage. But that was the past. Now in his day, the prophet pleads with God to open heaven, come down, and restore Israel in the hope of a new exodus.

The most poignant language in the Old Testament about the Fatherhood of God is contained in this prayer-poem (Isa 63:15–17).

> Look down from heaven and see,
>   from your lofty throne, holy and glorious.
> Where are your zeal and your might?
>   Your tenderness and compassion are withheld from us.
> But *you are our Father,*
>   though Abraham does not know us
>   or Israel acknowledge us;
> *you,* Lord, *are our Father,*
>   our Redeemer from of old is your name.
> Why, Lord, do you make us wander from your ways
>   and harden our hearts so we do not revere you?

> Return for the sake of your servants,
>   the tribes that are your inheritance. (italics added)

The Hebrew Scriptures seldom address God as "Father," so Isaiah's prayer here represents something new. This theme of God's Fatherhood becomes key to Jesus' message. Jesus will pray "Abba, Father!" and teach his disciples to pray, "Our Father in heaven . . ." (Mt 6:9).

Descending like a dove. Why is the Spirit of God described "like a dove" and not "like an eagle" or like some other sort of bird?

Later rabbis associated the dove with the creation account (Ge 1:2), noting that the Spirit hovered above the waters like a dove. But no dove is mentioned there, only that the Spirit hovered (like a bird) above the waters.

Within the Scriptures of Israel, the first mention of a dove is in the flood story (Ge 8). Over fourteen days Noah sends out a dove three times to determine if dry land had appeared. On the third attempt, the dove does not return. It had found a home on earth and so will Noah and his family; they realize that their exile from dry ground has come to an end. Given God's address to Noah (Ge 9), one could rightly conclude that flood story itself is a new creation account. It is not coincidental that early Jewish Christians found the story of Noah's safe passage through the water as a prefiguration of baptism (1 Pe 3:20–21). Maybe it was Noah's dove and their safe passage through the water that provided a scriptural focus to the Spirit's descent "like a dove." The Spirit comes at the dawn of a new creation reminiscent of the one following the flood.

But also consider Psalm 74, a communal lament begging God to remember his people. An enemy had vanquished them and razed the temple to the ground. God's people together beg him to reverse the shame of their defeat (74:19), "Do not hand over the life of your dove to wild beasts; do not forget the lives of your afflicted people forever." God's conquered people are called "your dove" and "your afflicted people." We see the same image reflected in the prophets as they describe the moaning of the dove like the mourning of the suffering people (Isa 38:14; 59:11; Eze 7:16).

So the dove comes to symbolize Israel in all of its sufferings at the hands of foreigners. If Jesus and his Jewish followers are aware of this image, the description of the Spirit coming down like a dove signals to Jesus his Spirit-directed role as sufferer representing all of the Father's people. If Jesus is to fulfill Israel's story and thus all righteousness, there can be no "way" except the way of suffering. This is borne out in what follows. The Spirit compels Jesus to the wilderness for forty days of fasting, and the adversary tempts him to sidestep his appointed task. But Jesus refuses to yield the road to any way other than the way of suffering.

What the Structure Means: Father, Son, and Spirit (Mt 3:13–17)

The baptismal scene provides the initial gospel reference to the interconnectedness of God the Father, the Son, and the (Holy) Spirit as Jesus is initiated into a new phase of life. We should note that this episode points ahead to the end of the gospel when Jesus commissions the disciples to teach *and baptize* into the name of the Father, the Son, and Holy Spirit. This is no full-bodied doctrine of the Trinity, but it is suggestive that thematically—at the beginning and the end of the story— we should see that Matthew and his community are already aware of the connection between these three.

3:17 *This is my Son, whom I love; with him I am well pleased.* Voices from heaven are not common in the Old Testament. When the Lord does speak from on high, the psalmist likens it to thunder in the heavens (Ps 18:13; cf. 2 Sa 22:14). But on certain occasions, God does speak from the heavens. Moses, on the plains of Moab, reminds Israel how God revealed himself to them at Mt. Sinai: "From heaven he made you hear his voice to discipline you. On earth he showed you his great fire, and you heard his words from out of the fire" (Dt 4:36). As a result of Nebuchadnezzar's pride over his accomplishments, a voice from heaven declared his temporary exile from human society (Da 4:31–32). Few people in the history of the world had heard God speak from the midst of the fire or from heaven and lived (Dt 4:32–40), but Moses and Israel had. Thus, the arrival of Jesus at the Jordan River is no ordinary event.

The initial introduction, "This is my Son" finds its closest scriptural parallel in Psalm 2. This psalm is one of ten royal psalms in the collection,[12] written likely as a coronation hymn for a Davidic king. It carries certain messianic themes, including the special relationship the Lord God would have with David's son (cf. 2 Sa 7:12–16).

In the psalm the Lord is unmoved and unimpressed by the raging of the nations against him and his anointed [king], and announces, "I have installed my king on Zion, my holy mountain" (Ps 2:6). Next, the king himself speaks of God's decree, a personal word (Ps 2:7): "I will proclaim the LORD's decree: He said to me, 'You are my son; today I have become your father.'" Psalm 2 is a messianic psalm used by the early church to speak to Jesus' special status as David's Son, and therefore the Messiah. Matthew hears in this psalm Jesus' presentation to the crowds, and thus to the world, God's affirmation of Jesus as his Anointed. All that the psalm claims about the Messiah coalesces in Jesus at this unique moment.

The phrase "whom I love" can also be rendered "the Beloved;" it signals Jesus' unique relationship with God and recalls again Hosea 11:1: "When Israel was a child, I loved him, and out of Egypt I called my son." As we saw before (regarding Mt 2:15), this situates Jesus squarely within the people of Israel as their representative.

As the voice from heaven declares "with him I am well pleased," our ear turns to the prophet Isaiah (42:1): "Here is my servant, whom I uphold, my chosen one, in whom I delight; I will put my Spirit on him, and he will bring justice to the nations."

The Servant Songs of Isaiah (42:1–4; 49:1–6; 50:4–11; 52:13–53:12) tell a long and debated story. At some points God has called Israel to be his servant (41:8–9), but at others there seems to be an individual, a prophetic figure who comes out of Israel to fulfill the servant's mission (Isa 53). Early Christ followers heard in this prophecy a word about Jesus and his significance.

Matthew 3 Through Old Testament Eyes

At his baptism, the heavenly voice introduces Jesus to the world through the words of Scripture. He is God's Anointed-by-the-Spirit king, the true Son of David as we saw both on and below the surface of the genealogy (Mt 1). As the liberating and justice-bearing servant, he embodies Israel and ultimately fulfills God's deepest pleasure. These images come from every corner of Scripture and cohere with the man from Nazareth.

In addition, Matthew presents us with "an apocalyptic Jesus, a seer and transmitter of visions."[13] For the evangelist the emphasis is not so much on the act of baptism—narrated with only a few words—but the attendant phenomena: divine manifestations, apocalyptic-symbolic visions. This is not to say that Jesus was a thoroughgoing apocalyptic-mystic, but that on occasion Jesus did receive visions and revelations consistent with other apocalypses.[14] John the Immerser, like Jesus, walks the apocalyptic line in his message and ministry, but it is Jesus who will go on to take center stage.

What Jesus does next will most define him. He will not give in to temptation but is delivered from evil (Mt 4:1–11). He will announce the imminence of God's kingdom and demonstrate it through miracles (Mt 10:7–8; 12:28); predict the destruction of the temple (Mt 24:1–29); and prophesy the coming of the Son of Man in power (Mt 24:30–33).

The central and prevailing feature of apocalyptic theology is the threat and promise of a heavenly intrusion into time and history to save and to judge, an intrusion that establishes a realm where God's will is done on earth as it is in heaven. As Zechariah 14 predicts, cosmic signs accompany God's visitation, and, when all is done, the Lord becomes king, not just over Israel and Jerusalem but all the earth. When the kingdom of heaven comes in full, the whole earth recognizes God as God and God as its rightful king. According to Matthew, Jesus is both its prophet and its king.

MATTHEW 4

The same Spirit that came down on Jesus "like a dove" now leads him into the wilderness for a time of testing (Mt 4:1–11; cf. Mk 1:12–13). If the dove symbolizes Jesus' destiny in suffering (see comments on Mt 3:16–17 at "Descending like a dove"), then the Spirit's guidance is intended to test his willingness to follow that path. But the Spirit is not alone, and the scene is complicated. The agent of testing is "the devil." The location is "the wilderness." The duration is forty days and forty nights. Each of these has resonance with the Hebrew Bible.

4:1 *Then Jesus was led by the Spirit into the wilderness to be tempted by the devil.* The fact that Jesus is Spirit-led to the wilderness indicates that heaven has mandated this period of trial. On many occasions in Scripture, God is said to lead his people (Dt 8:2) and often by the Spirit (Israel—Isa 63:14; the exiles—Ps 107:7; Elijah—1 Ki 18:12; Ezekiel—Eze 3:14). This is a well-trodden path in the Bible, and Jesus now joins that great company.

The Spirit leads him to a season of temptation. The word translated "tempted" (Mt 4:1, *peirasthenai*) could also be rendered "given a trial" or "tested." While there are many texts that describe God testing his people, there are two that come to mind here. First, God put Abraham to the test when he asked him to take his only son to Mt. Moriah and sacrifice him there. Abraham's obedience to God in both going to the mountain and restraining his hand in sacrifice indicate his willingness to follow God's instruction regardless of the cost. As a result, God once again affirms his promise to Abraham to make him a great nation and be a blessing to all (Ge 22:15–18):

The angel of the LORD called to Abraham from heaven a second time and said, "I swear by myself, declares the LORD, that because you have done this and have not withheld your son, your only son, I will surely bless you and make your descendants as numerous as the stars in the sky and as the sand on the seashore. Your descendants will take possession of the cities of their enemies, and through your offspring all nations on earth will be blessed, because you have obeyed me."

At the beginning of the gospel Jesus is introduced as "the son of Abraham," not only because he is related to him, but because Abraham's covenant is renewed and fulfilled in him. The Nazarene fulfills Abraham's covenant by extending his mission to the nations (Mt 28:19–20) and becoming a universal blessing. But he does so by treading the road of trial and suffering as his ancestor(s) did before him.

If this first example comes from the first book of the Pentateuch, the second comes from the last.[1] Before the former slaves return to the land of their ancestors—Abraham, Isaac, and Jacob—Moses reminds Israel who they are and whose they are on the plains of Moab. He rehearses the significance and stipulations of the covenant for them. While Israel is forbidden from putting God to the test (Dt 6:16), God affirms that he has led them for forty years in the wilderness to humble and test them (Dt 8:2). The tests revealed what was in their hearts and whether they would keep God's commandments. It may well be that the tests were not so much for God's benefit but for the people's: to know whether they had "what it took" to walk in his ways and worship only him (Dt 8:5–6): "Know then in your heart that as a man disciplines his son, so the LORD your God disciplines you. Observe the commands of the LORD your God, walking in obedience to him and revering him."

The tests were part of God's training program for his children. They were a loving parent's discipline for life ahead, life in the land that would present them with many challenges. God fed them in the wilderness with manna to humble them, test them, but ultimately to do them good (Dt 8:16). By recalling Jesus' tests at the outset, Matthew likens Jesus to Israel—her past, present, and future—throughout his gospel. Jesus not only recapitulates Israel's story but rewrites and fulfills it, replacing failure with faithfulness.

We should note that this extensive backstory to Israel and her testing took place in the wilderness, which gives shape and reason for Jesus' return to the wilderness for his time of testing. The duration of his testing—forty days and forty nights—corresponds to the forty years spent by Israel in the wilderness, as they are disciplined and prepared for their mission. We might sense here too a connection to the forty-day period when Moses ascended Mt. Sinai, entered the cloud, and received God's law for his people.[2] Up until now, Jesus had never preached a sermon, healed the sick, or called disciples. His mission awaited until after his time of trial.

Even if the Spirit led Jesus to the wilderness to test him, the agent who administered the test is the devil (4:1). The devil is known otherwise as "the

Satan" (see Mk 1:12–13) whose main objective in the Hebrew Scriptures is to stand as an "accuser" or "adversary." Satan is best known and most maligned for his role as prosecuting attorney in Job 1:6–9 as he appears to make a deal with the Lord for the blameless and upright Job. In Zechariah 3:1–2 Satan appears again as the accuser, this time of Joshua the high priest: "Then he showed me Joshua the high priest standing before the angel of the LORD, and Satan standing at his right side to accuse him. The LORD said to Satan, 'The LORD rebuke you, Satan! The LORD, who has chosen Jerusalem, rebuke you! Is not this man a burning stick snatched from the fire?'"

Jesus' name, of course, is the Hebrew name Joshua. And both Joshuas pass the test. Joshua, the high priest, assumes his priestly garb and is granted the right to intercede for the people. He and his colleagues are an omen of things to come when God brings "my servant, the Branch" (Zec 3:8–10, "the Nazarene"?). Jesus, too, passes the test and will assume a priestly role beyond any in Israel's past.

Going Deeper into Tests and Temptations: Matthew 4:1

A test can feel an awful lot like a temptation. To pass the test is to resist the temptation. To fail the test is to give in to temptation. When you give in to temptation, the result is often sin. That may be why the words for "test" and "temptation" in Greek are the same. James 1:13–14 insists that people who feel tempted should not blame God because he is beyond tempting us to evil. Instead, people are lured away into temptation by their own desires. It is when our desires find an agreeable opportunity provided by the devil that sin can be conceived and born in us; when it is, there are always bad consequences. Jesus never allowed his desires to get in the way of his mission.

Truly, tests and temptation come to us all. But sin can, and should, be resisted. Jesus was able to do so not because he was some hybrid human with superpowers. He did so by keeping his mission and his God first and foremost. He also did so by keeping Scripture in his ear and in his heart. To each temptation, regardless of how pleasant and positive it sounded, he responded with the words of Scripture. Not Scripture as a proof text, but Scripture as a deep text integrated with his true self. When Scripture resides deep within us, it forms our dispositions and habits; it rules our conscience and guides our way. Also, Jesus had a relationship with the author of these words, and that made all the difference. If we want to resist temptation and send the tempter away empty-handed, we would do well to follow the example of Jesus.

4:2 *After fasting forty days and forty nights, he was hungry.* Jesus fasted for forty days and nights, perhaps in imitation of Moses who remained on Mt. Sinai forty days and forty nights without bread and water (Dt 9:9; cf. Ex 24:18). We have seen already how often Matthew finds the correspondence between Moses and Jesus. Whether on the mount of temptation or Mount Sinai, both men were preparing for the next phase of their remarkable missions.

Fasting, of course, is part of Israel's discipline before God. Jesus affirms it in the lives of his own disciples (e.g., see comments at Mt 6:16–18). Throughout the Old Testament, fasting appears to come at various times for various purposes: (1) to mark seasons of joy (Zec 8:18–19); (2) to express deep mourning (Ne 1:4); (3) to ask for a safe journey (Ezr 8:21); (4) to demonstrate humility (Ps 69:10); (5) to seek answers (Da 9:3); (6) to accompany repentance (Joel 2:12). There are others too, but these represent some of the many faces of fasting. Scholars note that fasting seems to be on the rise with and after the exile.[3] By the time of Jesus, fasting appears as a regular feature of Jewish piety for the Pharisees and the followers of John (cf. *Did* 8.1; Tertullian, *On Fasting* 16; Tacitus, *Hist* 5.4.3). But fasting, in and of itself, may not have any rewards if it is not done in the right way for the right reason.

According to the prophet Isaiah, fasting without a life of repentance, a life turned Godward, leads to nothing (Isa 58:2–5). But fasting that addresses injustice and meets the needs of the poor brings healing and help in time of need (58:6–9). Proper fasting, the Scripture says, results in your light breaking forth like the dawn and God's glory standing watch over your rear guard. Perhaps Jesus fasts after his baptism—after this turning point in his life—inspired by the words of Isaiah 58. If he had meditated on the prophet's teaching, he leaves his wilderness experience expecting the Lord to guide him and satisfy his body and bones in these parched places.

4:3 *The tempter came to him and said, "If you are the Son of God . . .".* While there may have been more temptations, Scripture records three. In the first, "the tempter" lures Jesus: if you are the Son of God—as the voice from heaven declared—then "speak so that these stones become bread" (4:3, author's translation). The language here is reminiscent of the Lord's instruction to Moses to speak to the rock and command it to yield water (Nu 20:8). Whereas Moses is to do this in the company of the congregation, the devil wheedles Jesus while he is alone in the wilderness. The tempter knows Jesus is famished after so many days without food.

Jesus responds to this temptation (as he does all three) with Scripture, particularly the book of Deuteronomy. This was one of the best-known and most quoted books in the Second Temple period.[4] It has already taken a lead role in Matthew's account. Jesus answered (in the words of Dt 8:3): "It is written: 'Man shall not live on bread alone, but on every word that comes from the mouth of God" (Mt 4:4).

This teaching comes as a reminder in Moses's discourse to the people. Whatever success they have in the land of Canaan is not theirs; it is God's. Obedience to God and allegiance to his teaching must light the way if their future is to be secure. They must remember how God led and provided for them during their forty-year journey. The result ought to be humility and a recognition that whatever life they have comes from God. Bread may satisfy one kind of hunger, but there is another, deeper, more fundamental "hunger"; it is satisfied by the "word" that comes from God. Jesus refuses the tempter's whisper, opting instead to stay true to Scripture and to center himself squarely with God's sojourning people. He might have bypassed the suffering brought on by fasting; instead he trusted his life ultimately to God and his teaching.

4:5–7 *Then the devil took him to the holy city and had him stand on the highest point of the temple.* The second temptation takes place in the holy city, Jerusalem.[5] After placing Jesus on this high spot on the temple, he cajoled him: if you are the Son of God—again, as the voice from heaven declared— then you can jump, knowing that God will call in his angel army to catch you (Mt 4:6). Even the devil gets in on the act of quoting Scripture; here, Psalm 91:11–12. If there is a theme to Psalm 91, it is this: God is protector. He shelters his people from enemies, near and far, human and otherwise (Ps 91:13). In other words, it is the right passage to lean on in times of trouble. It introduces the idea that "guardian angels" stand at the ready to shield the faithful and protect them (Ps 91:11–12). The devil appeals to this text to urge Jesus to do something dramatic at one of the busiest spots in all of Israel, the temple itself. Had Jesus complied, he would immediately have had the attention of the crowds. Stories about his fall and miraculous, soft landing would have echoed in the streets. No one could survive a fall like that, but Jesus would—or so the tempter would have it.

Jesus refuses the tempter's urging, finding in Deuteronomy 6:16 the right stance before God: "It is also written, 'Do not put the Lord your God to the test'" (Mt 4:7). One may appeal to God in times of trouble, but there is no point in making trouble and asking God, or his angels, to swoop in at the last minute to save you. The passage Jesus cites comes from Deuteronomy 6, one of the most quoted chapters from all the Old Testament. It contains the Shema (Dt 6:4–6), the bold confession of God's oneness and reminder to love God with all your heart, soul, mind, and strength. Jesus quoted this chapter as part of his teaching on the first commandment (Mt 22:37; cf. Mk 12:29–30).

This commandment and its corollaries become the spiritual furniture in the minds of God's people; they are to place them strategically in their lives as a reminder of who and whose they are. In quoting this chapter, Jesus remembers both his identity as God's Son, the Messiah, and his mission. He must stay true to the path of hardship and suffering that lies ahead. No shortcuts, regardless of how dramatic they are, can be taken. The road is long and hard as Jesus reminds his disciples (Mt 7:13–14).

4:8 *Again, the devil took him to a very high mountain and showed him all the kingdoms of the world and their splendor.* The tempter comes to Jesus on this very high mountain and shows him all the kingdoms of the world and their splendor. He offers to give them to him if Jesus will fall down and worship him (Mt 4:9). He makes the offer as if he had them to give and could deliver the goods whenever he wished. In other words, the devil claims control and ownership over these kingdoms. Jesus never disputes that claim. He does not sing, "This Is My Father's World." He does not brush the claim aside, but takes it seriously; the devil, at least for now, appears to be in charge. If we pull back the veil, we see who is running the show. Paul describes him as "the god of this world" who blinds the minds of unbelievers so they cannot see the light of the gospel of the glory of God's Anointed (2 Co 4:4). So Jesus does not laugh it off; he takes it as true and responds once again with the words of Deuteronomy 6, this time verse 13: it stands written that you are to worship and serve YHWH, the God of Israel. All other worship is out of bounds and idolatrous.

The devil knows his time is short. Jesus is the herald and purveyor of the kingdom, a kingdom that, when it comes, will undo evil and render untrue every bit of sorrow and suffering the devil has ever conjured up. He bids Jesus to take a shortcut and make it so now, on this mountain. He urges Jesus to ignore the Spirit-dove he saw at his baptism that signaled the long, hard way of suffering that lies ahead. To put it another way, he mocks Jesus with the promise that if he worships the Satan, he could inherit the earth.

Matthew 4:8 Through Old Testament Eyes: Mountains

Many important events in Matthew take place on a mountain: (a) the last temptation (Mt 4:8); (b) the Sermon on the Mount (Mt 5–7); (c) the transfiguration (Mt 17:1–13); and (d) the commissioning of the disciples (Mt 28:16–20). We might even say that Matthew thematizes the mountain because these transcendent moments in the life of Jesus and his followers require a transcendent setting.

In the Old Testament, mountains are places of refuge and safety (Ge 14:10; Mt 24:15–16); dwelling places (Ge 36:8); sites to build altars and assemble the people (Dt 27:1–8; Jos 8:30–33); and places to send/receive signals (Isa 18:3) and prepare for battle (1 Sa 17:3). Mountains were the spot chosen by God to utter blessings and curses (Dt 27:11–13) as Israel entered the land of promise.

Ancient people regarded mountains as special places, "high places," where temples and altars were to be built. This was true for Israel as well as her neighbors. Israel's God had a special relationship to certain mountains. YHWH meets his people and gives them the law from Mt. Sinai (Dt 33:2). In Psalm 68:15–16, the psalmist poetically describes how God establishes Mt. Zion (Jerusalem) as his royal residence as other envious peaks look on. The point is this: mountains occupy a special place in Israel's geography and history. They will also do so in Matthew's story of Jesus.

4:10–11 *Jesus said to him, "Away from me, Satan! For it is written: 'Worship the Lord your God, and serve him only.'" Then the devil left him, and angels came and attended him.* Jesus will have none of it. Quoting Deuteronomy 6:13, he commands the Satan to leave and, at least for now, the adversary complies. Throughout the ordeal Jesus has been alone, but on the very high mountain, after the third and final temptation, Jesus becomes aware that he is attended by angels. Exactly what they do or how they serve him, we do not know. Occasionally in Scripture we read how God himself comes or sends his agents to comfort those who are faithful (e.g., 1 Ki 19:5–8). Earlier, the devil reminded Jesus of Psalm 91 and how God commands the angels to guard and carry the faithful in times of trial. Now it seems Psalm 91 has come true.

Going Deeper into God's Words in Our Hearts: Matthew 4:1–11

Jesus repels the devil with the words of Scripture. On this occasion at least, it was the book of Deuteronomy that held Jesus' attention and gave him the shield he needed to ward off the blazing darts of temptation. Scripture shaped Jesus' thought and directed his life. He did not wait until he had a problem to open his Bible and "find a verse." The words of Scripture already inhabited his mind and pervaded his thoughts. You don't have to be the Son of God to know Scripture well and let it direct you. Too many of us rely on technology to bring things to mind. We can google it or look it up on our phones. But that is not the same as having the Word in you, as a living Word. We can thank God for the technology we do have but recognize its limitations. Memorization and meditation remain the best ways to hide God's Word in our hearts so that we, like Jesus, will not fail the tests.

4:12 *When Jesus heard that John had been put in prison, he withdrew to Galilee.* News of John's arrest by Herod Antipas (Mt 14:3) reached Jesus, and he withdrew to his home in Nazareth of Galilee. We do not know the exact timeline here, but Galilee will become the focus of his initial work. After a while, he moved to Capernaum, a fishing village on the northwest shore of the Sea of Galilee. Matthew adds a few details, reminding his readers who know the geography of Galilee that this was the ancestral land of Zebulun and Naphtali.

4:14 *To fulfill what was said through the prophet Isaiah.* Once again Matthew indicates that Jesus' move to Galilee is not happenstance; it is the fulfillment of Scripture. Hundreds of years earlier the poet/prophet Isaiah spoke this oracle (Isa 9:1–2):

> Nevertheless, there will be no more gloom for those who were in distress. In the past he humbled the land of Zebulun and the land of Naphtali, but in the future he will honor Galilee of the nations, by the Way of the Sea, beyond the Jordan—
>
> The people walking in darkness
>   have seen a great light;
> on those living in the land of deep darkness
>   a light has dawned.

Isaiah prophesies a change that is coming, the birth of a new age. Gloom and anguish accompanied the Assyrian invasion. For a time, the people had "walked in darkness," but that time was coming to an end when a child would be born and a son given (Isa 9:6–7). The territories first to fall to the invaders' cruelty were in the north, Zebulun and Naphtali (namely Galilee). Now, in the providence of God, they would be the first to experience the light of the good news.

Matthew takes Jesus' move to Galilee as the fulfillment of Isaiah's prophecy. Jesus is the child born, the son given; he is the God-with-us one. Matthew does not quote Isaiah 9 as much as he paraphrases it. His phrasing may have more in common with the Greek version in the Septuagint than the Hebrew version, but the meaning is the same. The ancestral lands of Zebulun and Naphtali, the area known as Galilee, had become home to many non-Jews. Still, a majority of the population were Jews at this time (Josephus, *Ant* 13.337). The faithful who had lived there had seen great darkness; they dwelled in the shadow of death and dying as empire after empire swept in to conquer them. But darkness would be overcome by light, great light that would rise and shine

over them. For Matthew, the light-bearer is Jesus; perhaps better, Jesus himself
is the light. His arrival in Galilee after his baptism signaled that a change was
coming. In this case, we may wonder whether Jesus fulfilled this prophecy
intentionally. He set Capernaum strategically as the base of operations for his
itinerant ministry. Rather than go to Jerusalem, the location of the temple,
the city of King David, he went north because Isaiah said it would be so. After
all, those ancestral lands had been the first to fall into darkness and suffering.

In a sense, Jesus took his marching orders from Isaiah who had prophesied
where the light was first to shine. Giving up his builder's tools in exchange for
parables and a good pair of sandals, he leaves Nazareth to become an itinerant
teacher and healer with Capernaum as his headquarters.

4:17 *From that time on Jesus began to preach, "Repent, for the kingdom of heaven
has come near."* That light shone upon the people of Galilee as Jesus traveled
and spoke about the kingdom of heaven in synagogue after synagogue. It
shone upon the sick and infirm as well as many who came to Jesus with pain,
demons, and disease, and Jesus healed them. Great crowds began to follow
him as his fame spread throughout the region (Mt 4:23–25).

The essence of Jesus' message was this: "Repent, for the kingdom of heav-
en has come near." His message is no different from John's (see Mt 3:2). As we
saw earlier, the kingdom is rooted in scriptural hopes and imagination. The
kingdoms of this world have been under the rule of another for far too long;
through Jesus' life, teaching, and example heaven begins to exert its power
and influence in the world. Jesus himself is the presence of the kingdom.

4:18 *As Jesus was walking beside the Sea of Galilee, he saw two brothers.* It
was by the sea of Galilee and not in the hill country that Jesus called his first
followers. Though not called "disciples" until later, Jesus bids certain people
to follow him (Mt 4:18–22). The first followers named in the gospel are two
sets of two brothers: Simon (aka Peter) and Andrew; and James and John,
sons of Zebedee. The names are Jewish, as you might expect. *Simon (Shim'on)*
is a name that means "God hears/listens." It is similar to "Shema," which we
discussed earlier, the confession from Deuteronomy 6 of YHWH as Israel's
God and his oneness. Like some other Jews at the time, Simon has a second
name, Peter, a name likely given to him by Jesus (Mt 16:18; cf. Saul/Paul Acts
9–13).

4:19 *Come, follow me . . . and I will send you out to fish for people.* All four of
Jesus' first followers are fishermen. The men are temporarily in port to mend
their nets, and Jesus takes the occasion to urge them to take up the ranks of
discipleship and fish for people. There is little context in the Old Testament

for any positive notion of fishing for people. Most of the time, fish are just fish. Fish are a part of creation over which Adam and his kin are urged to exercise "dominion" (Ge 1:26; Ps 8:6–8). Sometimes they are a symbol of abundance (Nu 11:5). Death of fish near populated areas is recognized as indicative of God's judgment (Hos 4:3; Isa 50:2). But their return to the waters is a sign of future hope (Eze 47:9).

Fishermen are described as God's instrument of judgment against Judah (Jer 16:16–18). The fishermen will catch the unfaithful and the hunters will hunt them down because Judah polluted the land with idolatry and detestable acts. Prophesying against the Pharaoh and all of Egypt, Ezekiel declares that the Lord will soon put a hook in their jaws and fling the Egyptians into the wilderness (Eze 29:4). A similar image is found in Amos 4 in a message against the wealthy and wicked women of Samaria who oppress the poor, crush the needy, and bully their husbands. A time is coming, according to the prophet, when the Lord will take them away with fishhooks (Am 4:2).

Yet there is another possibility for understanding this text, and it comes from a close reading of the Hebrew text in Genesis 48:15–16:

Then he [Jacob] blessed Joseph and said,

> "May the God before whom my fathers
>   Abraham and Isaac walked faithfully,
> the God who has been my shepherd
>   all my life to this day,
> the Angel who has delivered me from all harm
>   —may he bless these boys [Ephraim and Manasseh].
> May they be called by my name
>   and the names of my fathers Abraham and Isaac,
> and may they increase greatly
>   on the earth."

As Jacob neared the end of his life, he gathered his sons and spoke a blessing over each of them. The patriarch begins with Joseph who brought to his father his two lads, Ephraim and Manasseh. Jacob accepted them as his own and uttered a blessing over them. The relevant line to our discussion is the last: "May they increase greatly on the earth." The Hebrew word translated "increase" occurs only once, here in the Old Testament, which makes its meaning obscure. The root of the word is the noun "fish" (*dag*) and its verbal cognate (*dûgâ*). With a bit of rabbinic imagination, it would not be hard to see how Jesus standing on the edge of the sea of Galilee in the company of fishermen might remember this text and import the word's root meaning "fish" into the discussion. In a sense it would mean "May these sons of Israel fish for a multitude in the midst of the earth." While a bit speculative, this reading takes into account Jesus' positive angle[6] on "fishers of men," and it takes seriously an obscure Hebrew word.

Whereas the presence of fish in the Old Testament indicates blessing and the absence of them is a sign of judgment, fishermen and their hooks cast an overall negative shadow. Jesus, it seems, turns this image inside out by assigning his followers the task of fishing for people. Theirs is not a ministry of judgment, but one of proclamation of God's kingdom, healing, and hope. They are to cast their nets through preaching the gospel, for such is the kingdom of heaven (Mt 13:47–50).

4:23 *Jesus went throughout Galilee . . . proclaiming the good news of the kingdom.* Regarding the kingdom of heaven, see comments on Matthew 3:1–2 and 4:17.

4:24 *And people brought to him all who were ill with various diseases, those suffering severe pain, the demon-possessed, those having seizures, and the paralyzed; and he healed them.* See "Matthew 11:4–6 Through Old Testament Eyes: Jesus' Miracles." All the Gospels foreground the miracles of Jesus. The proximity of Jesus' proclamation of the kingdom of heaven and a season of miracle working is no accident. Matthew wants his hearers and readers to understand something important about Jesus' miracles. They are certainly evidence that Jesus was a man of compassion, but they also signal what kind of kingdom Jesus would be bringing. The kingdom to come would be free of disease, pain, paralysis, and the agony inflicted by demons.

4:25 *Large crowds from Galilee, the Decapolis, Jerusalem, Judea and the region across the Jordan followed him.* Imagine walking an hour or two, a day or two, or a week or two in order to see and hear Jesus. That is what Matthew is telling us happened as large crowds gathered. The distances involved and the terrain made these journeys challenging. But there may be something else at work in Matthew's mind. Were you to plot these areas on a map, the scope of Jesus' "reach" would have spread to the extent of the kingdom of Israel during the days of King David. Perhaps Matthew is once again claiming Jesus is the proper Son of David, the rightful king of Israel.

What the Structure Means: The Galilean Ministry (Mt 5–18)

Jesus' baptism launches him into his mission. The season of Galilean ministry (Mt 5–18) will profoundly shape that mission in three ways, which Matthew sets up for us in 4:12–25. The first involves preaching and proclamation found in Matthew 4:12–17, which is expanded on in Matthew 5–7. Jesus arrives on the scene echoing John's proclamation of the nearness of the kingdom of heaven and the necessity of repentance.

The second has to do with calling disciples, noted in Matthew 4:18–22—that is, students who will call him teacher and follow him. Over the last years of his life Jesus will address the crowds, but he will pour his life into his disciples (Mt 8–10).

The third is introduced in Matthew 4:23–25 and developed in Matthew 12–14. This encompasses his ministry to the masses for which his fame spreads far and wide. Central to that are miracles he performs on the sick and demonized. For Matthew and Jesus, the miracles are not simply acts of benevolence performed for the suffering; they are manifestations of the kingdom. Though this age is characterized by sickness and evil, when the kingdom comes it will mean health, life, and goodness for all who enter.

MATTHEW 5

Wherever Jesus preached and healed in Galilee, crowds gathered. His fame and reputation grew and appears to have done so quickly (4:23–24). He preached in synagogues in Galilee, and his message about the good news to the kingdom spread to Syria and the land of the Gentiles, the Decapolis, in accordance with the prophecy (4:14–16).

5:1–2 *Now when Jesus saw the crowds, he went up on a mountainside and sat down. His disciples came to him, and he began to teach them.* As crowds gathered, Jesus ascended an undisclosed mountain in Galilee (5:1). By sitting, he assumed the posture of a teacher, and his disciples approached him. The crowds also gathered to overhear what he had to say in this, the first of five major discourses in Matthew (see Table 0.1). Once again, Jesus takes on the role as a new Moses. He has cheated death, gone down to Egypt and returned, and spent time being tested in the wilderness. His story has paralleled that of Moses. Now he ascends the mountain like Moses did on Mt. Sinai (Ex 19:1–3; and see "Matthew 4:8 Through Old Testament Eyes: Mountains").

Matthew 5–7 Through Old Testament Eyes: A Prophet Like Moses

The expectation that a prophet like Moses would appear is ancient. It goes back to Deuteronomy 18:18–19:

> [The Lord said to Moses] I will raise up for them a prophet like you [Moses] from among their fellow Israelites, and I will put my words in his mouth. He will tell them everything command him. I

myself will call to account anyone who does not listen to my words that the prophet speaks in my name.

God decreed that Moses would not be able to go with Israel into the land of promise, so the prophet of Sinai did everything he could to prepare the people for what was ahead. God promised them another prophet, a prophet like Moses who would arise one day from the people. Like Moses, the prophet would speak for God. Over time the prophecy took on an eschatological cast, that is, the expectation of a future coming of a prophet like Moses at the end of days. We see this reflected in literature from roughly the same period when Matthew was writing: Philo (*De Spec Leg* 1.65) and the Pseudo-Clementine *Preaching of Peter* (*Recogn* 1.43). The author of Acts clearly makes a connection between Jesus and the end-time prophet, intensifying the threat that those who do not listen to him will be rooted out of God's people (Ac 3:22–23; cf. Mt 7:21–23). Matthew makes the case that Jesus is the eschatological prophet like Moses not by stating the obvious but by paralleling their lives' stories. Now Jesus opens his mouth and speaks for God, as Moses had done before him.

5:3 *Blessed are the poor in spirit, for theirs is the kingdom of heaven.* The first part of this famous sermon consists of nine sayings, referred to as the Beatitudes (from the Latin *beatus,* "blessed, happy, fortunate, flourishing"[1]).

First, Jesus pronounces a blessing upon "the poor in spirit" (5:3). While not identical and translations vary, the notion owes its substance to Old Testament passages like Isaiah 61:1 (LXX) quoted regarding Jesus elsewhere (Lk 4:16–30):

> The spirit of the Lord is upon me,
>   Because he has anointed me;
> he has sent me to bring good news to the poor,
>   to heal the brokenhearted,
> to proclaim release to the captives
>   and recovery of sight to the blind,
> to summon the acceptable year of the Lord
>   and the day of retribution,
>   to comfort all who mourn
> so that to those who mourn for Sion
>   be given glory instead of ashes,
> oil of joy to those who mourn,
>   a garment of glory instead of a spirit of weariness.

They will be called generations of righteousness,
   a plant of the Lord for glory.
They shall build the desolate places of old;
   they shall raise up the former devastated places;
They shall renew the desolate cities,
   places devastated for generations. (Isa 61:1–4, LXX)[2]

The unnamed prophet described in Isaiah 61 has a distinct mission to preach to the poor and captives, heal the brokenhearted and blind, and call for the year of jubilee and the release of slaves from bondage. He is anointed directly by God and has the spirit of the Lord upon him. In this oracle we notice the confluence of several ideas regarding the people who are created through his mission. They are the poor and brokenhearted who mourn for Zion, whose mourning is comforted and, eventually, turns to joy. They are known for their righteousness. Their task is to rebuild the ancient ruins and renew destroyed cities: in other words, to erase the stain and shame of defeat at the hands of their enemies. The prophet's mission brings to mind another figure from earlier chapters, the servant of the Lord, who is also endowed with the Spirit and is God's delight ("in whom I delight," Isa 42:1–4; cf. Isa 49:1–7; 52:13–53:12). His task is to bring justice and righteousness to the nations. The reference to the "poor in spirit" recalls Isaiah 61 and other passages like it.

God's disposition toward people with humility is similar to his disposition toward the poor (e.g., Zep 2:3). For example, Isaiah 66:2 (LXX) reads:

   And to whom will I look
   but to the one who is humble and quiet
   and trembles at my words?

God's favor rests on those who are humble, quiet, and tremble at his word. The opposite are the lawless who sacrifice to YHWH but mock God through disobedience. This is not the way of the poor in spirit.

5:4 *Blessed are those who mourn, for they will be comforted.* Isaiah 61 may well shape the second beatitude too, for it announces comfort for those who mourn, particularly those who mourn over Jerusalem and the land of Judah. They are called the poor and the righteous. But in the beatitude the promise of comfort is for the future, not necessarily the present: "They will be comforted." It is eschatological, awaiting its complete fulfillment in the age to come.

In Jesus' "Bible," mourning has a variety of associations, but two are primary. First, there is the grief of loss and death (e.g., Ge 23:2; 50:11; Nu 14:39; 1 Sa 25:1). Second, the survivors mourn the plight of Jerusalem and those

Jews who suffered death and exile because of their enemies (Ne 1:4; Isa 66:10). There are triumphant notes as well. When God ends the exile and gathers his people home to Zion, mourning will turn to dancing and joy (Jer 31:13).[3]

5:5 *Blessed are the meek, for they will inherit the earth.* This third beatitude has obvious links to Psalm 37:11: "But the meek will inherit the land and enjoy peace and prosperity." Psalm 37 is a wisdom psalm built on the acrostic form. It makes various promises associated with the land and its abundance to the righteous, contrasting those who trust in the Lord with the wicked. The wicked will fade like the grass and vanish like smoke, while those who trust in the Lord and do good will live in the land and enjoy security. Five times the promise to inherit the land is made to: (1) those who hope in the Lord (37:9); (2) the meek (37:11); (3) those blessed by the Lord (37:22); (4) the righteous (37:29); and (5) those who hope in the Lord and keep his way (37:34). When the psalm was composed, the "land" referred to the territories traditionally settled by the children of Israel. But in the beatitude Jesus universalizes the blessing to extend to all the earth: the meek will inherit the earth. When the kingdom comes—"will inherit"—it will stretch to the four corners of the earth. So the meek, as described in Psalm 37, are the righteous, those who trust and wait on the Lord and follow his teachings. In keeping with the wisdom theme, the meek then are the truly wise (Pr 16:18–21).

5:6 *Blessed are those who hunger and thirst for righteousness, for they will be filled.* We have already seen how important Isaiah 61 was to the first and second beatitude regarding the poor in spirit and those who mourn. It is likely significant as well to the fourth, for in this oracle the poor and mournful are further described as the "oaks of righteousness" (61:3).

The dominical saying—"Blessed are those who hunger and thirst for righteousness"—is unique to Matthew (cf. Lk 6:21). There is no phrase precisely like this in the Old Testament, but the wise do "pursue" justice and righteousness.

> The way of the wicked is an abomination to the Lord,
>> but he loves the one who *pursues righteousness*.
>> (Pr 15:9 NRSV, italics added)

> Whoever *pursues righteousness and kindness*
>> will find life and honor. (Pr 21:21 NRSV, italics added)

> Listen to me, you who *pursue righteousness*,
>> you who *seek the* Lord.

Look to the rock from which you were hewn,
   and to the quarry from which you were dug.
(Isa 51:1 NRSV, italics added)

In Isaiah 51:1 the pursuit of righteousness is parallel to seeking the Lord. Each of these phrases interprets the other. Likewise, often "justice" parallels righteousness in the Old Testament (e.g., Job 29:14; Ps 36:6; Am 5:24). God's people are commanded by Moses, and therefore by God, to pursue justice so they will live well in the land God is about to give them (Dt 16:20). Such passages likely inform anyone with ears attuned to the Hebrew Scriptures.[4]

In Sirach 24:21, Wisdom claims that "those who eat of me will hunger for more, and those who drink of me will thirst for more" (NRSV). The language of hungering and thirsting is clear and parallels Jesus' beatitude. Although Sirach is not an Old Testament book, there is a good chance that Wisdom sayings like this circulated in instructional settings so that people would have been broadly familiar with hungering and thirsting for something (like wisdom or righteousness).[5] Those who hunger and thirst for more wisdom are commended and promised implicitly that there is more to come. Yet wisdom is identified with the book of the covenant, the law delivered to Moses and passed on to the people (i.e., Torah; Sirach 24:23). Therefore, knowing and following God's teaching is broadly construed as wisdom. In addition, trusting God and doing the commandments is widely interpreted as righteousness. Ultimately, God's law codifies justice.

5:7 *Blessed are the merciful, for they will be shown mercy.* In the Old Testament, the primary "person" described as merciful is God. There is a constant refrain that the Lord God is "compassionate and merciful, patient and very merciful and truthful and preserving righteousness and doing mercy for thousands . . ." (Ex 34:6 LXX; cf. Jer 3:12; Joel 2:13; Jnh 4:2). The quality of being merciful and showing mercy is primarily an attribute of God. But the people of Israel who are called into being by God and are commanded to imitate God in his holiness are required to extend mercy to one another as well (Mic 6:8). As we will see later in this gospel, the evangelist is fond of Jesus' teachings on mercy that appeal to the words of the prophet Hosea, "I [God] desire mercy, not sacrifice" (Hos 6:6; Mt 9:13). Again, the promise of receiving mercy is eschatological. Kingdom citizens (Mt 5:3) are expected to be merciful now, in this present age, but they may not experience mercy fully until the life to come.

5:8 *Blessed are the pure in heart, for they will see God.* When Jesus' followers heard this beatitude, Psalm 24 may have been in their minds. The psalm offers an entrance liturgy describing what qualities a person needs to approach the temple and the Lord of creation (24:1–2). It asks (Ps 24:3–6, italics added):

> Who may ascend the mountain of the LORD?
>   Who may stand in his holy place?
> The one who has *clean hands and a pure heart*,
>   who does not trust in an idol
>   or swear by a false god.
>
> They will *receive blessing from the LORD*
>   and *vindication from God their Savior*.
> Such is the generation of those who seek him,
>   *who seek your face*, God of Jacob.

Clean hands and a pure heart are required of anyone who wants to ascend the holy hill. There is nothing here about office or station. The Hebrew concept of "the heart" had to do with the center of thought, emotions, and decision; according to the Shema (Dt 6:4–6), the faithful are called to love the Lord God first "with all your heart." Those not fit to see God and approach the temple are those who pridefully exalt themselves to "what is false" (Ps 24:4 NRSV) and swear deceitfully. The "what is false" may be a not-so-subtle swipe at those who make gods out of what is not God at all. They are not ready to seek the face of the Most High. Those with pure hearts, however, are promised that they will receive a blessing from the Lord. These terms come together in Jesus' sixth beatitude with the promise that those with pure hearts will "see God." Jesus' teaching would have had the ring of familiarity.

Matthew 5:8 Through Old Testament Eyes: Seeing God

"Seeing God," of course, presents us with a problem in much of the Old Testament. It was not expected that someone could see God and live, and yet some do (Hagar—Ge 16:13; Jacob—Ge 32:30; Manoah and his wife—Jdg 13:22). Still the Lord is said to have spoken to Moses face-to-face as one speaks to a friend (Ex 33:11). This could be taken to say either (a) that Moses does see God or (b) that God communicates directly with and possibly through Moses. But almost immediately the text unravels that image. When Moses asks to see God's glory, God responds that no one can see his face and live. God compromises with his prophet, hiding him among the boulders and allowing him to see his back as he passes by but not his face (Ex 33:18–23). If Moses is not allowed to see God, then who is?

Job speaks with some confidence about a day when, after his skin has been destroyed, that in the flesh "I will see God" (Job 19:25–26). Isaiah describes a time when the Lord returns to his people and the glory of the Lord is revealed so that all people are able to "see it together" (Isa 40:3–5). Jesus' promise that the pure in heart "will see God" is best taken as a promise that awaits the pure-hearted on the other side of the general resurrection, when the kingdom has come on earth as it is in heaven.

5:9 *Blessed are the peacemakers, for they will be called children of God.* Jesus pronounces blessing upon "peacemakers," because they will be called the children (literally, the sons) of God (Mt 5:9; cf. Jas 3:18). The language of peacemaking is rare in the Old Testament.[6]

In Hebrew "peace" (*shalom*) refers to more than a cessation of conflict. Peace refers to an inner sense that all is well, despite whatever might be raging about you. It signifies harmony with God, oneself, others, and creation itself.[7] It depends upon God's reconciling act that calls into existence a people who dare to seek reconciliation (Mt 5:23–26; 2 Co 5:17–21). Peacemaking is active, not passive. It is not hoping for peace, thinking about peace, writing blog posts about peace, or walking in the streets for peace; it is peacemaking that is completely dependent upon God. The connection between blessing and peace is probably best expressed in the Aaronic blessing (Nu 6:23–26 NRSV):

Speak to Aaron and his sons, saying, Thus you shall bless the Israelites: You shall say to them,

The LORD bless you and keep you;
the LORD make his face to shine upon you, and be gracious to you;
the LORD lift up his countenance upon you, and give you peace.

Peace here is God's gift or grace, his blessing and presence. While it may be God's gift, it must be received and deployed toward one's friends, neighbors, and enemies for peace to truly take root in a person or community. Some in Jesus' day felt the right thing to do was to take up arms and make war against their Roman oppressors, but the teacher offered a peaceful, nonviolent vision of God's coming kingdom.

Those who make peace and actively seek reconciliation with God, others, themselves, and creation will be called "sons of God" (or "children of God"). In the Old Testament, that phrase has a variety of meanings, but primarily, in this context, it refers to inclusion within the people of God (Ex 4:22–23; Hos 1:10; 11:1). It implies a parental relationship marked by fidelity and trust.

5:10–12 *Blessed are those who are persecuted because of righteousness, for theirs is the kingdom of heaven. Blessed are you when people insult you, persecute you and falsely say all kinds of evil against you because of me. Rejoice and be glad, because great is your reward in heaven, for in the same way they persecuted the prophets who were before you.* Regarding "they persecuted the prophets," see comments on Matthew 21:34–36 and "Going Deeper into the Fate of the Prophets" also found there.

Jesus' final blessing is also an admonition; he predicts what is coming for those willing to enter the kingdom and give themselves completely to God's righteousness and Jesus' lordship. They will be persecuted; they will be reviled. He urges them to stay the course and find joy in it because a reward awaits, and they can find inspiration and comradery in the prophets (cf. Heb 11). Isaiah 51:7 speaks to the same challenges:

> Hear me, you who know what is right,
>   you people who have taken my instruction to heart:
> Do not fear the reproach of mere mortals
>   or be terrified by their insults.

Isaiah assures his audience that salvation is coming, and their enemies will come to nothing. Despite what others do to you, say about you, Jesus urges his followers to persevere in the faith for righteousness sake, his sake, and the future reward. Whatever persecution they endure, regardless of its severity, will be short-lived compared to the reward coming their way in the kingdom of heaven.

The Beatitudes begin and end with the phrase "for theirs is the kingdom of heaven." The promise of entering and belonging to the kingdom form the frame of these eight sayings. As a result, each saying is best read against a kingdom perspective. The qualities they advance and the blessings they pronounce characterize the community of kingdom citizens that begins to emerge from the movement Jesus inspires.

Matthew 5:3–12 Through Old Testament Eyes:
The Beatitudes

The Beatitudes—the opening of Jesus' most famous sermon—are thoroughly bathed in the Old Testament.

The beatitude form is familiar to any who have read the Old Testament. It is found in the opening line of the Psalter (Ps 1:1–2):

> Blessed is the one
>   who does not walk in step with the wicked
>   or stand in the way that sinners take
>   or sit in the company of mockers,
>   but whose delight is in the law of the LORD,
>   and who meditates on his law day and night.

We see other examples, but most of those are one-off statements (e.g., Job 5:17; Da 12:12–13) and not a series of blessings as we see in Matthew 5:1–12. Two beatitudes are found back-to-back in Sirach 14:12. Though the text is fragmentary, the Dead Sea Scroll identified as 4Q525 (also designated *4QBeatitudes*) has a series of "blessed are/is . . ." statements configured around the pursuit of wisdom and walking in the law of the Most High (2.2.1–6). So when Jesus sits to deliver his Beatitudes—his own brand of wisdom—he is not inventing a new form of address; he is employing a form familiar to those who know the Scriptures and Jewish tradition.

5:13 *You are the salt of the earth. But if the salt loses its saltiness, how can it be made salty again? It is no longer good for anything, except to be thrown out and trampled underfoot.* When kingdom citizens are living out the qualities of the Beatitudes and expectantly waiting for the fulfillment of God's promises, they will be the salt of the earth and the light of the world (Mt 5:13–16). Both images find various resonances within the Old Testament.

As God instructs Moses on the recipe to make incense for the altar of incense, he directs that it be salted, pure, and sacred. No other incense is to be made with this recipe because it is to be "holy to the LORD" (Ex 30:34–38). Similarly, the people of Jericho petitioned Elisha to help them when their spring became unproductive and dangerous. The prophet placed salt in a new bowl and poured it into the spring, declaring that God had healed the water and it would never again make the people sick or the ground unproductive. Thereafter, the water remained pure (2 Ki 2:19–22). Midwives apparently rubbed salt on the skin of newborns after washing them, as a regular part of their duties to clean and purify the baby's skin (Eze 16:4). Each of these passages demonstrate the custom of using salt to purify and clean.[8]

Salt was the additive for other offerings as well (Lev 2:13; Ezr 6:9; in Ezekiel's restored temple, Eze 43:24). Salt was so closely identified with all holy offerings that these priestly sacrifices were referred to as "a covenant of salt forever." For example, Numbers 18:19 reads: "Whatever is set aside from the holy offerings the Israelites present to the LORD I give to you and your sons and daughters as your perpetual share. It is an everlasting covenant of salt before the Lord for both you and your offspring." The constancy of this practice likely had some impact on how Jesus' first followers heard the statement "You are the salt of the earth." Worshipers who came to the temple had to bring salt as well as their offering before God. In bringing these offerings they were bringing a piece of themselves and offering themselves to God. The connection between salt and worship is strong.

But Jesus goes on to press the point about salt.[9] Does the potency of salt concern its flavor? Surprisingly, there is little in the Old Testament that refers to that specific quality of salt (cf. Job 6:6). It is the notion of salt's purity, sacrifice, and holiness that characterizes the Old Testament Scriptures.

5:14–16 *You are the light of the world. A town built on a hill cannot be hidden. Neither do people light a lamp and put it under a bowl. Instead they put it on its stand, and it gives light to everyone in the house. In the same way, let your light shine before others, that they may see your good deeds and glorify your Father in heaven.* When Jesus declares his disciples to be "the light of the world,"[10] the poetry of Isaiah could not have been far away in his thoughts. Israel is called to be "a light for the Gentiles" (Is 42:6) and to extend righteousness and justice to the world. That language is repeated and intensified (Is 49:6): "I will also make you a light for the Gentiles, that my salvation may reach to the ends of the earth." Both passages form a fitting backdrop to Jesus' saying that deputizes his disciples into fulfilling God's original design for Israel. When they embody in themselves the qualities of the Beatitudes, their lives, words, and deeds will be a light to the nations that inhabit the earth. Note that the "you" in both 5:13 and 14 is not singular but plural. The community of faith stands as "the salt of the earth" and "the light of the world," not any one person. The "you" is you together, doing life together with good works standing out to the Father's glory.

5:17 *Do not think that I have come to abolish the Law or the Prophets; I have not come to abolish them but to fulfill them.* Apparently, opponents accused Jesus—and by inference Matthew and his community—of setting aside the Law and the prophets. By "the Law and the Prophets" (Torah and Nevi'im), Jesus is referring to what we today call the Old Testament. Similar charges are made throughout Jesus' ministry, as later chapters reveal, because his interpretation and performance of the Scriptures did not square with that of his detractors. But Jesus insists that he keeps the law: "I have not come to abolish . . . but to fulfill." By now the language of "fulfillment" should be familiar. Many aspects of Jesus' birth, life, and ministry are said to fulfill Scripture. Contrary to some recent interpretations, Jesus' fulfillment of Scripture does not mean it is no longer valid for his followers: "Jesus fulfilled the law so I don't have to." That is not the point, as Jesus goes on to affirm the continuing validity of the commandments. Jesus lives the law to the fullest. His words, deeds, and teachings are a living example of proper interpretation of God's teachings. Jesus' entire demeanor stands in contrast to the many Old Testament kings (shepherds) who were charged but failed to live up to the law. Israel, too, never lived up to her promises (2 Ki 10:31; 1 Ch 22:12; 2 Ch 12:1; Is. 5:24; Jer 6:19; Hos 4:6; 8:1; Am 2:4).

Going Deeper into Fulfilling the Law and the Prophets: Matthew 5:17

To follow Jesus means more than to believe in him; it means to imitate his life. As with the Scriptures' earlier fulfillment, there is an escalation and intensification that takes place with Jesus now that the kingdom of heaven is breaking in. Fulfillment takes on an eschatological and transcendent reality. Jesus takes the law to a new level. Breaking the commandments and teaching others to do so is not an option for Jesus or his followers. Disciples will be called "great in the kingdom of heaven" (Mt 5:19) as long as they do and teach the Scriptures in their entirety.

5:20 *For I tell you that unless your righteousness surpasses that of the Pharisees and the teachers of the law, you will certainly not enter the kingdom of heaven.* When Moses delivered God's teachings to the children of Israel at Mt. Sinai, the people had a univocal response. They promised to fulfill God's commandments.

> When Moses went and told the people all the Lord's words and laws, they responded with one voice, "Everything the Lord has said we will do." (Ex 24:3)

> Then he [Moses] took the Book of the Covenant and read it to the people. They responded, "We will do everything the Lord has said; we will obey." (Ex 24:7)

The people pledge obedience and fidelity to all the words of the Lord, the ordinances, and the book of the covenant. While not exactly equivalent to what becomes the Old Testament, it expresses the right posture God's covenant partners are to take toward his teaching.

Jesus told his followers that they must have a righteousness greater than that of the scribes and Pharisees to enter the kingdom of heaven (Mt

5:20). From one perspective he could not have set a higher standard; for the Pharisees were known for being deeply righteous people. But from another, he showed how far the Pharisees had to go before they could enter the kingdom of heaven.

What the Structure Means: Greater Righteousness (Mt 5)

In Matthew 5:21–48 Jesus illustrates what greater righteousness (5:20) looks like in the life of kingdom citizens through a series of Old Testament quotations. They are sometimes described as antitheses because of the pattern the teacher adopts: "You have heard it said . . . but I tell you . . ." But Jesus' teachings do not *stand in opposition* to the Scripture—a charge he has already denied—they exhibit what it means to fulfill the Law and the Prophets. The Pharisees and scribes were regarded by many as champions of an outer, public righteousness, but they had much to learn—if they dared—from Jesus about a lived theology that surpasses public piety. With Jesus, there is always more.

In fact, Jesus is doing what the Pharisees and the rabbis do all the time—they are debating the meaning and significance of Scripture. For the seriousness with which they addressed Scripture, the Pharisees should be applauded. In order not to violate God's teaching, the rabbis made a "fence" around the Torah (*m. Avot* 1.1). Another way of saying this is that they established layers of protection around God's teaching so they might live it rightly. Jesus does the same thing. If you do not give in to anger (the fence), you will not murder. If you do not lust after a person (the fence), you will not commit adultery.

Jesus situates himself as an authority on par with Scripture itself, an audacious thing to do: "The Scripture says, but I say to you." His exegesis stands in continuity with Scripture and elevates it by interiorizing its teaching and showing how it fits a new pattern of righteousness, righteousness fit for the kingdom. These examples of dominical exegeses are given weight simply because they are spoken by Jesus himself.

5:21-22 *You have heard that it was said to the people long ago, "You shall not murder, and anyone who murders will be subject to judgment." But I tell you that anyone who is angry with a brother or sister will be subject to judgment. Again, anyone who says to a brother or sister, "Raca," is answerable* *to the court. And anyone who says, "You fool!" will be in danger of the fire of hell.* The first illustration (Mt 5:21–26) has to do with the sixth commandment and its corollaries: "You shall not murder" (Ex 20:13; Dt 5:17) and "whoever murders will be subject to judgment" (see Ex 21:12; perhaps Ge 9:6). The Ten Commandments are central to the Sinai covenant and Jesus affirms their importance and ongoing validity. Jesus peels back the commandment and exposes the motive that often leads to murder, that is, anger: "But I tell you that anyone who is angry with a brother or sister will be subject to judgment" (5:22). A kingdom citizen must be a person who is not ruled by anger, who does not hurl insult or resort to name-calling. Well-placed words can murder a person's reputation, cost them their livelihood, and destroy relationships. Insulters will be liable to the council: in Jerusalem, the Sanhedrin; in other regions, a local court. Name-callers will be in danger of the fire of hell.

The Hebrew that underwrites the translation of "hell" is *Gehinnom*, the valley of the son of Hinnom, a valley southwest of Jerusalem that in earlier days was associated with child sacrifice (2 Ki 23:10; Jer 7:30–34). Though the law expressly forbids the practice (Lev 18:21), some Israelites engaged in it nonetheless.

Jewish literature composed up to two centuries prior to Jesus described Gehenna as an accursed valley in the midst of a blessed land (*1 Enoch* 27). This likely reflects a more general sentiment toward the unseemly gorge. The valley, an angelic guide describes, is meant for those whom God will curse forever. At some day of his choosing ("the last days"), God will gather the blasphemers into one place and punish them "forever," apparently in full view of the righteous. Such a display causes the righteous and merciful to bless God for the mercy he has shown them.

Jesus apparently links "hell" (Gehenna) with the very last words of the prophet Isaiah (66:24): "And they will go out and look on the dead bodies of those who rebelled against me; the worms that eat them will not die, the fire that burns them will not be quenched, and they will be loathsome to all mankind." It should be noted that the bodies of the accursed are dead and decomposing; they are (slowly) burning. This is not an image of conscious suffering but one of utter destruction with no hope for life.[11]

5:23–24 *Therefore, if you are offering your gift at the altar and there remember that your brother or sister has something against you, leave your gift there in front of the altar. First go and be reconciled to them; then come and offer your gift.* The upshot of Jesus' teaching on murderous anger is worked out in some concrete examples he gives. Apparently, he assumes that his followers will continue to travel to Jerusalem and make offerings at the temple. Since the time of King Josiah, Jerusalem was the only legitimate place to sacrifice.

What Jesus does insist on is that reconciliation with a brother or sister must be undertaken prior to an act of worship. As you remember others with whom you have "issues," it is incumbent upon you to leave the altar and be reconciled, so that you can properly offer your gift (Mt 5:23–24). It is as if he says, "You cannot be right with God until you are right with your brothers and sisters." It is interesting how Jesus relates murder to anger and anger to a lack of reconciliation.

5:25 *Settle matters quickly with your adversary who is taking you to court. Do it while you are still together on the way, or your adversary may hand you over to the judge.* Similarly, when it comes down to it, you must come to terms quickly with someone ready to accuse you before a court or else the judgment could be harsh. Jesus' teaching echoes the wisdom of Proverbs 6:1–5: act quickly— without sleep if necessary—to settle matters with a neighbor to whom you are in debt.

5:27–28 *You have heard that it was said, "You shall not commit adultery." But I tell you that anyone who looks at a woman lustfully has already committed adultery with her in his heart.* The next illustration also comes from the Decalogue as well. This time it is commandment seven: "You shall not commit adultery" (Ex 20:14; Dt 5:18). The gravity of the commandment comes to light through its penalty (Lev 20:10), but often the penalty for adultery fell disproportionately on the woman (e.g., Jn 7:53–8:11). Jesus appears to level the playing field through his interpretation: "But I say to you that *every man* who looks at a woman with lust has already committed adultery with her in his heart" (Mt 5:28, author's translation). Once again Jesus peels back the skin on the commandment to expose the interior thoughts that lead to adultery. By this standard, adultery takes place—prior to any sexual act—in the way a man regards a woman, how he looks at her, how he thinks about her.

The lustful look could be associated keenly with the last of the ten commandments: "You shall not covet your neighbor's wife" (Ex 20:17; Dt 5:21).[12] In this case, coveting is an overwhelming desire for the wife of another man, not just a wife in general; it is a desire that demands thought and action. It often begins with a lustful look. Job knew the danger of lust of the eyes and how it could lead to crime. He made "a covenant" with his eyes so that he would not even look at a virgin (Job 31:1). If his heart had been enticed by his neighbor's wife and he acted on his impulse by waiting at her door, then "let my wife grind for another, and let other men kneel over her" (Job 31:9–10 NRSV).He went on, "That would be a heinous crime . . . a fire consuming down to Abaddon" (Job 31:11–12 NRSV). Job denied both the lustful look and crime of desiring his neighbor's wife. He knew that in the end everyone would lose.

We should exercise caution here. The point Jesus is making has nothing to do with what a person happens to see. That often cannot be helped. Furthermore, there is nothing inherently wrong in the appreciation of beauty. But what can be helped is what all too often happens next, when a person continues the look until the look becomes desire. Likewise, desire frequently objectifies the other until he/she is considered merely a sexual object. The lustful look, Jesus would warn us, is intentional not accidental. It is act one in adultery. On the ideal of marriage see Matthew 19:1-9.

5:29-30 *If your right eye causes you to stumble, gouge it out and throw it away. It is better for you to lose one part of your body than for your whole body to be thrown into hell.* Jesus underscores the severity of the lustful look and the immodest touch by what he says next. But the teacher is not advocating self-mutilation. The Old Testament speaks directly against such practices (Dt 14:1-2), which pagans engaged in (1 Ki 18:27-28). Jesus is speaking hyperbolically, a common form of speech in the ancient Middle East (Dt 1:28; Jdg 20:16; 2 Sa 17:13; 2 Ch 1:15; Job 29:6). It is enough to say that kingdom citizens must control what the eyes see and hands touch. For "hell," see comments on Matthew 5:21-22.

5:31-32 *It has been said, "Anyone who divorces his wife must give her a certificate of divorce." But I tell you that anyone who divorces his wife, except for sexual immorality, makes her the victim of adultery, and anyone who marries a divorced woman commits adultery.* Jesus' teaching on the seventh commandment leads naturally to his instruction regarding divorce.[13] A person could get around the seventh commandment through easy divorce and then remarriage to another.

We should notice that, once again, the wife is in a weaker position legally; husbands often initiated divorces. Jesus' interpretation of that commandment presses the question: What are the legitimate grounds for divorce? Any man, Jesus says, who divorces his wife for any reason other than her sexual misconduct violates the seventh commandment: he commits adultery against her.

The issue has to do with a close reading of Deuteronomy 24:1-4. It is a complex passage but at the heart of it is this situation: "If a man marries a woman who becomes displeasing to him because he finds something indecent about her, and he writes her a certificate of divorce, gives it to her and sends her from his house . . .". The law allowed for divorce and remarriage, but it did not clearly stipulate the legitimate grounds for it. So Jesus enters the debate of what "something indecent" means. How high or low should that bar be set? What if the wife just cannot cook your meals? What if she grows old and tired and you find someone young and trim? To borrow Job's language, what if your wife decides to grind with another man? Well, according to Jesus' standard, the only legitimate grounds for divorce is sexual misconduct (*porneia*). A husband is not required to divorce his wife on such grounds, but he is permitted.[14] Once again Jesus calls for greater righteousness (Mt 5:20) than was apparently practiced by many "religious" men of the day.

5:33–37 *Again, you have heard that it was said to the people long ago, "Do not break your oath, but fulfill to the Lord the vows you have made." But I tell you, do not swear an oath at all: either by heaven, for it is God's throne; or by the earth, for it is his footstool; or by Jerusalem, for it is the city of the Great King. And do not swear by your head, for you cannot make even one hair white or black. All you need to say is simply "Yes" or "No"; anything beyond this comes from the evil one.* In this next example of greater righteousness, a number of biblical texts might come to mind. The closest parallel may be Leviticus 19:12: "Do not swear falsely by my name and so profane the name of your God. I am the LORD." The context of this and other laws spoken by God to Moses had to do with holiness. "I am the LORD, who brought you up out of Egypt to be your God; therefore be holy, because I am holy" (Lev 11:45). The laws in Leviticus 19 and beyond demonstrate what a life of holiness looks like in action. It is fair dealing, honesty, and a refusal to swear dishonestly, especially if one invokes the incomparable name of God. This leads, of course, back to the Ten Commandments which prohibit the use of God's name (YHWH) in any wrongful way, including magic, divination, or any deceitful action/manner (Ex 20:7; Dt 5:11). When the covenant people misuse his name and undertake deceitful actions and lies, God gets a bad name/reputation.[15]

Any vow made to the Lord must be taken seriously and fulfilled unless there are extenuating circumstances (e.g., Nu 30:3–15). Vows made to God anticipate heaven's blessing. But Deuteronomy warns against making vows and not completing them in the first place (Dt 23:21–23; cf. Ecc 5:4). If a vow is made, one should not postpone fulfilling it. At the same time, no one is forced into making a vow; there is no guilt in refraining to do so. Ecclesiastes 5:5 puts a finer point on it: "It is better not to make a vow than to make one and not fulfill it."

But Jesus' interpretation presses harder than anything in the Old Testament. He does not say with Deuteronomy and Ecclesiastes to make sure you fulfill your vows to God. He says, "Do not swear an oath at all" (Mt 5:34; cf. Jas 5:12) Then he lists several formulas by which vows were made and why they are wrongheaded: heaven is God's throne; earth is God's footstool; Jerusalem is the city of the Great King. Centuries earlier, Isaiah described heaven as God's throne and earth as God's footstool (Isa 66:1). The language had likely become commonplace among those quick to utter a vow. But vows have no purpose for the kingdom citizen; to express them smacks of evil and its harmful twin, deception. It is enough to let your word, not your vow, be your bond.

5:38–39 *You have heard that it was said, "Eye for eye, and tooth for tooth." But I tell you, do not resist an evil person. If anyone slaps you on the right cheek, turn to them the other cheek also.* The first statement of the law of retaliation (*lex talionis*) in the Old Testament occurs in a context where a pregnant woman receives an injury and loses her baby (Ex 21:22–25). Abortion advocates and opponents alike cite the passage to support their positions because there are ambiguities in the text. But a clearer version of the retaliation standard is given in a more neutral context (Lev 24:19–20; cf. Dt 19:21): "Anyone who injures their neighbor is to be injured in the same manner: fracture for fracture, eye for eye, tooth for tooth. The one who has inflicted the injury must suffer the same injury."

To modern ears this law seems to promote cruelty, but, when it was given, the standard curbed cruelty and limited liability. If someone fractures your leg in a struggle, you are not allowed to send others to fracture two of your opponent's legs or worse. Violence escalates. One eye for one eye. One tooth for one tooth. No more.

What the Structure Means: Foreshadowing Jesus' Arrest and Death (Mt 5:38–39)

When Jesus said, "You have heard that it was said, 'Eye for eye, and tooth for tooth'" (Mt 5:38), he is presuming the entire statute (Lev 24:19–20) not excising only part of it. Others who overheard him could have filled in the rest. But Jesus' take on this likely turned his hearers inside out: "But I tell you, do not resist an evil person. If anyone slaps you on the right cheek, turn to them the other cheek also" (Mt 5:39–42). In one sense, Jesus is describing what will happen to him prior to the crucifixion: not resisting arrest, being struck on the cheek, having his clothes taken away, being forced to walk with the cross by Roman soldiers (Mt 26:1–2, 12, 24, 46–56, 67; 27:27–37). So Jesus will practice what he preached in the sermon.[16]

Lamentations accounts for such nonaction as waiting on the Lord and seeking God. "It is good to wait quietly for the salvation of the Lord. . . . Let him offer his cheek to one who would strike him, and let him be filled with disgrace." Why? For the Lord will not reject his people forever (La 3:25–31). For now, Jesus and his hearer-disciples lived in the shadow of empire with recurring abuse, insults, loss of freedom, injustices, and financial hardships. With all the strains of rebellion afoot, Jesus' teaching on nonviolent resistance must have sounded naïve and completely ineffective. But Roman power would not yield, and violent resistance was futile. Jesus' way ended up being the right way.

5:42 *Give to the one who asks you, and do not turn away from the one who wants to borrow from you.* Jesus' teaching on generosity falls in line completely with Deuteronomy 15:7–11:

> If anyone is poor . . . be openhanded and freely lend them whatever they need. . . . Give generously to them and do so without a grudging heart; then because of this the LORD your God will bless you in all your work and in everything you put your hand to. There will always be poor people in the land. Therefore I command you to be openhanded toward your fellow Israelites who are poor and needy in your land.

Generosity toward the needy was a part of God's covenant expectations. Yes, the needy would always be with them, but the generous should outnumber the poor as God consistently blessed their work and made their lands productive. Money was not to be lent to the needy with interest (Ex 22:25). Charity was not business, and none should make a business of charity. No one should profit from the poor. In ancient economies people could quickly become dependent on others, but they should be able to expect the support of their countrymen. Fully aware of these teachings, Jesus offers his own kingdom interpretation regarding generosity.

Some might say it is generosity to the extreme: give to everyone who asks; do not refuse anyone who wants to borrow from you (Mt 5:42). Is Jesus serious? If we give to everyone who asks, we will not have anything left; people always have their hands out. If we do not refuse anyone who wants to borrow from us, then we become the destitute. These things are hard to reconcile. On the one hand, we wonder if Jesus is exaggerating to make a point . . . yet again. On the other, we see the radicalness of his generosity and imagine he is asking his followers to be generous in the extreme.

5:43–47 *You have heard that it was said, "Love your neighbor and hate your enemy." But I tell you, love your enemies.* Another example of greater righteousness has to do with love of enemies. The pattern Jesus has set is repeated.

Every Jew who heard the Torah read in synagogue would have been familiar with "love your neighbor" (Lev 19:18), but they would have scratched their heads at the second part, "hate your enemy." No clear instructions are in the Torah that Israelites are to hate their enemies. Some Psalms speak (apparently) favorably of hatred of enemies (Ps 31:6; 139:21). So it may have been a sentiment that drifted into the consciousness of people who had been oppressed for centuries by power and brutality. That attitude of hating one's enemy was expressed among the sectarians who copied and collected the Dead Sea Scrolls (*1QS* 1.9–11): "in order to love all the sons of light, each one according to his lot in God's plan, and to detest all the sons of darkness, each one in accordance with his blame in God's vindication." Or (*1QS* 9.21–22): "And these are the rules of behaviour for the Inspector in these times, concerning his love and his hatred. Everlasting hatred for the men of the pit in clandestine spirit."[17] Clearly, this sect of Judaism—and perhaps others—taught that hatred of the enemy was pleasing to God. How prevalent was this attitude in society? It is hard to say, but Jesus frames the teaching ("you have heard it said") in a way that points to a pattern of thought and not a random opinion.

Greater righteousness demands that kingdom citizens love their enemies and pray for their persecutors. Rabbi Hillel said famously to a Gentile who wished to convert, "That which is hateful to you, do not do to your fellow; this is the whole Torah, and the rest is commentary, go and learn it" (*b. Shabb* 31a). Yet not mistreating another person is not the same as loving them and praying for them (cf. Pr 25:21). Jesus presents his followers with a standard which had to seem out of touch, especially in light of the horrors the Jewish people had suffered. Such love, however, is to be an identity marker for Jesus followers. When they love their enemies, they demonstrate they are unique in the world; who else does that? As a result they will be known as children of the Father in heaven. Their love for enemies reflects on God.

That you may be children of your Father in heaven. The Fatherhood of God to Jesus and his followers is a well-known theme in the New Testament (Mt 6:9; Jn 1:12; Ro 8:14–15), but it is rooted in the Hebrew Scriptures (e.g., Isa 63:16; 64:8; 2 Sa 7:12–14; Ps 82:6). The question of identity continues in Jesus' teaching because he contrasts the "you" (my disciples) with the tax collectors and the Gentiles who engage only in reciprocal love and greetings. There is nothing special in such behavior; the mark of a disciple is a commitment to love enemies who do not return love and pray for those actively seeking their harm.

5:48 *Be perfect, therefore, as your heavenly Father is perfect.* Jesus' emphasis upon greater righteousness concludes with urging his disciples to be perfect (*teleioi*), recognizing that the heavenly Father is perfect (*teleios*). Again, the identity of the disciples is wrapped up in the identity of their heavenly Father. Their lives are to reflect his unique person and character. Yet "perfect" may not be the best translation of the Greek *teleioi*. There is a notion of maturity and wisdom connected with this word and how it echoes from the Hebrew

Scriptures. Jonathan Pennington makes the case that we should think of this as disciples are to be "whole," and "complete," just as God is.[18] Whole in this sense means that the inside matches the outside. Disciples are to be consistent in their actions because their actions are rooted in who they are. Rule-keeping creates . . . well, rule-keepers, not highly integrated, consistent Christians marked by character and virtue. We might hear a gentle echo of Leviticus 19:2 and 20:26 where God says, "Be holy because I . . . am holy." For any who imagined holiness had to do primarily with matters of purity and performance, Jesus transposes it into the key of wholeness and integrity. Such is the kingdom of heaven.

Going Deeper into Greater Righteousness: Matthew 5

Righteousness is an important theme in Jesus' Sermon on the Mount. His mind was so immersed in Scripture that he could not discuss righteousness without reference to it. That which is right, good, true, and beautiful is found in the Bible's teaching. Over and again he said, I know what you have been taught from the Scriptures, but let me tell you what that really means. He is not replacing the Scriptures with his own teachings; he is putting a finer point on them. What you look like on the outside needs to match what is on the inside. If not, there is no *shalom*, no peace. Eventually, you and your life will break down. What we do is important, but who we are is important as well. Some focus only on their private spiritual lives and experience. Others emphasize action and give little thought to their interior lives. Greater righteousness demands, as Jesus teaches, that we do what is right because on the inside we are right—with God, others, and ourselves.

MATTHEW 6

6:1 *Be careful not to practice your righteousness in front of others to be seen by them. If you do, you will have no reward from your Father in heaven.* The theme of greater righteousness (Mt 5:20) continues into chapter 6, but rather than continuing to illustrate how Scripture is interpreted in light of kingdom righteousness, Jesus shifts his emphasis to the *practice* of righteousness. He deals with three well-known biblical practices: (a) giving to the poor (Mt 6:2–4); (b) prayer (Mt 6:5–15); and (c) fasting (Mt 6:16–18).

The teacher begins with a principle. Righteousness must be practiced for God's eyes only. If it is performed for the eyes of people, then there is no reward with God. Human praise and adulation are, of course, rewards. As any performer can tell you, they are intoxicating benefits of being in the limelight. If that is what you seek, then that is what you will have. But you will lose out on heaven's rewards. A similar standard is reflected by the Jewish leader, Shimon the Righteous; he was fond of urging the faithful not to be like slaves who serve their master for the sake of reward; instead they should serve out of the fear of heaven (*m. Avot* 1.3; cf. Col 3:22). Righteousness, in this sense, means doing the right thing for the right reason: that is, doing what God prescribes for God's pleasure and heaven's reward.

6:2–4 *So when you give to the needy, do not announce it with trumpets, as the hypocrites do in the synagogues and on the streets, to be honored by others. Truly I tell you, they have received their reward in full.* The giving of alms to the poor is a practice rooted in the Old Testament. Though there are a number of places this teaching is expressed, Deuteronomy 15:10–11 is key. It urges God's people to give generously to the needy and underscores the promise that the Lord God will bless their work and continue to provide for them. Since the needy will always be in the land, those wealthier are commanded to open their hands to the poor. Similarly, the principle of gleaning (Dt 24:19–22) allowed for the poor and needy to eat but required them to collect what was not harvested in the fields. The grapes, grain, and olives left by those who have are given to those who have not. Every third year, a full tithe is to be brought and stored in local towns and villages so that the Levites, resident aliens, orphans, and widows in these areas can have all they need. Again, if his people do as the law prescribes, the Lord God promised to bless them and all the work they undertake (Dt 14:28–29).

Passages like these directed God's covenant people to give to the poor and provided Jesus with a framework consistent with the practice of greater righteousness. He urged his disciples when they gave alms to do so in secret so that the Father who sees in secret would reward them (Mt 6:2–4). Implicit within this is the Old Testament notion that God would bless and provide for those who give to the poor.

Jesus is a master of exaggeration and humor. He painted his opponents as hypocrites so interested in the praise of others that they hired trumpets to announce their offerings. The term *hypocrite* comes from a Greek word meaning "actor"; an actor could change masks and instantly change his character. Jesus used the term often to describe his opponents (e.g., Mt 6:2; 7:5; 15:7; 22:18). The kingdom righteous are not hypocrites; they are so concerned not to seek human attention that they give to the poor in such a way that their left hands do not know what their right hands are doing. Another exaggerated, humorous image. As they give, the Father will see their secret gifts and reward them.

Going Deeper into Giving to the Needy: Matthew 6:2

Giving to the poor today is a regular feature of Christian worship and practice (see also comments at Mt 26:11).[1] It is not enough for Christ followers to say, "This is why I pay taxes. Let the government take care of the poor." While we hope our governments are attuned to the poor and their needs, that does not release us from Jesus' teaching about meeting the needs of the hungry and homeless. Giving is not only right; it brings with it blessings and opportunities to spread the good news of the kingdom. Yet, providing alms to the poor for God's eyes only is a challenge in our economic systems of credit cards and increasingly cashless exchanges. Someone somewhere will know about our gift, and we cannot avoid that. Jesus' point has to do with our motives, not the detailed mechanics of the gifts. Are we giving for God's pleasure and in obedience to his teaching or are we doing so for a tax credit? Are we genuinely trying to meet the needs of the poor or impress the right people?

6:5–7 *And when you pray, do not be like the hypocrites, for they love to pray standing in the synagogues and on the street corners to be seen by others. Truly I tell you, they have received their reward in full.* Another practice Jesus highlights in kingdom righteousness is prayer. He expected his disciples to be people of prayer: "when you pray, do not be like the hypocrites" who pray standing in prominent places to be seen by others. The praise of people is all the reward that will be coming to them. (See "Going Deeper into Prayer: Matthew 23:5.")

Daniel reflected the traditional Jewish practice of prayer three times daily: morning, afternoon, and evening (Da 6:10). In defiance of King Darius's edict, Daniel did so in his own house before open windows that faced Jerusalem. He knelt when he prayed in an act of contrition and praise. Exactly when the practice of prayer toward the land of Israel began is unclear, but it is likely inspired by Solomon's prayer at the time the temple is dedicated (e.g., 1 Ki 8:35, 44, 48). Early Christians adopted the threefold practice of prayer for their own. Peter and John go up to the temple at the hour of prayer, about 3:00 p.m. (literally the ninth hour—Ac 3:1). And the early Christian document known as the *Didache* appears to direct the praying of the Lord's Prayer three times daily (*Did* 8:2–3). Jesus' instructions on kingdom righteousness likely presumes these practices. He is not forbidding public prayer, of course, but he is criticizing the public performance of prayer for the eyes of any but God. He directs his followers to go into their rooms, shut the doors, and pray to the Father who will see and reward them. Likewise, Jesus followers are not to babble on and on like other peoples who imagine their many words will gain God's attention.

6:9 *This, then, is how you should pray: "Our Father in heaven."* In Matthew 6:9–11 Jesus offers what we call the Lord's Prayer as a model for his disciples. Not only should one pray this prayer, but also prayers inspired by it. Nearly every element in the prayer has its roots somewhere in the Hebrew Scriptures. The address to God as "Our Father in heaven," for example, is language inspired by Isaiah's prayer (63:15–16, italics added):

> Look down from heaven and see,
>   from your lofty throne, holy and glorious.
> Where are your zeal and your might?
>   Your tenderness and compassion are withheld from us.
> But *you are our Father,*
>   though Abraham does not know us
>   or Israel acknowledge us;
> *you,* LORD, *are our Father,*
>   *our Redeemer from of old is your name.*

God is clearly in heaven. The "our Father" is repeated twice in an intimate request for him to be present and mighty with them as Redeemer. The prayer continues with a direct appeal to God to rend the heavens, come down, and rescue his people (Isa 64:1–3). It pleads with God to forgive their sins, confessing YHWH as their Father (64:8).

Hallowed be your name. The first petition is often mistaken as "a word of praise"; in fact, it is a request. Father, hallow (make holy) your name. The connection with God's name and holiness is expressed powerfully in Isaiah's vision as the seraphs call out to each other: *Qadosh, Qadosh, Qadosh*/"Holy, holy, holy is the LORD Almighty; the whole earth is full of his glory" (Isa 6:3).[2] In various sectors of the Scripture the correlation of God's name and holiness are obvious. For example, in one of Isaiah's poems of renewal the prophet speaks of a day when the deaf hear, the blind see, the meek find joy, and the neediest among them exult in the Holy One of Israel. When that day comes, God reverses the shame and "they [his people] will keep my [YHWH's] name holy" (Isa 29:23).

Ezekiel 36 contains an influential prophecy of God's future restoration. At the heart of it is God's concern for his name, a refrain that is repeated throughout the oracle. In former days, the house of Israel profaned God's good name among the nations with violence and idolatry (Eze 36:16–21). So God dispersed them among the nations. But now God had determined to act to restore their fortunes, not for their sakes, but for the sake of his holy name (36:22). God promises to sanctify his own name so that the nations will know that "I am YHWH" when he displays his holiness before them. God will sprinkle them with clean water and remove their uncleanness and idolatry. He will give them a new heart and a new spirit so they will follow his sensible teachings. Then the nations will recognize YHWH as God and Israel as God's own people (Eze 36:23). But again, God claims not to act for their sake but for his own, that is, to restore his good name. When all is done, then God will make the land uber-productive once again, to his glory (Eze 36:29–32).

Leviticus relates keeping God's commandments and observing the Torah to not profaning God's holy name so that "I [God] may be sanctified among the people of Israel: I am YHWH" (Lev 22:31–33, author's translation). Jesus' prayer recognizes that God alone can protect his good name. More often than not, people who claim to be his damage God's name through the sinful ways they live. As such, the prayer cuts two ways: God, do not let your people spoil your good name, but act as Redeemer among them to protect your name and reputation in the world.

6:10 *Your kingdom come, your will be done.* The second petition also has roots deep in Scripture. The two phrases stand in parallel. For God's kingdom to come is for God's will to be done on earth, for heaven already experiences the uninterrupted benefits of God's will. We can define the kingdom then as the time and place in history when God's will is done on earth as it is in heaven. By asking for God's kingdom to come, the prayer assumes that God's will is not yet being done on earth. Ironically, the juxtaposition of "kingdom" and "God" are rare in the Old Testament. But nearly everything in Israel's Scriptures recognizes YHWH's sovereignty over Israel as her king. The so-called enthronement psalms are filled with lines such as "The LORD is king, he is robed in majesty . . ." (Ps 93:1 NRSV; e.g., Ps 97:1 and Ps 47, 95, 96, 97, 99). Regarding "kingdom," see also comments on Matthew 3:1–2 and 4:17.

Matthew 6:10 Through Old Testament Eyes: "Your Kingdom Come"

Scholars have long recognized that the Mosaic covenant as established is a theo-political act.[3] Over time the kingdom is associated with the royal house of David (2 Sa 7:12–16) and related to the coming Messiah (e.g., Isa 2:1–4; 9:1–7; 11:1–9). Still, there are prophecies that envisage God's personal revelation and actions to judge, restore, and renew (Isa 40:1–11; Jer 30–31; Eze 36). As N. T. Wright has pointed out, a central feature of Second Temple Judaism was a robust conviction that Israel's God had promised to return to his people one day. His return would be in person and in glory (e.g., Isa 40:1–11). When he comes, he will judge and save; he will initiate a new exodus and establish a new creation (Isa 65–66). In other words, God would return to be king.[4] Perhaps no prophet states it more succinctly than Zechariah: "Then the LORD my God will come, and all the holy ones with him. . . . The LORD will be king over the whole earth. On that day there will be one LORD, and his name the only name" (Zec 14:5–9). As Beasley-Murray writes, "Thus, the goal of history is reached in the revelation and universal acknowledgement of Yahweh's sovereignty, the triumph of righteousness, and the establishment of peace and salvation in the world."[5]

When God's kingdom comes in full and God's will is done, then all the nations will turn to God and acknowledge the Lord as God. All nations will find their destiny salvation in Israel's God (e.g., Isa 25:6–7; Zep 3:8–9; Zec 8:20–21). This is not universalism, but universal access to God by all nations. In that kingdom, sins and debts are forgiven, righteousness and justice prevail (e.g., Isa 1:25–26; Jer 31:31–32; Eze 36:25–26). As justice and righteousness spread across the earth, peace will settle in. War will be a thing of the past (Isa 2:2–4; 9:5–6). Humans and animals will live in a peaceable kingdom without fear (Isa 11:6–7; 35:9), and the land will be exceedingly bountiful (Isa 35; Eze 47; Am 9:13). Peace with God. Peace with others. Peace with creation. God's shalom filling the earth. The Messiah is God's agent to effect these eschatological realities. He is God's Son, in whom God is present and through whom God acts to bring heaven to earth.

6:11 *Give us today our daily bread.* Bread here is symbolic of all that humans need to live well. Already we have seen how Jesus quoted Deuteronomy (8:3), recognizing that people need more than bread to flourish (Mt 4:4). Yet those needs are concretized at the table where God provides daily bread. The phrase may be better translated "God give us today the bread we need for tomorrow." In other words, do not give us too much that we might think we are providing for ourselves. And do not give us too little that we might worry and steal and so profane your name.

The creation story relates how God has already fed the children of Adam and Eve with seed-bearing plants and fruit-bearing trees (Ge 1:29). The proverbs of Solomon assert that "the LORD does not let the righteous go hungry" (Pr 10:3). The Psalms often celebrate God's provision for animals and humans alike (e.g., Ps 104:10–23; 147:7–9). These texts provide a likely backdrop for the kind of petition expressed. As with global water crises and food insecurity today, in biblical times poverty and hunger had causes in famine, diseases, lack of rain, insect plagues, and political threats from enemies. Despite these challenges, God's people are to seek his provision, which often comes through the generosity of others.

One of most memorable provisions God supplied the Israelites on the way to Sinai and beyond was the bread that rained down from heaven six days a week to feed and nourish them (Ex 16; Nu 11:7–9). The miracle grain sustained them during their wilderness wanderings. Moses directed Aaron, his brother and high priest, to gather an omer of it, and place it in the ark of the covenant so generations to come would be reminded of God's faithfulness (Ex 16:32). Here again we see a connection between Jesus and Moses. Later in the gospel, Jesus' multiplication of the loaves and fish (Mt 14:13–21) echoes this often-rehearsed tradition.

6:12, 14–15 *Forgive us our debts, as we also have forgiven our debtors.* The fourth petition is the only one based on a condition. Luke states it differently, but the meaning is the same: "Forgive us our sins, for we also forgive everyone indebted to us" (Lk 11:4, author's translation). "Debts" is a metaphor for sins and has roots deep in the Hebrew Bible (Dt 15:1–6). In the year of Jubilee (Lev

25:8–12), property is to be returned, families reunited, and a perfect sabbath of rest for the people and the land enacted. The connection between sins and debts is clarified by what Jesus says after the prayer: "For if you forgive other people when they sin against you, your heavenly Father will also forgive you. But if you do not forgive others their sins, your Father will not forgive your sins" (Mt 6:14–15). The Greek word translated "sins" typically refers to a false step or offense against another person.

The parable of the unforgiving servant/slave (Mt 18:23–35) provides the best story illustrating what Jesus meant by this teaching. The "punch line" of the parable comes in Matthew 18:35: "This is how my heavenly Father will treat each of you unless you forgive your brother or sister from your heart." Jesus begins the parable with reference to the kingdom of heaven, demonstrating that the forgiveness of sins and cancellations of debts characterize the kingdom when it comes in full. In the meantime, Jesus followers are to pray for the Father's forgiveness and effect it through their own forgiving acts.

6:13 *Lead us not into temptation, but deliver us from the evil one.* The fifth and sixth petitions are related and stand somewhat in parallel; they ask the Father not to lead them into the time of trial but to deliver them from the evil one. This is a hard petition to understand especially since, as we have seen (4:1–11), the Spirit leads Jesus into the wilderness for a time of trial and testing. And Jesus sets his disciples up to expect persecution or times of trials. Some translations render the word *peirasmos* as "temptation," but God does not "tempt" people to do evil and thus bring about their downfall (cf. Jas 1:13–15; also see "Going Deeper into Tests and Temptations: Matthew 4:1"). As we saw in Jesus' trial in the wilderness, God tested Abraham at Mt. Moriah and Israel in the wilderness, but the tests were not to see whether they would measure up. They were for their good, to humble and discipline them. They were, in a sense, part of God's training program for his people (Dt 8:2–3).

So perhaps we should read this petition of protection as: "Father, do not let us fall into temptation." It is plausible, however, given the eschatological bent of Jesus' kingdom proclamation, that he has in mind a particular season of trial "in the last days" (see the eschatological discourse, Mt 24:4–29). In a sense then, the final petitions beg God to deliver them from falling away in the great trial that is to come and thus fall prey to the evil one. By evil one, Jesus has in mind "the Satan," his adversary in the wilderness (Mt 4:1–11; see comments at Mt 4:1).

6:16–18 *When you fast, do not look somber as the hypocrites do.* Jesus practiced and recommended fasting as a regular aspect of kingdom righteousness (Mt 6:16–18). The early church order known as the *Didache* regularized the practice to twice weekly on days we call Wednesdays and Fridays (*Did* 8.1). This was to distinguish the Jesus followers from the hypocrites who fasted on Mondays and Thursdays. Exactly how often Jesus and his disciples fasted is unclear, but he is questioned later by John's disciples about why they are not fasting on a recognized, prescribed fast day, and we will consider Jesus' answer then (Mt 9:14–17). Still, there is the expectation that Jesus' disciples will fast.

In the Old Testament, fasting typically accompanied acts of repentance and mourning. *Yom Kippur,* the day of atonement, was to be a fast day practiced on the tenth day of the seventh month every year to atone for the sins of the people (Lev 16:1–34; Nu 29:7–11). King David fasted before God for the life of his child, hoping "the LORD may be gracious" and the child live (2 Sa 12:20–23), but it was not to be. The most thorough critique and presentation of fasting is in Isaiah 58:1–14 (cf. Joel 2:12–17). The oracle condemns fasting without an accompanying righteousness. God does not hear prayers said or recognize fasts carried out in self-interest and injustice, regardless of how pious they might appear. The fast that God wants deals with injustice, releases the oppressed, and feeds, clothes, and houses the poor. Then, and only then, can God's people expect him to hear and answer.

As with almsgiving and prayer, Jesus teaches his followers to do their fasting in secret, for God's eyes only. So, they are not to go around grumbling and unkempt, letting everyone know by their appearance they are denying themselves. If they do, the only reward they can expect is the praise of others. Instead, they should wash their faces and put oil in their hair (see 2 Sa 12:20; Ecc 9:8) (a brush or comb is also a good idea). Fasting may be the right practice, but is it done for the right reason? The right reason is to please the Father who can and will reward them (also see comments on fasting at Mt 4:2).

6:19–20 *Do not store up for yourselves treasures on earth. . . . But store up for yourselves treasures in heaven.* The Sermon continues, contrasting treasures on earth with treasures in heaven (6:19–21); this teaching pulls together Jesus' instruction on the practice of greater righteousness. It also provides a point of transition to how kingdom righteousness relates to "things" that people often put their trust in (other than God): particularly, wealth and what money can buy. The Father's rewards are now recast as "treasures in heaven," as human accolades and praise are recast as treasures on earth that will fade over time. The message overall is similar to what is found in Ecclesiastes, which describes everything gained on earth as fleeting (literally, a mist/*hebel*) and striving after the wind (e.g., Ecc 1:2, 14). Isaiah says that you should not fear those who revile you, for the moth will eat them like a garment and a worm will gnaw them like wool (Isa 51:8).

Nothing in the Hebrew Bible condemns personal property or the acquisition of wealth (Dt 28:1–14; Pr 3:9–10). The fruit of the womb, the crops from the ground, and the birth of livestock are taken as evidence of God's blessing and obedience to his law. There are, however, concerns expressed over a preoccupation with wealth. Riches profit nothing in matters of righteousness. Wealth does nothing to forestall death (Pr 11:4). So disciples must focus their efforts on treasures in heaven rather than rewards on earth that are subject to decay, corruption, and theft. A complete rethinking is in order. What matters on earth is kingdom righteousness which lays up treasure in heaven. And how is this ideally expressed? Through almsgiving, prayer, fasting and other righteous acts conducted for God's eyes only.

6:21 *For where your treasure is, there your heart will be also.* Jesus makes explicit what is implicit in the Old Testament. Psalm 52 Contrasts the way of the arrogant with the way of the righteous. The "mighty" are described in various ways—plotting destruction against the godly, loving evil more than good, having deceitful tongues—but the righteous see God's judgment of them and mock those who trusted in riches and sought refuge in wealth (Ps 52:7). Psalm 62 is a hymn of trust that urges God's people not to engage in extortion or robbery and not to set their heart on riches; rather, they are to trust in God, their refuge (Ps 62:8–10). Finally, in the second code of the law, God says he will allow his people to have a king after they enter and settle the land, but he warns them against a king who seeks horses, wives, gold, and silver because in seeking such riches his heart will turn away from God. Instead, he is to have a copy of the law with him at all times, and he is to read it all the days of his life (Dt 17:17–19).

6:22 *The eye is the lamp of the body. If your eyes are healthy, your whole body will be full of light.* Jesus' teaching about the lamp and the light (Mt 6:22–23) is not disconnected from what comes before (storing up treasures) and what follows (serving God or money). Properly understood, this hinge verse/teaching is about how one "sees" earthly treasure and earthly goods. How one sees reveals what is on the inside. We have all witnessed how some people "light up" when they see a new car, new clothes, a chef-inspired meal, or a chance to make a lot of money. Others might "light up" when they see a good opportunity to serve and love others. The appearance of the eye in those moments reveals what is on the inside. Our phrase "light up" is equally metaphorical, but we also recognize that when people "light up" it involves the entire body. In that sense, the eye is a lamp of the whole body. At the heart of the image is the mystery of sight itself. How does sight work? Do our eyes take in light or give off light? In a way it is both. By saying our eyes are a lamp, Jesus is saying our light shines in the world. The image also poses a philosophical question: What is life about? Is life about getting or about giving? Is it about opening the hand or keeping a tight fist?

Jesus paints a stark picture between two polar opposites: the healthy/light side and the unhealthy/dark side. Healthy/unhealthy (NIV, NRSV) may not, however, be the best way to translate the Greek words. A good case can be made for "whole"/"evil." This lines up with the earlier beatitude about the "pure in heart" (Mt 5:8). The issue is not one of health and 20/20 vision, but a moral disposition toward wealth and what it affords. A person whose eye is "whole" is not fixated on wealth, but a person with an evil eye is (cf. Dt 15:9; Pr 23:6).

The contrast made by Jesus is not unique; the people who collected the Dead Sea Scrolls had similar thoughts about the two poles. The Hebrew Bible is filled with images of light and darkness, good and evil (Isa 60:20). To offer a few examples, Proverbs 15:30 says: "The light of the eyes makes the heart rejoice, good news refreshes the body" (author's translation). According to Psalm 82:5, without wisdom and knowledge people walk in darkness. In the wisdom tradition, the ways of evil are said to parade about in darkness (Pr 2:13), and wisdom is to folly as light is to darkness (Ecc 2:13). The prophet Isaiah warned against seeing evil and calling it good or seeing darkness and calling it light (Isa 5:20). After a vision in the night, Daniel blesses the God of heaven and confesses that God reveals deep and hidden things because he knows what dwells in darkness since light is in him (Da 2:22). In the teachings here, Jesus draws deeply from the symbolic world of the Hebrew Scriptures.

6:24 *No one can serve two masters. Either you will hate the one and love the other, or you will be devoted to the one and despise the other. You cannot serve both God and money.* The contrast shifts away from light and darkness to two other opposites represented by two masters: God and money. A servant must decide whom to serve because you cannot serve two masters, especially when they are diametrically opposed. Some English versions read God and wealth (NRSV) or God and money (ESV, NIV). But the word translated as *wealth*, *riches*, or *money* is actually a Greek transliteration of an Aramaic word, *mamona*.[6] The root of the word means "trust" or "reliance." It refers to anything one puts their trust in or relies upon other than the one, true God. Money would certainly seem to fit the context of Jesus' teaching and our addiction to it in the modern world. But it could be much more. The J. B. Phillips translation has the right idea: "You cannot serve God and the power of money at the same time." Here the emphasis is on what money can do for you. Money itself is not the problem; it is value-neutral. Yet when it is valued ultimately, we grant it soul-destroying power. As Paul said to Timothy, the love of money is the root of all sorts of evil and many have been ruined by it (1 Ti

6:10). Ecclesiastes affirms that the love of money can never be satisfied; it is all vanity (Ecc 5:10). Wealth can be gained and easily lost in some misadventure.

Jesus' teaching depends in large measure on the wisdom tradition. Among the words to the wise (Pr 22:17–24:34) are cautions regarding wealth. The wise trust in the Lord and pursue wisdom (Pr 22:17–21), not mammon.

> Do not wear yourself out to get rich;
>   do not trust your own cleverness.
> Cast but a glance at riches, and they are gone,
>   for they will surely sprout wings
>   and fly off to the sky like an eagle. (Pr 23:4–5)

Whatever can be gained on this earth can also be lost. The miser might hurry to get rich, but his head will spin when he/she sees how quickly it is lost (Pr 28:22). Perhaps it is the antithetical parallels in Israel's poetry that have the most in common with Jesus' teaching on God and mammon:

> The greedy stir up conflict,
>   but those who trust in the LORD will prosper. (Pr 28:25)

> Those who give to the poor will lack nothing,
>   but those who close their eyes to them receive many curses. (Pr 28:27)

Matthew 6 Through Old Testament Eyes

In this central section of the Sermon on the Mount, Jesus focuses on the allure and danger of materialism. While he never quotes Proverbs and its wisdom, the wisdom of Proverbs courses throughout his teaching. Human beings are at their best when they are giving to others; we are at our worst when we are building our own kingdoms, treasuring *ultimately* money and what it can buy us. Greed for gain (mammon) is the opposite of trust in the Lord. Greed leads to strife, trust in God to true riches. Those who give can expect God's blessing, but those who turn a blind eye (again, the eye) will suffer his curses. Jesus, informed by Israel's Scripture and the wisdom of Proverbs, casts a similar vision of earthly goods and the limits of what they can do for you.

6:25 *Therefore I tell you, do not worry about your life, what you will eat or drink; or about your body, what you will wear.* The final section dealing with kingdom righteousness and earthly goods is rich in scriptural memory; it is also some of the most elevated prose in the New Testament. Jesus contrasts the human habit of worrying with the disciple's call to strive for the kingdom and God's righteousness (6:25, 33). As with each of these contrasts, there is likely some reliance on a teaching expressed in the Deuteronomic theme. Simply stated: obedience to God brings blessings, disobedience brings curses. While it is stated clearly (in absolute terms) in several places and illustrated richly in the history of Israel, Deuteronomy 28:1–14 demonstrates how blessings flow and needs are met when God's people seek God and keep his teachings. It is also a clear example of how the Deuteronomic covenant builds on and expands the Abrahamic blessing (e.g., Ge 12:1–3). The passage is too long to quote in its entirety, but we can summarize some of its salient features. If God's people obey him by observing his commandments, "all these blessings" will come upon them and overtake them (Dt 28:1–2). Then follows a list of those blessings: (1) life in the land God promised; (2) abundant children, produce, and livestock; (3) victory over their enemies; (4) prosperity in what they do; (5) rain; and (6) primacy of place and respect among the nations. All of this is predicated upon obedience to and trust in the Lord. The national blessings come down to the individual disciples most clearly in what they have to eat, drink, and wear—the Nazarene's emphases—three sources of insecurity and worry then and now.

6:26 *Look at the birds of the air; they do not sow or reap or store away in barns, and yet your heavenly Father feeds them.* When Jesus asks his disciples to consider the birds and how the Father feeds them, he is invoking imagery found in Israel's poetry. In Job's defense of himself to his friends, he notes that nature itself—the animals and the birds—can instruct the wise if they pay attention (Job 12:7–9; cf. Pr 6:6–11). God is the one who feeds the critters what they need; when baby ravens call out from the nest, it is God who provides (Ps 147:9). God answers the prayers of the poor and needy when they seek water and there is none; he makes rivers flow and fountains rise. He plants the wilderness thick with trees (Isa 41:17–20). Those who heard Jesus teach would find nothing strange in Jesus' call to consider the birds and how the Father feeds them.

Yet Jesus escalates the image with a simple question: "Are you [my disciples] not much more valuable than they [the birds]?" (6:26). Indeed, they are. As the crown of creation, human beings have a special place in God's world. That is expressed in Genesis 1–3, but also in Psalm 8. Made just a little lower than the *Elohim,* crowned with glory and honor, human beings exercise dominion over the works of God's hands, including the birds of the air and the fish of the sea (Ps 8:5–8).[7] This escalation from light to heavy, lesser to greater, characterizes Jewish rabbinic readings of biblical texts at the time and in the centuries following (e.g., *m. Qidd* 4.14; in the Old Testament see Dt 31:27; Pr 11:31; Jer 12:5; Eze 15:5).[8] A similar argument is made by Rabbi Shimon ben Eleazar that neither beast nor bird has a trade, but they earn their living without anguish. They do exactly what their Creator made them to do. Human beings, however, have to deal with the consequences of sin (Jer 5:25; *b. Qidd* 82b).

6:28-29 *And why do you worry about clothes? See how the flowers of the field grow. They do not labor or spin. Yet I tell you that not even Solomon in all his splendor was dressed like one of these.* Kingdom citizens must not worry about clothing. God clothes the lilies of the field and gives them a glory greater than Solomon's. King Solomon himself had become proverbial for great wealth and wisdom. When the Queen of Sheba visited his kingdom, she saw with her own eyes the splendor of it, and it took her breath away (1 Ki 10:1-13; 2 Ch 9:1-12). But the flowers of the field have a greater splendor, even if that splendor is temporary like the grasses that grow, are cut, and become fuel for the ovens. The psalms recognize the brevity of human life and the splendor of Solomon. We come from the dust and shall return to dust. Like grass that springs up in the morning, we live, fade, and wither (Ps 90:3-6). Isaiah 40:6-8 echoes these sentiments and contrasts them with the permanency of God's word:

> All people are like grass,
>   and all their faithfulness is like the flowers of the field.
> The grass withers and the flowers fall,
>   because the breath of the Lord blows on them.
> Surely the people are grass.
> The grass withers and the flowers fall,
>   but the word of our God endures forever.

If God is concerned to clothe the grasses and lilies, he will also clothe the faithful.

6:33 *But seek first his kingdom and his righteousness, and all these things will be given to you as well.* So Jesus concludes with an admonition not to worry like the Gentiles; instead his followers are to trust God to provide all they need as they seek the kingdom life first and go after righteousness (Mt 6:31-34). On pursuing righteousness, see Matthew 5:6. Although Jesus does not quote Psalm 37, he could have, because it fits perfectly with his teaching to his disciples. It sits comfortably in the background of everything Jesus says in this part of his sermon. It is a wisdom psalm constructed as an acrostic. One of the most relevant passages reads:

> Trust in the Eternal, do what is good,
>   Then you will live in the land and feed on faithfulness.
> Take great joy in the Eternal
>   And he will grant you what you desire.
>   (Ps 37:3–4, author's translation)

Trusting in the Eternal, finding joy in him, and feeding on faithfulness translate well into what it means to strive for the kingdom and his righteousness. In fact, the phrase "do what is good" might well be rendered "do what is right." Implicit within this wisdom text is a promise that resembles the positive aspect of the Deuteronomic code: trust in God, do what is right, feed on faithfulness, and God will grant your desires (that is, obedience brings blessing). Similarly, Jesus urged his disciples to seek the kingdom first and its righteousness, then all these things—what you eat, drink, and wear—will be given to you.

6:34 *Therefore do not worry about tomorrow, for tomorrow will worry about itself. Each day has enough trouble of its own.* In Psalm 37 the sage urges, "Do not fret—it leads only to evil" (v. 8). Fretting and worrying accomplish nothing toward meeting one's needs. In fact, they lead to trouble, and as Jesus said, tomorrow will have enough trouble of its own.

MATTHEW 7

The Sermon on the Mount concludes with a variety of teachings by Jesus that touch on topics consistent with his call to seek the kingdom and its righteousness.

7:1–2 *Do not judge, or you too will be judged. For in the same way you judge others, you will be judged, and with the measure you use, it will be measured to you.* Not every pericope in the gospel or saying of Jesus has direct or even indirect connections with the Old Testament. Such is the case with Jesus' admonition about judging (Mt 7:1–5). This appears to be a unique and innovative teaching of the Master. There are Old Testament roots, however, in the general admonition in Scripture to pursue justice. God directed Israel to appoint judges and officials to render just decisions for the people (Dt 16:18–20). They were not to show partiality, accept bribes, or distort justice. They were to pursue justice with all their might so that they could continue to live in the land the Lord had given them. The language here is insider language. The local courts were established to render just decisions for the people of Israel, not their Canaanite or Philistine neighbors. Still, inherent with rendering just judgments is the obligation of some to judge others, establish codes of fairness (beyond those expressed explicitly in Scripture), and at times to condemn the behavior of others.

The prophets often expressed judgments consistent with the Law. While Amos famously said, "Let justice roll on like a river, righteousness like a never-failing stream!" (Am 5:24), it was only after speaking oracles that criticized all the religious activities (festivals, assemblies, offerings, songs) by people who failed to act morally and justly. The prophet announced "woe" to all those seeking the day of the Lord and warned it would be "darkness, not light!" (Am 5:18–20). The prophets could be forgiven, however, because they were speaking for God. Still the prophets were the moral conscience of Israel; they formed judgments and expressed them and held nothing back.

Some take Matthew 7:1, "Judge not, that ye be not judged" (KJV),[1] as an absolute prohibition against forming and expressing a judgment. But that seems odd given the Old Testament background about the pursuit of justice and the fact that Jesus forms and expresses judgments often in his teachings in no uncertain terms. For example, disciples are not to give what is precious to dogs or cast their pearls before swine (Mt 7:6). It is unlikely Jesus is talking about farm animals here. As the context shows, he is characterizing some people in derogatory terms—about as derogatory as you find in the Gospels— to warn his disciples against sharing the good news of the kingdom with those who consistently reject it. The false prophets are like hungry wolves, dressed in sheep's clothing; they must be recognized for what they are (Mt 7:15–16). Jesus pronounces "woe!" on some Pharisees and teachers of the law for being blind guides, hypocrites, sons of hell, and whitewashed sepulchers (e.g., Mt 23:15–16, 27). Jesus has made and expressed judgments in keeping with the Law and the Prophets.

7:3–5 *Take the plank out of your own eye, and then you will see clearly to remove the speck from your brother's eye.* It is best to approach Matthew 7:1–5 within its context, that is, an admonition in a wisdom formula that has four parts:

1. Admonition—do not judge
2. Rationale—you will be judged by how you judge
3. Illustration—the speck in the eye of your brother and a plank in your own eye
4. Admonition restated—remove the plank in your eye so you can see well enough to remove the speck for your brother

If this is the correct way to interpret the text, what we have is not an absolute prohibition against judging, but a way for humble Christ followers to go about bringing correction to one another in the church. Again, notice the insider language. "Your brother" has a speck, that is, the believing brother or sister. This is consistent with the Old Testament admonition to establish courts of justice and has nothing to do with how the faithful are to approach those outside the community. If there is to be shalom and justice in the church, judgments must be made, expressed, and carried out, even if it gets messy. The assumption driving this teaching is that the church—like Israel of old—will need correction from time to time, and the church is to be a self-correcting body. It is not to look to outsiders to solve its problems (see 1 Co 6:1–7). Then, as now, courts were corrupt, and justice was seldom done. They could not be trusted to do what is right

in God's eyes. Throughout history, with injustice on the rampage, Jesus' teaching showed a better way; anyone who judges should examine themselves first.

7:6 *Do not give dogs what is sacred; do not throw your pearls to pigs. If you
do, they may trample them under their feet, and turn and tear you to pieces.*
If correction is prudent inside the community, then what posture should
disciples take toward offering what is holy to those outside the circle?

As John Stott noticed, we have to keep this teaching in balance.[2] On
the one hand, Jesus followers are called to make disciples of the nations (Mt
28:19–20); that is where the story is ultimately headed. On the other, Jesus
recognizes that some people will be hostile to the gospel and will, in days to
come, turn on the disciples to tear them to pieces. Jesus referred to these as
"dogs" and "pigs." But how will disciples know whom they should share with
and whom they should not? Two types of enemies to the gospel exist. Some
present themselves from the first as antagonists to believers and will often
seek them out to ridicule and publicly shame them. They work actively to tear
down the Christian faith. There is no use casting gospel pearls before people
like this. Others become hostile over time, after repeatedly hearing and rejecting the message. Their hearts become harder and harder, and eventually it
becomes obvious they are not fertile ground for the good news to take root.

The most likely scriptural influences for thinking about what is holy
comes from purity passages like Exodus 29:33.[3] The teaching makes clear that
only Aaron and his sons are allowed to eat the ram of ordination. Because it
was holy (devoted to God), no one else was permitted to taste of it. The divide
between pure and impure, holy and unholy was so wide that any meat left
over had to be destroyed by fire the next day rather than given to another.
Similarly, Leviticus 22:1–16 instructs that only priests in a state of purity are
permitted to eat the holy donations. Any priest in a temporary state of impurity—as well as a lay person—was prohibited from eating it. Why? Because
the donations were holy; they were given to God.

The holiness and purity codes stand in the background of Jesus' instruction not to give what is holy to dogs or throw pearls before swine. The language
is harsh, but it is not as harsh as the reality of the persecutions the followers of
Jesus would face (5:11–12). Some are going to trample you and turn on you,
so refrain from placing before them "what is sacred." The "sacred" here could
refer to a variety of things, but in the context it makes sense to see it in line
with Jesus' teaching regarding the kingdom and righteousness.

7:7–8 *Ask and it will be given to you; seek and you will find; knock and the door
will be opened to you. For everyone who asks receives; the one who seeks finds; and
to the one who knocks, the door will be opened.* When Jesus urges his disciples to

ask, seek, and knock, he does so in concert with a variety of scriptural witnesses. The story of Hannah comes to mind as a good example of a woman who asked the Lord for an extraordinary gift and received her heart's desire (1 Sa 1:1–2:11). Hannah's song (1 Sa 2:1–10) resonates within the gentle verse of the Magnificat of Mary from Nazareth (Lk 1:46–56). When Wisdom cries out in the city, she promises that those who seek her find her (Pr 8:17). Jeremiah's letter to the exiles in Babylon (Jer 29:1–32) is an extraordinary document because it invalidates the other so-called prophets and sages who promised a speedy return home. The prophet instructs the exiles to build houses, plant gardens, and plan to be there for a while as they seek the good of the city where God had sent them. In due course (seventy years) God will fulfill his promise to bring them back home. But in the meantime, they are to call upon God and pray and trust the promise: "'You will seek me and find me when you seek me with all your heart. I will be found by you,' declares the LORD" (Jer 29:13–14). A verse from the oracles of Isaiah sounds a similar note: "Seek the LORD while he may be found; call on him while he is near" (Isa 55:6). The backdrop to Jesus' instruction may well be found in passages like these and others that portray God as answering prayer and providing an opening for his people.

The three appeals—ask, seek, and knock—invite believers into a proactive relationship with God. They are not magical formulas that somehow obligate God to any person's desired outcome. In the language of the New Testament, these commands imply a constancy of action and thought. Ask and keep on asking. Seek and keep on seeking. Knock and keep on knocking. At the heart of the matter is constancy in prayer even when what we ask is not forthcoming. Likewise, the assumption is that disciples are moving deeper in faith; when that happens, one's desires coalesce around kingdom priorities. With time and growth, what disciples ask for and seek begins to move closer to the will of God.

7:9–11 *Which of you, if your son asks for bread, will give him a stone? Or if he asks for a fish, will give him a snake? If you, then, though you are evil, know how to give good gifts to your children, how much more will your Father in heaven give good gifts to those who ask him!* The illustration Jesus uses to clarify this wisdom is exaggerated. What mother would give her son a chunk of granite if he asked for bread? What father would give his daughter a water moccasin if she asked for a fish? Obviously, no one. Since even human beings with their propensity for evil know how to give good gifts, "how much more" will the Father give you good things when you ask? As we saw earlier, the "how much more" technique is typical of Jesus and the rabbis (see Mt 6:26). Jesus' insistence that disciples are to consider God in heaven as their "Father" (see 5:45; 6:9) is a regular feature of his teaching.

7:12 *So in everything, do to others what you would have them do to you, for this sums up the Law and the Prophets.* The Golden Rule summarizes Jesus' overall teaching on how disciples are to relate to neighbors. In the Scriptures the disposition a covenant member is to have toward the neighbor is commanded in Leviticus 19:18: do not seek revenge on your neighbor, instead love your neighbor as you love yourself. There are two parts to this: "do not" and "do," inasmuch as love is an action not a feeling. Act in such a way that you seek the best for your neighbor. How is that discerned? One way is to consider what you yourself regard as favorable and do that.

When asked by a lawyer, Jesus describes the love of neighbor as the second commandment (Mt 22:34–40). What does this look like in real life? In every situation, treat the other as you would like to be treated. That is the whole of the Law and the Prophets. (See also "Going Deeper into Fulfilling the Law and the Prophets: Matthew 5:17.")

Going Deeper into the Golden Rule: Matthew 7:12

There is a similar saying among the rabbis, but it is stated negatively. Whereas Jesus says "do," Rabbi Hillel told a Gentile who would be a Jew to "do not." Hillel taught: "That which is hateful to you do not do to another; that is the entire Torah, and the rest is its interpretation. Go and study" (*b. Shabb* 31a; Tobit 4:15; Philo, *Hyp* 7.6).[4]

The sayings of Jesus and Hillel are similar but stated differently. What is key is that both Hillel and Jesus see this action or nonaction as the whole or entire Law. Jesus includes "the Law and the Prophets." Those two parts represent the whole of Scripture. For Hillel there is both an oral and written Torah, so the prophets could be included.

7:13–14 *Enter through the narrow gate. For wide is the gate and broad is the road that leads to destruction, and many enter through it.* Jesus concludes the sermon with a variety of appeals. In the first, he encourages his disciples to enter by the narrow gate. We can visualize the text as two similar but opposing paths (see Table 7.1).

Table 7.1. The Two Ways of Matthew 7:13

Narrow gate → narrow road → hard way → few are on it → leads to life

Broad gate → broad road → easy way → many are on it → leads to destruction

Jesus has restated a theme common to the Old Testament. The offer would ring true to those who heard him on the mountain that day. The initial statement of it is in the book of Deuteronomy (30:11–20). It is often called the Deuteronomic theme, but it continues into the historical books as well (what Jews called the former prophets). It is also called the doctrine of the two ways because it offers two possibilities: "See, I set before you today life and prosperity, death and destruction" (Dt 30:15).

What the Structure Means: The Two Ways (Mt 7:13)

God gives his people two options. One way is this: obey the commandments, love your God, walk in his ways, and you will live and become numerous and prosperous in the land God provides. But there is another way: disobey the commandments, be led astray, worship other gods, and you will perish and be exiled from the land God provides. He repeats the invitation of verse 15 and calls heaven and earth as witnesses (Dt 30:19–20):

> This day I call the heavens and the earth as witnesses against you that I have set before you life and death, blessings and curses. Now choose life, so that you and your children may live and that you may love the LORD your God, listen to his voice, and hold fast to him. For the LORD is your life, and he will give you many years in the land he swore to give to your fathers, Abraham, Isaac and Jacob.

The wisdom tradition picks up on this theme (Pr 11:19; 14:27) and recasts it as wisdom and folly. Those who pursue wisdom find happiness and life, while those who neglect her find injury and death (Pr 8:32–36). The pursuit of wisdom is linked clearly to doing what is righteous and thus obeying God's law.

The Sermon on the Mount offers a number of examples of Jesus following this binary pattern. He uses such stark contrasts to grab the attention of people and call them to the way of righteousness: be salty, not unsalty (5:13); shine your light, don't hide it (5:14); do not seek treasures on earth but in heaven (6:19–20); choose God, not money (6:24). Are there middle roads, halfway measures, lukewarm ways of following Jesus that don't involve out-and-out rejection of God? Of course, but the reason Jesus offers only two opposing choices is pastoral. It is a way of saying, "Don't even consider that third, middle option. You know you shouldn't turn away from God completely. Therefore, make the only choice you really have left—to be fully committed to God."

Jesus' teaching about the narrow gate leans heavily on the Deuteronomic and wisdom themes. The path to life is entered by a narrow gate; it is a difficult road and only a few choose it. But the path to death and destruction is entered by the broad gate; it leads to a broad way and is an easy street. But it ends in destruction. Although Jesus does not mention it explicitly in this invitation, one enters the narrow gate and the path to life by listening to and following his teachings. And his teachings and example fill full what is, in fact, the Old Testament. That becomes explicit in the parable of the person who built his house on the rock (Mt 7:24–27).

7:15 *Watch out for false prophets. They come to you in sheep's clothing, but inwardly they are ferocious wolves.* When Jesus warned his followers about false prophets (Mt 7:15–20; see also comments on Mt 24:24), he joined a chorus of voices from the Law and the Prophets. Deuteronomy warns against following any diviner or prophet who encourages his hearers to go after other gods and serve them (Dt 13:1–5). So dangerous were they that they were to be purged from the land of Israel. Similarly, any prophet who presumes to speak in the name of YHWH, Israel's God and whom God has not sent is not to be followed (Dt 18:20–22). But how do the people know? One test is this: any prophet who makes a prediction that does not come true is to be considered false.

Similarly, among the prophets Jeremiah cautioned (5:30–31):

> A horrible and shocking thing
>   has happened in the land:
> The prophets prophesy lies,
>   the priests rule by their own authority,
> and my people love it this way.
>   But what will you do in the end?

Both prophet and priest appear here as vocations recognized by the people. The masses follow and seem to relish doing so, because the false message is pleasing to the ears ("'Peace, peace,' they say, when there is no peace," Jer 6:14). Some are false primarily because they prophesy for financial gain and not because they are sent by YHWH. Micah alerts his hearers to avoid prophets who lead the people astray because they speak favorably to those who fill their mouths with good things to eat and unfavorably to those who do not (Mic 3:5–8). Ezekiel utters an oracle against every class of leaders in

Judah—the princes, the priests, the officials, and the prophets (Eze 22:23–31). He rails (Eze 22:27–28): "Her officials within her are like wolves tearing their prey; they shed blood and kill people to make unjust gain. Her prophets whitewash these deeds for them by false visions and lying divinations. They say, 'This is what the Sovereign LORD says'—when the LORD has not spoken."

Warnings against false prophets are plentiful in the Hebrew Scriptures. Jesus echoes them here to his own followers in his day. The day of false prophets has not yet come to an end.

When Jesus depicts the false teachers as ravenous wolves in sheep's clothing, he may have in mind Ezekiel's characterization above of officials who are like wolves shedding the blood of their prey. Throughout Scripture the people of God are portrayed as sheep and their leaders—whether true or false—as shepherds (e.g., Ps 23:1–3; 78:70–72; Eze 34:6; Jer 23:1–4; 50:6; Zec 10:3).

7:16–20 *By their fruit you will recognize them. Do people pick grapes from thorn bushes, or figs from thistles? . . . Thus, by their fruit you will recognize them.* Twice in this section Jesus makes the statement that the true and the false (prophets) will be known by their fruits (Mt 7:16, 20). The question appears to be, What do their lives produce? Fruit is a metaphor for the words and deeds of these leaders.

Isaiah's "Song of the Vineyard" (Isa 5:1–7) provides a memorable image of the promise of good fruit. "My loved one" planted a vineyard on a fertile hill and did everything imaginable to make it a success, but it yielded only bad fruit. In the parable the owner of the vineyard is the Lord of hosts; its vines are the people of Israel and Judah. God had expected good fruit (justice and righteousness) but instead harvested only bad (bloodshed and cries of distress). In Isaiah's day the fruit of the beloved's vineyard reveals the pitiful state of God's people.[5] Now in Jesus' time the threat of false prophets is real too, but his emphasis appears to be on the false prophets, not the general populace itself.

Good grapes and delicious figs are not gathered from thorns, thistles, and briers. Only good vines produce good fruit. Likewise, only good trees yield good fruit.

7:21 *Not everyone who says to me, "Lord, Lord," will enter the kingdom of heaven, but only the one who does the will of my Father who is in heaven.* Jesus' teaching about false prophets and false prophecy carries over into the next segment of the sermon (7:21–23). Some of the bad fruit producers will know his name and will even address him as "Lord" (*kyrie*), but they are not doing the will of the Father; these will not enter the kingdom. The scene of the teaching shifts dramatically to "that day," that is, the eschatological judgment. It is a day well described by the prophets who could foresee such a day coming (e.g., Isa 2:11; Hos 1:5; Joel 3:18; Am 5:18–24). It is a day in which "the many" will be confident because they prophesied in his name, cast out demons, and performed other works of power. But they will be surprised. As Amos says, it will be a day of darkness and not light (Am 5:18–20). Jesus is featured in the Matthew passage as the eschatological judge, an audacious claim on the face of it for a Galilean teacher.

The address to Jesus as "Lord, Lord," (κύριε, κύριε) occurs also in Matthew 25:11 in a similar judgment context where the bridegroom of Jesus' parable appears as judge who utters a similar reply, "I don't know you." (Mt 25:12). The double vocative (address) occurs sixteen times in the Greek version of the Old Testament and is always an address to God employing the divine name (either as Adonai YHWH or YHWH Adonai). Jesus' use of it as a self-reference would have registered with any biblically literate audience. He seems to lay claim to God's unique covenant name for himself.[6]

7:22 *Many will say to me on that day, "Lord, Lord, did we not prophesy in your name and in your name drive out demons and in your name perform many miracles?"* Jeremiah complained to God about false prophets in his day who promised safety and security for Jerusalem and its temple (Jer 14:14–15). The Lord was quick to respond that they were prophesying lies "in my name," a phrase similar to that used by Jesus to describe the false activities of the false prophets. In Matthew's account, Jesus will soon commission the Twelve to engage in a future mission (Mt 10:1–15). Jeremiah's account sits comfortably within Jesus' teaching. In his day, though God had not sent these false prophets, they claimed to have a revelation—whether through divination or vision. But the word of the Lord came to Jeremiah, indicating that these lying prophets would die soon by sword and famine as would those taken in by their message (Jer 14:15–16). Prophesying in the name of Jesus appears a regular feature of the early church. The teaching here likely means it is a practice which the deceitful will counterfeit for their own purposes. They might gain a foothold here but not in the judgment as Jesus himself presides over it.

7:23 *Then I will tell them plainly, "I never knew you. Away from me, you evildoers!"* Jesus takes part of Psalm 6:8 as his final word when he dismisses the false prophets in the judgment. The psalmist wrote: "Away from me, all you who do evil, for the LORD has heard my weeping." In context, the psalm is a prayer for healing, yet it turns to praise in the midst of one's enemies. The line is spoken by the psalmist, who orders his enemies to get away now that God has clearly heard his prayers for help and apparently has come through. Not only was the psalmist dealing with the effects of disease, but there were ongoing threats from enemies that made the weariness and grief

that much more intense. Jesus now turns the psalmist's words into a word of
final judgment.

7:24 *Therefore everyone who hears these words of mine and puts them into*
practice is like a wise man who built his house on the rock. The teacher brings
his sermon to a close with what might be called an invitation. He returns to
the theme of the two ways (cf. Mt 7:13–14). Now instead of the narrow or
broad gate he talked about earlier, he reformulates the two options into the
stories of two people, one who built his house on the sand, the other who built
on the rock. We might represent this as seen in Table 7.2:

Table 7.2. The Two Builders (Mt 7:24–27)

The Builder on Rock	The Builder on Sand
Hears Jesus' words	Hears Jesus' words
↓	↓
acts on them	does not act on them
↓	↓
like a wise man	like a foolish man
↓	↓
built his house on rock	built his house on sand
↓	↓
storms come	storms come
↓	↓
the house stands	the house falls

Again, this is a version of a Deuteronomic theme:

Obedience → blessing/the house stands
Disobedience → curse/the house falls

If we factor in wisdom (see comments on Mt 7:13–14):

Obedience → wisdom → blessing/the house stands
Disobedience → folly → curse/the house falls

The difference between the two people and their futures is simple: what
do they do with Jesus' teaching? Both hear Jesus' words, but the wise man
acts on them while the fool does not. Their destinies could not be more
different. It is not enough to know Jesus' words, or even be a good student
of them; what matters here is action (cf. *m. Avot* 1.17). In both scenarios,
storms rage. Knowing Jesus' words and acting on them is no guarantee

against the coming storms; what is guaranteed is that the foundation laid by the wise will hold. When the storm is over, the house continues to stand.

When reading this part of the Sermon on the Mount, the adept reader of Scripture may recall Ezekiel's oracle against the false prophets who misled Israel with false visions and lying divinations (Eze 13:8–16). In the prophetic imagination, the people are said to build a wall and the prophets plaster it over. Yet God is going to send a storm, a flood of rain, hail, and strong winds to topple the wall and expose the foundations. Rather than believing Ezekiel, God's prophet who predicted heaven's judgment, the people chose to hold on to nationalistic hopes: peace, peace, when there is no peace.

The final words of the sermon are a call to action. True faith, saving faith, is faith that goes to work. True discipleship is more than having a notebook filled with notes about Jesus and what he said; true discipleship involves hearing and doing. That is the essence of wisdom. That guarantees one's future.

7:28–29 *When Jesus had finished saying these things, the crowds were amazed at his teaching, because he taught as one who had authority, and not as their teachers of the law.* Matthew finishes and transitions this sermon as he does the other four main collections of Jesus' messages (11:1; 13:53; 19:1; 26:1): "When Jesus had finished saying these things . . . " (Mt 7:28). This sounds curiously like the end of Moses's speeches in Deuteronomy, especially from the Greek version we call the Septuagint: "And Moses finished speaking all these words to all the sons of Israel . . . " (Dt 31:1, LXX, author's translation; cf. Dt 32:45). There are several key differences, however. Moses's time with the people is nearly over; Jesus, it appears, is just getting started. Years of teaching and miracles await. Moses spoke to all the sons and daughters of Israel; Jesus spoke only to his small band of disciples on a mountain in Galilee, overheard by a crowd. Moses turned the reins of leadership over to Joshua; Jesus (the new Joshua) is readying his followers to carry on in his absence (Mt 28:19–20).

What the Structure Means: Five Sermons (Mt 5–25)

As discussed in the introduction, Matthew's gospel is structured around five sermons. The first and most famous is the Sermon on the Mount (see Table 0.1). The number five is important because it references the five books of Moses. Once again, we are in "new Moses" territory with this gospel as it carefully and programmatically links Jesus to Moses. While all the sermons are different—the setting, content, audience—what is common among them is a narrative conclusion that announces the end of the "sayings" and then transitions to what is next in the story (Mt 7:28; 11:1; 13:53; 19:1; 26:1). These transitional moments mark the end of the sermons.

These five sermons do not exhaust the teachings of Jesus. The teacher finds opportunity here and there to address the crowds and his followers in a variety of contexts.

MATTHEW 8

8:1 *When Jesus came down from the mountainside, large crowds followed him.* Matthew again portrays Jesus like Moses, who came down from Mt. Sinai with the covenant tablets (Ex 34:29). Yet there are differences. Moses descended the mountain alone until he met Aaron and the people of Israel. But Jesus is not alone on the mountain; he is surrounded by disciples and the crowds. Moses had the covenant tablets in his hands, but Jesus brings with him no written record, only his disciples. The teachings he delivered are written on the hearts and memories of the people with him. It is at this point that Matthew shifts his focus to a different part of Jesus' mission: healing the sick and performing miracles. (See also "Matthew 4:8 Through Old Testament Eyes: Mountains.")

8:2 *A man with leprosy came and knelt before him and said, "Lord, if you are willing, you can make me clean."* For months, if not years, this man had a skin disease that caused anxiety, discomfort, and social ostracism. He turns to Jesus, convinced the Nazarene could heal him.

The biblical term for "leprosy" covers a variety of skin diseases and is not necessarily the disease we know today as leprosy (i.e., Hansen's disease). Regardless, the Scriptures legislate what is to be done for people who find themselves with various skin diseases that create a state of ritual impurity or uncleanness. The prescriptions are not just for skin diseases but for mold growing on fabrics and walls in the house (Lev 13–14). Like other impurities, these can be spread by contact, so people with skin diseases became instant outsiders, separated from their families and villages.

There are Old Testament examples of similar people who were cleansed or healed of their various diseases. The prophet Elisha is directly involved in the healing of a leper named Naaman, the commander of the army of

Aram (i.e., Damascus; 2 Ki 5:1–19). Naaman learned from a captive girl that there was a prophet in Samaria who could heal him. The warrior took hundreds of pounds of silver and gold for payment for his healing to Israel's king, who scoffed at the idea and figured it was some sort of political ploy. When Elisha, the man of God, heard of the situation, he invited Naaman to come to him. The man of God told him to go and wash in the Jordan River seven times, but the commander went away in a rage about the prophet's direction. Finally, his servants got him to do what the prophet ordered, and he was cleansed of the disease. The punch line of the story comes when Naaman, the consummate outsider and enemy of Israel, confessed that there was no God in all the earth except the One who reigned in Israel (2 Ki 5:15).[1]

In addition to the prophetic implications of cleansing lepers, there is also a messianic, eschatological angle. When Jesus is asked by John the Baptist's disciples whether he is the one or is another coming, Jesus answered (Mt 11:4–5, author's translation), "Go and announce to John the things you hear and see: the blind are seeing, and the lame are walking, lepers are being cleansed and the deaf are hearing, the dead are being raised and the poor are receiving the good news." Jesus' answer to the question comes as no surprise to anyone who knows well the prophecies of Isaiah about the coming age (e.g., Isa 26:19; 29:18; 35:5–6; 42:18). We will deal with this text more fully later (regarding Mt 11:1–7), but for now it is enough to note that Jesus includes the cleansing of the lepers as a sign of the age to come. It is part of what the Messiah comes to do.

8:3–4 *Jesus reached out his hand and touched the man. "I am willing," he said. "Be clean!" Immediately he was cleansed of his leprosy. Then Jesus said to him, "See that you don't tell anyone. But go, show yourself to the priest and offer the gift Moses commanded, as a testimony to them."* Nothing in the law prohibited Jesus' physical contact with the "leper" (Lev 13:45–46).[2] When he speaks the words "Be clean," immediately the leper is healed. After Jesus encourages the leper to keep his healing a secret, he directs him to do what the law of Moses prescribes (Lev 14). According to the law, the priests are to examine any who think they are healed. And if they are, there is a ritual sacrifice to be performed involving two birds: the first is to be sacrificed, the second is to be released, in a sense carrying away the impurity. The rite takes a week, and it involves bathing, washing clothes, and shaving all hair. The ritual does not enact the healing but merely confirms it. It is a witness, most likely to the priests, who are the representatives of the people and who can officially restore those who were sick to full participation in the community.

What the Structure Means:
Jesus the Healer
(Mt 8:1–9:37)

Matthew augments his portrayal of Jesus the teacher (Sermon on the Mount) with Jesus the healer by using three clusters each with three miracle stories. As seen in Table 8.1, each cluster ends with a penetrating teaching on some aspect of discipleship. For Matthew, the miracles demonstrate the authority Jesus has over disease, nature, evil spirits, and death.

Table 8.1. Three Miracle Clusters

First Cluster (8:1–22)
- Healing of a leper (8:1–4)
- Healing the centurion's servant (8:5–13)
- Healing of many at Peter's house (8:14–17)

Discipleship sayings—the demands of discipleship (8:18–22)

Second Cluster (8:23–9:17)
- Stilling of the storm (8:23–27)
- Healing of the demonized in Gadara (8:28–9:1)
- Healing of the paralytic (9:2–8)

Calling of disciples and question of fasting (9:9–17)

Third Cluster (9:18–38)
- Resuscitation of the synagogue leader's daughter and healing of a woman (9:18–26)
- Healing of two blind men (9:27–31)
- Healing of a mute man (9:32–34)

Discipleship sayings—the plentiful harvest, the few laborers (9:35–37)

8:5–6 *When Jesus had entered Capernaum, a centurion came to him, asking for help. "Lord," he said, "my servant lies at home paralyzed, suffering terribly."* The healing of the centurion's servant (Mt 8:5–13) continues Matthew's emphasis on the inclusion of the Gentiles in the promises of God (see Mt 2:1–12). In itself this fills full or begins to fill full oracles spoken by Isaiah (42:1–7), who introduces a figure called the "servant of YHWH" whom God promises to bring forth; he will be endowed with the Spirit and given the task of taking justice to the nations. That phrase "to the nations" is key, for it refers to all peoples who are not Jews (aka Gentiles), like the centurion and perhaps his servant. Speaking directly to the servant of YHWH, the Creator and Covenant-maker rehearses the servant's call (Isa 42:6–7):

I, the Lord, have called you in righteousness;
    I will take hold of your hand.
I will keep you and will make you
    to be a covenant for the people
    and a light for the Gentiles,
to open eyes that are blind,
    to free captives from prison
    and to release from the dungeon those who sit in darkness.

Not only is Jesus sent to the lost sheep of the house of Israel, but he is sent as "a light to the nations/Gentiles." By "nations," we should not think of the nation-states we know today, but "people groups" with distinct languages, cultures, histories, and hopes. Today many "nations" might live in one city. The miracles that follow and the liberation of political prisoners are part of the justice and righteousness that is to extend to the nations.

A similar endowment or task is given to one called "the root of Jesse" (Isa 11:1–10). Jesse, the father of King David, holds a prominent place as the progenitor of this future ruler, described as a kind of architect of a peaceable kingdom. Endowed with the Spirit, clothed in righteousness and justice, this figure becomes key regarding the promise of a coming Messiah. Again, the followers of Jesus considered Jesus *God's yes* to this promise. He is the root of Jesse, and the root of Jesse has important tasks in the days to come (Isa 11:10, LXX, author's translation):

And in that day it will be that the root of Jesse,
    he will arise to rule the nations;
the nations will place their hope in him,
    and his rest will bring honor.

The oracle continues to describe how God is about to show his hand, and while he attends to the nations, he will also gather the lost of Israel, and bring back the dispersed of Judah from the four corners of the earth. This dual mission is imprinted on Matthew's Jesus as this miracle story demonstrates (cf. Mt 12:18–21). Through his portrait of Jesus, the evangelist demonstrates that he owns the promise of Gentile inclusion as part of his and his community's mission.

8:11–12 *I say to you that many will come from the east and the west, and will take their places at the feast with Abraham, Isaac and Jacob in the kingdom of heaven. But the subjects of the kingdom will be thrown outside, into the darkness, where there will be weeping and gnashing of teeth.* In this chapter, the first to be healed was likely a son of Israel (8:1–4), though the text does not say explicitly. The second was a paralyzed servant to a Roman centurion, that is, a Gentile army officer (8:5–13). The ethnic identity of the servant is not given and does not seem to be the point of the story. The Gentile's request is granted because he shows extraordinary faith in Jesus and his ability to heal (8:8–10). But the man's extraordinary faith highlights the fact that Jesus has not found anyone in Israel with such faith. Regardless of the little faith he finds around him, Jesus is inspired by the psalms and the prophets to describe a day when Abraham and his sons, including some of the lost sheep, will gather—from east and west—at a great banquet in the kingdom of heaven (8:11).

Several Old Testament texts describe such a day. It is a theme and a hope not far from the hearts of the first gospel's audience. Psalm 107 considers those redeemed by God, describing them as gathered from all the lands—east, west, north, and south (Ps 107:3). Again, Isaiah speaks of a day of redemption when God promises, "I am with you" (Isa 43:5–6) and that he will bring Israel's children from the ends of the earth—east, west, north, and south. But not all ethnic Israel is faithful Israel, as the Jewish apostle to the Gentiles makes clear (Ro 9–11).

Some who thought they were sons and daughters of the kingdom will find themselves cut off, cast into outer darkness. The phrase "weeping and gnashing of teeth" (Mt 8:12) echoes the final verse of Psalm 112. This acrostic wisdom psalm contrasts the future of the righteous and the wicked. When the wicked see the happiness and prosperity awaiting the generous and righteous, the wicked rage and grind their teeth. Ultimately, they melt away, and their desires come to nothing (Ps 112:10). For Jesus, the healing of the centurion's servant becomes an opportunity to cast a disturbing yet hopeful vision of future judgment. Disturbing for those "subjects of the kingdom" who think they are okay. Hopeful for Gentiles who come to Jesus in expectant faith.

8:16–17 *When evening came, many who were demon-possessed were brought to him, and he drove out the spirits with a word and healed all the sick. This was to fulfill what was spoken through the prophet Isaiah: "He took up our infirmities and bore our diseases."* Demonic spirits are not a regular feature of Old Testament stories and prophecies. However, where they do figure in Hebrew Scripture, they figure prominently. For example, in God's directive to Moses and Israel regarding the Day of Atonement, two goats are to be offered to YHWH before the tent of meeting. After casting lots—that is, sorting out God's choice—one is to be offered as a sin offering before the Lord, the other is to be sent off into the wilderness to Azazel (Lev 16:8, 10, 26 ESV, NET, NLT). Azazel likely refers to a desert-dwelling demon. The "scapegoat" is not offered to Azazel as a "sacrifice" nor is it vicarious suffering that takes place. It is, however, the means by which all the culpabilities and transgressions of the Israelites are banished.[3]

In another context, the prophet Isaiah utters an oracle against Babylon announcing its doom and devastation. After the day of YHWH, the splendor of Babylon will be turned to ruin, its cities inhabited by wild animals, howling creatures, jackals, and "goat-demons" (Isa 13:21–22 CEB, NRSV). Later, Isaiah speaks a similar oracle against Edom—this with cosmic proportions (Isa 34:1–17). Again, after the day of vengeance, the good land of Edom becomes a wasteland not unlike Sodom and Gomorrah (Ge 19:24–28). The land will be named "No Kingdom There," and it will be turned into a haunt of jackals, wildcats, demons, and a particularly nasty female demon known by the name of Lilith (Isa 34:14 CEB, NRSV). In the Second Temple period, there is a growing recognition of the spirit realms (both angelic and demonic).[4] By the time of Jesus, there is a robust awareness of the havoc the spirit world can inflict on poor, unfortunate souls.

After relieving Peter's mother-in-law of a fever (in Capernaum, 8:14–15), Jesus goes out in the evening and liberates the demonized and heals all who were sick. Then Matthew claims (8:17), "This was to fulfill what was spoken through the prophet Isaiah: 'He took up our infirmities and bore our diseases.'" The passage Matthew quotes comes from Isaiah 53, one of the most quoted and echoed by early Christians. There are at least forty quotations, allusions, or echoes in the New Testament to Isaiah 53. Many of those have to do with redemption from sin, others with physical healing. The quotation is part of a Servant Song that begins in Isaiah 52:13 and carries through the end of chapter 53. At the heart of the Song is vicarious suffering, although Matthew does not link the citation to Jesus' suffering in any way. Jesus does not take on the sickness of others or become demonized to heal or free them. He releases the agonized from their maladies with what Robert Gundry calls a "lordly 'word.'"[5] Still, the healing and exorcizing ministry of Jesus is such an important feature of his life that we might find it strange if Matthew did not see some Old Testament connection. Not just in this phase of his ministry but in all phases, whenever Jesus heals, he does so in fulfillment of Scripture.

What the Structure Means: Fulfillment Quotations

There are twelve fulfillment quotations in Matthew's gospel (see Table 8.2). The number is not coincidental. As we will see, the number twelve represents the people of God. Jesus' choice of "the Twelve" to be with him is the yeast of the new community that is forming around him. This numerology is reinforced by these twelve quotations which show how well the prophets line up with the life and ministry of Jesus.

With some of these fulfillment quotations Matthew identifies the prophet quoted, but with others he simply mentions the prophet(s). In some cases of fulfillment, more than one prophet bears witness, but we are not always sure what texts Matthew and his community may have had in mind. At the arrest of Jesus, for example, no specific text is quoted but, generally speaking, early Christians recognized that the prophets spoke with a single voice that the Messiah must suffer. A number of psalms speak of a righteous sufferer (e.g., Ps 22:6–8, 12–21; 80:14–17; 118:10, 13, 18, 22), and the Messiah is tasked with extending righteousness to the world. We might also consider here the suffering of the servant of YHWH (Isa 53).

Table 8.2. The Twelve Fulfillment Quotations

Passage	Topic	Prophesier	Old Testament Source
Mt 1:22–23	The Virgin Conceives	"the prophet"	Isaiah 7:14
Mt 2:15	Out of Egypt	"the prophet"	Hosea 11:1
Mt 2:17–18	Rachel Weeping	"the prophet Jeremiah"	Jeremiah 31:15
Mt 2:23	Called a Nazarene	"the prophets"	Isaiah 11:1(?)
Mt 4:14–16	Ministry in Galilee	"the prophet Isaiah"	Isaiah 9:1–2
Mt 8:17	Took Our Infirmities	"the prophet Isaiah"	Isaiah 53:4
Mt 12:17–21	"Messianic Secret"	"the prophet Isaiah"	Isaiah 42:1–4
Mt 13:14–15	Dullness of Hearing	"the prophecy of Isaiah"	Isaiah 6:9–10
Mt 13:35	The Use of Parables	"the prophet"	Psalm 78:2
Mt 21:4–5	"Triumphal" Entry	"the prophet"	Isaiah 62:11; Zechariah 9:9
Mt 26:54–56	Betrayal and Arrest	"the writings of the prophets"	Isaiah 53:4–9(?)
Mt 27:9–10	Purchase of the Potter's Field	"Jeremiah the prophet"	Zechariah 11:13; Jeremiah 32:6–15

8:18–19 *Then a teacher of the law came to him and said, "Teacher, I will follow you wherever you go."* When Jesus saw the crowd, he ordered the disciples to prepare a boat to take them to the other side of the Sea of Galilee. As he is waiting, Jesus is approached by two admirers. Among Jesus' would-be disciples is a scribe who promises to follow Jesus wherever he was going. Jesus' response, however, tests the limits of his devotion: "Foxes have dens and birds have nests, but the Son of Man has no place to lay his head" (8:20). We should not take this to mean that Jesus is "homeless" and liken his situation to the modern, social problem of homelessness. He is not "homeless" in the modern sense. He has a house in Capernaum (Mk 2:1) but has chosen the life of itinerancy; that is, he travels from place to place with the message of God's kingdom.

8:20 *The Son of Man has no place to lay his head.* This is the first time in this gospel that Jesus refers to himself using the cryptic, third-person phrase: "the Son of Man." He does so repeatedly throughout the remainder of the gospel (e.g., 9:6; 10:23; 12:8). It is probably the most debated title in the New Testament. Part of that has to do with the Old Testament settings.

Depending upon the translation, the phrase occurs frequently in poetic texts as a way to refer to a human being (e.g., Ps 8:4 NASB 1995 [italics added]): "What is man that You take thought of him, and *the son of man* that You care for him?" The NIV translates the phrase as "human beings."

Consider also Job 16:21 (ESV, italics added): "that he would argue the case of a man with God, as *a son of man* does with his neighbor." The NIV translates the phrase as "one," referring to a person. There are many other examples (e.g., Ps 80:17; 144:3; Job 25:6; 35:8). So "son of man" is used often in the Old Testament as an idiom that refers to a human being.

Another specialized use of the phrase "son of man" occurs in the prophecy of Ezekiel. Nearly one hundred times in the book YHWH addresses Ezekiel as "son of man" (e.g., Eze 2 [4x]; 3 [6x]; 8 [6x]; 12 [6x]; 20 [4x]; 21 [7x]). Translations will vary here also, ranging from "son of man," (NIV, RSV, NET, VOICE), "O mortal" (NRSV), "human one" (CEB), and "human" (NCV). Many of these addresses occur when YHWH is giving directions to his prophet (e.g., 2:1—"stand up on your feet"; 3:1—"eat this scroll; then go and speak to the people of Israel"; 20:3—"speak to the elders of Israel"; 24:16—"do not lament or weep or shed any tears"). There do not appear to be any messianic overtones in Ezekiel related to the address. It seems merely a poetic way to refer to one who is born of (wo)man and "stands in stark contrast to the 'glory of the Lord.'"[6]

Jesus' use of the phrase "the Son of Man" as a self-reference is unique. It does not seem to be merely a clever or mysterious way of saying "I." But it does have a riddle-like quality similar to some of the parables. There are three ways Matthew's Jesus uses the title: (1) to refer to his present, earthly ministry (e.g., Mt 8:20; 9:6); (2) to refer to his suffering, dying and rising on behalf of others (e.g., Mt 17:22–23; 20:17–28; 26:2); and (3) to refer to his arrival as judge and savior at the end of the age (e.g., Mt 10:23; 16:27–28; 25:31).[7]

Perhaps the most important Old Testament reference to the phrase for Jesus and his early followers hearkens back to a spectacular vision recorded in Daniel 7:13–14:

> In my vision at night I looked, and there before me was one like a son of man, coming with the clouds of heaven. He approached the Ancient of Days and was led into his presence. He was given authority, glory and sovereign power; all nations and peoples of every language worshiped him. His dominion is an everlasting dominion that will not pass away, and his kingdom is one that will never be destroyed.

There are complexities and ambiguities to the designation that we cannot explore here.[8] What does seem important for the current passage are two things. The "one like a son of man" is described as "coming with the clouds of heaven." This depiction implies a theophany, that is, an appearance of a divine being who as "the son of man" has human aspect (cf. Eze 1:26–28). Second, the Ancient of Days (God) grants him authority, glory, and an everlasting kingdom. The language deployed here is reminiscent of God's covenant with King David (2 Sa 7:12–16). So it is no surprise that Daniel 7 figures into late Jewish (*1 Enoch*) and early Christian messianic aspirations (*b. Sanh* 98a). Jesus adopts the designation to refer to himself likely because of its cryptic and enigmatic nature. Because it had a somewhat uncertain meaning in his own day, the teacher could more easily fill it with his own content for his own purposes.[9]

8:21-22 *Another disciple said to him, "Lord, first let me go and bury my father." But Jesus told him, "Follow me, and let the dead bury their own dead."* Matthew does not tell us how the scribe responded to Jesus' saying regarding the Son of Man (8:20). He immediately shifts to "another disciple" who wants to follow Jesus but says he must first go bury his father. At that time, as in our own day, Jewish burials and the initial period of mourning last seven days (cf. Judith 16:24), and burying the dead is taken as a sign of righteousness (Tobit 1:16–20; 4:3). If the dead remain unburied, their bodies will be eaten by the birds and wild animals, a sign of God's displeasure (Dt 28:26; 1 Ki 14:11). But the scene does bring to mind an episode from the lives of Elijah and Elisha (1 Ki 19:19–21). When Elijah selects Elisha to be his young apprentice, Elisha is plowing a field with twelve oxen. He asks permission to "kiss" his father and mother before he "follows" him. Elijah allows it, and Elisha goes back, slaughters the oxen, cooks them, and gives the meat to the "people." In other words, Elisha effects a quick, decisive break with his old life as he takes on a new one, following and serving Elijah.

Likewise, Jesus' statement to the would-be disciple calls for a decisive break with his past. On the surface, Jesus' statement is strange and disturbing: let the dead bury the dead. But understood against burial customs of the time, it is less so.[10] During this era of Jewish history burials took place in two phases. First, within a short time of a person's death, the body would be laid in a tomb. Second, after the flesh had decomposed—perhaps a year or more later—the bones would be collected, placed in an ossuary (a bone box), and then reburied. This would seem to make sense of letting "the dead bury their own dead," which probably implies his father is *already dead and buried* (i.e., among the dead) and the son is waiting for the second burial when the bones will be collected up and the tomb reused. If so, then Jesus' reply still asks for a decisive break but the command seems not as strange.

8:24–27 *Suddenly a furious storm came up on the lake, so that the waves swept over the boat. But Jesus was sleeping. The disciples went and woke him, saying, "Lord, save us! We're going to drown!"* The episode, often referred to as "the stilling of the storm," is set against the backdrop of the book of Jonah. In it, the God who appointed a prophet to cry out against Nineveh also appointed a storm when the prophet disobeyed and embarked on a ship to Tarshish away from the Lord (Jnh 1:1–6). As the storm rages on the sea, Jonah is fast asleep in the cargo compartment of the ship. Likewise, as Jesus and his disciples embark on a ship to the other side of the Sea of Galilee, a storm arises quickly and threatens to swamp the vessel, and where is Jesus? He is relaxed and sleeping in the hull of the ship, an exemplar of faith in a raging storm (Ps 3:5). The disciples frantically wake him: "Lord, save us! We are about to die!" (Mt 8:25, author's translation). At that, Jesus rebukes those of little faith for being crushed with fear. But he does get up, rebuke the winds, and the sea becomes calm. Someone greater than Jonah is here!

There is a feature of Matthew's account that is different from Mark's (Mk 4:35–41). Whereas the disciples in Mark refer to Jesus as "Teacher," the disciples in Matthew address him as "Lord." This is intentional on Matthew's part because he wants to bring his account in line with Psalm 107:25–32. In that psalm, seafaring merchants go down to their ships and set sail for distant markets. And then the Lord raises up a storm and the waves lap the edges of the heavens itself. As the men's courage begins to melt away, they stagger and reel, but they cry to the Lord in their trouble, and God hears. He hushes the waves and stills the storm. Matthew aligns his account with Psalm 107 to make a staggering claim about Jesus.

The disciples' address to Jesus as "Lord" rather than "Teacher" is a way of teasing out the implications that Jesus is Immanuel, "God with us" (Mt 1:23). As Ulrich Luz said, for Matthew Jesus is "an occurrence of *God*."[11] He is more than a prophet, healer, teacher of the law, new Moses, son of Jesse. He fulfills Scripture, but he does so as "Lord," a reference to the divine name, YHWH. Jesus is YHWH-with-us. He is the embodiment of the God of Israel. When the disciples ask at the end of the episode, "What kind of man is he that the wind and sea obey him?" (Mt 8:27, author's translation), there is only one right answer.[12]

The Lord of hosts is depicted in other psalms as ruling the raging sea and stilling the roaring waves (Ps 89:9). Psalm 65 celebrates the awesome deeds of God among which are silencing the roaring seas, soothing the angry waves, and settling the tumult of the people (Ps 65:7). The seas here refer to the forces of chaos. Matthew has the disciples call upon the Lord Jesus to save them. The close association of Jesus with the divine name has significant implications for how he and his community regarded Jesus. It unfolds yet another aspect of what it means to call him "Immanuel."

8:28 *When he arrived at the other side in the region of the Gadarenes, two demon-possessed men coming from the tombs met him. They were so violent that no one could pass that way.* Earlier in this chapter Matthew refers to Jesus performing a variety of miracles, including exorcisms. The episode in Gadara offers the first, in-depth look into this kind of miracle. Jesus and his disciples make their way by boat across the Sea of Galilee to a territory populated by non-Jews. He is met by two demoniacs (cf. Mk 5:2) who are said to come out of the tombs. We may detect a subtle echo of Isaiah 65:4. As we saw in our discussion of Jesus' baptism (Mt 3:13–17), Isaiah 64 offers a communal prayer to God to rend the heavens, come down, and do awesome deeds as he has done in the past. Isaiah 65 is God's answer to that prayer and offers the reason why God had not yet responded (in Isaiah's day). God says that he is ready to be found by those who do not seek and to be present to those who do not call on his name, yet they have been a rebellious people. Among their faults is that they sit inside tombs and eat pig.

While citizens of Gadara did not catch the reference, Matthew's Jewish audience, knowledgeable of Isaiah, may well have remembered the connection. Tombs and swine are symbols of impurity in Jewish law, and in Gadara they are on full display.

8:29 *What do you want with us, Son of God?" they shouted.* The demoniacs address Jesus as "Son of God," an address not spoken by any in the gospel since the tempter referred to him as such (Mt 4:3, 6). But that title, of course, originated not with him but with the voice from heaven at his baptism (Mt 3:17). Exactly what is meant by that becomes clear throughout the gospel as the story progresses. Matthew employs it at key moments in his story. In the Old Testament, the title "son of God" is used in three ways: (1) to refer to angels (Job 1:6 ESV, NASB, RSV; Psa 29:1 ASV, NASB, NLV, etc.); (2) to refer to Israel (Ex 4:22; Hos 11:1); and (3) to refer to the Davidic king (2 Sa 7:14–16; Ps 2:7; cf. 4QFlor 1 I, 10–11). As we have seen already, Matthew has interest in describing Jesus both as true Israel (2) and as Messiah, that is, a Davidic king (3). But there is no reference in Matthew to Jesus in angelic terms. Still, there is more to the title than that. Jesus never refers to himself as the Son of God; he refers to himself consistently as the Son of Man. But "the Son of God" is spoken by a variety of witnesses in a variety of contexts. In this case, the demons have it right; Jesus is the Son of God, as the voice from heaven declared and as the tempter taunted. As Matthew weaves his story, the title "Son of God" takes on more transcendent interest as it coheres with other titles (like "Lord" and "Son of Man").

Have you come here to torture us before the appointed time? The demoniacs pose the question whether the Son of God has arrived early, "before the time" to torment them. The "time" likely refers to the final judgment. Matthew may have in mind Psalm 82, a psalm of God's condemnation of subordinate beings who walk in darkness and wickedness and fail to pursue justice. Ironically, they are referred to as "sons of the Most High" in the psalm, but they will die like any other mortal (in the judgment).[13]

8:30–32 *Some distance from them a large herd of pigs was feeding. The demons begged Jesus, "If you drive us out, send us into the herd of pigs."* The presence of a herd of swine in the vicinity demonstrates that Jesus is no longer in Jewish lands. According to God's law, pigs are not ritually clean (Lev 11:7; Dt 14:8; Isa 65:4; 66:3, 17) and are not to eaten (or kept) by the covenant people. The demons ask Jesus to cast them into the herd of swine. For reasons only he knows, he agrees and casts them there. The pigs rush to the sea, and the entire herd perishes. As the story shows, the one known to the evil spirits as the Son of God has authority over nature and over them. That authority may be questioned and tested by some, but it is made sure through Jesus' words and deeds. The mission of the demons is revealed in and through the swine: death and destruction. Left unchecked, the demons would have done to the two men what they did to the pigs.

MATTHEW 9

9:1–3 *Some men brought to him a paralyzed man, lying on a mat. When Jesus saw their faith, he said to the man, "Take heart, son; your sins are forgiven."* Jesus crossed the sea again and landed at Capernaum, his new hometown. Jesus' statement to the paralyzed man is audacious because it is well known that God is the one who forgives sins. In fact, some of the most beautiful and memorable passages on forgiveness in the Bible are found in the Old Testament.

Following Solomon's prayer at the dedication of the temple, God responds (2 Ch 7:13–14, italics added), "When I shut up the heavens so that there is no rain, or command locusts to devour the land, or send a plague among my people, if my people, who are called by my name, will humble themselves and pray and seek my face and turn from their wicked ways, then *I will hear from heaven, and I will forgive their sin and will heal their land.*" Forgiveness is not automatic; it depends on God's people humbling themselves, praying and repenting of their sins. But notice: God is one who forgives.

The book of Micah concludes with what might be considered an antiphonal liturgy that celebrates God's faithfulness to his people and loyalty to the sons of Abraham (7:18–19, italics added):

> Who is a God like you,
>> who *pardons sin and forgives the transgression*
>> of the remnant of his inheritance?
> You do not stay angry forever
>> but *delight to show mercy.*
> You will again have compassion on us;
>> *you will tread our sins underfoot*
>> *and hurl all our iniquities into the depths of the sea.*

Wherever the Scripture asks, "Who is like you, God?" the answer is always "no one." No human being, no god does what the one, true God does. One of the most vivid images of God's absolute forgiveness is found in Psalm 103:11–13 (italics added):

> For as high as the heavens are above the earth,
>   so great is his love for those who fear him;
> *as far as the east is from the west,*
>   *so far has he removed our transgressions from us.*
>
> As a father has compassion on his children,
>   so the LORD has compassion on those who fear him.

The upshot of these passages and many others in Scripture (e.g., Ex 34:6–7; Isa 43:25; Da 9:9) is that God alone has the authority to forgive sins. The scribes pick up on Jesus' presumptuous statement and should be applauded because they are trying to protect God's honor from this upstart preacher from Capernaum. But Jesus' identity as Immanuel, God-with-us, may be known to hearers of the gospel but not to the scribes in Capernaum. The episode reveals something new about Jesus and his earthly authority, an authority he will share with his followers.

9:4 *Knowing their thoughts, Jesus said, "Why do you entertain evil thoughts in your hearts?"* Jesus did not have to be omniscient to know what some scribes were thinking and murmuring to one another. The question Jesus asked here has an uncanny resemblance to the oracle of Zechariah that describes a series of things God's people are and are not to do, including devising evil in their hearts against a neighbor (Zec 8:14–17 ESV, NASB, NRSV, etc.). It seems that Jesus' opponents here are doing what God expressly forbids.

9:6 *"But I want you to know that the Son of Man has authority on earth to forgive sins." So he said to the paralyzed man, "Get up, take your mat and go home."* Jesus responds to their challenge by healing the paralyzed man to show that the Son of Man has authority on earth to forgive sins.[1] Again, Jesus deploys the phrase from Daniel 7:13–14 of the heavenly Son of Man to whom God has given authority and a kingdom. Here we see him doing what only God can do, namely, forgive sins. (For "Son of Man," see also comments on Mt 8:20.)

Going Deeper into Sin and Sickness: Matthew 9:2–8

This is the only healing episode where Jesus announces the forgiveness of sins along with performing the healing. The relationship of the man's sin to his paralysis remains veiled. Was his sin a direct or indirect cause of his ailment? Jesus' Bible was full of passages that connect physical ailments with sin and transgression. Leviticus 26:14–17 affirms that if God's people do not obey his commandments, the result could be sickness. During Jehoram's brief reign as king, he sacrificed to other gods and led Judah astray. Elijah wrote him a letter which said that as a consequence of his sins, plagues and severe illness would strike him and his family (2 Ch 21:12–15). One of the most famous episodes of the ultimate penalty for sin is found in the stories of King David. His court prophet, Nathan, confronted him and brought to light his sins against Uriah the Hittite—adultery and murder.[2] When David does repent, the Lord puts away his sin. David does not die, but the son born of his illicit relationship does (2 Sa 12:13, 19). This is a clear example of the sins of the father falling on their children. Scripture is clear that the consequences of sin can be intergenerational (Ex 34:6–7).

This does not mean, however, that all disease and sickness are directly or even indirectly related to "sin." When Jesus encountered a man blind from birth, his disciples asked whether he or his parents had sinned to cause him to be blind. Neither was the case, Jesus said (Jn 9:1–3). Some diseases are congenital or genetic; tragically, they just happen. Some people are paralyzed as a result of an injury or accident they did not cause. Still others develop cancers for no clear reasons. As COVID-19 rampaged the world in 2020, millions died after being exposed to a virus only the most sophisticated microscopes could image. In these and other cases, no behaviors, actions, or sins on the part of the sick or dying had anything to do with the tragedy of their conditions.

Sickness may get our attention and cause us to reflect on our lives and God. We might ask God "why?" and never know. Sometimes such thoughts lead to confession and repentance. That can be a good thing, but we should never assume that sickness in us or others was necessarily caused by sin.

9:7-8 *Then the man got up and went home. When the crowd saw this, they were filled with awe; and they praised God, who had given such authority to man.* The paralytic's encounter with Jesus left him forgiven and able to walk and go home. The scribes charged Jesus with blasphemy for usurping the authority of God and claiming to forgive sins (Mt 9:3). It will not be the last time he is charged with blasphemy (Mt 26:65). But his pronouncement is clear: the Son of Man has the authority to forgive sins. The crowds that witnessed this scene were gripped with fear, but they did the proper thing. They gave God glory because heaven had allotted such authority to humanity in and through Jesus.

9:12-13 *On hearing this, Jesus said, "It is not the healthy who need a doctor, but the sick. But go and learn what this means: 'I desire mercy, not sacrifice.' For I have not come to call the righteous, but sinners."* Jesus is stating a principle a majority of people in his day could probably agree on: the sick, not the healthy, need a doctor. Jesus, of course, is not dismissing preventative medicine. But with his final pronouncement, he gets directly to the point: "I have not come to call the righteous, but sinners" (Mt 9:13).

Jesus is swimming upstream from the conventional wisdom of the day that is ensconced in passages like Tobit 4:17: "Place your bread on the grave of the righteous, but give none to sinners." Another morsel of Jewish wisdom is found in praise offered to God who separates the righteous from the sinners and repays sinners for their actions (*Psalms of Solomon* 2:33-37). The divide between the righteous and sinners is wide and is maintained by God himself. So, who is this man from Nazareth who tries to bridge it?

Such teaching reflects the wisdom traditions that encourage the righteous not to walk in the path of evildoers (Pr 4:14; Ps 1). The righteous, we are told, choose their friends carefully while the wicked are easily led astray (Pr 12:26). Even as the wicked crave evil, their neighbors receive no mercy (Pr 21:10). One of the clearest bits of wisdom is this: "Do not envy the wicked, do not desire their company" (Pr 24:1). Old Testament texts like these stand in the background of those who criticize Jesus for desiring the company of sinners.

Matthew's gospel tracks well with Mark's account (Mk 2:13-17). What is different is that Matthew inserts an important lesson from Hosea (6:6): "I desire mercy, not sacrifice."[3] Jesus' mission is a mission of mercy: to extend mercy to those who know they need it. The Pharisees bristle with Jesus' extension of mercy to "sinners"; it is a stumbling block. They may have worn a groove in the stones leading up to the temple to sacrifice, but they would not give the time of day to "sinners." But Jesus' invitation to the kingdom is open to sinners who turn and become disciples. No one is to be left out.

Now, Hosea's statement does not nullify the sacrificial system, but it does prioritize mercy ahead of it. Another way to say this is that sacrifices must be carried out by those who practice mercy (Mt 5:7). Without that, sacrifices simply become something abhorrent to God (see Am 5:21–24). And the context of Hosea's statement is telling as well. As the people say they will repent and come back to the Lord (Hos 6:1–3), God seems to agonize, to vacillate over what to do with Ephraim and Judah; even if they do return, their love will vanish like the dew as they beat a path to the temple without pondering any sort of lived theology or knowledge of God (Hos 6:7, LXX; "For I desire mercy, not sacrifice, and acknowledgment of God rather than burnt offerings."

Another prophet, Samuel, made a similar statement (1 Sa 15), when he confronted King Saul for failing to carry out God's directives against the Amalekites. Instead of putting all the animals of the conquered to the sword, Saul keeps flocks, supposedly to sacrifice them to YHWH at Gilgal. Now this miscalculation was not Saul's first big infraction, but it marks the beginning of the end of his kingdom. Ironically, Saul appears proud of his decision to disobey God and set up these sacrifices, but Samuel, the man of God, utters a memorable word: "To obey is better than sacrifice" (1 Sa 15:22). Wisdom, too, expresses herself in this: "The beginning of the good way is to do the things that are just, it is more acceptable to God than to offer sacrifices" (Pr 21:3, LXX, author's translation). Again, these are not criticisms of the sacrifices or the system; after all, God established them. Rather, it is ranking obedience and justice—and mercy (*eleos*), according to Hosea—before them in maintaining covenant faithfulness.

9:14 *Then John's disciples came and asked him, "How is it that we and the Pharisees fast often, but your disciples do not fast?"* The disciples of John (and John himself?) appear to be puzzled by the behavior of Jesus and his disciples. It was a regularly scheduled fast day (according to them and the Pharisees), but Jesus' band of followers were eating and drinking as usual. According to one textual variant, this was not a one-time fast but something that happened over and over.[4]

We have already seen that Jesus expected his disciples to practice fasting, not for public consumption but for God's eyes only (Mt 6:16–18). We do not know what fast Jesus and his followers were neglecting here. It was probably not the Day of Atonement, which is described as an everlasting statute and a day of self-denial (Lev 16; Nu 29:7–11). Zechariah 8:18–19 describes a series of fasts throughout the Jewish year that appear to commemorate the destruction of Jerusalem and its aftermath by the Babylonians. There were many dark days scattered through those years, and unfortunately history has a tendency to repeat itself.[5] But one day, Zechariah prophesied, these times of mourning and sorrow would be turned to joy and cheer. The rabbis debated Zechariah 8:18–19 and its implications (*b. Rosh Ha Shanah* 18b). Some said that when the Jews are at peace, they are to feast, and when they are not at peace, they are to fast. Fasting was often an act of mourning and pleading with God for mercy (2 Sa 12:15–23; 1 Ki 21:20–29).

9:15–17 *Jesus answered, "How can the guests of the bridegroom mourn while he is with them? The time will come when the bridegroom will be taken from them; then they will fast. No one sews a patch of unshrunk cloth on an old garment, for the patch will pull away from the garment, making the tear worse. Neither do people pour new wine into old wineskins."* Jesus' response to the question comes in images drawn from daily life. It would be bad form for wedding guests to mourn during a wedding celebration. No one would argue with that, and Jesus portrays his presence as a bridegroom at the wedding. As long as he is in the world, fasting is inappropriate. But a day is coming when the bridegroom will be taken away—a cryptic reference to his arrest and execution. Then they will fast.

In Jesus' Bible, the figure of the bridegroom is associated primarily with YHWH as a covenant partner with Israel (Isa 62:5; Jer 31:32; Hos 2:16–20). The prophet Isaiah (54:5) assures a people who have suffered in exile that a wedding is in their future: "For your Maker is your husband—the LORD Almighty is his name—the Holy One of Israel is your Redeemer; he is called the God of all the earth." Perhaps no prophet is better known for acknowledging the covenant of marriage between God and Israel than Hosea (2:16, 19–20):

> "In that day," declares the LORD
> > "you will call me 'my husband';
> > you will no longer call me 'my master.'. . .
>
> "I will betroth you to me forever;
> > I will betroth you in righteousness and justice,
> > in love and compassion.
> I will betroth you in faithfulness,
> > and you will acknowledge the LORD."

Both prophets envision a day on the horizon when Israel will be wed to YHWH (the Lord). The relationship will be based on intimacy, love, and affection. It will not be a marriage of convenience or an arrangement; it will be bathed in righteousness, justice, and faithfulness. For Jesus to situate himself in an illustration like this as a bridegroom is a bold move, one that will register with his disciples on a day on the horizon.

Jesus' brief lesson on mending cloth and making wine would not be controversial to seamstresses or winemakers. But these images are intended to imply that something new is in their midst. Jesus is not declaring the end of traditions; he is saying that the newness of the kingdom requires new traditions to contain it.[6]

What the Structure Means: Matthew's Pairs

Matthew often tells his story with an emphasis on the number two. Like any good author, he does not tell us why; he leaves it up to his readers and hearers to sort it out. But the reason appears to be rooted in the Old Testament. Deuteronomy 19:15 insists that a single witness is not sufficient to establish a charge. Two or three witnesses are required. Paul quotes this divine directive prior to his third visit to Corinth: "Every matter must be established by the testimony of two or three witnesses" (2 Co 13:1). Matthew was certainly aware of this teaching. He thus constructs special moments in his gospel by bringing forth two witnesses. We saw in chapter 8 how Jesus liberates the two men possessed by demons (8:28). In chapter 9 Jesus heals two women: one has died, the other has suffered for twelve years from vaginal bleeding (9:18–26). Then somewhere in Galilee he heals two blind men who pled for mercy (9:27–31). He performs a similar miracle on two blind men as he is leaving Jericho (20:29–34). These pairs stand as witnesses to Jesus as healer.

9:18 *While he was saying this, a synagogue leader came and knelt before him and said, "My daughter has just died. But come and put your hand on her, and she will live."* The first pair of miracles demonstrate Jesus' remarkable authority over death and disease. The stories are told together, not consecutively. The resuscitation of the synagogue leader's daughter begins and ends the account. In a way, it frames the story of the healing of the woman with the bleeding problem. In addition, it is the first example in Matthew of Jesus' power over death.

The synagogue leader approaches Jesus in a reverent fashion; he gets on his knees and asks Jesus to come and lay hands on his daughter, so she can live. As the master and his disciples are on their way, a woman approaches Jesus from behind. She too needs to be made whole. For twelve years she has bled uncontrollably, and she had lived with the pain, shame, and stigma of it.

9:20–22 *Just then a woman who had been subject to bleeding for twelve years came up behind him and touched the edge of his cloak.* The law prescribes what must be done for such a woman (Lev 15:25–30). Any woman who has a discharge of blood that is not part of her regular menstruation is unclean and everything she sits on or touches is rendered unclean as well. The prescription for women during their regular menstruation cycles is the same (Lev 15). For us with our modern hygienic practices and conveniences, these commandments sound strange. All who touch such a woman or these unclean things become unclean themselves. The remedy for those who touch her involves washing one's clothes, taking a ritual bath, and recognizing one's uncleanness until the evening. The woman is unclean as long as there is a discharge of blood—in this woman's case, twelve years. Once the blood stops, the woman is to wait seven days. On the eighth day, she is to make a sacrifice.[7]

The woman who approaches Jesus has lived as an outsider, a stranger to her family and friends for a dozen years. She has suffered the ill effects of her condition and has heard that a healer is on the move in Galilee. She hopes that she might touch the fringe of his garment.

She said to herself, "If I only touch his cloak, I will be healed." Every pious Jew wore a garment with fringes on its corners in compliance with the law (Nu 15:37–40). Jesus was no exception. On each corner of the garment was a blue cord. The rationale for this teaching is given: whenever someone sees the fringe, they are reminded of the commandments God gave them (cf. Dt 22:12).

The woman possessed a simple yet profound faith: she thought, even if all I can do is touch the fringe of the garment, I will be made whole. When she touched him, Jesus noticed, turned, and addressed her. He told her to take courage because her faith had made her well. And it was so.

9:23–24 *When Jesus entered the synagogue leader's house and saw the noisy crowd and people playing pipes, he said, "Go away. The girl is not dead but asleep." But they laughed at him.* Jesus and his disciples continued on their mission to raise the daughter of the synagogue leader. When they arrived, he found them in full mourning mode. After the crowd was ushered out of the house, Jesus went in, took the girl by the hand, and she got up.

Going Deeper into Death and Resuscitation: Matthew 9:23–24

Someone who has died looks at first like a person in a deep sleep, but it does not take a doctor to know the difference. Modern people have done everything in their power to separate themselves from death and dying, but the ancients did not have access to hospitals, hospices, and funeral homes. We have outsourced the end of life to specialists to distance ourselves from the discomfort of it all.

Every culture has euphemisms for death because it is such a distressing subject to talk about. Instead of saying this person died, we say he/she "passed away," "passed," "went home," or is "in a better place." In the Hebrew Bible, the old and ailing King David is said to soon "rest with his ancestors" (1 Ki 1:21). In Daniel 12:2 the dead are described as sleeping in the dust of the earth. Paul described Christian death as falling asleep in Jesus (1 Th 4:13–18), in part because the resurrection at the second coming awakens all to life. But what Jesus did for this young girl was not to resurrect her—because she went on to die a natural death later—but to resuscitate her. That is, he brought her back to life, for now. Resuscitations like this are not common in the New Testament, but they do point beyond themselves to a greater reality: through Christ's death, burial, and resurrection all who believe in him will be resurrected to eternal life at the end of the age (see Jn 11). For now, death seems to have an absolute power, but the pain, fear, separation, and sorrow of death are rendered untrue in the coming of Christ. See also "Matthew 16:18 Through Old Testament Eyes: 'The Gates of Hades.'"

9:25–26 *After the crowd had been put outside, he went in and took the girl by the hand, and she got up.* There are a few examples of resuscitations of the dead in the Hebrew Scriptures. Elijah, the prophet, raised the son of the widow living in Zarephath, a city along the coast about ten miles south of Sidon. The man of God had taken refuge with her for a time after declaring a drought on the land of Israel to the wicked king Ahab (1 Ki 17:17–24). Elisha, Elijah's apprentice, prayed to the Lord for the dead son of the Shunammite woman. She had provided the man of God with food and lodging on a number of occasions, and he repaid her kindness by resuscitating her son (2 Ki 4:18–37). On both occasions, the prophets pled with God for the lives of the young, and God raised them and gave them back to their families. The prophets did not raise them on their own authority; they merely interceded for the grieving parents. It was God who raised them.

There is another resuscitation, however, of a different character. The prophet Elisha died and was buried. During a funeral for another Jewish man, Moabite raiders appeared. As the dead man's friends were fleeing, they threw his corpse into Elisha's tomb. When his corpse touched the bones of the prophet, the man came back to life and stood on his feet (2 Ki 13:20–21). Even from the dead, it seems, Elisha had power.

Reports of the girl's awakening to life spread throughout the district. If they knew their Bibles, they would have thought a prophet had arisen in their midst along the order of Elijah and Elisha. The difference, however, is that Jesus is Immanuel, God-with-us, and he raises the dead on his own authority.

9:27–29 *As Jesus went on from there, two blind men followed him, calling out, "Have mercy on us, Son of David!"* We have already seen the import of the title "Son of David" as it refers to Jesus (Mt 1:1; cf. Mt 12:23; 15:22). On the face of it, it is clear that these men are confident that Jesus is the Messiah, and they are convinced he can give them back their sight. It was Isaiah who best painted a hopeful future when he talked about a day when the deaf shall hear the words of a scroll and the blind shall see (Isa 29:18). Jesus himself appealed to Isaiah (35:5) in answering John's question from prison (Mt 11:5): "The blind receive sight, the lame walk, those who have leprosy are cleansed, the deaf hear, the dead are raised, and the good news is proclaimed to the poor." The hope of this better world is grounded deep in the prophets and is taken up in Matthew's portrayal of Jesus, his messianic role, and his divine identity. Jesus enacts a world the prophets could only dream of. This is the first account in Matthew of Jesus healing the blind, but it will not be the last. He touches their eyes and says, "According to your faith let it be done to you" (Mt 9:29). Their eyes are opened.

Going Deeper into Spiritual Blindness: Matthew 9:2–31

The problem of blindness in Matthew is not restricted to those who are literally blind. Some are spiritually blind, and yet they insist on being spiritual leaders. Many of these opposed Jesus and found themselves at the tip of his rhetorical sword. Jesus calls them "blind guides" who "strain out a gnat but swallow a camel" (Mt 23:24). They are blind fools who take oaths but carefully nuance their words to say literally nothing (Mt 23:17–22). Jesus' healing of those who are physically blind offers some hope that those who are spiritually blind might too receive sight.

Jesus' parables apparently both reveal and conceal the secrets of the kingdom of heaven (Mt 13:10–17). Beyond the circles of discipleship, the teacher expects many to see but *not truly see and understand*. Yet even among insiders, some of the parables require explanation. The revelation of secrets is part of God's activity leading up to the end of days (Da 12:8–10; Ro 16:25–26). Jesus regards his own role in line with that of the prophet Isaiah (Isa 6:9–10).

9:32–34 *While they were going out, a man who was demon-possessed and could not talk was brought to Jesus. And when the demon was driven out, the man* *who had been mute spoke. The crowd was amazed and said, "Nothing like this has ever been seen in Israel."* As this time of healing and teaching gives way to the disciples' commission (Mt 10), Matthew has one more miracle to share and one more challenge to leave the disciples. The miracle is an exorcism; this time a man is demonized and not able to speak (9:32–34). And after further healings and teachings, Jesus gives his disciples a bit more insight into the kingdom of God and a special prayer they would be wise to pray (9:35–38).

Jesus has already met and liberated some who were troubled by evil spirits (Mt 8:16–17, 28–34). What is unique now is that the man he meets is not only demonized; he is not able to speak (Mt 9:32–34). The reason may have been his inability to hear *(kophos)*. When the demon exited, the man was able to speak. The crowds marveled. Sitting on the sidelines were some Pharisees who were not at all pleased with Jesus. They did not—perhaps could not—deny that Jesus was casting out demonic spirits and freeing people from their tyranny. But they began to mutter among themselves a charge that will later become public (12:24–27): the only reason Jesus can cast out demons is that he is in league with the devil himself. (Regarding demons, see comments at Mt 10:24–25.)

9:35–36 *Jesus went through all the towns and villages, teaching in their synagogues, proclaiming the good news of the kingdom and healing every disease and sickness. When he saw the crowds, he had compassion on them, because they were harassed and helpless, like sheep without a shepherd.* With just a few words Matthew summarizes a period of itinerant ministry. Anyone familiar with the Law and Prophets would have recognized Matthew's intentional use of the phrase "like sheep without a shepherd." When leadership is transferred from Moses to Joshua, Moses asks YHWH to appoint someone to lead them so that the congregation would not be like sheep with no shepherd (Nu 27:17). That same language occurs with a little variation when King Jehoshaphat inquires of the Lord regarding a battle. The prophet Micaiah reports that he saw Israel scattered on the mountains like sheep without a shepherd (2 Ch 18:16; 1 Ki 22:17 [3 Ki 22:17, LXX]). Scattered Israel is a reference to the coming invasions and forced exiles the people would have to endure. Ezekiel voices an oracle against the bad shepherds of Israel who took care of themselves but not the sheep: "So they [God's people] were scattered because there was no shepherd, and when they were scattered they became food for all the wild animals. My sheep wandered over all the mountains and on every high hill. They were scattered over the whole earth, and no one searched or looked for them" (Eze 34:5–6).

Again, a later prophet, Zechariah, recycles that same image in an oracle encouraging God's people to seek YHWH for rain, showers, and an abundance of produce. Appealing to idols or consulting diviners is foolish and offers only lies and nonsense. Because they have not prayed to YHWH and sought his blessing, they are like sheep, suffering because they have no shepherd (Zec 10:1–2).

Matthew is no doubt familiar with this Old Testament trope and employs it here to link Jesus with the Law—perhaps even a hint of transfer of leadership to Joshua (i.e., Jesus)—and Prophets. Now that the true King of Israel has arrived, everything must change. (See also "Going Deeper into Micah's Bad Shepherds: Matthew 2:5–6.")

9:37–38 *Then he said to his disciples, "The harvest is plentiful but the workers are few. Ask the Lord of the harvest, therefore, to send out workers into his harvest field."* The disciples will have a role to play, as we will see in chapter 10, but they also have a prayer to pray.

The image of harvest has deep prophetic roots. An agricultural people are accustomed to several harvests a year. They know the disappointment of a poor crop and the joy of a bountiful one. They know, too, the labor it takes to harvest the crops. The biblical prophets use "harvest" in a metaphorical sense. Isaiah, for example, employs the image in an oracle of restoration. The day will come, he says, when the Lord will thresh the world from the Euphrates to the Wadi el-Arish (Egypt) and will gather his people back from exile. On that day, a great trumpet will sound and the lost and exiled will return to Jerusalem to worship on the holy mountain (Isa 27:12–13). The prophet Joel may have the most memorable verses on sowing, reaping, and harvesting (Joel 3:13–15):

> "Swing the sickle,
>   for the harvest is ripe.
> Come, trample the grapes,
>   for the winepress is full
>   and the vats overflow—
> so great is their wickedness!"
>
> Multitudes, multitudes
>   in the valley of decision!
> For the day of the LORD is near
>   in the valley of decision.
> The sun and moon will be darkened,
>   and the stars no longer shine.

The harvest is a time of cutting, dividing, and ultimately separation. The harvest comes as both a threat and a promise. Some are cut down by the sickle; others are gathered and redeemed. In all cases, the harvest is an eschatological action of God.[8] That is why Jesus urges the disciples to pray to the Lord of the harvest to send workers. The Lord of the harvest determines the right time. There is a sense of urgency to this moment. The harvest is abundant. The time could be soon.

The "Lord of the harvest" could refer to God the Father or it might refer to Jesus himself, though it would not be clear simply from this text. When you factor in how early Christians saw the relationship of Jesus and God in "last things,"[9] and how, for example, the day of the Lord had become the day of the Lord Jesus Christ as early as Paul (e.g., 1 Co 1:8; Php 1:6), then a good case can be made that Matthew and his community would have understood Jesus to be the Lord of the harvest. Consider the vision the seer saw of one like a Son of Man seated on a white cloud. He is wearing a golden crown, and he carries a sharp sickle in his hand. When the angel comes out of the temple and announces that the time of the harvest has come, with one motion the Son of Man swings his sickle and the earth is reaped (Rev 14:14–16).

In Matthew there are no coincidences. Jesus' teaching, healing, and calling of disciples are done with a view to the harvest that is and that is to come. Some will choose to follow Jesus; others Jesus himself will chose to be his followers. As Matthew's story unfolds, the mission of Jesus and his Twelve will become clear.

MATTHEW 10

The harvest prayer that Jesus teaches his disciples (9:35–38) anticipates the mission that begins in chapter 10. He has been the example par excellence of the itinerant preacher, teacher, and healer; now he sends out his disciples with authority into the plentiful harvest.

10:1–4 *Jesus called his twelve disciples to him and gave them authority to drive out impure spirits and to heal every disease and sickness.* "The Twelve" make their first appearance in Matthew's story at this point. They are named, beginning with Simon, aka Peter, and given the title "apostles" (a transliteration of a Greek word meaning "the one sent"; Aramaic *shaliach*).[1] "The Twelve" recall the twelve tribes of Israel (Ge 35:22–26; Nu 1). If there is a question whether the number twelve is intentional, that question is answered in Matthew 19:28 where Jesus himself makes the correlation between his Twelve and the twelve tribes. We should likely see Jesus' action of naming and creating "the Twelve" as a prophetic action. As a prophet, Jesus not only spoke his message but at times acted it out. The well-attuned audience can both hear and see the message as he dramatically enacts it. Some have concluded that Jesus' message creates a new people of God, thereby replacing the twelve tribes with the twelve apostles. But given the fact that Jesus sends the Twelve out to "the lost sheep of the house of Israel" (Mt 10:6 ESV, NRSV), we should probably view his act as naming his representatives to Israel or sending out twelve missionaries to the lost and scattered sheep.

What the Structure Means:
The Mission of the Twelve (Mt 10)

Matthew 1:21 says that Jesus came to save his people from their sins, and the genealogy that precedes that statement (1:1–17) has the effect of naming his people, that is, the people of Abraham. For centuries they had been scattered among the nations. As Israel's Messiah and God's Son, Jesus' task is to gather them from the four corners of the earth and lead them as the rightful King. The mission of the Twelve on this occasion anticipates their mission to the wider world after the crucifixion and resurrection of Jesus (28:19–20).

Matthew 10, in which Jesus gives instructions to the disciples as they go out to do ministry in pairs, is the second of the five main teaching sections found in the gospel (see "What the Structure Means: Five Sermons [Mt 5–25]" at Mt 7:28 and Table 0.1).

10:5–6 *Do not go among the Gentiles or enter any town of the Samaritans. Go rather to the lost sheep of Israel.* Jesus instructs them (for now) where not to go (among the Gentiles and Samaritans) and where to go, namely, to "the lost sheep of Israel." Whether they are lost of their own accord or because they have had bad leaders (bad shepherds; Eze 34), Jesus does not say. The point is they are now lost and must be saved. So Jesus sends the Twelve out on a rescue mission to cast out wicked spirits, preach the good news, and extend his authority to heal over the diseased and dying. Jesus' memorable phrase owes its substance to the prophecy of Jeremiah (Jer 50:4–7, italics added):

> "In those days, at that time,"
>   declares the LORD,
> "the people of Israel and the people of Judah together
>   will go in tears to seek the LORD their God.
> They will ask the way to Zion
>   and turn their faces toward it.
> They will come and bind themselves to the LORD
>   in an everlasting covenant
>   that will not be forgotten.
>
> *"My people have been lost sheep;*
>   *their shepherds have led them astray*
>   *and caused them to roam on the mountains.*
> *They wandered over mountain and hill*
>   and forgot their own resting place.
> Whoever found them devoured them;
>   their enemies said, 'We are not guilty,
> for they sinned against the LORD, their verdant pasture,
>   the LORD, the hope of their ancestors.'"

Jeremiah 50–51 is a collection of oracles with two major emphases: the destruction of Babylon and the return of the exiles. There is coming a day, the prophet says, when Babylon, the aggressor, is laid waste and her gods put to shame. At that time Israel and Judah together will return to the Lord, make their way to Zion, and join in an everlasting covenant with the Lord. But that day is not yet, according to the prophet. At present, God's people are "lost sheep" scattered and beaten down; they are harassed and helpless like sheep with no shepherd (Mt 9:36). Even their enemies recognize their plight and the cause of it: they have sinned against YHWH, the one in whom their ancestors had hoped.

10:7–13 *As you go, proclaim this message: "The kingdom of heaven has come near."... Do not get any gold or silver or copper to take with you in your belts ... for the worker is worth his keep.* Like a finely polished mirror, the mission of the Twelve is to reflect Jesus' words and deeds in towns and villages across Galilee. They are to preach the good news of the kingdom of heaven, heal the sick, raise the dead, and cast out demons. They are the model of itinerancy, begging from no one but dependent on everyone for their food and lodging.

Like the prophet Elisha, they are to take no money for their services regardless of the offer. As the story goes, Naaman the Aramean came to Elisha and was healed of leprosy. He attempts to give Elisha a gift but Elisha refuses with this oath: "As surely as the LORD lives, whom I serve, I will not accept a thing" (2 Ki 5:16). Instead, Naaman asks the prophet for two mule-loads of dirt (earth) from Israel to take back to Syria, most likely to build an altar to YHWH whom he now recognizes as the one true God. As Naaman leaves, the prophet says, "Go in peace" (2 Ki 5:19). The disciples are to do likewise. They are to take no reward, and they are to let their peace come upon worthy houses.

10:15 *Truly I tell you, it will be more bearable for Sodom and Gomorrah on the day of judgment than for that town.* Those houses and villages that are unworthy must be left behind with no peace. Jesus invokes the memory of Sodom and Gomorrah; on the day of judgment, it will be worse for those who reject Jesus' apostles than for those ill-fated cities (Ge 19:24–28). Sodom and Gomorrah had become watchwords of how God judged and destroyed wicked cities. Babylon and its splendor will become like Sodom and Gomorrah when God overthrows it (Isa 13:19). Similarly, God vows to make Moab like Sodom and the Ammonites like Gomorrah; the land will become a wasteland and its inhabitants will become slaves to the Jews (Zep 2:9). Ezekiel describes the sin of Sodom and Gomorrah—the sin for which God judged them—as lack of justice toward the poor and needy, pride, living in luxury, and doing abominable things before God (Eze 16:46–50).

10:16 *I am sending you out like sheep among wolves. Therefore be as shrewd as snakes and as innocent as doves.* As part of his commission to the Twelve, Jesus warns them of what is to come. He begins with a word he typically uses to urge his hearers to pay close attention ("behold," Greek *idou*): "I am about to say something important." He is sending them out into dangerous and hostile territory. The Twelve will be like sheep among the wolves, so they must be as prudent as serpents and innocent as doves.

Invoking these animal images, Jesus draws deeply from culture, characterizations, and scriptural memory. Sheep are known as fragile and silly creatures. Up until now sheep have been a symbol for the "lost" (Mt 9:36; 10:6); in this passage they signify the vulnerability of the disciples sent with a message of good news and salvation. Wolves are fearsome and powerful animals, enemies of shepherds and sheep everywhere; night especially is a dangerous time for sheep, particularly when they are isolated. Often wolves signify Israel's enemies, ripping, tearing, and leaving nothing of their prey (Eze 22:27; Hab 1:8; Zep 3:3).

The serpent, of course, is clichéd as the craftiest creature the Lord God made (Ge 3:1). Jesus urges his disciples to be as shrewd as serpents. He employs the same adjective found in the Septuagint to describe the creature in Genesis (*phronimos*), crafty or prudent.[2] The Twelve will have to exercise good judgment and caution as they go on mission. We have already seen some of the characterizations associated with the dove regarding Jesus' baptism (see Mt 3:13–17). In this passage, Jesus emphasizes the "innocence" of doves. The Greek word (*akeraios*) has a variety of senses and virtues associated with it. Literally, it means "unmixed," and so comes to imply "pure" and "innocent."[3] As Jesus explains the trials to follow, the Twelve are to be above any charge of evil or mischief.[4]

10:17–19 *Be on your guard; you will be handed over to the local councils and be flogged in the synagogues.* The warnings Jesus sounds have an eschatological ring to them. They will characterize their upcoming mission and missions to come (cf. Mt 24–25). Authorities in cities and synagogues will detain and flog the apostles. The Twelve will stand before governors and kings on Jesus' account "as a testimony to them and the gentiles" (Mt 10:18 NRSV). This intimates that the mission soon will extend beyond the lost sheep of the house of Israel. The testimony statement echoes the time when, after writing down the book of the law, Moses sets it before the people as a testimony against them (Dt 31:26). In Matthew's case, it is no written law that stands as a testimony; it is the lives of men who have forsaken all to follow Jesus.

When they are examined before officials—whether synagogue or council—the Twelve have no need to prepare their remarks because God will give them what to say when the time comes (Mt 10:19–20). Moses had a similar gift. Though Moses was slow of speech when God commissioned him, the Lord told Moses not to worry because he would give him what to say (Ex 4:12). Similarly, the Twelve can rest assured that the Spirit of the Father will speak through them. God will do for the Twelve what he had done for Moses centuries earlier.

10:20 *For it will not be you speaking, but the Spirit of your Father speaking through you.* Those with Old Testament eyes might remember the occasion when Moses gathered seventy elders and placed them around the tent of meeting. The Lord descended in a cloud. After speaking to Moses, the Lord took some of the spirit that was on Moses and put it on the seventy elders and they prophesied. But the text is quick to say they did not prophesy again (Nu 11:24–25). The difference is that the elders prophesied only in the camp.

The Twelve will be required to move throughout the towns and villages of Galilee (and later to the ends of the earth Mt 28:19–20), endowed with the authority of Jesus and trusting in the Spirit of the Father to give them the words they need. And their endowment is not for a one-off mission. Their mission and commission will continue to the end of the age.

10:21 *Brother will betray brother to death, and a father his child; children will rebel against their parents and have them put to death.* When Jesus remarks that brothers will betray one another and that parents and children will rise against each other, he likely has in mind the prophecy of Micah. The prophet describes a dark and desperate time. The faithful will have disappeared. The righteous cannot be found. Justice is perverted and families are in disarray (Mic 7:6):

> For a son dishonors his father,
>> a daughter rises up against her mother,
> a daughter-in-law against her mother-in-law—
>> a man's enemies are the members of his own household.

We find the same caution expressed by Jesus in his final "sermon," known as the eschatological discourse (Mt 24:9–14). A similar sentiment is expressed in the rabbis. In days to come, the world spirals out of control, the righteous and wise are nowhere to be found, families disintegrate, and young people put their elders to shame (*m. Sot* 9.15). Jesus is teaching his followers to expect rejection and abuse in this upside-down world that desperately needs redemption.

10:22 *You will be hated by everyone because of me, but the one who stands firm to the end will be saved.* Though the language here is different, we are reminded of the final chapter of Daniel. A time of anguish is coming, the vision goes, such as the world has never seen (Da 12:1). At the same time, Daniel's people are delivered, those whose names are written in the book. The dead shall awake, some to eternal life, others to shame and eternal contempt. Until then, his heavenly guides instruct him to keep his words secret as evil waxes strong. When one guide asks another, "How long until the end of the wonders?" the other guide responds cryptically, "time, times, and half a time" (Da 12:6–7). Daniel is told, happy are those who persevere and make it one thousand three hundred and thirty-five days, roughly the same period as "time, times and half a time" (that is, a year, two years and one half a year—or three and a half years). Daniel is assured that once he falls asleep in death, he will rise for his reward at the end of the days (Da 12:12–13). Daniel 12 contains the clearest reference to the resurrection of the dead in the Old Testament (cf. Eze 37; Hos 6:2; Isa 26:19). Jesus' warning to his disciples comes with the promise that perseverance and endurance will be rewarded, a reward similar to Daniel's. Though they may sleep in the dust, they too will be awakened to eternal life.

10:23 *You will not finish going through the towns of Israel before the Son of Man comes.* (For "Son of Man," see comments on Mt 8:20.) Perseverance sometimes means suffering; at other times it means fleeing persecution. A dead apostle cannot proclaim the good news, so they are to do their best to stay alive and stay healthy. But the mission will not be complete before the Son of Man comes in judgment and power (Mt 24:30–31). This title likely owes its substance to Daniel's vision of one like a son of man who comes on the clouds and is granted an everlasting kingdom by the Ancient of Days (Da 7:13–14). Some Son of Man sayings have to do with Jesus' present work (e.g., Mt 8:20; 9:6; 13:37); others, his glorification and future coming (e.g., various in Matthew 24–25). This is the first statement in Matthew of the Son of Man "coming." His coming is "the end" of the mission but the beginning of salvation for those who endure.

10:24–25 *If the head of the house has been called Beelzebul, how much more the members of his household!* Meanwhile the disciples should expect to be maligned by their enemies. If the master (*kurios*) of the household has been called Beelzebul, those who belong to him, namely, the household of disciples, will be treated as demons as well. Already we have seen how Jesus is accused of being in league with the devil because he has the ability to cast out demons (Mt 9:32–34). This is a charge that will be made again and again (Mt 12:22–32). If Jesus has been treated this way, how much more likely is it that those who follow and seek to imitate him as teacher and master will be decried as demonic as well.

"Beelzebul" transliterates the name of a Canaanite god. We find reference to it in the Old Testament when the king of Samaria, Ahaziah, appeals to the "god" of Ekron, *Baal-zebub* (literally, "lord of the flies"; 2 Ki 1:1–16). This is probably a deliberate corruption of the real name *Baal-zebul*, which means "lord of the exalted abode." The apostle Paul refers to the so-called gods and lords worshiped by the nations as demons (1 Co 8:4–5; 10:19–21). Beelzebul refers to the prince of the demons, that is, Satan.[5]

10:26-27 *So do not be afraid of them, for there is nothing concealed that will not be disclosed, or hidden that will not be made known.* Before Jesus releases the Twelve for their mission, he has a few final words of instruction. Although opposition will be fierce, he urges them not to fear those who will malign and persecute them. Three times Jesus says, "Do not be afraid" (10:26, 28, 31). His commission sounds a lot like the words YHWH speaks to the prophet Jeremiah when he is called to be "a prophet to the nations." Initially, the young man objects because he is only a boy. But God has an answer for that (Jer 1:6–8): "'Alas, Sovereign Lord,' I said, 'I do not know how to speak; I am too young.' But the Lord said to me, 'Do not say, "I am too young." You must go to everyone I send you to and say whatever I command you. Do not be afraid of them, for I am with you and will rescue you,' declares the Lord." Jeremiah's excuse will not stand because (a) God will direct his mission and command him what to say, and (b) God will be with him to deliver him. So Jeremiah is not to fear.

Similarly, the disciples of Jesus are to go where they are sent with the words Jesus has told them: "What I tell you in the dark, speak in the daylight; what is whispered in your ear, proclaim from the roofs" (Mt 10:27). They are to be confident the Spirit of the Father is speaking through them (10:19–20). Moreover, readers and hearers of this gospel know that Jesus is Immanuel, "God with us" (Mt 1:21–23). For those who know the end of the story, they know that Jesus promises to be with his followers in their disciple-making mission to the end of the age (Mt 28:19–20). As we have suggested, the entire gospel should be read against this claim that Jesus himself is God-with-us, taking courage from his presence in/with them.

10:28 *Be afraid of the One who can destroy both body and soul in hell.* Regarding hell, see comments at Matthew 5:21–22.

10:29-31 *Are not two sparrows sold for a penny? Yet not one of them will fall to the ground outside your Father's care. And even the very hairs on your head are all numbered. So don't be afraid; you are worth more than many sparrows.* These encouraging words of God's care evoke two stories in the Hebrew Scriptures. In the first, Jonathan, son of King Saul, is threatened with death because he has violated the king's foolish vow. The people challenge the king, saying Jonathan will not die and not a hair of his head will fall to the earth (1 Sa 14:45). And it is so. In the second, another king, David, pronounces an oath of protection based on a fictional story told him by a woman of Tekoa. He says: "As YHWH lives, not one hair of your son shall fall to the earth" (2 Sa 14:11, author's translation). The saying "not one hair . . . will fall to the earth" may have been a common phrase at the time to underscore a person's well-being despite uncertainty. In Jesus' teaching, the juxtaposition of the sparrow falling to the ground and the hairs on the head being numbered sounds a similar chord. Those who heard Jesus' encouragement to his apostles that day may well have thought of these stories of protection and safety for the faithful.

10:32-33 *Whoever acknowledges me before others, I will also acknowledge before my Father in heaven. But whoever disowns me before others, I will disown before my Father in heaven.* This kind of reciprocal promise does not appear first in the words of Jesus. As you might expect, this relational reciprocity has precedent in the Old Testament. When a man of God approached Eli, the senior priest at Shiloh, with a word of judgment about him and his scoundrel sons, he reported the Lord to declare, "Those who honor me I will honor, but those who despise me will be disdained" (1 Sa 2:30). Although God had established a permanent priesthood with Moses and Aaron, it became clear that their heirs, Eli and his family, had abused the privileges. The priesthood remains, but it cannot be disconnected from the actions of its agents. Eli's sons had helped themselves to the choicest parts of the sacrifices, sexually abused women worshipers, and thus dishonored God. God, therefore, had no choice but to judge them and raise up a faithful priest (Samuel) who would do God's will.

10:34-36 *Do not suppose that I have come to bring peace to the earth. I did not come to bring peace, but a sword.* The inevitable result of fidelity to Jesus and the arrival of God's kingdom will be family division (Mt 10:34–39). Not peace, but a sword. Peace might be the ultimate destination for peacemakers, but in the interim trouble abounds. Every revolution in history has divided before it united. And what Jesus is proposing is not just minor reform; his arrival ("I have come") and teachings are fomenting revolution, kingdom revolution. The kingdom is especially tough on families. As noted above in 10:21, Micah had prophesied centuries earlier about a similar time of woe for Israel (Mic 7:6).

Seasons of woe and human suffering have come and gone throughout Israel's history with various bad actors seeking their own way. Micah envisaged such a day. As the kingdom dawns bright in the world, opposition unfurls even inside of families. The Messiah found Micah's lament a good way—a familiar way—to help his disciples piece together their immediate future when family discord, not peace, arises.

10:37 *Anyone who loves their father or mother more than me is not worthy of me; anyone who loves their son or daughter more than me is not worthy of me.* Jesus' person and message will divide but will not permit divided loyalty.

Going Deeper into Discipleship: Matthew 10:34–39

Allegiance to Jesus must take precedence over any other. Three times Jesus describes followers who were not worthy of him: those who love father and mother more than him, those who love a son or daughter more than him, and those who do not take up their cross and follow him (Mt 10:37–39). Here we find the first hint in Matthew's gospel that Jesus' and his disciples' destinies are moving toward the cross. The re-statusing of family as a result of kingdom commitments may have its antecedent in a blessing uttered by Moses to Levi (Dt 33:9). The family of Levi is to receive the sanctions and apparatus to be priests over the people, that is, to teach Torah to Israel and to officiate at the altar. The Levites loyalty to the covenant would come at the expense of their families: parents disregarded, relatives ignored, and children not recognized. Moses's "blessing" may not appear to be a blessing at all to those attuned to "family values" in the twenty-first century, but Jesus' remarks about who is worthy and who is not regarding the kingdom burrows heavily beneath the surface of culture and its norms.

10:40–42 *Anyone who welcomes you welcomes me.* Jesus ends his instruction to the Twelve on a positive note. Up until now, he has tutored them to anticipate and respond to opposition and rejection. But not everyone will react this way. Some are going to welcome the disciples. And when they do, they will be welcoming Jesus and the one who sent him (God the Father). The identity of the Twelve is closely connected to Jesus and his heavenly Father; they are, as Jesus' high priestly prayer declares (Jn 17), one. Such statements could have contributed to the Pauline notion that developed later that those "in Christ" form his body (e.g., 1 Co 12:12–26).

Matthew 10 Through Old Testament Eyes

In the past, people have received prophets and other righteous folk and received a reward. Those who know the Old Testament will recall the occasion when the widow of Zarephath welcomed the prophet Elijah (1 Ki 17:9–24). She offered him food and drink as he was on his journey. All she had was a little meal in a jar; the drought was so severe she reckoned that she and her son would soon die. But as long as she showed hospitality to the prophet, the meal never ran out. The greatest reward, however, came when her son died and the prophet raised him to life. We might recall, too, the woman from Shunem who welcomed and showed extraordinary hospitality to Elisha (2 Ki 4:9–37). She prepared many meals for the traveling man of God, and eventually she and her husband built a chamber for him to lodge with them. The woman wanted a child but was barren. In due time she had a child as the prophet predicted. But the child became sick and died. Elisha came to her house, prayed to the Lord, and after some time, the child came back to life. In both cases, the women receive rewards for welcoming the prophets, but the ultimate reward was the resuscitation of their sons from the dead. One of the features of the movement founded by Jesus is the mutual support followers share with those in need (e.g., Ac 2:43–47).[6] Jesus' disciples can expect to be welcomed by some as his representatives. Ultimately, the reward they receive will be the resurrection from the dead and life in the world to come (Mt 10:22).

MATTHEW 11

Jesus finishes his mission instruction and then moves on to preach in the cities of Galilee. When we last heard about John the Baptist, the fiery prophet had been arrested (Mt 4:12). Matthew does not give us further detail, but now we know he remains in custody. Josephus records that John was imprisoned in Machaerus, east of the Dead Sea (Josephus, *Ant* 18.116–119).

11:2–3 *Are you the one who is to come, or should we expect someone else?* Reports of Jesus' ministry had reached John in prison; apparently, he still had some access to the outside world and his disciples. What he had heard about Jesus or its context is unclear. So he sent disciples to Jesus with an important question. John draws from several Old Testament hopes and aspirations about the "one who is coming" to redeem God's people. We might begin with Psalm 118:26: "Blessed is the one who comes in the name of the LORD" (NRSV). Psalm 118 is one of the most quoted and alluded to Scriptures in the New Testament (twenty-three times). It provides the refrain chanted by the crowds during Jesus' triumphal entry into Jerusalem (Mt 21:9, author's translation): "Hosanna to the son of David, blessed is the one coming in the name of the Lord." The reference to the son of David fits well into Matthew's theme and demonstrates the psalm is messianically understood. The Messiah, the true King of Israel, is the one who is to come. But Jesus often describes the Son of Man as "coming," suggesting the two figures are the same.

We have already seen (see comments at Mt 8:20) how often Jesus refers to himself cryptically as the Son of Man, an expectation drawn from Daniel 7:13–14: one like a Son of Man "coming with the clouds" is presented to the Ancient of Days and is given an everlasting kingdom. Many of the "I have come" and "the Son of Man comes" sayings could fit into the expectation of "the one who comes."[1] Finally, given Matthew's interest in Jesus as Immanuel,

God with us, the "coming" of God back to Zion and his temple should probably figure into the question "Are you the one who is coming?" Consider, for example, Malachi 3:1–2:

> "I will send my messenger, who will prepare the way before me. Then suddenly the Lord you are seeking will come to his temple; the messenger of the covenant, whom you desire, will come," says the Lord Almighty.

> But who can endure the day of his coming? Who can stand when he appears? For he will be like a refiner's fire or a launderer's soap.

Malachi does not tell us initially the identity of the messenger in this passage, but later he indicates it is Elijah (Mal 4:5). In the New Testament, John the Baptist is linked to Elijah and is given the task of announcing the procession and preparing the way of the Lord, whom Matthew identifies as Jesus (cf. Isa 40:3; Mt 3:1–3; 11:10; Mk 1:2). The prophecy of God's return to his people to dwell with them is fulfilled in the coming of Jesus, the Son of Man, Israel's true King. We should probably see various hopes of a "coming one" from Scripture converging in the Baptist's poignant question.

11:4–6 *Go back and report to John what you hear and see: The blind receive sight, the lame walk, those who have leprosy are cleansed, the deaf hear, the dead are raised, and the good news is proclaimed to the poor. Blessed is anyone who does not stumble on account of me.* Jesus responded to John's question by commissioning ("go back and report") the Baptist's disciples to bear witness to what they hear and see. As we might expect, Jesus' answer is itself immersed in Scripture: the blind see, the lame walk, lepers are cleansed, the deaf hear, the dead are raised, and the good news is preached to the poor (Isa 35:5–6; 61:1). The catalogue of wonders listed shows Jesus' authority over disease and death and the inclusion of the poor in this kingdom message. For those with Old Testament ears, this list rings familiar; each of these is derived directly from Scripture.

Matthew 11:4–6 Through Old Testament Eyes: Jesus' Miracles

Jesus instructs John's disciples to bear witness to what they hear and see. Then he lists a series of miracles he has performed. Each of these has resonance deep in the Old Testament. A day is coming, Isaiah prophesied, when the deaf hear, the blind see, and the meek and the neediest experience joy (Isa 29:18–19). In another oracle about the return of the exiles, the prophet says that one day the barren land will bloom and everyone will see the revelation of YHWH's glory as he comes to judge his enemies and save his people. On that day the eyes of the blind will see, the ears of the deaf will be opened, the lame will leap for joy, and those who cannot speak will speak; the ransomed of the Lord will return to Zion in joy (Isa 35:4–6, 9–10; cf. Isa 42:18). Lastly, Isaiah 26 contains an apocalyptic psalm that foresees a time when the Just One (God) will make the path for the righteous smooth (v. 7). YHWH will bring about peace (v. 12), the dead will live, corpses will rise, and those who dwell in the dust will awake (v. 19). But from the seer's perspective this was a big "not yet." Now is a time for yearning and longing; the devout must wait longer for salvation.

That such yearnings were in the air is evidenced by a document found at Qumran (4Q521). Though fragmentary, there is a significant, legible portion in fragment 2 ii. It begins:

> heaven and earth will obey his messiah. . . . For the Lord will seek out the pious and call the righteous by name, and *his spirit will hover over the poor* and he will renew the faithful by his might. For he will glorify the pious on the throne of an eternal kingdom, *releasing captives, giving sight to the blind* and *raising up those who are bo[wed down]. . .* for *he will heal the wounded, give life to the dead* and *preach good news to the poor . . .*[2]

Because the text is fragmentary, scholars debate who the "he" is who performs such wonders. Is it God? Is it the Messiah? Is it Melchizedek or some other heavenly agent? We cannot solve the debate, but we can note the correlation of these hopes with those Jesus lists as he is responding to the Baptist's question. Both seek the fulfillment of prophecies in a glorious future for God's redeemed. Such hopes belong to a wider Jewish and now Christian audience.

11:9-10 *This is the one about whom it is written, "I will send my messenger ahead of you, who will prepare your way before you."* When John's disciples depart with Jesus' Scripture-infused reply, the Nazarene takes the opportunity to offer a testimony of praise for John and his greatness. Who, after all, is John? Jesus testifies that John is a prophet, and yet he is more. His life and work were envisaged by the prophet Malachi centuries earlier. Malachi, in turn, was reflecting upon the rich divine-warrior tradition (e.g., Ex 14:13–14, 27–28; 15:3–4; Dt 1:29–30; 3:22; 20:3–4; Jos 10:8, 14; 2 Ch 20:29; Ne 4:14, 20; Ps 18:13–14; Zec 9:10–13; 14:1–5) from the Torah: So where is the God of justice? Who can endure the day when he comes or stand when he appears? (Mal 2:17–3:2). As the people of Jacob were receiving the covenant and wondering what was next, God told them that he would send an angel ahead of them to guard them and bring them to the land he had prepared. *Angel* translates the same Hebrew word as "messenger," underscoring the agent's commission and message. The divine warrior was about to go ahead of them and conquer the land (Ex 23:20); they were not on their own. God would fight the battle for/with them. From Malachi's perspective, that was the past, as Israel moved out of Sinai into Canaan. But Malachi foresaw a future when God would again send "my messenger" (ironically, the meaning of Malachi's name) for an important task (Mal 3:1): "'I will send my messenger, who will prepare the way before me. Then suddenly the Lord you are seeking will come to his temple; the messenger of the covenant, whom you desire, will come,' says the LORD Almighty."

We should not miss that the way is prepared "before me," that is, God, the Lord, is about to come suddenly to the temple (Mal 3:1). The identity of the messenger at this point is ambiguous. Is it the prophet himself? Is it the angel of the Lord?[3] But Malachi makes it explicit later when he writes, "See, I will send the prophet Elijah to you before that great and dreadful day of the LORD comes. He will turn the hearts of the parents to their children, and the hearts of the children to their parents; or else I will come and strike the land with total destruction" (Mal 4:5–6). The book of Sirach[4] proves that such sentiments were in the air at the time. Toward the end of that book, the sage composes poetry in praise and honor of Israel's ancestors, and Elijah figures prominently in that list. He rehearses some of Elijah's deeds from the past but gives him a prominent place in the future as he comes to calm God's wrath, turn the hearts of the parents to their children, and restore the tribes of Jacob (Sirach 48:1–11). Clearly, the author of Sirach is reflecting on Malachi, as well as other passages.

11:13 *For all the Prophets and the Law prophesied until John.* Matthew refers to the Law[5] and Prophets four times (Mt 5:17; 7:12; 11:13; 22:40). Only here does he reverse the order and name the Prophets first. He likely does so to privilege the prophetic function of both sections of the Hebrew canon. The two form a hendiadys to describe the whole of sacred Scripture. (See also "Going Deeper into Fulfilling the Law and the Prophets: Matthew 5:17.") Traditionally Hebrew Scripture is described as three parts: Law, Prophets, and Writings. In one of Luke's unique resurrection appearances, the risen Jesus reminded his disciples that everything written about him "in the Law of Moses, the Prophets and the Psalms" must be fulfilled (Lk 24:44).

11:14 *And if you are willing to accept it, he is the Elijah who was to come.* As Jesus offers his commendation of the Baptist, he makes clear John is the one about whom Scripture had been written. What high praise indeed! He is the Elijah to come (Mt 11:14). In effect, Jesus is saying that Malachi's future has arrived. John, Jesus, and the disciples are living in the day Malachi hoped for. Again, we see lines of convergence drawing around Jesus. Jesus is the Lord who is to come. Jesus takes Malachi's "before me" and personalizes it to "before you [singular]" (Mt 11:10).[6] The pronouns have shifted to make clear that Jesus is God with us, the one who is coming to us after the forerunner, John, aka Elijah. So even as Jesus praises John for his significant place in God's providence, we see more clearly how Jesus and John are related and complementary, through the lens of Scripture.

11:16–19 *For John came neither eating nor drinking, and they say, "He has a demon." The Son of Man came eating and drinking, and they say, "Here is a glutton and a drunkard, a friend of tax collectors and sinners."* (For "Son of Man," see comments on Mt 8:20.) Regardless of the high calling both Jesus and John have in their day, they are subject to condemnation by "this generation" (Mt 11:16–19). Those who reject John will also reject Jesus. Jesus likens the situation to the taunts of children sitting in the market. One group wants to play, and the other flatly refuses. One group plays a catchy tune, but the other will not dance. One group sings a sad song, but the other refuses to join in. The people of "this generation" are out of step with God's messengers, John and Immanuel, regardless of whether their message is one of blessing or grief. They get their backs up at the slightest provocation, and so they will miss out on what heaven is doing.

The charge "glutton and a drunkard" is taken directly from Torah's instructions on what parents are to do with a rebellious son (Dt 21:18–21), that is, take him before the elders of the town, accuse him, and have him stoned. The charge was considered a capital crime which may speak to what some in the crowd are thinking. Ironically, it is this generation of unbelieving, rebellious sons and daughters of Israel who look John and Jesus square in the eye and reject them as unfit shepherds.

11:19 *Wisdom is proved right by her deeds.* Jesus' praise of John comes to an end with the Master associating John's and Jesus' actions and words with wisdom. For Matthew and his community, both Jesus and John are envoys of wisdom. Ultimately, their ways—though distinct—will be vindicated from every detractor. Wisdom has rich Old Testament tones probably best expressed in the wisdom psalms (e.g., Ps 1) and Proverbs. Wisdom is personified as a woman, a companion of God in creation (Pr 8:1–31). Wisdom calls to young people to enter her finely built house, feast, and follow her ways because they are good and just and right.

11:20-21 *Then Jesus began to denounce the towns in which most of his miracles had been performed, because they did not repent. "Woe to you, Chorazin! Woe to you, Bethsaida! For if the miracles that were performed in you had been performed in Tyre and Sidon, they would have repented long ago in sackcloth and ashes."* Jesus' praise of John the Baptist is countered by his denunciation of the cities which had witnessed his deeds of power, yet failed to repent: Chorazin, Bethsaida, Capernaum. These Galilean cities had an unmatched opportunity but blew it. The word *woe* has an Old Testament ring to it; it occurs often in the poetry of particular prophets who appear fond of pronouncing "woe" against the nations and injustice among God's elect. Isaiah uttered woe against the wicked, Assyria, Cush (Ethiopia), Ariel, and the sorry leaders of Ephraim and Judah, among others (Isa 3:11; 10:5; 18:1; 28:1; 29:1). The word implies a coming disaster that God is orchestrating to right wrongs. Jeremiah spoke a word of "woe" regarding Moab (cf. Nu 21:29) and Jerusalem (Jer 13:27; 48:1). Ezekiel brings things closer to home by pronouncing calamity on the shepherds of Israel and the city of bloodshed (Eze 24:6-9; 34:2). The complacent of Zion are the object of Amos's oracle (Am 6:1). While oracles against foreign nations are common in the prophets, "woe" is most often an immediate threat to unsavory elements of Judah and Ephraim. So Jesus echoes the prophets when he pronounces "woe" against the cities of Galilee.

The reference to repentance in sackcloth and ashes reflects some well-known Old Testament stories. Daniel turns to God (similar word to repentance), prays, fasts, wears sackcloth, and sits in ashes in light of perilous times (Da 9:3). The book of Jonah describes the people of Nineveh, from greatest to least, repenting, fasting, and donning sackcloth in response to Jonah's preaching (Jnh 3:5). They were hoping to ward off God's judgment, which they did.

11:22 *But I tell you, it will be more bearable for Tyre and Sidon on the day of judgment than for you.* On judgment day, the citizens of Tyre and Sidon will fare better than the citizens of these Galilean cities. Tyre and Sidon were Phoenician cities that sat along the coast. They were known for their trade, but according to Isaiah they were consumed with materialism (Isa 23). Soon, from Isaiah's perspective, the Lord would send Assyria and Babylon to punish them. Ezekiel's oracle (ch. 28) is directed against the prince of Tyre who set himself up as a god and pursued wealth and pride. God said that he would die a violent death as a mortal and not as a god. The thrust of Joel's prophecy (3:4-7) is reciprocal justice. The Phoenicians sold the people of Judah into slavery. Now Phoenicia's sons and daughters would be enslaved and sold to the Sabeans who lived far away in Arabia (see also Zec 9:1–4). Imagine for a moment Jesus' audacious statement that one of Israel's vilest enemies would fare better in the final judgment than "God's people."

11:23 *And you, Capernaum, will you be lifted to the heavens? No, you will go down to Hades. For if the miracles that were performed in you had been performed in Sodom, it would have remained to this day.* Capernaum is singled out for its unbelief. This language may be some of the harshest of all, for it recalls an enscripturated taunt song against the king of Babylon (Isa 14). Though unnamed in the text, this Babylonian king was known for inspiring fear, destroying the environment, and killing some of his own people (Isa 14:20). Like other eastern monarchs, he had the nerve to think he was divine. He said to himself that he would ascend to the heavens, raise his throne above the stars, take to the throne, and make himself like the Most High God (Isa 14:12–14). In fact, he would be cut down to size, die like any other mortal, and his body would remain unburied (Isa 14:19–20). Sheol, the abode of the dead, would snatch him up. Those who gazed on his corpse would wonder, "Is this the man who made the earth tremble, shook kingdoms, overthrew cities, and refused to release the captives of war?" (Isa 14:16–17, author's translation).

Some have interpreted part of this taunt song as relating to the arrogance and fall of Satan, but it should be read in its context which clearly states that the foe was a human being (the king of Babylon) who claimed divine status but, in the end, died a mortal's death.[7]

Capernaum could suffer a fate similar to that of the king of Babylon (Isa 14:4–21). Exactly how the people have exalted themselves, Jesus does not say. But like the king of Babylon who attempted to take heaven by storm, Capernaum would go down to Hades, a Greek word describing the shadowy abode of the dead (see "Matthew 16:18 Through Old Testament Eyes: 'The Gates of Hades'"). Now the comparison is between Capernaum and Sodom in all its infamy (see also the comments at Mt 10:15).

11:25–26 *At that time Jesus said, "I praise you, Father, Lord of heaven and earth, because you have hidden these things from the wise and learned, and revealed them to little children. Yes, Father, for this is what you were pleased to do.* Jesus voices a prayer of thanksgiving (cf. Ps 136:1–2, 26) to the Father, the Lord of heaven and earth. God's wisdom is revealed in his hiding some things from the (so-called) wise/understanding and revealing them to babes. Proverbs gives us a context to understand the statement. Solomon composes his book primarily (Pr 1:4): "for giving prudence to those who are simple, knowledge and discretion to the young . . .".

Yet Solomon's teaching and instruction can bring them to wisdom, righteousness, justice, and equity. That is the point of it, the reason for it. Wisdom here is not street smarts or earthly wisdom, but God's wisdom codified in Scripture. We see the same emphasis in Psalm 19:7:

> The law of the LORD is perfect,
>   refreshing the soul.
> The statutes of the LORD are trustworthy,
>   making wise the simple.

The connection between law/statutes and wisdom/refreshing the soul (finding rest) is clear. The simple are made wise. The educated may think they are wise already, but in fact may miss divine wisdom altogether because God is actively hiding it from them until they are humble enough to receive it. (Also see comments at Mt 21:16.)

The prophet Isaiah draws from this tradition in one of his oracles when he describes how the people's worship of YHWH had grown stale; they were just going through the motions. Now God is promising/threatening to do shocking and amazing things in their midst so that the wisdom of the wise will perish, and the discernment of the discerning will be hidden (Isa 29:14). Revealing and concealing are God's prerogative. The simple will shame the wise, and the wise will be confounded by heaven's wisdom.

11:27 *All things have been committed to me by my Father. No one knows the Son except the Father, and no one knows the Father except the Son and those to whom the Son chooses to reveal him.* Throughout this gospel Jesus invites his followers to enter a relationship with him. By entering that relationship, the disciple also comes face to face with God because of Jesus' unique Sonship with God (Mt 11:27). The Father has handed all things (*ta panta*) over to Jesus, the Son. Here "Son" is not shorthand for "Son of Man" but "Son of God." The language of Jesus' baptism is back, underscoring his unique identity and connection with God. This identity was forged in Scripture (see comments on Mt 3:13–16). Father-Son language is concentrated so much that it sounds like we are reading the gospel of John (e.g., Jn 5:19–20; 8:28; 10:14–15, 30; 17:25). No one knows the Father but the Son of God, yet there is an exception. Any to whom the Son chooses to reveal the Father can come to know the Father as well.

11:28–30 *Come to me, all you who are weary and burdened, and I will give you rest. Take my yoke upon you and learn from me, for I am gentle and humble in heart, and you will find rest for your souls. For my yoke is easy and my burden is light.* Jesus' offer to "come to me" is an invitation to relationship and discipleship.

His promise—I will give you rest—assumes a variety of Old Testament shades depending on the contexts.[8] For example, at Mt. Sinai Moses is busy interceding for his people and taking advantage of his special relationship with God. As Moses presses God further, he wants assurance that God will go with them along the journey to the promised land. YHWH seems reluctant at first to make the pledge, but finally he says: "My Presence will go with you, and I will give you rest" (Ex 33:14). Ambiguity resides in this text (in English); "you" could be singular (Moses) or plural (the people). But the Hebrew is not ambiguous. God's pledge appears to be focused on Moses: "My Presence will go with you, Moses, and I will give you rest." But Moses was not content with that. Three times in his pleading he brings God back to his people: "Remember that *this nation is your people*" (Ex 33:13, italics added) and "For how shall it be known that I have found favor in your sight, *I and your people*, unless you go with us? In this way, we shall be distinct, *I and your people*, from every people on the face of the earth" (Ex 33:16 NRSV, italics added). It is not too much to say that Moses demands that YHWH accompany his people and give them rest; eventually, the Lord agrees to everything Moses asks (Ex 33:17).[9] In this context, entering rest has to do with entering the promised land. The slaves of Egypt under Moses's governance would not remain nomads forever. There is a long journey ahead, but they will have the land God has promised. Then they will have rest.

Sabbath rest constitutes a different kind of rest, a cessation of labor (Ex 20:8–11). For those who had been slaves in Egypt, the command not to work one day in seven likely sounded strange. But Sabbath rest is based on God's rest in creation. In six days YHWH made the heavens, the earth, the seas, and all their inhabitants, and then he rested on the seventh (Ge 1:1–2:3). Sabbath rest, then, forms a type of imitation of God. On day seven his people are to lay their burdens down.

Going Deeper into Rest: Matthew 11:28–30

In Jeremiah, the people are in the land. They had been for hundreds of years, but there are threats against them from ancient superpowers that filled them with dread. Through the prophet, the Lord says (Jer 6:16):

> Stand at the crossroads and look;
>   ask for the ancient paths,
> ask where the good way is, and walk in it,
>   and you will find rest for your souls.

"Rest for your souls" sounds remarkably like what Jesus promised. YHWH's offer to Jerusalem was an opportunity to seek the right road, the ancient path. If they discovered it, it would be "the good way" and they ought to walk in it. We are dealing here with deep, ethical metaphors for what God wants for his people now, in this world. Another way of putting this is to say that obedience to God and his way will lead his people into soul-rest. It echoes Jesus' invitation toward the end of the Sermon on the Mount. Enter by the narrow gate. The narrow gate leads to a narrow road. Few are on it. The end of that road is life (Mt 7:13-14). When we read passages like this, we should be careful not to default immediately to thinking "rest" means the assurance of life after death. That may well be the end to which all things are headed, but in the present we are not meant to live insecure, frazzled existences. Rest can be, ought to be, a here-and-now reality for kingdom citizens.

This squares perfectly with what Jesus says next: take my yoke upon you, learn from me, my yoke is easy, my burden light. A yoke consisted of a wooden frame that joined two oxen for pulling a load (Nu 19:2; Dt 21:3; 1 Sa 6:7). But the idea of a yoke became a ready symbol for subjection of one person to another (Ge 27:40) or one nation to another (Jer 27:8-11). On most occasions the symbol is deployed negatively. The people, for example, came to Rehoboam with the complaint that his father, Solomon, had placed on them a heavy yoke of servitude and asked him to lighten their load. After consulting with advisors, the new king decided to make a statement, saying in effect, "You think my father's yoke was heavy, I will add to your yoke and make it even heavier" (1 Ki 12:1-15). Often the prophets describe God as shattering the yoke of the oppressors (e.g., Isa 9:4; Jer 30:8; Na 1:13). Jeremiah chastises the rich of Israel for breaking the "yoke" of the covenant; by that he meant that they did not know the way of YHWH nor did they live according to God's law (Jer 5:5). Positively, it could be said that a person who spent time learning the way of God and living by God's law was yoked to the covenant.

The rabbis took these ideas, developed them in their own unique way, and the yoke image became a useful way to describe a person who undertakes the study of Torah (m. Avot 3.5; cf. Sirach 51:23-27). It is probably this meaning that is closest to what Jesus is talking about. Taking Jesus' yoke stands in parallel with "learn from me." Likewise, "my yoke is easy" stands in complement to "my burden is light." Taking on Jesus' yoke refers to anyone who decides to learn Jesus' teachings and then live by them. Jesus fulfills Torah, every jot and tittle—to borrow the King James language—so following Jesus and his teachings means fulfilling Torah, Jesus' way.

Following Jesus does not mean that God promises we can take wonderful, long naps every day. Nor does it mean that all of our sleep will be restful. It means we have the security and safety of leaning on the power and love of God to do his will rather than the exhausting work of relying only on our own energy or understanding in life.

Matthew 11 Through Old Testament Eyes

The Old Testament shaped Jesus' ministry. From prison John the Baptist heard little of what was happening with Jesus, and what he did hear was filtered mainly through unsympathetic reports. But John's messengers asked the right question: Are you the coming one or is there another? Jesus did not answer the question "yes" or "no." He answered it in scriptural echoes that were easily picked up by anyone with Old Testament ears and eyes. Miracles, such as those described in Isaiah, were taking place: the blind see, the lame walk, lepers are cleansed, the deaf hear, the dead are raised, and the good news is preached to the poor (Mt 11:5). The inevitable conclusion, still yet unvoiced, is this: Jesus is the Messiah, the one to come. But John the Baptist himself is prefigured in the Scriptures, not just Jesus, as Malachi 3–4 makes clear. Themes of judgment roll down like water on Galilean cities from Isaiah and Joel, and wisdom like an ever-flowing stream sourced in Proverbs and Psalms. The chapter ends with an appeal to rest, not the kind of rest that awaits the disciple in the world to come but rest for the here and now (Jer 6:16).

MATTHEW 12

Jesus was a deeply polarizing person. People either loved him or they hated him. He did not leave any room for indifference. He did not mean to. We have already seen how Jesus is accused of trying to abolish the law, befriending sinners, and casting out demons by the power of the devil himself. All are serious charges. Now opponents come to Jesus with another charge: he is a Sabbath breaker.

12:1–2 *Look! Your disciples are doing what is unlawful on the Sabbath.* Jesus' disciples are hungry as they walk through the grain fields, so they rake their hands up the stalks, pull off a few grains and pop them in their mouths. Some Pharisees must have been watching closely . . . critically, and did not like what they saw; they come to Jesus with the complaint that his disciples were doing what is not permitted on the Sabbath. They were harvesting grain. Jesus should have done something to stop them.

At the heart of this challenge is Sabbath law, rooted in the commandments, the top ten commandments. There is hardly anything more distinctively Jewish than Sabbath observance. The covenant people have six days to work, but the Sabbath is to be kept holy. And how do they do that? By doing no work on the Sabbath regardless of the season (Ex 20:8–11; Dt 5:12–15). To observe this commandment properly, the faithful had to know three things: (1) What day is the Sabbath? (2) When does that day begin and when does it end? And (3) what constitutes work? These were essential for those who had the audacity to think God said it, he meant it, and it mattered. It is the third question that shapes this public disagreement. Rabbinic scholars over the decades and centuries developed thirty-nine categories of work not permitted on the Sabbath, including sowing and reaping. Clearly the Pharisees regard what the disciples were doing to be work; Jesus did not.[1] Jesus is not saying the Sabbath is just like any other day, nor is he claiming that anything goes on the Sabbath.

12:3–4 *Haven't you read what David did when he and his companions were hungry?* To answer his detractors, Jesus takes them to Scripture. This is Jesus' default mode. Whenever he is asked a question or presented with a challenge, he goes to Scripture. In a way Jesus is goading the Pharisees. They were supposed to be experts in Scripture, so he asks (in effect), "Haven't you read the Bible?" Of course they had, but they had missed something crucial.

Jesus finds two witnesses in Scripture. First, consider David, the shepherd from Bethlehem, turned fugitive from King Saul (1 Sa 20). On his way to meet some compatriots, David stops at Nob, a village not far from Jerusalem. He meets Ahimelech, the priest who presides over the shrine of YHWH. David is hungry, and he knows his men are as well, but all Ahimelech has is holy bread (1 Sa 21:1–6).

Leviticus 24:5–9 describes God's design for some of the furnishings for the tabernacle, including a table for holy vessels and the holy bread (aka, the bread of the Presence). Every Sabbath, twelve loaves (one each for the twelve tribes of Israel) were to be placed before God as an offering. At the end of the week, the priests, and only the priests, were allowed to eat them after placing the next twelve loaves before YHWH. But after some discussion with David, Ahimelech was satisfied and gave the holy bread to David and his companions. Human hunger and need somehow trumped the letter of the law.

12:5 *Or haven't you read in the Law that the priests on Sabbath duty in the temple desecrate the Sabbath and yet are innocent?* There is a second witness. The law itself prescribes that the priests "break" the law every Sabbath. How? By performing their priestly duties (Nu 28:9–10); that is, they are required every Sabbath to offer two one-year old lambs without defect, a drink offering, and a grain offering. Technically, by performing their duties on the Sabbath, they were "working." Yet no one accused the priests of breaking the Sabbath. In effect, they were guiltless as Jesus said.

12:6 *I tell you that something greater than the temple is here.* All this talk of shrines, the temple, and offerings led Jesus to make this pronouncement. What or who is greater? There is only one possible answer: Jesus himself. The primary activity of the temple is the worship of the one, true God. As Immanuel, God-with-us, Jesus himself occupies divine space and is the object of their temple devotion,[2] even though no one yet in the story recognizes it. The evangelist Matthew would recognize it and so would his audience, but first there is more to the story.

12:7–8 *If you had known what these words mean, "I desire mercy, not sacrifice," you would not have condemned the innocent. For the Son of Man is Lord of the Sabbath.* For all their piety the Pharisees missed something essential. Had they not, they would not have been so eager to assign guilt to Jesus' hungry disciples. Again, Matthew and Jesus bring us back to Hosea 6:6 and an unrelenting theme in the prophets: "I desire mercy, not sacrifice" (see comments at Mt 9:12–13; cf. Am 5:22–24; Mic 6:6–8). He who is greater than the temple prioritizes mercy over ritual. This is not to say that ritual and offerings are bad; it is to say that mercy must be the lens through which Torah and Sabbath are viewed. The Pharisees have gone astray because they insist on observance without a nod to mercy. Torah is not set aside, but it is configured around mercy. Richard Hays is correct when he says, *"For Matthew, the story of Israel is carried forward through a particular, prophetically shaped, interpretation of Torah within a community called to embody the mercy of God."*[3] The episode ends with yet another pronouncement: "For the Son of Man is Lord of the Sabbath." As Lord of the Sabbath, Jesus has the authority to interpret what is work and what is not work regarding the Sabbath. (For "Son of Man," see also comments on Mt 8:20.)

12:9–14 *Going on from that place, he went into their synagogue, and a man with a shriveled hand was there.* The exact cause of the man's disability is not clear. But since it was still the Sabbath, the question comes, "Is it lawful to heal on the Sabbath?" (Mt 12:10). Now, Matthew makes clear that this was not a real question but an opportunity to make yet another accusation against Jesus. Scripture is silent on whether healing is actually considered "work" on the Sabbath. So Jesus responds to the question with a question: "If any of you has a sheep and it falls into a pit on the Sabbath, will you not take hold of it and lift it out?" (Mt 12:11). The Master Teacher is not speaking theoretically here: "If a person has a sheep and it falls into a pit . . .". No. He is speaking directly to them. For Jesus, this is deeply personal and pointed.

Not everyone was agreed on this situation as it pertained to Sabbath law. Some Jews followed this interpretation: "No man shall assist a beast to give birth on the Sabbath day. And if it should fall into a cistern or pit, he shall not lift it out on the Sabbath" (*CD* 11.13).[4] But Jesus probably knew his audience would not have practiced the law in this way. Jewish law in the main shows a great deal of respect and kindness to animals (*b. Shabb* 128b). Expecting that sheep-owners would go down into the pit and bring up the injured sheep on the Sabbath, Jesus deploys a common rabbinic device of comparison: If you would do this for a sheep on the Sabbath, would you not also do good for a human being who is so much more valuable than the sheep? The implied answer: of course, you would (Mt 12:12). Here we see another extension of mercy as the principal lens through which one observes Torah and the Sabbath. Mercy requires the observant to do good, regardless of the day. So Jesus healed the man, which led the Pharisees to go away and conspire against him (Mt 12:13–14).

12:16–18 *He warned them not to tell others about him. This was to fulfill what was spoken through the prophet Isaiah: "Here is my servant whom I have chosen, the one I love, in whom I delight."* Jesus could see that his words and actions caused offense to the Pharisees. He did not have to be omniscient to spot it on their faces or hear it in their grumblings. So he left (Mt 12:15). Many followed him and he continued his ministry of healing with this caveat: he directed them not to point him out to others. We have seen this before (Mt 8:4) and will see it again. Many refer to these directives as the "messianic secret" because Jesus regularly tells others not to make him known. People have debated why Jesus insisted on this, but Matthew tells us that this "secret" is based in Scripture (Isa 42:1–4).

12:19–21 *He will not quarrel or cry out; no one will hear his voice in the streets.* While Matthew quotes all of Isaiah 42:1–4 in 12:18–21, in particular he has in mind verse 2, which describes "my servant" as one who does not quarrel or make a lot of noise. In fact "no one will hear his voice in the streets." Jesus appears to take this as a directive to keep a low profile. There may have been practical reasons as well—to avoid unnecessary run-ins with the authorities— but Matthew recognizes the priority of Scripture. Jesus did this to "fulfill" the word of the prophet Isaiah.

Matthew 12:15–21 Through Old Testament Eyes: The Servant Poem

Matthew's quotation of the servant poem demonstrates that early Christians saw these and similar passages as another line of prophecy that converges on the person and work of Jesus (e.g., Isa 49:1–6; 50:4–6; 52:13–53:12). At Jesus' baptism the voice from heaven echoes this same language (Isa 42:1; Mt 3:16–17). Jesus is "my servant," "my chosen/ beloved," in whom God is well pleased. God places his Spirit upon him. Jesus' task is to announce and enact justice among the nations. He is not going to shout or cry out or raise his voice in the streets. He will not stop until he has made justice victorious. Matthew's language does not match precisely either the Hebrew or the Greek texts of Isaiah we know, but we do not have access to every Hebrew or Greek edition of these texts that might have been available to Matthew. Still, it is clear the evangelist intends to bring to light all these lines of hope toward the servant and his mission. Ultimately, in his name (the servant's name) the Gentiles will hope (Mt 12:21). This last line echoes another passage from Isaiah (11:10, LXX, author's translation): "On him the nations will hope." The extension of Jesus' ministry to the Gentiles is a constant theme throughout Matthew.

Some people regard the "servant" in these servant-of-YHWH poems as the people of Israel. There is some textual basis for that (Isa 41:8–9; 42:18–25; 45:4; 49:3–7), and that position has much to commend it, but others have viewed these texts as references to a single individual who comes out of Israel to represent Israel before God and the world. Early Christians could be counted in that camp because they saw Jesus not only as an idealized Israel—everything Israel could be—but also as Israel's Messiah, Israel's representative par excellence (cf. 2 Baruch 70:9).

12:22–23 *Then they brought him a demon-possessed man who was blind and mute, and Jesus healed him, so that he could both talk and see. All the people were astonished and said, "Could this be the Son of David?"* Another healing miracle and exorcism is an opportunity for Matthew to remind us of Jesus' authority as "the Son of David." Here Jesus exhibits his authority over foul spirits and disease. We saw the title first in the opening and genealogy (Mt 1). It sets the tone for what comes in the gospel. We heard it again in the pleas of the two blind men (Mt 9:27). "The Son of David" was a special messianic title that underscored Jesus' royal identity. He is Israel's true king. The miracle is recorded quickly; it is the controversy that ensued where things got interesting.

12:24 *But when the Pharisees heard this, they said, "It is only by Beelzebul, the prince of demons, that this fellow drives out demons."* This charge has been made against Jesus before. For a bit of history on Beelzebul and his other name, Satan, see comments at Matthew 10:24–25. We have in this pericope Jesus' most complete response to the charge.

12:25–26 *Jesus knew their thoughts and said to them, "Every kingdom divided against itself will be ruined, and every city or household divided against itself will not stand. If Satan drives out Satan, he is divided against himself. How then can his kingdom stand?* Jesus begins with a bit of self-evident logic about divided kingdoms and households. In doing so, Jesus suggests that Satan has a kingdom. If so, then Satan must be the prince. Likewise, he must have subjects in his kingdom. Jesus has battled Satan before, in the wilderness, and came out on top, but not until Satan offered Jesus all the kingdoms of the world (Mt 4:1–11). Perhaps we should read the temptation account and this charge in light of each other. But we must wait for the pronouncements Jesus is about to make. First, Jesus asks a probing question: If my power to cast out demons is derived from Beelzebul/Satan, then what about your own exorcists (Mt 12:27)?[5]

12:28 *But if it is by the Spirit of God that I drive out demons, then the kingdom of God has come upon you.* Jesus makes a bold pronouncement, and he places it in an if-then statement. People must decide for themselves whether Jesus is telling the truth: Is Jesus driving out demons by the Spirit of God or another spirit (cf. Lk 11:20)? If it is the Spirit of God and not Satan—as some Pharisees allege—who is the means by which Jesus performs his exorcisms, then another kingdom is laying claim to the world. It is the kingdom of God, the same kingdom John the Baptist proclaimed (see Mt 3:2). The miracles Jesus performs are manifestations of that kingdom; they provide a sense of reach and priority for what God is accomplishing through the Son of David.

12:29 *Or again, how can anyone enter a strong man's house and carry off his possessions unless he first ties up the strong man? Then he can plunder his house.* Jesus punctuates his pronouncement with a parable of a strong man and a robber who plans to plunder the strong man's possessions. We typically don't like robbers and we admire strong people. So we can casually make the mistake of thinking of Jesus as the strong man. But in fact, Jesus is using the characters in this parable the other way around. Satan is the strong man. Jesus is the robber intent on plundering his house. Satan has a kingdom (house) and all the goodies (possessions). But before they can be plundered, the robber has to bind the strong man. Then what should we make of this? Whenever Jesus performs any miracle or exorcism, he is binding the strong man so he can take back the world one soul, one life at a time. For such is the kingdom of God.

Going Deeper into Binding the Strong Man: Matthew 12:29

The parable Jesus tells has its antecedent in an oracle of hope spoken by the prophet Isaiah. The prophet describes a day when the cities defeated by Babylon will again be rebuilt and repopulated (Isa 49:14–26). Put another way, Babylon had once been the strong man that held God's people captive. The oracle ends (Isa 49:24–26):

> Can plunder be taken from warriors,
>   or captives be rescued from the fierce?

But this is what the LORD says:

"Yes, captives will be taken from warriors,
    and plunder retrieved from the fierce;
I will contend with those who contend with you,
    and your children I will save.
I will make your oppressors eat their own flesh;
    they will be drunk on their own blood, as with wine.
Then all mankind will know
    that I, the LORD, am your Savior,
    your Redeemer, the Mighty One of Jacob."

The enemy is portrayed as battled-hardened warriors, ferocity etched in every line of their faces. The rhetorical question is asked, "Can plunder be taken from warriors?" The implied answer is, no way. On a human level you cannot take plunder away from the warriors and rescue the captives from the fierce. But Israel is not on its own. YHWH joins the battle, fights, and defeats those who oppressed Israel. When that day comes, all humanity will know that YHWH is the Savior, Redeemer, and Mighty One of Israel.

The situation has changed, but the categories are the same. The enemy is strong, and he has the house and its possessions, but it is no longer Babylon. Satan himself has a kingdom, a realm, and subjects. Disease, death, evil, and chaos are his policies. Enter the robber who, empowered by the Spirit, slips in the house, ties him up, and then plunders his possessions, one wonder at a time. All in the name of the kingdom of God. In the end, this is no contest, for the warrior on the side of Israel and God's people is the Son of David, the Lord, their Savior, their Redeemer, the Mighty One of Israel. Not only for Jesus' contemporaries but for us as well, all these hopes and aspirations converge around this one man, Jesus of Nazareth.

12:31-32 *And so I tell you, every kind of sin and slander can be forgiven, but blasphemy against the Spirit will not be forgiven.* The forgiveness of sins is an important theme in the Hebrew Scriptures. The sacrificial system, in part, exists for the penitent sinner to seek and find forgiveness. People who sin *unintentionally* are directed to make a sin offering. Priests make atonement for them, and they are forgiven. The same rule applies to both covenant people and resident aliens (Nu 15:27–29). But if anyone sins intentionally, in a high-handed way, there is no sacrifice that atones for them. They are to be cut off from the people, which could mean divine punishment by early death, capital punishment, or possibly the end of their family line (Nu 15:30–31).

Intentional sins, then, appear to be beyond forgiveness. Likewise, we ought to consider the following commandment: "You shall not misuse the name of the LORD your God, for the LORD will not hold anyone guiltless who misuses his name" (Ex 20:7). Carmen Imes makes a compelling case for a proper meaning of this commandment in the context of its day and ours. She uses the phrase "bearing God's name" to describe the force of the commandment. The directive is not exclusively focused on how one speaks but how one lives. Israel was "branded" with God's name, and often God's reputation was sullied by their misdeeds. Living the command properly means that the Lord is magnified in the world and among the nations.[6]

The Jews who heard Jesus' teaching were likely primed to think that at least some sins (intentional sins and misuse of God's name) were beyond forgiveness. If these two commandments are brought together, then we can say there is no unintentional misuse of God's name. Every time God's name is misused, it is high-handed and calculated. If the same rules apply, then there is no unintentional blasphemy of the Holy Spirit; a person who blasphemes the Spirit does so deliberately and with malice. There is no need for anyone to wonder whether or not they had somehow misspoken and thereby blasphemed the Spirit. Blasphemy, by its nature, is premeditated and not accidental.

The way Matthew links (*dia touto*) the charge leveled against Jesus that he is in league with the devil (Mt 12:24) with the statement about blasphemy against the Spirit suggests that these Pharisees have, in fact, crossed that line. They have committed the unforgiveable sin. Nothing here suggests Jesus is speaking in the abstract. He claims to cast out demons by the Spirit of God (Mt 12:28), not by any other power. These opponents, having seen Jesus' actions, have equated the work of the Spirit with Beelzebul. They have blasphemed the Holy Spirit.

12:34 *You brood of vipers, how can you who are evil say anything good? For the mouth speaks what the heart is full of.* In Matthew 12:33–38 Jesus makes the point that good fruit comes from good trees, and bad fruit from bad trees. Likewise good words and actions come from a good person, bad words and bad actions from an evil person (see comment on Mt 7:16–20). This discussion follows the question of whether Jesus is linked with the devil (12:22–29). Thus when Jesus says here that the Pharisees are a "brood of vipers" (children of the serpent?), he may be recalling Genesis 3 where a snake uses deceptive words to bring about bad fruit in the lives of Adam and Eve.

While certain qualities of snakes are sometimes seen positively (e.g., Pr 30:19; Mt 10:16), here Jesus is picking up on negative associations, such as connecting the image of a snake with evil words (Ps 140:3), as well as with lies and injustice (Isa 59:4–5). In this way, Jesus is turning the tables on the Pharisees. He is not the one who is in league with that "ancient serpent" (Rev 12:9)—*they* are![7]

12:39 *He answered, "A wicked and adulterous generation asks for a sign!"* The generation Jesus addressed was not the first generation to be called evil and adulterous. Jesus' language echoes two significant moments in Scripture. First, God referred to the generation of Israelites who decided not to take the land because of the bad report from the majority of spies as "this evil generation" (Dt 1:34–35). God swore that they would not see the good land he had promised to their ancestors. Then, second, we might consider the book of Hosea, which persistently refers to the people of Israel as committing adultery against the Lord. God said to the prophet: "Go, marry a promiscuous woman and have children with her, for like an adulterous wife this land is guilty of unfaithfulness to the LORD" (Hos 1:2). Hosea's marriage is an enacted parable, an account of how Israel has committed spiritual adultery against the Lord by going after other gods and ignoring his sensible teachings. The generation Hosea addressed was the quintessential "adulterous generation."

12:39–40 *But none will be given it except the sign of the prophet Jonah. For as Jonah was three days and three nights in the belly of a huge fish, so the Son of Man will be three days and three nights in the heart of the earth.* It is not the preaching of Jonah or the repentance of the Ninevites that garners Jesus' attention; it is the miracle of the prophet's survival despite being in the belly of the big fish for three days and three nights (Jnh 1:17–2:10). So, what was he doing in there besides being slowly digested in the fish's gastric juices? One school of thought says he was praying, praying a lot. That makes sense given what we find in chapter 2, a psalm-like prayer of thanksgiving. But as Mark Lanier points out, it is also possible to interpret this as . . . Jonah died and was resuscitated. He makes a strong case, noting that Jonah appeals to God "out of the belly of Sheol" (Jnh 2:2 ESV, NRSV); *Sheol* is a "Hebrew word for the underworld, the grave, or death."[8] Furthermore, Jonah speaks of going down to the land whose bars closed over him forever (Jnh 2:6). That sounds permanent! Yet God brought him up from the pit, again *Sheol,* the land of the dead. For God to bring him up *from there, he had to be there.* So Jonah offered Jesus a sign of resurrection.[9]

Whether Jonah suffered death or a near-death experience, this was a miraculous escape for the reluctant prophet. Jesus took advantage of the people's knowledge of the story to begin to predict a similar future for the Son of Man. Early Christians apparently picked up on this story and often portrayed Jonah's deliverance from the belly of the fish as a symbol of Jesus' resurrection. According to Matthew, Jesus himself was the first to make the connection, but early Christians created the art to visualize it.[10] (For "Son of Man," see comments on Mt 8:20.)

12:41 *They [the people of Nineveh] repented at the preaching of Jonah, and now something greater than Jonah is here.* Jesus dug deeper into the story of Jonah to remind his audience how the people of Nineveh—the great and the small—turned to God when confronted with the prophet's message (Jnh 3–4), yet the evil generation Jesus confronted with his message and miracles were refusing to repent. When the judgment comes, the people of Nineveh will "rise up" and call for their condemnation. "Rise up" here has a double meaning. First, they will be resurrected with the righteous because they repented. Second, they will "rise up" as a witness against the evil, adulterous generation. Why can they do so? Because something, someone greater than Jonah is here (Mt 12:41). And just who could that be? Again, it must be Jesus. There is no other candidate.

12:42 *The Queen of the South will rise at the judgment with this generation and condemn it; for she came from the ends of the earth to listen to Solomon's wisdom, and now something greater than Solomon is here.* Not only will the Ninevites call for the evil generation's condemnation, so will the Queen of Sheba (or Saba; her story is told in 1 Ki 10:1–13 and then retold in 2 Ch 9:1–12). The fame of Solomon (because of the name of YHWH) reached the Queen of Sheba, so she and her retinue traveled an enormous distance to meet Solomon, question him, and observe him in action (both politically and cultically). The encounter left her breathless. Before she returns to her land, she gives Solomon an elaborate gift of gold, spices, and precious stones. She offers praise to YHWH and blesses him for making Solomon king and granting him such wisdom.

Her story would have been familiar to Jesus' audience. The teacher bears down on the fact that she traveled from the ends of the earth to listen humbly to Solomon's wisdom. Jesus' opponents, on the other hand, were attentive to his words and actions only to find fault and challenge his honor in public. No humility there. Their offense is even greater because something/someone greater than Solomon is here (Mt 12:42). If Solomon had his glory—and he did—Jesus has more.

What the Structure Means: Something Greater (Mt 12)

Three times Jesus speaks of something greater being in their midst. Someone greater than the temple (12:6), Jonah (12:41), and Solomon

(12:42) is here. The temple, of course, represents *the place* where heaven touches earth and where God chooses to meet his people. It is sacred ground. The first temple was built and dedicated by Solomon nine centuries before the birth of Jesus. Jonah could stand for the prophets in general who spoke for God and called for the nations (in Jonah's case, Assyria) to repent. Solomon represents *the ruler of Israel at the height of its glory.* He too is visited, not by the lost sheep of Israel, but by an outsider, the woman who reigned over parts of what we know today as Arabia. Her encounter with Solomon and his realm left her ready to praise the God of Israel. How much more shall the nations of the earth be drawn to Jesus and his glory.

In the Old Testament, the number three can be associated with completeness (Ge 40:10–19; Nu 22:28; 1 Sa 3:8; 1 Ki 18:33–35; Jnh 1:17). Jesus' greatness, suggests Matthew, is evident not just in these three ways, but in every way.

Matthew Through Old Testament Eyes: Solomon

Solomon was the first son of David to reign during the brief period of a united monarchy (c. 970–931 BC). His name appears twice in Jesus' genealogy (Mt 1:6–7), along with the reminder that David fathered him through Bathsheba, who had been the wife of another man. Earlier in the gospel, Matthew compares the "glory" of the flowers of the field with Solomon's (Mt 6:29). The king's stories are recounted in the Hebrew Scriptures (1 Ki 1–11; 2 Ch 1–9). Through him and his descendants, God's covenant with King David (2 Sa 7:12–16) is carried on. Solomon is known both for his wisdom and for his apostasy (1 Ki 11). His legendary wisdom becomes a type that is imitated and replicated throughout Scripture in psalms and proverbs. Among the works of the Apocrypha is the Wisdom of Solomon. He is celebrated as a master builder and is remembered primarily for building and dedicating the first temple of YHWH in Jerusalem (1 Ki 8). There are a number of parallels between Solomon and Jesus: his status as David's son, his wisdom, and his legacy as builder of the first temple. Jesus will pronounce judgment on the temple in Jerusalem (Mt 21:12–13) but go on to build his own "not made with hands" (Mk 14:58; see Mt 26:61). Solomon's mistakes eventually caught up with him and the united kingdom is divided into two during the early days of his son's reign.

12:43–45 *That is how it will be with this wicked generation.* The expression "this wicked generation" links the parable of the possessed person with the Pharisees who asked for a sign in Matthew 12:38–39 (see comment).

12:48–50 *He replied to him, "Who is my mother, and who are my brothers?" Pointing to his disciples, he said, "Here are my mother and my brothers. For whoever does the will of my Father in heaven is my brother and sister and mother."* Jesus redefines the family. Blood only goes so far, but there is "something greater." For Jesus, that something was living according to the will of the Father in heaven. The language Jesus uses is not gendered. When asked about his mother and brothers, he points to his disciples: these people are my brother and sister and mother. The Master did not invent this frame of reference for family, but he did adopt and adapt it for his purposes from the Bible. Deuteronomy 33 contains the blessings Moses spoke over the sons of Israel before his death. Preeminent among them are the words he spoke over Levi (Dt 33:8–11), whose tribe God set aside to be the priests before and of the people. He notes especially that Levi had no regard for his father or mother, ignored his family, and did not acknowledge his children. Why? Because they (the sons of Levi) are to devote themselves to the will of God revealed in the word, covenant, ordinances, law, and offerings. In adopting this framework, Jesus acts as a priest and priest-maker, for all his disciples are now to relate differently to family and one another. For such is the kingdom of heaven.

MATTHEW 13

13:2–3 *Such large crowds gathered around him that he got into a boat and sat in it, while all the people stood on the shore. Then he told them many things in parables.* Jesus takes everyday situations for people (planting, harvesting, baking bread, fishing, and joyful discovery) and compares them with some kingdom reality. The idea is that what is valid in one sphere (the earth) is equally valid in the other (the kingdom).

13:3 *A farmer went out to sow his seed.* The parable of the sower (13:3–9) is one of the parables Jesus explains privately to his disciples (13:18–23). While the sower is not identified in either the parable or its explanation, the Son of Man is named specifically as the sower in the parable of the weeds (13:37). With the earlier commission of the disciples (Mt 10), it is reasonable to see them as sowers as well. The seed sown, however, the seed that falls on different qualities of soil, is clearly identified as "the message about the kingdom" (13:19). Sowing plays an important part in a number of Jesus' parables as it has played in the Old Testament.

The act of sowing is integral to Jeremiah's message. At his call the Lord said to him (Jer 1:10): "See, today I appoint you over nations and kingdoms to uproot and tear down, to destroy and overthrow, to build and to plant." Four infinitives describe judgment and destruction: uproot, tear down, destroy, overthrow. Two infinitives portray elements of hope and restoration: build and plant (or sow). Jeremiah's message of judgment and restoration included Israel but is to extend to the nations (cf. Mt 28:19–20). Throughout the book of Jeremiah, the oracles are peppered with the same language (e.g., Jer 31:27–28).

Ezekiel also has in mind Israel's restoration as a day when the people of Israel come home, when the mountains and hills of Israel will be plowed and sown (Eze 36:8–12). Those who plow and sow the land of Israel participate in Israel's good future. Likewise, in one of Hosea's restoration oracles, he speaks of a day when the Lord responds to the skies and the earth responds to grain and those who were "Not my people" will be planted again in the land (Hos 2:21–23). Generally, the act of sowing itself is part of a motif of God's mercy and redemption of his people.

What the Structure Means: Eight Parables (Mt 13)

In this third major teaching portion of the First gospel (see "What the Structure Means: Five Sermons [Mt 5–25]" at Mt 7:28 and Table 0.1), Matthew expands on Mark's parables of the kingdom to eight parables in all (see Table 13.1). The number eight has resonance within the Jewish and Christian tradition with new creation. Circumcision was on the eighth day (Ge 17:12). Firstborn animals were dedicated on the eighth day (Ex 22:30).[1] Sunday (the first day of creation, Ge 1) is completed in the Sunday we know as resurrection/Easter Sunday (the new creation). Since Sunday to Sunday is eight days, the number eight held special importance for early Jesus followers as the day of new creation.

Table 13.1. The Eight Parables of Matthew 13

Passage	Parable
Matthew 13:3–9	Parable of the Sower
Matthew 13:24–30	Parable of the Weeds and Wheat
Matthew 13:31–32	Parable of the Mustard Seed
Matthew 13:33	Parable of the Yeast
Matthew 13:44	Parable of the Treasure Hidden in the Field
Matthew 13:45–46	Parable of the Pearl of Great Value
Matthew 13: 47–50	Parable of the Net
Matthew 13:52–53	Parable of the Treasures New and Old

13:7 *Other seed fell among thorns, which grew up and choked the plants.* The third unfit soil will not let the seed grow because the good seed fell among the foul thorns that grew and choked them out (see Job 31:40). Thorns and thistles are part of the story of the "fall" in Genesis 3. When Adam and Eve disregarded God's instructions not to eat from the tree of the knowledge of good and evil, God cursed the ground, making it difficult to bring in a crop. Instead of grain, fruit, and nutritious plants, the earth easily grows thorns and thistles which stand in unfair competition to the plants people need for sustenance (Ge 3:17–19). As we will see in Jesus' explanation in Matthew 13:22, just as Adam's sin is related to thorns, the sin of deceitful wealth is a thorn that prevents Jesus' word from taking root in people's hearts.

Going Deeper into the Parable of the Sower: Matthew 13:1–9 and 13:18–23

The parable of the sower is open to a variety of interpretations. Let's consider one of them. The followers of Jesus, those charged to take the message of the kingdom to the nations (Mt 28:19–20), need some sort of explanation for the kind of results they can expect. Some people will hear the message but never be open to the gospel; evil, in all its manifestations, swoops in and steals away whatever seed has been planted. Others will hear the gospel and spring to life, it seems, just to wither away when trouble and persecution arises. They are here one day and gone another. Still others will seem to grow in the gospel only to become unfruitful when worries and the pursuit of wealth overwhelm them. But there are some people who not only receive the message, they also grow in it and become great producers of kingdom crops. These are results Jesus achieved in his ministry. The disciples should expect the same.

There is disappointment in kingdom work. Much effort is expended to see limited results at times. Disappointment sometimes leads to ministry burnout. But servants, armed with this parable, know what to expect. Some kingdom preaching and teaching will be wasted. Then there are moments when something fresh happens, something unusual and unexpected. A day is ahead when the kingdom grows like a mustard seed in the midst of the garden. How does it happen? As the other parables demonstrate, the kingdom comes shrouded in mystery.

13:11 *The knowledge of the secrets of the kingdom of heaven has been given to you, but not to them.* This is why Jesus spoke in parables. The word *secrets* could also be translated "mysteries." This refers to aspects of God's plan hidden for a time but now revealed in and through Jesus. Of all the Old Testament prophets, Daniel is probably best known as revealer of mysteries. On one occasion the king of Babylon had a troubling dream and wanted to know its interpretation (Da 2). He called for the magicians and sages of his kingdom and asked them to both describe the dream and offer an interpretation. The wise responded over and again to the king that no human being on earth could know both the dream and its interpretation (Da 2:10). The king flew into a rage and sent them all to the executioner until Daniel, an exile from Judea, stepped in. He urged his companions to pray to the God of heaven for mercy, and later that night God gave him a vision revealing both the dream and its interpretation (Da 2:17–23). The first thing Daniel did after waking was to bless God and acknowledge that God reveals deep and hidden secrets. This notion of secrecy and mystery is typical of the apocalyptic mindset Daniel shared with Jesus (cf. *1QpHab* 7.8).

13:13 *This is why I speak to them in parables: "Though seeing, they do not see; though hearing, they do not hear or understand."* While the disciples have the mysteries of the kingdom revealed to them, Jesus spoke to the crowds in parables. The parables, it seems, have both a revealing and concealing function as the next verses will show. But Jesus' language is broadly reminiscent of Jeremiah's oracle, a recurring warning about how the people's service to foreign gods will leave them as exiles serving strangers in days to come.[2] They are described as foolish and senseless people who have eyes but do not see and ears but do not hear (Jer 5:21). So Jeremiah's prophecy sounds strangely like Isaiah's, which Jesus quotes next.

13:14–15 *In them [the crowds] is fulfilled the prophecy of Isaiah: "You will be ever hearing but never understanding; you will be ever seeing but never perceiving."* Though they did not know it, the crowds that attended Jesus' teaching that day were fulfilling Isaiah's prophecy (Isa 6:9–10). The same could probably be said for other crowds that heard Jesus on other days.

When God called Isaiah to be his voice to his generation, he told him to speak a message that would dull the minds, blind the eyes, and stop the ears of the people. The message reminds the careful reader of how sometimes the presence and speech of a prophet hardens the heart. Who hardens whose hearts *first* may be part of the mystery. The prophecy had an earlier fulfillment in the eighth century BC both prior to and as the land is laid waste and people are sent into exile by the Assyrians. But Jesus sees in the patchy response of the crowds another fulfillment, an ultimate fulfillment of Isaiah's prophecy, because history has reached a crossroads and the kingdom of heaven is at hand. Perhaps the most cited example of hardening the heart involves the unnamed Pharaoh of the exodus. Does the Pharaoh harden his heart (Ex 9:34–35) first or does YHWH harden it (Ex 10:1–2)?

Matthew Through Old Testament Eyes: Parables

As David Garland points out, the parables are "not brain teasers intended to stump people."[3] There is nothing inherently difficult about hearing and grasping a parable unless a person is already set in their ways and unwilling to repent. So the parables reveal the obduracy of people even as they conceal (to the obdurate) the message of the kingdom.[4] It is not that people cannot repent; it is that they choose not to. When that happens, the later state is worse than the first. It was as true in Isaiah's day as in Jesus'.

But the disciples were different. As for them, they could hear and see because God had granted them the blessing of sight and sound understanding. They also had private access to Jesus so they could ask Jesus about the meaning of the more obscure parables.

13:17 *Many prophets and righteous people longed to see what you see but did not see it, and to hear what you hear but did not hear it.* The current batch of disciples has a leg up on the ancients because of what they are now hearing and seeing in the life of Jesus. The teacher does not give us names or specific references, but the author of Hebrews concludes the roll call of faith (Heb 11) by acknowledging that the heroes died in faith not receiving what was promised (Heb 11:13, 39).[5] It could well be that Jesus and, more to the point, his disciples would have had a similar list in mind. Craig Keener is correct when he notes that the followers of Jesus—compared to the crowds—had taken seriously the cost of discipleship and *"pressed close enough to Jesus to understand the rest of the teaching he was giving them."*[6] Therefore, they were the rich to whom more was given (Mt 13:12); they were the good soil in the parable of the sower (13:8, 23).[7]

13:18 *Listen then to what the parable of the sower means.* Some Old Testament parables have explanations (e.g., 2 Sa 12:1–14). See comments at Matthew 13:3. Jesus leaves most of his parables "hanging," which explains the rich diversity of opinion and commentary on them.[8]

13:19 *The evil one comes and snatches away what was sown in their heart.* For "the evil one," for references to him as the devil and [the} Satan, see comments at Matthew 4:1.

13:22 *The worries of this life and the deceitfulness of wealth choke the word.* See comments at Matthew 13:7.

13:25 *While everyone was sleeping, his enemy came and sowed weeds among the wheat, and went away.* The "enemy" pays another visit in the parable of the wheat and the weeds (Mt 13:24–30). In Jesus' explanation of the parable, the farmer's enemy stands for "the devil" (Mt 13:39). See Matthew 13:19.

13:30 *Let both grow together until the harvest. At that time I will tell the harvesters: First collect the weeds and tie them in bundles to be burned; then gather the wheat and bring it into my barn.* Harvest and harvesting are metaphors in Scripture to refer to a time of judgment, in some cases final judgment. In Jesus' parable the reference is clearly to wheat, though Israel was known for three main crops; grains, grapes, and olives. Consider Joel's oracle against the nations (Joel 3:13):

> Swing the sickle,
>   for the harvest is ripe.
> Come, trample the grapes,
>   for the winepress is full
>   and the vats overflow—
> so great is their wickedness!"

Joel indicates that the Lord will call all the nations to gather in the valley of Jehoshaphat as he sits in judgment, described here as harvesting grain (sickle), grapes (winepress), and olives (vats). Their fruit is the fruit of wickedness. Proximate to the statement "I desire mercy not sacrifice" (Hos 6:6), God says that a harvest is appointed for Judah, citing offenses such as violence, transgression, and spiritual adultery (that is, worshiping other gods; Hos 6:11). Jeremiah (51:33) employs the image of the threshing floor (grain) as a place of judgment against the daughter of Babylon. Jesus agrees with the prophets that a time of harvest is coming.

13:31-32 *The kingdom of heaven is like a mustard seed, which a man took and planted in his field.* The parable of the mustard seed is one of the best known of Jesus' sayings. As with most parables, Jesus is expressing something essential about the kingdom of heaven. Some of the language in the parable is familiar. For example, Ezekiel offers an allegory of the Messiah as a sprig of a cedar which God takes and plants on a high mountain in the midst of Israel. Eventually, the sprig grows into a noble cedar where every kind of bird lives and builds a nest in the shade of its branches (Eze 17:22–24). He employs a similar image of a cedar of Lebanon in an oracle addressed to the king of Egypt and his people (Eze 31:1–9).

Daniel records a dream of King Nebuchadnezzar and its interpretation (Da 4). In the center of the earth the king saw a great tree that reached into the heavens. Its foliage was beautiful; its fruit abundant. The animals of the field and the birds of the air found shelter and shade beneath its limbs. It presented an idyllic setting that was disturbed by the message of a watcher from heaven (Da 4:13–17).

Psalm 104 is dedicated to God's good creation and providential care for the earth. At one point (vv. 10–13), God is described as making the springs flow from the mountains to water the valleys. Wild animals and birds find their habitation there, and the birds sing among the branches. God waters the trees and plants the cedars of Lebanon, and the birds of the air build their nests on its trustworthy branches (vv. 16–17).

The prophets and psalmist were tapping into a common image people had about the world, a hope of safety and plenty beneath the shelter of a massive tree. The irony of Jesus' parable begins with the mustard seed itself, described as the smallest of all seeds.[9] But it does grow into an impressive bush; an agricultural people would have known that. One person might call it a bush, another a tree. The language of comparison is imprecise and depends on what you are accustomed to. One person's hill is another's mountain. But clearly the contrast is between the small seed and the large bush/tree. The kingdom might begin small, almost imperceptible, but it will grow and become a place for the birds to build their nests and find shelter. By closing out the parable of the mustard seed this way, Jesus is connecting his audience to a primal story of hope and plenty. The contrast between a mustard bush/tree and a cedar of Lebanon may have generated more than one smile, like watching a king descend the Mount of Olives on a donkey.

13:33 *The kingdom of heaven is like yeast that a woman took and mixed into about sixty pounds of flour until it worked all through the dough.* The parable of the yeast has a similar theme to the parable of the mustard seed, but another thing is added. Once the yeast is hidden and worked into the dough, it permeates the whole so that there is no non-yeasty portion. Sixty pounds of flour is an enormous quantity and stands in contrast to the small mustard seed; it would create enough dough to feed a megachurch congregation. Perhaps, this is another example of Jesus' tendency to exaggerate to make a point. The point is: the kingdom of heaven infuses and influences the whole of the earth.

When the Lord appeared to Abraham by the oaks of Mamre, Abraham instructed his wife Sarah to prepare three measures (thirty-six pounds) of the best flour and make cakes for his three visitors (Ge 18:1–8). Then as now, Middle Eastern hospitality was a picture of abundance. Not only would the visitors have had plenty for a satisfying meal, but they'd have enough for the journey.

13:34–35 *Jesus spoke all these things to the crowd in parables; he did not say anything to them without using a parable. So was fulfilled what was spoken through the prophet: "I will open my mouth in parables, I will utter things hidden since the creation of the world."* Matthew returns to a familiar theme: the fulfilment of Scripture. He interrupts the series of parables with a summary to let his readers know that Jesus' habit of speaking to the crowds in parables is called for in Scripture. Then he quotes Psalm 78:2. Some may find it strange that he says, "So was fulfilled what was spoken through the prophet" (Mt 13:35), and then goes on to quote a psalm. But the term "prophet" here does not refer to a "canonical" prophet. Prophets speak throughout Scripture, not just in the categories *we designate* as prophecy.

We find ample evidence that David was considered a prophet in early Christianity and in Second Temple Judaism. Josephus writes that David began to prophesy when the Spirit left Saul and came upon him (*Ant* 6.8.2). Furthermore, he claims that David had special access to visions of things past and to come (*Ant* 8.4.2). The sectarians who composed the Dead Sea Scrolls regarded David's psalms as spoken through a prophetic spirit (*11QPsa*). Early Christians agreed. The author of Acts confidently declares that David was a prophet who knew that his dynasty would continue beyond him and who spoke of the resurrection of the Messiah (Ac 2:29–31). Likewise, he writes that David prophesied by the Spirit regarding Judas, Jesus' betrayer (Ac 1:16). David, then, is clearly regarded as a prophet, and the psalter identified with him possessed a particular prophetic power.

Prophets in Israel do a variety of things. Not only do they foretell God's plans for the future, they often interpret what God is up to in the present. In some cases, prophets reflect over Israel's history and bring that history to bear on God's people past, present, and future. So prophets were also teachers, teachers of God's word and will. Psalm 78 functions in exactly this way;[10] it recites Israel's history for the instruction of future generations (Ps 78:1–4). Matthew sees Jesus' instruction to the crowds as serving the same purpose and employing the same methods.

13:36–40 *His disciples came to him and said, "Explain to us the parable of the weeds in the field." He answered, "The one who sowed the good seed is the Son of Man."* Jesus explains the parable allegorically. It has to do with the way of the kingdom in this age and the end of the age. The kingdom consists of both wheat and weeds until a future day of reckoning. Not only does the Son of Man sow good seed, but he also executes the harvest by sending out angels who will separate the sinners and unrighteous from the righteous. (For "the Son of Man," see comments on Matthew 8:20.)

13:41–43 *The Son of Man will send out his angels, and they will weed out of his kingdom everything that causes sin and all who do evil. . . . Then the righteous will shine like the sun in the kingdom of their Father. Whoever has ears, let them hear.* Jesus' description of the judgment has an apocalyptic flair, in part because it echoes the final chapter of Daniel. The prophet tells of a future when Daniel's people, those whose names are found in the book, are delivered. Many who sleep in the dust awake to eternal life, and others awake to eternal shame. The wise shine like the stars in the sky (Da 12:1–3). The forever-destinies of the two, like the wheat and the weeds, are set after the general resurrection. Similarly, we read the final words of King David who describes two destinies. The just ruler of the people is like the light of the morning, like the sun rising on a cloudless day. But the godless are to be cast aside and consumed with fire (2 Sa 23:1–7). (For "Son of Man," see comments on Mt 8:20.)

13:42 *They will throw them into the blazing furnace, where there will be weeping and gnashing of teeth.* The furnace represents judgment, in this case, final judgment. This accords with the harvest-judgment theme. Hearers and/or readers of the gospel may recall the time when Nebuchadnezzar fashioned an immense golden statue and ordered all the nations under his rule to fall down and worship it. Those who refused were to be cast into a furnace that blazed with fire (Da 3:1–7). Shadrach, Meshach, and Abednego, out of allegiance to YHWH, refused the order but escaped the king's ire (Da 3:8–30). But from the furnace Jesus describes there is no escape.

For the expression "weeping and gnashing of teeth," see comments at Matthew 8:11–12.

13:44–46 *The kingdom of heaven is like treasure hidden in a field. When a man found it, he hid it again, and then in his joy went and sold all he had and bought that field.* In this parable Jesus appears to be trading on passages from the wisdom tradition. Proverbs 2:1–4 speaks of treasuring God's commandments, wisdom, and understanding. The one who searches for it (wisdom) will find the knowledge of God. Proverbs 3 goes on to itemize the benefits that accrue to one who seeks and finds wisdom (e.g., a long life, health, a good reputation, guidance through life, sufficient to abundant wealth). Another wisdom book offers a proverb, noting that as long as wisdom is hidden and treasure undiscovered, it has no value (Sirach 20:30). Jesus relates the kingdom of heaven to wisdom and its acquisition to joy.

The merchant's search for the pearl of great price (Mt 13:45–46) deals with a similar theme.

13:47 *Once again, the kingdom of heaven is like a net that was let down into the lake and caught all kinds of fish.* The parable of the net is similar to the parable of the wheat and the weeds. There are two ways, two destinies, portrayed in the catch of fish. The two ways are reflected in Psalm 1, a wisdom psalm that poetically illustrates the lives and future of the righteous (a tree planted by streams of water) and the wicked (chaff that the wind drives away). The righteous prosper in all they do, and they will stand in the judgment. By contrast the wicked are temporary, and their way will perish.

Jesus' parable assumes the practices of those who fished on the Sea of Galilee. Their nets would indiscriminately drag up all sorts of fish, kosher and nonkosher.[11] Their first task after catching the fish would have been to divide them into two groups. Habakkuk 1:14 does depict people like the fish of the sea and crawling things (on the ground) that have no leader. The parable of the net may have to do with Jesus' commission to his disciples to fish for people (Mt 4:19). Images of judgment are often linked with fishing language as well (Jer 16:16; Eze 32:3; Am 4:2).

13:50 *And throw them into the blazing furnace.* Jesus' language here echoes the Greek version of Daniel 3:6. See comments at Matthew 13:42.

There will be weeping and gnashing of teeth. For this expression, see comments at Matthew 8:11–12.

13:53–57 *A prophet is not without honor except in his own town and in his own home.* Jesus finished his parables and went back to his hometown, Nazareth, to preach and teach in the synagogue. At first the people were astounded and moved by his teaching, but as they thought about it, Jesus was just too familiar. After all, he grew up in that town and was the carpenter's son. They knew his mother and his siblings. Their amazement turned to resentment. Chris Keith makes a compelling case that part of what put Jesus in jeopardy with the "scribal elite" was his status as a "teacher."[12] According to them, he was a simple laborer, untrained, and illiterate, and because of his popularity, they resented and deplored him.

Jesus' statement about a prophet's honor has roots in Jeremiah, who, for good reason, is called "the weeping prophet." There are series of laments in the book of Jeremiah.[13] The first is recorded in Jeremiah 11:18–23. Apparently, in his hometown, Anathoth, there was a plot to assassinate him. At the heart of the complaint against Jeremiah is that he apparently brands their prophets and priests as false. He brings his grievance to God, and God promises to intervene and punish the sons and daughters of Anathoth for their gall and evil schemes. Jeremiah describes himself as a gentle lamb led to the slaughter, which sounds like Isaiah 53:7. There are other plots against his life alluded to in the book (Jer 18:18–23). It is clear from the public persecution that his message and actions are unwelcome among his own people.

Amos too had his troubles. Amaziah, the royal priest of the shrine at Bethel, sent a message to King Jeroboam of Israel that Amos was conspiring against him in the center of Israel. He banned the seer from the sanctuary and told him to flee south, to the land of Judah. He told him never to show his face again in the king's shrine (Am 7:10–17).

There are other cases too, not all of which are documented in Holy Scripture, but the writer of Hebrews describes some of what he has heard (Heb 11:36–38): "Some [heroes of faith] faced jeers and flogging, and even chains and imprisonment. They were put to death by stoning; they were sawed in two; they were killed by the sword. They went about in sheepskins and goatskins, destitute, persecuted and mistreated—the world was not worthy of them. They wandered in deserts and mountains, living in caves and in holes in the ground."

The rejection of the Hebrew prophets is further documented in Scripture. For example, the spirit of God came upon Zechariah, the son of the priest Jehoiada, who prophesied a message that offended King Joash. The king directed officials to stone Zechariah to death in the court of the temple (2 Ch 24:20–22). Jeremiah recounts the story of another prophet, Uriah, son of Shemaiah from Kiriath-jearim, whose ministry and message were like his own. Uriah's word disturbed King Jehoiakim so much that he ordered him killed. The doomed prophet fled for a time to Egypt, but officials there cooperated in his capture and extradition back to the king, who struck him down with the sword (Jer 26:20–24). Other stories of the martyrdom of prophets found their way into oral traditions. Citing other biblical and extrabiblical evidence, William Lane says calmly, "The price of fidelity to God was often intense suffering."[14]

Jesus did not do many wonders there in Nazareth because of their unbelief. It is not that Jesus needed their faith in order to do a miracle; he chose not to do them.[15]

Jesus' comment on the harsh treatment that prophets endured leads directly into the story of the death of John the Baptist (Mt 14), another prophet without honor.

Matthew 13 Through Old Testament Eyes

Matthew collects a number of parables Jesus told—likely at many times throughout his ministry—and concentrates them in what we call Matthew 13. This is the third of five discourses in the gospel. He is addressing both the crowds gathering around him—some just curiosity seekers— and his disciples. The parable (Hebrew, *mashal*) form itself is found in Jewish literature from the period. We see it, for example, in the story the prophet Nathan told King David (2 Sa 12:1–7). Nathan sets before David a presumably real account of a rich man taking a lamb from a poor man to throw a party for friends. Nathan then asks the king to decide what should be done to deliver justice to the poor man. When David passes judgment on the rich man, he passes judgment on himself, for he was the rich man Nathan had in mind in his parable. We find another, prominent example in Isaiah's poetry, the song of the vineyard (Isa 5:1–7). The comparison made is between a select vineyard that yielded only sour grapes and Israel/Judah who were God's pleasant planting where injustice and unrighteousness reigned. As a result, judgment was sure to come.

MATTHEW 14

14:4 *John had been saying to him [Herod Antipas]: "It is not lawful for you to have her."* John's steady attack on Herod Antipas over marrying Herodias, his brother's wife, led to the prophet's capture, arrest, and imprisonment at Machaerus (Josephus, *Ant* 18.109–19). John's criticism was based on the part of the Torah dedicated to regulating against sexual improprieties. It rules out bestiality (Lev 18:23), sexual intercourse with menstruating women (18:19), male homosexuality (18:22), adultery (18:20), and incest (18:6–18). Perhaps the most relevant commandment to Herod's situation was this (18:16): "Do not have sexual relations with your brother's wife; that would dishonor your brother." God himself punishes this kind of impurity by making sure the illicit couple remain childless (20:21). The law of levirate marriage (Dt 25:5–10) was not applicable in this case because Herodias' first husband, Herod Philip (not the tetrarch) still lived. Herod Antipas had to desert his first wife in order to marry Herodias. So, against any meaningful reasoning with the law, Herod's marriage with Herodias was illegitimate.[1]

14:6–12 *On Herod's birthday the daughter of Herodias danced for the guests and pleased Herod so much that he promised with an oath to give her whatever she asked.* Herod's rash oath has much in common with the promise made to Queen Esther by King Ahasuerus (Xerxes I). The queen uncovered a plot to kill all of the Jews in the Persian Empire; it had been created and sanctioned by one of the king's advisors, Haman. The king, however, had been kept in the dark on the plan. In an attempt to stop it, Esther put herself in jeopardy by presenting herself before the king unannounced. When the king saw her standing in the court, he gave the signal and invited her into his presence. He was so enraptured by her beauty and poise, he invited her to make a request and promised it would be given to her, up to half of the kingdom. Esther's initial request was modest, on the surface: she proposed a royal dinner party for Haman, the would-be exterminator of the Jews. Three times the king speaks the brash vow to his beloved: "What is your request? Even up to half of my kingdom, it will be given you" (Est 5:3, 6; 7:2). Eventually, the plot to rid the empire of the Jews is revealed, and actions are taken to head off the pogrom. Haman gets his due when he is hung on the gallows he had built for the Jew Mordecai, Esther's uncle (Est 7). Poetic justice is justice after all.

Herod had kept John alive in prison because the Baptist enjoyed broad support among the people. The ruler uttered an oath in the presence of his guests, a word he could not easily take back. He spoke it not to his wife but to her daughter, which has a tawdry feel. Prompted by her mother, she asked for the head of John the Baptist on a platter. The king regretted his promise made in the haze of wine and desire, but he complied.

John the Baptist was in a long line of prophets who suffered at the hands of their own people. See comments at Matthew 13:53–57.

14:13–16 *Jesus replied, "They do not need to go away. You give them something to eat."* The episode known as "the feeding of the five thousand" (Mt 14:13–21) is the only miracle found in all four canonical Gospels. Some are surprised to know that Jesus' multiplication of the fishes and the loaves is not the first account of such a miracle. In 2 Kings 4:42–44 we read how a crowd of people had their fill and had some left over. A man from the village of Baal-shalishah brought to Elisha the first fruits of his garden. Elisha directed him to give it to the people so they could eat. The man expressed alarm because there was not enough food, he thought, for such a crowd. But Elijah insisted because he had had a word from the Lord. So the man complied with the prophet, and people were well fed with some left over.

Matthew Through Old Testament Eyes: Elijah and Elisha

In Matthew's gospel, we see a variety of contrasts and connections between Matthew's Jesus and the two Old Testament prophets, Elijah and his successor, Elisha (1 Ki 19:16; 2 Ki 2).[2] Both prophets represented God in the centuries following the division between the northern and southern kingdoms. They were public figures who often clashed with powerful people, just as Jesus did throughout his ministry. In the Hebrew Bible, their accounts are part of the former prophets who spoke for God in their day. For those who have not read their stories, they may be surprised to know the kind of miracles they performed. Jesus was not the first miracle worker in Israel (see Table 14.1).

Table 14.1. Elijah, Elisha, and Jesus

Elijah	Elisha	Jesus
Elijah worked alone.	Elisha worked in the company of prophets (2 Ki 2:3–18; 6:1), or with his "bumbling sidekick," Gehazi (2 Ki 4–5; 8).	Jesus worked in community with his often "bumbling sidekicks," the disciples (Mt 8:25–26; 16:21–23; 17:14–20; 26:56; etc.).
Elijah worked behind closed doors (1 Ki 17:8–24); conducted much of his ministry through dramatic, public confrontations (1 Ki 18:16–40; 2 Ki 1:10–12; etc.).	Elisha worked both behind closed doors (2 Ki 4) and publicly (2 Ki 2:19–22; 5:1–19; 6:1–23; etc.).	Jesus worked both behind closed doors (Mt 9:25) and publicly (Mt 8, etc.).
Elijah spent most of his time outside Israel.	Elisha spent most of his time within Israel.	Jesus spent most of his time within Israel's borders. Exceptions included his time in Egypt (Mt 2:13–21) and in Tyre and Sidon (Mt 15:21–28).
Elijah performed miracles publicly and privately: some challenged the authorities (1 Ki 17–18); he multiplied food (1 Ki 17:8–16); raised the dead (1 Ki 17:17–24); performed nature miracles (1 Ki 17:1–7); in the end he was taken up into heaven (2 Ki 2:1–12).	Elisha performed miracles publicly and privately: he purified water and food (2 Ki 2:19–22; 4:38–41); multiplied food (2 Ki 4:1–7, 42–44); raised the dead (2 Ki 4:8–37); healed the sick (2 Ki 5:1–18); performed nature miracles (2 Ki 6:1–7).	Jesus performed miracles publicly and privately: some challenged opponents (Mt 12:9–14); he healed the sick (Mt 9:2–8); performed nature miracles (Mt 8:23–27); exorcized demons (Mt 8:28–34); raised the dead (Mt 9:18–26); in the end he is taken up into heaven (Lk 24:50–53). (See "Matthew 11:4–6 Through Old Testament Eyes: Jesus' Miracles" and "Matthew 11 Through Old Testament Eyes").

14:19 *Taking the five loaves and the two fish and looking up to heaven, he gave thanks and broke the loaves. Then he gave them to the disciples, and the disciples gave them to the people.*

Jesus' particular prayer posture is described in Psalm 123, a prayer for deliverance from one's enemies. It begins (123:1–2):

> I lift up my eyes to you,
>> to you who sit enthroned in heaven.
> As the eyes of slaves look to the hand of their master,
>> as the eyes of a female slave look to the hand of her mistress,
> so our eyes look to the LORD our God,
>> till he shows us his mercy.

The psalmist's posture is one of a servant who is always attuned to the hand of the master. Since God is high and lifted up, enthroned in heaven, then God's servants look up into the heavens to seek God where he can be found. Jesus, the ultimate Servant of YHWH, models the posture of prayer for his disciples.

Going Deeper into Blessing God for Food: Matthew 14:19

Prayerfully, Jesus gives thanks to God for the food. Some interpret the word translated "give thanks" as "bless," as if Jesus "blesses the food." That is not Matthew's intent. The food is already a blessing, since it comes from God's hand and the good earth. What is right and proper is for the servant of God to give thanks or *to bless God for the food*. We do not know the exact words of Jesus' blessing, but one of the earliest blessings (*birkat hamazon*) is this:

> *Barukh ata Adonai Eloheinu, melekh ha'olam, hamotzi lehem min ha'aretz.*

> Blessed are you Lord our God, king of the world, who brings forth bread from the earth.

The biblical basis cited for blessing God for food is found in Deuteronomy 8:7–10. Before the children of God enter the land of promise, Moses warns the people to remember God's provision for them or else they may give themselves credit for their successes. The Lord, he said, is bringing you to a good land crisscrossed with streams and dotted with cool springs flowing through valleys and hills. It will grow wheat, barley, grapes, figs, pomegranates, olives, and honey. The people will eat without scarcity. The prophet concludes (Dt 8:10), "When you have eaten and are satisfied, praise the LORD your God for the good land he has given you." A later Jewish tradition describes Moses as instituting the first blessing when manna descended from heaven (*b. Berakhot* 48b).

When we eat a meal or receive any good gift in life, we ought to give thanks the way Jesus did. God is the source of every good meal or good gift. The words we use do not matter. A rote prayer of thanks can be as genuine as some prayer you make up on the spot. What matters is stopping and recognizing God, remembering God daily. It is harder to fall headlong into sin when, on a regular basis, you are stopping to say "thanks."

14:20 *They all ate and were satisfied, and the disciples picked up twelve basketfuls of broken pieces that were left over.* The feeding of the crowd of more than five thousand reminds a careful listener how God fed Israel in the wilderness with manna (Ex 16:15–18) and a miraculous catch of quail (Nu 11:31–32). The twelve basketfuls of fragments of fish and bread left over may correspond to the Twelve, Jesus' insider disciples. Each apparently participated in the distribution of the food and the collection of fragments at the end. None were idle during this miracle. (See comments at Mt 10:1.) John Nolland describes the number as "symbolic: food for all Israel."[3]

14:23 *He went up on a mountainside by himself to pray.* Moses likewise went up on a mountain by himself to be with God (Ex 19:3; see also "Matthew 4:8 Through Old Testament Eyes: Mountains.")

14:25 *Shortly before dawn Jesus went out to them, walking on the lake.* The episode of Jesus walking on the water has some resonance with the earlier account, when Jesus calmed the storm (Mt 8:23–27). At the heart of it is the conviction that Jesus has power over nature; such miracles resonate with Old Testament texts that describe God's authority over creation, especially the seas. Perhaps the most memorable miracle involving God's power over the sea is the exodus when the Lord drove back the sea so the former slaves might walk through on dry ground, the quintessential Old Testament act of redemption (Ex 14:21–22). Prophets and poets celebrate that miracle in a variety of ways. Isaiah, for example, echoes how God dried up the sea, creating a highway through the depths so the redeemed could cross to the other side (Isa 51:9–10). Similarly, Psalm 77 offers the following recollection of the miracle (77:19–20):

> Your path led through the sea,
>   your way through the mighty waters,
>   though your footprints were not seen.
>
> You led your people like a flock
>   by the hand of Moses and Aaron.

God left no footprints on the sea or dry land as he made his way ahead of his flock on the way to freedom. Though the gospel does not say, we'd scarcely see Jesus' footprints on the water either. Only God can make a way through the sea, especially the chaotic, turbulent waters. They have been defeated by YHWH (cf. Job 9:8). This fundamental belief informed Matthew's audience of hearers and readers. Jesus clearly must be recognized as one with God. His next words underscore his divine status.

Richard Hays proposes that Mark's account of Jesus walking on the water (Mk 6:45–52)—which likely Matthew uses with some modification—is shaped by Job 9:4–11. In Job's poetic response to Bildad, he describes God as the Creator who moves mountains, shakes the earth, stretches out the heavens, and *tramples the seas*. He does things far beyond human comprehension. The passage ends (Job 9:11 NRSV): "Look, he passes by me, and I do not see him; he moves on, but I do not perceive him." Uniquely, Mark records that Jesus came toward his disciples as they strained against the oars, walking on the lake and "was about to pass by them" (Mk 6:48). That phrase has baffled interpreters but may well be explained by appeal to Job 9:11.[4] For reasons only Matthew knows, he did not include it in his gospel. Regardless, with Mark as the most likely source for Matthew's gospel, the account echoes and links Jesus to Job's description of the acts of God.[5]

14:27 *But Jesus immediately said to them: "Take courage! It is I. Don't be afraid."* In the Old Testament, only YHWH walks on the water (Job 9:8; Ps 77:19; Isa 43:2, 16), but in the gospel so does Jesus. Like YHWH, Jesus demonstrates power over the storm. Uttering three "staccato phrases"—"Take courage! It is I. Don't be afraid."—Jesus gives them a reason to be calm.[6]

When the disciples saw Jesus walking toward them on the sea, they were understandably terrified. They had never experienced anything like this before. Jesus spoke words of comfort, words that echo excerpts of Moses's final speeches to the children of Israel before they set foot in the promised land (Dt 31:3, 6):

The LORD your God himself will cross over ahead of you. He will destroy these nations before you, and you will take possession of their land. Joshua also will cross over ahead of you, as the LORD said. . . .

Be strong and courageous. Do not be afraid or terrified because of them [the peoples in the land], for the LORD your God goes with you; he will never leave you nor forsake you.

Moses is one hundred twenty years old and will not accompany the children of Israel any further, but the Lord God is going ahead of them, crossing over the Jordan. The water will once again part, not so that God can go through but so the people can. In a sense, God has already gone ahead. And God will take on the nations so Israel can possess the land. Still the people were understandably afraid, so Moses spoke words of comfort, inspiring strength and courage with the assurance the Lord goes "with you." That phrase "with you" takes us back to the beginning of Matthew's gospel when Jesus is given the name Immanuel, God with us.

Matthew 14:27 Through Old Testament Eyes: "I AM"

The interpretation above is not far-fetched because of what Jesus said in the midst of his encouragement to the disciples. After he says, "Take courage!" he identifies himself. The translation "It is I" is probably too weak. Literally, he says, "I AM." Though capable of multiple levels of interpretation, a seasoned reader of Scripture would think immediately of Moses's first encounter with YHWH on Mt. Sinai. The reluctant prophet asks God for his name (Ex 3:14–15, author's translation):

God said to Moses, "I AM WHO I AM, This is what you are to say to the Israelites: 'I AM has sent me to you.'"

God also said to Moses, "Say to the Israelites, 'YHWH, the God of your fathers—the God of Abraham, the God of Isaac and the God of Jacob—has sent me to you.'

"This is my name forever,
    the name you shall call me
    from generation to generation."

It would be hard to overestimate the significance of Moses's encounter. God's name, YHWH, becomes the covenant name of God. It is found more than six thousand times in the Old Testament. It is the name protected by one of the ten commandments (Ex 20). The name is built on the Hebrew verb "to be," and at the heart of it is God's promise to "be there" with his covenant people and to go *with them* on their mission to be his chosen.[7] Jesus' self-identification is a not-so-subtle link connecting Jesus with the unspeakable name of God.[8]

14:32-33 *And when they [Peter and Jesus] climbed into the boat, the wind died down. Then those who were in the boat worshiped him, saying, "Truly you are the Son of God."* As in the earlier account (8:23–27), the storm roils to a stop, this time when Jesus entered the boat. The disciples seem to hear and understand something more of his significance as a result of this experience. The people in the boat worshiped Jesus, confessing that he is truly the Son of God. The word *worship* here means essentially to bow down. It is a word about their posture, but also about their allegiance. They are professing "faith" in Jesus. The same word "worship" will be used again, on the other side of the resurrection, as the disciples encounter Jesus on the mount of commission (Mt 28:17–20). The title "Son of God" could mean no more than Israel's rightful king, but there is more to it in this story, especially in light of the disciples' worship of Jesus. The title "Son of God" takes on an increasingly potent significance in the gospel, directing the hearers and readers to see Jesus as a man of transcendent stature.[9]

In one of Job's descriptions of God in his majesty, he depicts him as having the power to control the seas (Job 26:12). Likewise, in a psalm of thanksgiving God is hailed as one who silences the roaring of the waves of the sea (Ps 65:7). In yet another psalm giving thanks to God for rescue, YHWH is credited with both creating the storm (Ps 107:23–27) and stilling it (Ps 107:28–29) in response to prayers for help. In the Old Testament, God is the only one with such powers. Matthew seems to suggest that this ability of Jesus comes from his participation in God's unique identity.

14:36 *[The people] begged him to let the sick just touch the edge of his cloak, and all who touched it were healed.* The "edge of his cloak" could also be translated "the fringe of his cloak." Perhaps the story of the woman healed by touching the fringe of his garment earlier (see comments at Mt 9:20) had become common news.

MATTHEW 15

15:2 *Why do your disciples break the tradition of the elders? They don't wash their hands before they eat!* Another charge leveled against Jesus by his opponents was that he ignored the tradition of the elders and taught his disciples to do the same. In this case, it had to do with a ritual of washing the hands prior to a meal (literally, "bread"). The charge is made by Pharisees and scribes who had traveled to Galilee from Jerusalem. The Pharisees were champions of tradition. In addition to Scripture (written Torah), they had developed an oral Torah that they claimed went back to Moses at Sinai (*m. Abot* 1.1). The oral Torah is otherwise known as "the tradition of the elders," and it applied the Scripture to everyday life and practice.

There is no explicit teaching in Scripture about washing prior to a meal. But the Pharisees found ample basis for this tradition in the ways they read and interpreted the Old Testament. Consider God's instruction to Moses to fashion a bronze basin and a stand that stood between the tent of meeting and the altar. The priests (Aaron and his sons) were to wash their hands and their feet prior to going into God's presence to offer a sacrifice. This was described as a perpetual ordinance for them and their descendants (Ex 30:17–21).

Over time the instruction is expanded, in part, because after a meal one is to recite a blessing to God. Filthy hands were unworthy of a priest in the temple; likewise, they are not appropriate to recite a blessing to God after meals (*b. Berakhot* 53b). It ends up a matter of holiness (Lev 20:26). We might also point to Leviticus 15:11, which implies that washing one's hand removes ritual uncleanness. For the Pharisees, it was not so much an issue of hygiene but striving toward ritual cleanliness. It is difficult to tell how deeply entrenched this practice was for most people at the time. But Pharisees were not most people. Compared to the *hoi polloi*, they were more rigorous in their observance of the law and traditions that protected them.[1] From their perspective, Jesus and his disciples were styling themselves as righteous, yet they were not doing what righteousness required.

15:3-4 *For God said, "Honor your father and mother" and "Anyone who curses their father or mother is to be put to death."* Jesus answered their question with a question: Why do you violate the clear teaching of the commandments in order to observe your traditions? The example he gives comes from the Ten Commandments and their application. The truly pious are to prioritize the respect for parents and protecting their honor. The command to honor father and mother is found first in Exodus 20:12; it is repeated in Deuteronomy 5:16. Jesus summarizes the commandment but does not include the promise that their days may be long in the land the Lord God is giving them (Ex 20:12; Dt 5:16). He quickly refers to another commandment based upon a situation when a child curses either father or mother (Ex 21:17; Lev 20:9). A curse was considered a powerful word (Nu 22:6), so it must be dealt with powerfully. Its punishment is the same as when someone strikes a parent (Ex 21:15). In both cases the child is to be put to death.

15:5 *But you say that if anyone declares that what might have been used to help their father or mother is "devoted to God."* There is no expiration date on honoring one's parents. The care of aging parents is part of what it means to honor them. But the so-called pious had figured out a way around that commandment by devoting some of what they had to the temple and its upkeep. Once some property or possession was declared "Corban" (Mk 7:11), it could not be sold because it was temple property. But the owners could still make use of it as long as they wished. Parents could and did become destitute in the shadow of this vow.[2] The misuse of Corban provided a way to avoid keeping God's law. The fault was not with the law but with those who misappropriated it. The tradition of honoring one's parents is a noble one and should be followed. But those who intentionally misuse the tradition are the culprits here.

15:7-9 *You hypocrites! Isaiah was right when he prophesied about you: "These people honor me with their lips, but their hearts are far from me. They worship me in vain; their teachings are merely human rules."* Ironically, the Pharisees and scribes who had come from Jerusalem to chastise and check up on Jesus were fulfilling Scripture—not in the way Jesus did, but in their own, hypocritical way. Isaiah prophesied about them (and people like them) in an oracle we read in Isaiah 29. Jesus' quotation follows closely the Greek version of the prophecy (Isa 29:13, LXX). The accusation is that these "pious ones" are only going through the motions. They are incapable or perhaps unwilling to do the harder stuff, drawing near to God with their hearts. They can make rules and enforce them. They can "worship," but it comes to nothing. Publicly, they shine; privately, they hide in shadows (Isa 29:15–16). Remarkably, the oracle goes on to a complete reversal. Despite the growing darkness, God promises to do wonderful things, startling things, for his people. He gives no detail as to what he will do, except to render every expression of human wisdom null and void (Isa 29:14). It is probably not too hard to say—from Matthew's and Jesus' perspective—that the shocking and amazing things God planned were taking place in Galilee right before their eyes.

15:11 *What goes into someone's mouth does not defile them, but what comes out of their mouth, that is what defiles them.* When Jesus wanted to explain himself, he often turned to the crowds. In this saying, he makes clear what the Pharisees had obscured by their allegiance to the traditions of the elders: what comes out of you defiles you, not what goes in.

With Matthew's ample use of Isaiah, we might expect that the narrative of the prophet's call would have a prominent place within Jesus' teaching. In the year of King Uzziah's death (758 BC), Isaiah experienced a theophany, a vision of YHWH in his temple (Isa 6). The vision of absolute holiness made him cry out (Isa 6:5): "'Woe to me!' I cried. 'I am ruined! For I am a man of unclean lips, and I live among a people of unclean lips, and my eyes have seen the King, the Lord Almighty.'" For a sinful person to see God is to approach death. And what issue causes Isaiah the most angst? Answer: what has come out of his mouth and through his lips. From Isaiah it is clear that what comes out of a people can defile them. Jesus reflects Isaiah's depiction of his awe-filled visionary experience.

Going Deeper into Legalism: Matthew 15:1–20

For good reason, Jesus accused *some* Pharisees of legalism, but that did not mean that the Jewish religion was inherently legalistic. The same criticism could be leveled against Christianity, or any religion for that matter—just because some Christians approach life legalistically does not mean the Christian faith in and of itself is legalistic. We must distance the faith from those who practice it wrongfully. But in Jesus' day, as in ours, the question of what "defiles" was a matter of significant debate. Jesus comes down on a side with scriptural precedents.

We should be clear. The problem is not the law, but how to keep the law. Jesus never advocated that the law be set aside. He came to fulfill it, not abolish it (Mt 5:17). But legalism lurks around the edges. It is tragically common to transform a living faith into judgmental attitudes about others who do not live the life the way we do. Perhaps you have felt the harsh gaze or heard the hateful words of people ready to condemn but not extend mercy. When rules regulate a person's life more than anything else, those rules or standards become idols.

When Hezekiah cleansed the city of Jerusalem before he led the nation in celebrating the Passover, it became clear that many of the "worshipers" had not followed the purity regulations. Yet the king prayed to God for their pardon and God granted his request (2 Ch 30:18–20). On this occasion, purity was not achieved by performance of rituals but by the intercession of the king. Similarly, Psalm 24 asks an important question: Who can enter the sanctuary and be in the presence of "the King of glory"? The requirements are not ritual but moral—that is, the person with clean hands, pure heart, and in whom there is no deception. In both cases, purity is not a matter of performing a particular ritual; it is a matter of personal and communal morality.[3]

15:13–14 *He [Jesus] replied, "Every plant that my heavenly Father has not planted will be pulled up by the roots. Leave them; they are blind guides. If the blind lead the blind, both will fall into a pit."* It was not uncommon for the prophets to describe Israel as a people God had "planted." Agricultural people, like those who lived in the Fertile Crescent, were constantly planting wheat, barley, and grapes. We see this theme expressed memorably in the song of the vineyard (Isa 5). God plants the best land with the best vines, yet it yields only bad fruit. God threatens to abandon it and leave it to the elements.

Jeremiah, from the other side of judgment, laments over Jerusalem's destiny as God's vineyard. Wicked shepherds had crept in, trampled the vines and turned it into a wasteland (Jer 12:10–12). Yet even this is mysteriously God's doing. We see the planting theme expressed in judgment but also in restoration. Isaiah speaks of a time when God's covenant with Abraham (e.g., Ge 12:1–3; 18:18) will at last be fulfilled. God's righteous people will possess the land because they are the shoot that God planted (Isa 60:21).

Yet not all who can trace their lineage back to Abraham are righteous. They are not the people the heavenly Father has planted; they will be pulled up like weeds in the harvest. No doubt Jesus has in mind those who appear constantly as his accusers and detractors in the gospel. He describes them as "blind guides" (Mt 23:16; 23:24) who will fall into a pit. So it would be foolish to follow them.

We have several examples from Scripture of the unrighteous or the enemies of God's people likened to those who fall into a pit. Isaiah addresses the inhabitants of the earth who deal treacherously with God's elect. When the sound of terror arises, they will flee and fall into a pit; then they will make their way out of the pit only to be caught in a snare (Isa 24:17–18). Jeremiah has a similar oracle, but it focuses on the nation of Moab (Jer 48:44). Proverbs describes the essence of poetic justice: whoever sets a trap will be caught by it; whoever digs a pit will fall into it (Pr 26:27). That principle is liturgized in a prayer of deliverance (Ps 7). Surrounded by enemies, the psalmist begs God to intervene, and God rescues his servant by turning the adversaries' mischief back on their heads. They will build a pit and a snare, only to be caught by them (Ps 7:14–17).

15:22 *A Canaanite woman from that vicinity came to him, crying out, "Lord, Son of David, have mercy on me! My daughter is demon-possessed and suffering terribly."* For those with Old Testament eyes, Jesus' encounter with the Canaanite woman evokes Elijah's with the widow of Zarephath (1 Ki 17:8–24). Elijah the prophet stood toe-to-toe with King Ahab when he prophesied a period of drought in Israel that would be eased only by his word. Afterward, God told the prophet to go hide east of the Jordan River. Then he directed him to travel to Zarephath, in the vicinity of Sidon (Gentile territory), not far from where Jesus ran into the Canaanite woman. The woman Elijah met there was so poor she had reached the end of her means, but God provided miraculously for her through the prophet whom she welcomed and assisted. When her son became ill and died, the prophet Elijah cried to the Lord three times so that the child might live. And God granted the boy life once again. A miracle had come through a son of Israel to a daughter of Eve and son of Adam—premonitions of things to come.

Tradition has it that the Canaanites descended from Ham, the cursed son of Noah (Ge 9:25). They were the people who inhabited the land prior to the slow and gradual conquest that pushed them north and toward the sea.[4] The people of Israel lived among the Canaanites, intermarried with them, and took to their gods, including Baal (Jdg 3:5–7). The prophet Hosea describes how God will punish his people for going after other lovers/gods (Hos 2:13). The history between Israel and the Canaanites was tense and fraught with difficulties. So it is no wonder that the disciples wanted to see Jesus dismiss this woman with hardly a thought.

The woman calls out to Jesus in words reminiscent of the psalms: "Have mercy on me, Lord" (e.g., Ps 6:2; 30:10; 86:3).[5] This is the language of prayer. She addresses Jesus as "Lord," which in the psalms could refer to only one, the God of Israel. This address is completely in keeping with the designation of Jesus from the beginning as Immanuel, God with us.

For the address, "Son of David," see comments at Matthew 1:1 and 9:27. Though an outsider, she is turning to Israel's Messiah to help her and her daughter in their distress.

15:24–27 *He [Jesus] answered, "I was sent only to the lost sheep of Israel."* Jesus had instructed his disciples not to go to the Gentiles or Samaritans, only to "the lost sheep of Israel." See Matthew 10:6. Yet Jesus' acquiescence to the pleas of the centurion (Mt 8:5–13) and to the Canaanite woman (Mt 15:21–28) signal that a time had come to expand his mission. This appears to be confirmed by yet another centurion, a Gentile indeed, who saw what happened at Jesus' death and said, "Truly, this man was the Son of God!" (Mt 27:54, author's translation). Jesus' response, of course, was not to the woman but to the disciples. Yet, the woman's persistence, prostration, and skillful answer to Jesus about the children's food demonstrated a laudable level of faith. In the feeding miracle a chapter earlier (Mt 14:13–21), Jesus anticipated the woman's skillful answer to him; each disciple collected "twelve basketfuls of broken pieces" (Mt 14:20). In the leftovers of the miraculous meal, we can also see the table scraps to feed the "dogs" (Mt 15:27; cf. Mt 15:29–39).

15:28 *Then Jesus said to her, "Woman, you have great faith! Your request is granted."* And her daughter was healed at that moment. The prophet Isaiah foresaw such a day when he wrote (Isa 60:1–3):

> Arise, shine, for your light has come,
>   and the glory of the LORD rises upon you.
> See, darkness covers the earth
>   and thick darkness is over the peoples,
> but the LORD rises upon you
>   and his glory appears over you.
> Nations will come to your light,
>   and kings to the brightness of your dawn.

In Jesus and the movement he spawns the light of the world had come (Mt 5:14–16). And the nations stream to the light. The woman's faith in Jesus who is light is rewarded, and the darkness of disease is dispelled from her home. The same sentiment is found in Psalm 67, a prayer by the people seeking God's blessing. Once again, the image of light dawns when the psalmist asks God to be gracious and to let his face shine upon them. But this is no self-centered desire. The blessing makes it possible for God's ways to be known throughout the earth and for all the peoples of the earth to praise him (67:1–4; cf., Ps 148, a hymn of praise for all creation). Likewise, we should probably note the final chapter of Malachi. He speaks of a day to come when the sun of righteousness rises; he has healing in his wings for everyone who reveres God's name (Mal 4:1–2). The healing that graces the Canaanite woman's home stands in fulfillment of that prophecy.

15:29 *He went up on a mountainside and sat down.* See "Matthew 4:8 Through Old Testament Eyes: Mountains."

15:31 *The people were amazed when they saw the mute speaking, the crippled made well, the lame walking and the blind seeing. And they praised the God of Israel.* Instinctively the crowds respond to these wonderful miracles with praise and adoration to "the God of Israel." That phrase, "the God of Israel," is repeated over and over in the Hebrew Bible. Most often it stands in apposition to the divine name: YHWH, the God of Israel (e.g., Jos 13:33; 24:23; Jdg 4:6; 11:23; 1 Sa 10:18). From his deathbed King David uttered this blessing: "Praise be to the LORD [YHWH], the God of Israel, who has allowed my eyes to see a successor on my throne today" (1 Ki 1:48). The occasion was his selection of Solomon to be king after him in fulfillment of 2 Samuel 7:12–16. Psalm 68, a psalm filled with intertextual echoes, celebrates the victory of YHWH over his foes. The divine warrior rides upon the clouds as he takes his place of authority over the people of Israel (Ps 68:4). The nations are called to sing to God, awesome in his sanctuary, the God of Israel (Ps 68:32–35). As God of covenant and victory, he now shows his hand by extending a healing hand to the sick and diseased. For such is the kingdom of heaven.

What the Structure Means:
The Feeding Miracles (Mt 14:13–21 and 15:32–39)

The feeding of the four thousand is a second witness to Jesus' power to feed the crowds. The two episodes stand in parallel to one another (see the comments on Mt 14:16, 19, 20). As we have seen, Matthew has an affinity to things in twos; that is built into the structure of his gospel. As God had fed the hungry Israelites in the wilderness (Ex 16), so now Jesus will feed those who are on the margins of discipleship. For three days they have been "with him" who is God with us (Mt 15:32). They had hung on his words and watched his wonders. Their presence with him for three days anticipates the three days of waiting between the crucifixion and resurrection. In this feeding uniquely, there is the note of Jesus' compassion for the crowd.

The seven rounds of (flat) bread are enough to feed the crowds to satisfaction and then have seven baskets full of leftovers (Mt 15:37). The number seven, of course, is related to completeness and to creation (Ge 1:1–2:4), and ultimately to the Sabbath, a day God blessed and hallowed (Ex 20:8–11; Dt 5:14–15). Seven is also the number of nations surrounding Israel. Moses lists seven nations that God will drive out despite their superior strength (Dt 7:1; see also Ac 13:19). Though it is unclear, the crowd Jesus addresses, heals, and ultimately feeds may have been comprised mainly of Gentiles. The location is unknown, but the fact that Jesus took a boat to the area of Magadan, or Magdala (Mt 15:39), appears to support a predominately Gentile territory, north or east of the town. If so, the number seven could suggest that Jesus' mission extends to all nations. The two feedings, then, would together represent all people, since the twelve baskets left over at the first feeding of the five thousand suggested that Jesus abundantly feeds the twelve tribes of Israel (see comments on Mt 14:20). Thus we may see in this second feeding Jesus' deeper investment in a Gentile mission.

15:32–38 *They all ate and were satisfied. . . . The number of those who ate was four thousand men, besides women and children.* How Jesus provided food in public rhymes with what Elijah and Elisha did in private homes. Elijah, when fleeing from King Ahab, came into the company of the widow of Zarephath, who benefited from prophet's presence by having a seemingly endless supply of flour and oil (1 Ki 17:14–16). Similarly, Elisha happened upon a widow in danger of losing her two sons to creditors, and he provided her with a home business through a supply of oil sufficient to be sold to provide for her family (2 Ki 4:1–7).

MATTHEW 16

16:1 *The Pharisees and Sadducees came to Jesus and tested him by asking him to show them a sign from heaven.* As in Matthew 12:38, scribes and Pharisees come to Jesus seeking a sign; once again Jesus decries them as a wicked and adulterous generation (Mt 12:39–40; Mt 16:4). The real purpose of their public request, Matthew tells us, is to test Jesus. But it is unclear exactly what they are looking for. Are they looking for Jesus to engineer some kind of astronomical phenomenon like an eclipse or a star or a comet (Jer 10:2)? Are they challenging him to validate his ministry with some sort of incontrovertible proof from God? As we have seen with the oft-repeated phrase "kingdom of heaven," the word *heaven* had become a pious circumlocution for God in Jewish texts from the time. We see this only once in the Hebrew Bible, that is, in Daniel 4:26: [Daniel to Nebuchadnezzar] "The command to leave the stump of the tree with its roots means that your kingdom will be restored to you when you acknowledge that Heaven rules." So it could be that they are asking for Jesus to show them a sign from God.

16:4 *A wicked and adulterous generation looks for a sign, but none will be given it except the sign of Jonah.* Jesus' response to the request for a sign mirrors his response to an earlier request from the same parties. For "the sign of Jonah," see comments on Matthew 12:39–40. See also "What the Structure Means: Matthew's Pairs" at Matthew 9:15–17.

16:6–12 *Be on your guard against the yeast of the Pharisees. . . . He was not telling them to guard against the yeast used in bread, but against the teaching of the Pharisees.* In the parable of the leaven/yeast (Mt 13:33), Jesus likened the kingdom of heaven to the action of yeast in a big batch of dough. In that context, leaven had a positive influence. In this saying, however, Jesus probes the negative connotations of yeast. If the influence of the kingdom spreads and affects the whole, then so can the influence of the Pharisees.

God's instructions to the Israelites prior to leaving Egypt were to make and eat bread without yeast as they prepared for the exodus (Ex 12:8; see also 12:34, 39). Subsequent commandments regarding celebration of the Passover included cleaning out all leaven in the house for seven days and eating only unleavened bread during that time (Ex 12:19; 13:7; Dt 16:4). Offerings to YHWH were not to contain leaven with the grain (Lev 2:11). The apostle Paul, instructing the Corinthians regarding the new Passover, encourages them to clean out the old leaven of malice and evil and replace it with the unleavened bread of sincerity and truth (1 Co 5:6–8).

16:13 *When Jesus came to the region of Caesarea Philippi, he asked his disciples, "Who do people say the Son of Man is?"* According to the Gospels, the furthest north Jesus traveled was to Caesarea Philippi, a majority Gentile city about twenty-five miles north of the Sea of Galilee. It was there that Jesus posed to his disciples a question that stands at the center of Matthew's story. For the phrase "the Son of Man," see comments on Matthew 8:20. It is clear that Jesus identifies himself with "the Son of Man" because of the question he asks next: "Who do you say *I am*?" (Mt 16:15, italics added).

16:14 *They [the disciples] replied, "Some say John the Baptist; others say Elijah; and still others, Jeremiah or one of the prophets."* So who is this Son of Man? The disciples go down a list of apparently what they are hearing in the markets. For John the Baptist, see comments at Matthew 3:1–12; 11:1–15; 14:1–12. We have seen how often episodes from the life of Jesus mirror stories of Elijah. But see especially the comments at Matthew 11:14. Malachi bears witness to a robust belief that one day Elijah would return (Mal 4:5–6).

Jeremiah is also included here, but for what reason? Jeremiah is known broadly as the weeping prophet whom people opposed and persecuted (Jer 19:1–20:6; 26:1–24). He prophesied against the temple and mourned its coming destruction (Jer 7; 26:1–6). These too are characteristics of Jesus' public life. He is opposed, persecuted, and ultimately martyred. Likewise, he prophesies against the temple and mourns the coming destruction of Israel. Although his temple sermon (Mt 24) comes later in the gospel, Jesus could very well have said similar things on other occasions that were not recorded. John's gospel uniquely portrays an early incident between Jesus and the temple authorities (Jn 2:13–22). Jesus may have been known as a troublemaker on more than one Jerusalem visit. At the very least, we should note that here Jesus is described as "one of the prophets." Many Jews today regard prophecy to have ceased at the time of Ezra and Nehemiah, not long after the destruction of the first temple.

16:15–16 *"But what about you?" he [Jesus] asked. "Who do you say I am?" Simon Peter answered, "You are the Messiah, the Son of the living God."* Jesus pressed the question, made it personal. What about you? Answering for the whole, Simon Peter says, I/we believe you are the Messiah. Some translations render the statement: "You are the Christ." But "Christ" is a transliteration of the Greek word χριστός which is the translation of the Hebrew *meshiach*, the Messiah, that is, literally, the Anointed One (of God). For Messiah, see comments at Matthew 1:1.

It might look on the surface that Simon Peter is saying two things: (1) you are the Messiah; (2) you are the Son of the Living God. In fact, the second phrase stands grammatically in apposition to the first. That is to say, the second unpacks and draws out the first. To be the Messiah is to be the "Son of God." See Matthew 3:13–17 and comments. The confession by the disciples that Jesus is the Messiah is one of the highpoints of the gospel. Whatever expectations they had about the Messiah (his identity and work) had been unwritten or perhaps overwritten in light of Jesus' person and deeds.

16:18 *And I tell you that you are Peter, and on this rock I will build my church, and the gates of Hades will not overcome it.* Peter's place of primacy in church history has been built in the main on this episode. Simon's given name is supplanted by Jesus' new name for him, *Petros* (Peter), a play on the word *rock* (*petra*).[1]

Of the four New Testament Gospels, only Matthew uses the word *church*. It comes to refer to the "assembly" of Jesus followers and has its antecedents in Old Testament covenantal texts such as Deuteronomy 4:10 (Hebrew, *qahal*, "congregation" or "assembly"). In encouraging the Israelites to observe Torah and teach God's ways to their children, Moses reminds them of the time the Lord directed him, "Assemble the people." That gathering is referred to as "the day of assembly" (Dt 9:10; 18:16); it is the time when the covenant people gathered to hear the recitation of the law and agreed to follow it.

The Hebrew word *qahal* ("assembly") is *ekklesia* in Greek. While often translated "church," *ekklesia* does not refer to ecclesiastical structures or hierarchy; it refers to the intentional gathering of God's people for the express purpose of hearing God and responding to him (in other words, worship). But the gathering generates a community of people who are like-minded even when they are not gathering, and they are engaging in mission in between times.

Matthew 16:18 Through Old Testament Eyes: "The Gates of Hades"

The "gates of Hades" refers to the realm of the dead. Jesus employs the Greek mythological term "Hades" to talk about the underworld since it receives the dead to an unknown, shadowy existence. It is not heaven or hell, but an interim place roughly synonymous with *Sheol* or *Gehenna* (see comments at Mt 5:21–22).[2] While Jesus' phrase is not present in the Old Testament, similar phrases are. For example, when God finally responds to Job's petitions, he does so in a series of rhetorical questions about creation and the ongoing administration of the earth. Each question drives home the reality that human beings lack knowledge, experience, and understanding (Job 38:16–18, italics added; cf. Job 17:16).

> Have you journeyed to the springs of the sea
>   or walked in the recesses of the deep?
> Have *the gates of death* been shown to you?
>   Have you seen *the gates of the deepest darkness*?
> Have you comprehended the vast expanses of the earth?
>   Tell me, if you know all this.

The answer to all these questions is, of course, no! For the reality of "the gates of death" is unknown to Job. Similarly, the psalmist uses the poetic expression "the gates of death" to express how low he sank before God's rescue of him. Appealing to God for grace, he recognizes that God and God alone can lift him up from the gates of death. He contrasts the gates of death with "the gates of Daughter Zion" (Ps 9:12–14). Only in Zion can he express praise and rejoice in God's deliverance.

When King Hezekiah became sick and was at the point of death, the prophet Isaiah visited him and told him to set his house in order for he would surely die (Isa 38). Hezekiah pled and wept before God for his life, reminding his Maker how he had walked in faithfulness all his days. The Lord heard his prayer and relented; he granted Hezekiah fifteen more years to live and then rescued Jerusalem from the grip of Assyria's king (Isa 38:1–6). In the aftermath of that dark night of the soul, Hezekiah penned a writing (*miktav*) that sounds like a biblical psalm. In poetic verse he describes his situation: "In the prime of my life must I go through *the gates of death* and be robbed of the rest of my years?" (Isa 38:10, italics added). That phrase "the gates of death" is better rendered "the gates of *Sheol*."

So when Jesus employs the phrase "the gates of Hades," it is likely his disciples would hear an echo from Hebrew poetry regarding death and its ever-present threat. The church's main task is to engage in an all-out assault on death. While death may remain a reality (for now), it is not the final word. The church bears the final word, the message of the cross and resurrection. (See also "Going Deeper into Death and Resuscitation: Matthew 9:23–24.")

16:19 *I will give you the keys of the kingdom of heaven; whatever you bind on earth will be bound in heaven, and whatever you loose on earth will be loosed in heaven.* Those with Old Testament eyes and ears may recall an oracle from the prophet Isaiah when Eliakim is made the head steward of the house of David. Among other endowments, God grants to Eliakim the key to the house of David (Isa 22:22). "I will place on his shoulder the key to the house of David; what he opens no one can shut, and what he shuts no one can open." As head steward, Eliakim is granted royal authority and is established as a "father" to the inhabitants of Jerusalem and Judah. God says further that he will fasten the steward like a peg in a secure place and the whole weight of David's house will rest upon him. Indeed, Eliakim will temporarily be granted a lofty role. However, the Lord also says that the peg will give way and the load will be lost. Perhaps we have here, ensconced in Scripture, a premonition of Peter's rebuke of Jesus (Mt 16:21–23) or of his denials as Jesus is being interrogated by powerful people in Jerusalem.

Before Eliakim's downfall, he had great authority to open and shut access to the king and his palace. In reality, he probably had a big ring of keys that allowed him to open and lock rooms and courtyards around the palace. The language of opening and shutting is not far removed conceptually from binding and loosing, which are legal terms found in rabbinic discussions for deciding whether an action is permitted or forbidden according to the law. We should be careful not to imagine that somehow "heaven" is bound by any decision Peter makes. Rather, Peter's decisions express the reality of God's will, on earth as it is heaven.

16:21 *From that time on Jesus began to explain to his disciples that he must go to Jerusalem and suffer many things at the hands of the elders, the chief priests and the teachers of the law, and that he must be killed and on the third day be raised to life.* The confession by Peter and the disciples that Jesus is the Messiah marks a turning point in the story. From this point forward, Jesus would teach his followers that he will be heading to Jerusalem to suffer at the hands of religious leaders, but ultimately to be resurrected on the third day (see Mt 17:22–23 and 20:17–19). Intense suffering is to be his lot, as the Scriptures have said, not only the physical suffering of crucifixion but also the psychological pain of rejection (cf. Isa 52–53). Zechariah describes an occasion when the shepherd of the community is attacked and only one third of the people remain in the land; even those must be refined (Zec 13:7–9).

Jesus says he will be raised on the third day. For adept readers of Scripture, the third day rings familiar. First, as we saw with the sign of Jonah (see Mt 12:39), Jonah was in the belly of the great fish for three days and three nights before he was "raised" (Jnh 1:17; 2:10). Second, another prophet urges repentance and turning back to the one, true God who has punished his people (Hos 6:1–2, italics added):

> Come, let us return to the LORD.
> He has torn us to pieces
>   but he will heal us;
> he has injured us
>   but he will bind up our wounds.
> *After two days he will revive us;*
>   *on the third day he will restore us,*
>   *that we may live in his presence.*

Hosea offers a pounding critique of the people of the northern kingdom and recognizes the hand of God in the rise of the Assyrians and their coming conquests. Israel will be defeated for a host of sins as they had departed from God's way for their own. Yet, there is always hope that even on the other side of judgment God will have compassion on his people and restore them. Jesus' role as the Messiah links him inextricably with the suffering people of God throughout history. "After two days . . . on the third day . . ." provides him a scriptural link to the conquered people through the message of a not-so-minor prophet. Jesus identifies with them so closely that he is willing to suffer by them and for them. Yet God's vindication of him, as with Israel, is sure.

What the Structure Means: Matthew's Numbers

The first evangelist appears to have had a fondness for numbers. This is expressed in a variety of ways structurally in the gospel. Consider how often Matthew groups into threes. The genealogy that opens the gospel constructs Jesus' family history into three groups of fourteen names (Mt 1:1–17). As we saw earlier, the number fourteen is important because it is the number associated with the name of King David. As another example, in Matthew 16:21 we have the first of three predictions of Jesus' suffering, death, and resurrection as he travels to Jerusalem (see "What the Structure Means: Three Predictions of Jesus' Passion" at Mt 17:22–23). In the Sermon on the Mount, Jesus illustrates the greater righteousness of the kingdom by appealing to three acts of piety: almsgiving, prayer, and fasting (Mt 6:1–18). The number three may come in multiples as well. For example, the Sermon on the Mount begins with nine Beatitudes (3 x 3, Mt 5:1–12). Likewise, there are three sets of three miracles recorded in a series in Matthew 8–9. Each set of three miracles concludes with discipleship sayings, three in all.[3]

16:22–23 *Peter took him aside and began to rebuke him. "Never, Lord!" he said. "This shall never happen to you!" Jesus turned and said to Peter, "Get behind me, Satan! You are a stumbling block to me; you do not have in mind the concerns of God, but merely human concerns."* Peter, empowered by receiving the "the keys," takes the initiative to set Jesus straight. "Not going to happen," he says. For an instant, it is as if Jesus is back in the wilderness of temptation (Mt 4:1–11), but now Peter is the Adversary's agent. Jesus addresses him as Satan and calls him a stumbling block (*skandalon*) because his mind is fixed on the way humans see things, not God.

In his day, the prophet Isaiah had a strong word from God not to walk in the way of others or fear them (Isa 8:11–15). Instead, he should regard the Lord of Hosts as holy and fear him. Indeed, YHWH himself is described as a stumbling stone, a trap, and a snare for the inhabitants of Jerusalem. Matthew's account reverses the language and makes Peter, the rock, the stumbling stone. According to the prophecy, God and his Messiah are supposed to be the stumbling stone (see Ro 9:30–33) for those who pursue righteousness the wrong way. But now Peter is marching out of step with God's plan of suffering, death, and resurrection for Jesus. It will not be the last time.

16:26 *What good will it be for someone to gain the whole world, yet forfeit their soul? Or what can anyone give in exchange for their soul?* How many good people have been lost in the pursuit of wealth? Not only lost for the life to come but for this life? The pursuit of wealth changes a person and not (usually) for the good. Jesus addresses the challenge of the now and the hereafter through a discipleship saying based in part on Psalm 49. Like Ecclesiastes, this wisdom psalm speaks to the fleeting nature of this life and whatever humans can achieve. Life is like a mist, like trying to catch hold of a breath (Ecc 1:1 VOICE). Those who trust in their riches, those who brag about all they have achieved cannot ransom their lives; there is not enough money in the world to save a person from the grave (Ps 49:5–9). When people die, they carry nothing with them. They might count themselves fortunate as long as they live, but what about when they perish (Ps 49:16–20)? Jesus' teaching relies on such wisdom about wealth and its limits.

16:27 *For the Son of Man is going to come in his Father's glory with his angels, and then he will reward each person according to what they have done.* For the title "Son of Man," see comments on Matthew 8:20. Matthew's Jesus often speaks of his coming again (e.g., Mt 24:27, 30, 37, 39, 41; 25:31; 26:64) with apocalyptic overtones.[4] Early Christians picked up on this teaching though they did not associate it with the title "Son of Man." Paul, for example, encouraged the persecuted in Thessalonica that their afflictions would end when the Lord Jesus is revealed from heaven with his fiery angels and avenges their suffering. On that day, he will come and be glorified among all the saints/ holy ones (2 Th 1:6–10). In an earlier letter, Paul offers a blessing on the faithful at Thessalonica so that they may stand blameless before God and Father at the arrival (Parousia) of the Lord Jesus with his holy ones (1 Th 3:11–13).[5] Old Testament passages like Zechariah 14:5 ("then the LORD my God will come, and all the holy ones with him") and Isaiah 66:15–16 ("The LORD is coming with fire. . . . For with fire . . . the LORD will execute judgment") likely factored into both Jesus' and Paul's frames of reference.

Matthew 16:27 Through Old Testament Eyes: Rewards

Jesus was not the first to say that each person will be rewarded or paid back according to what they have done. It was a sentiment expressed in his Bible as well as other Jewish literature (cf. Sirach 35:14–26, esp. v. 24). Let's consider two examples.

First, Psalm 62 is a psalm of trust in God who demonstrates time again that he is strong and able. Twice we hear the refrain: God alone "is my rock and salvation, my fortress, I will never be shaken" (Ps 62:2, 6). Then the psalm ends (62:11–12):

> One thing God has spoken,
>   two things I have heard:
> "Power belongs to you, God,
>   and with you, Lord, is unfailing love";
> and, "You reward everyone
>   according to what they have done."

A similar lesson in Proverbs is difficult to translate, but what seems the case is that a person becomes aware of a situation when violence and injustice are directed toward others (Pr 24:10–12). How will he/she respond? With courage, depression, or cowardice? It might be understandable that a person might not want to "get involved" and maybe turn and look the other way, but "cowardice in the face of injustice is reprehensible."[6] If you feign ignorance, the teacher says, does not God who watches over your soul know it; likewise, will he not repay all according to their deeds? The time of payback is never stated exactly in either Old Testament example. It could be in this or the life to come. But Jesus makes clear that—at least some—payback comes in the future, after the Son of Man comes with his angels.

16:28 *Truly I tell you, some who are standing here will not taste death before they see the Son of Man coming in his kingdom.* For the "Son of Man," see comments at Matthew 8:20. As we indicated earlier, many Son of Man sayings have to do with "the coming" of the Son of Man. This is a particularly knotty passage because it can be interpreted to mean that the Son of Man's coming into his kingdom will take place in the lifetimes of at least "some" of his earthly disciples. In other words, soon! Similarly, Jesus told his disciples that their mission to the cities of Israel would not be complete before the Son of Man comes (Mt 10:23). But what does it mean for the Son of Man to come into his kingdom? He has already come into the world and exercised authority to forgive sins (Mt 9:6), heal, teach, and be Lord of the Sabbath (Mt 12:8). Jesus' miracles, particularly his exorcisms, are taken as a sign of the kingdom and its authority (Mt 12:28). Currently, the Son of Man is on mission (Mt 13:37), a kingdom mission no less, that will end with him being handed over to authorities to suffer on the cross, giving his life as a ransom for many (Mt 17:12, 22; 20:18, 28; 26:2). But that is not the end of the Son of Man. God will vindicate him and raise him from the dead (Mt 12:40), and he will be seated at the right hand of power and come on the clouds in power and glory (Mt 24:27, 30–31; 26:64) to the dismay and horror of the unrighteous (Mt 25:31–46). If Jesus' prediction causes us consternation, it did not seem to bother Matthew. Had this been an unfulfilled promise, then Matthew could have left it out, embarrassed that Jesus could have been so wrong. But Matthew might well have considered what happens next in his story as its fulfillment.

MATTHEW 17

17:1 *After six days Jesus took with him Peter, James and John the brother of James, and led them up a high mountain by themselves.* The episode of Jesus' transfiguration has aspects in common with the covenant-sealing ceremony officiated by Moses (Ex 24). Like Moses, Jesus takes three people with him up the mountain to share in this revelatory experience. (See also "Matthew 4:8 Through Old Testament Eyes: Mountains.") He took Peter—the holder of the keys—and two brothers, James and John. Since they are often named and present with Jesus at key moments, these three formed a kind of inner circle of followers. Moses took others, but three people in particular are named: Aaron and his two sons, Nadab and Abihu (Ex 24:9). Since Aaron and his sons were priests, we might expect some priestly role coming out of the transfiguration experience from Jesus' inner circle.

Matthew seldom gives his readers the kind of precise chronology we find in this passage; the "after six days" reference may reflect another aspect of the covenant ceremony as it describes a cloud covering Mt. Sinai/Horeb for six days (Ex 24:15–16).

Since Elijah figures prominently in this encounter (Mt 17:3, 10–13), we ought to remember Elijah's meeting as well with God on Mt. Horeb. After fleeing from Queen Jezebel, the prophet journeys forty days and forty nights to the mount of God. He returns to the site where God gave the Law/Torah to Moses (Dt 5:1–3). There he has a dramatic experience with God that resets and reorients his life and mission (1 Ki 19:1–18).

17:2 *There he was transfigured before them. His face shone like the sun, and his clothes became as white as the light.* Jesus' appearance changes (metamorphoses) as his disciples look on. He takes on a glorious aspect that resembles the kind of splendor seen by those who witness an angelic appearance (Da 10:5–9). In

Revelation, for example, John the seer describes the face of Jesus as shining like the sun at full strength (Rev 1:16). Moses's face, too, changes after he meets and talks with God. His face shines and creates concern for those who see him, so Moses takes to wearing a veil in the company of others, but he removes it to speak to God (Ex 34:29–35).

The description of Jesus' clothes as white as light takes us back to the moment when Daniel sees the Ancient of Days on his throne, and his clothes are white, as white as snow (Da 7:9). As Peter recounts the episode in his letter, he says it was a time when Jesus received honor and glory from God the Father (2 Pe 1:17–18).

17:3 *Just then there appeared before them Moses and Elijah, talking with Jesus.* Few events in Jesus' life link him more clearly with the Hebrew Scriptures. Moses is mentioned directly seven times in Matthew (8:4; 17:3, 4; 19:7, 8; 22:24; cf. 23:2). His main role has to do with being a giver or interpreter of the Law. Elijah is mentioned directly nine times primarily as one who has come or is to come at the end of the age (11:14; 16:14; 17:3, 4, 10, 11, 12; 27:47, 49), in keeping with Malachi 4:5–6.[1] Their presence appears to validate Jesus' ministry as it moves toward its end.

Jesus is portrayed as the prophet like Moses whom God said he would raise up (Dt 18:15, 18):

> The LORD your God will raise up for you a prophet like me from among you, from your fellow Israelites. You must listen to him. . . . "I will raise up for them a prophet like you from among their fellow Israelites, and I will put my words in his mouth. He will tell them everything I command him."

Moses may have been the lawgiver—or better, law-mediator—but he sets the standard for what it means to speak for God and to be a prophet. He hears God's voice and speaks with heaven's authority. Note: the Lord commands the people to "listen to him," a command that is echoed to Jesus' three disciples. Elijah continues the prophetic tradition. He is an interim prophet like Moses to the kings and people of his day. But his appearance on the mount of transfiguration points the way to the final, definitive prophet from Nazareth.

Malachi concludes his prophecy and sums up the prophetic witness by urging the people to remember the teaching, the Torah, of God's servant, Moses (Mal 4:4). In the Hebrew tradition, the (former) prophets begin with Joshua who opens his book by referencing the death of Moses, the servant of God (Jos 1). As the prophetic ideal, Moses forms a kind of frame around the prophets (*nevi'im*). They begin and end with him. The statutes and ordinances

God revealed to him at Mt. Horeb are not set aside; they continue to be the blueprint for the future of God's people. Finally, through Malachi God indicates he will send the prophet Elijah again before the great day of the Lord comes (Mal 4:5–6).

17:4–5 *While he was still speaking, a bright cloud covered them, and a voice from the cloud said, "This is my Son, whom I love; with him I am well pleased. Listen to him!"* As we have seen, the transfiguration is presented as a typology of events surrounding Israel at Mt. Sinai (Ex 24; 34): (1) the glory of the Lord settled on the mountain and a cloud covered it for *six days* (24:15–16); (2) a select group ascend the mountain (24:1); and (3) the skin of Moses's face shone because he had talked with God (34:29–35). Now we have two other elements: (4) a cloud covered the mountain (24:15–17); and (5) God spoke to Moses from the cloud (24:16).[2]

Peter's offer to build three booths for Jesus, Moses, and Elijah is upstaged by a bright cloud that represents the presence of God. When the voice from the cloud speaks, it echoes the heavenly voice that spoke at Jesus' baptism (Mt 3:17). As we saw then, the voice recapitulates potent phrases from the psalms (Ps 2:7) and the prophets (Isa 42:1), but it adds one other word for those fortunate enough to see this sight: "Listen to him." We should regard this as an echo of God's instructions to Israel; when the prophet like Moses comes, they must "listen to him" (Dt 18:15–19). This heavenly voice is for all who will follow Jesus, not just for the inner circle. Those with ears to hear could not help but notice how God's directive to Israel regarding the prophet like Moses (listen to him) finds its fulfillment in Jesus.

What the Structure Means: Two Witnesses

We have seen Matthew's proclivity to marshal witnesses, at least two, in keeping with the law (see "What the Structure Means: Matthew's Pairs" at Mt 9:15–17). In this episode we have a second witness to Jesus' connection with God ("my Son"). By the mouth of two witnesses everything is confirmed. Twice in the gospel heaven offers an opinion in condemnation of Jesus' enemies and validation before the followers. The first comes at Jesus' baptism before the beginning of his public ministry (Mt 3:17); the second comes during his transfiguration as his ministry moves geographically more towards Jerusalem and socially more toward his disciples. Within the scriptural endorsement we hear echoes of both the psalms (Ps 2:7) and the prophets (Isa 42:1), again in twos, and this time augmented with the voice of God from Deuteronomy (18:15–19).

17:6 *When the disciples heard this, they fell facedown to the ground, terrified.* The disciples' response to seeing the vision they encountered is typical of what happened in the Old Testament (cf. 1 Ch 21:16).[3] When Daniel had the vision of the glorious man (likely the angel Gabriel) as he stood on the edge of the Tigris River, he fell into a trance and fell to the ground (Da 10:9). On another occasion, the prophet had seen a vision and the angel Gabriel came to interpret it for him. As the angel approached, Daniel became frightened and fell prostrate to the ground (Da 8:15–18). When Ezekiel witnessed the appearance of the glory of YHWH, he fell on his face (Eze 1:28). The prophet had a second vision of the glory of YHWH like he had seen by the Chebar river; he again fell on his face and was instructed by God to isolate himself and remain silent (Eze 3:22–27). And another time, as the glory of the Lord filled the temple, the seer fell upon his face (Eze 44:4). It is impossible to say whether the response of falling prostrate is voluntary or involuntary. Is there an irresistible force that drives people to the ground? Or do they recognize the gravity of the moment and out of fear and obeisance, humble themselves? Fear and terror go hand in hand with these kinds of experiences.

17:9–13 *As they were coming down the mountain, Jesus instructed them, "Don't tell anyone what you have seen, until the Son of Man has been raised from the dead." The disciples asked him, "Why then do the teachers of the law say that Elijah must come first?"* In keeping with Jesus' other instructions to those who had seen and experienced marvelous things (the messianic secret), he now instructs Peter, James, and John not to talk about this vision until the Son of Man has been raised from the dead. Apparently only in the light of the resurrection will what they have seen make sense. For "Son of Man," see comments on Matthew 8:20.

The teachers of the law were teaching that Elijah will precede the coming of the Messiah based on Malachi 4:5–6 (see Sirach 48 for a hymn in praise of Elijah). Seldom does Jesus affirm the scribal readings of Scripture, but on this occasion he did. Then he added something new: Elijah had already come, and they (the religious leaders) did to him what they wished (Mt 17:12). Matthew concludes the pericope by letting us, his readers, know that the disciples understood. They knew—without Jesus saying it plainly—that John the Baptist was the Elijah-to-come.

In reality John's execution did not bode well for Jesus. Powerful people considered both men trouble. Jesus did not have to be omniscient to recognize that he could share a fate similar to John's. A different time. A different place, perhaps. But both would be executed.[4]

17:14–15 *When they came to the crowd, a man approached Jesus and knelt before him. "Lord, have mercy on my son," he said. "He has seizures and is* *suffering greatly. He often falls into the fire or into the water."* The man's appeal to the "Lord" Jesus for mercy sounds a great deal like the appeal made by the Canaanite woman (Mt 15:22; cf. Mt 9:27). But instead of mercy for himself, he asks on behalf of his son. Once again, the language of appeal has much in common with psalms for healing (e.g., Ps 6:2: "Have mercy on me, Lord") where the word Lord translates the covenant name of God (YHWH). Likewise, Psalm 41:4 ("Have mercy on me, Lord; heal me, for I have sinned against you"; also 41:10) appeals to God for personal healing. Since the gospel passage contains a plea for healing of the man's son, the formula used gives the request a prayer-like quality, with Jesus identified as "Lord." The man's approach to Jesus and kneeling before him takes on a different character in light of psalms for healing. This passage continues the theme sounded in chapter 1 that Jesus is God-with-us.

17:16 *I brought him to your disciples, but they could not heal him.* The disciples' inability to heal the man's son has precedence in the miracle stories of Elisha. When the woman of Shunem, a village in the Jezreel Valley, lost her only son, she went to request the help of the man of God (2 Ki 4:25–37). Elisha was content to send his servant, Gehazi, but the woman insisted the prophet himself go. Well, Gehazi went ahead and did as the prophet had directed to no avail; the child did not awake. It was not until the prophet arrived, prayed, and bent over her son that death beat a hasty retreat. Similarly, the man who sought the disciples' help was disappointed his son did not get any better when they tried to heal him. It took the personal presence of Jesus to turn away this demon.

17:17-18 *"You unbelieving and perverse generation," Jesus replied, "how long shall I stay with you? How long shall I put up with you? Bring the boy here to me." Jesus rebuked the demon, and it came out of the boy, and he was healed at that moment.* Jesus returns to a familiar tone, even if the language is different. When asked for a sign (Mt 12:38–39) by the scribes and Pharisees, Jesus condemned "the wicked and adulterous generation" for the request. He said the same when the Pharisees and Sadducees were seeking a sign from heaven (Mt 16:1–4). Now he casts a hard eye against his own disciples or perhaps some of those lurking in the crowd, calling them "you unbelieving and perverse generation." Earlier, Jesus had given his disciples authority over spirits and sicknesses like this boy suffered (Mt 10:8). But for some reason they could not help the boy. Jesus names the reason here (Mt 17:20): they lack faith (*apistos*).[5]

Jesus' reprimand resonates with similar reproofs uttered about God's people in the Song of Moses as the aging prophet waxed poetic about Israel's future. God is faithful, just, and upright, yet his children form "a warped and crooked generation" (Dt 32:5). Still, God had acted toward them all along like a loving father, providing and guiding them. Ultimately, however, "Jacob" turned from God, rejected the Rock of their salvation, and pursued other gods. Therefore, the Lord spurned his children and decided to hide his presence from them because they were a perverse generation, children in whom there is no faithfulness (Dt 32:20).

Jesus' rebuke of those present sounds eerily like the Greek version of God's rebuke of Israel. At the heart of it is God's decision not to punish his people, for that might lead the nations to dishonor the one, true God. Instead, God decides to punish Israel's enemies and so vindicate his people despite their unfaithfulness. One parallel at least arises: the disciples' lack of faith reflected badly on Jesus and the movement he was establishing. It effectively undercut his honor because disciples are supposed to be "apprentices in training to assume the roles of their teachers."[6] This may account for Jesus' harsh tone and quick fix of the boy's problem.

17:20 *Faith as small as a mustard seed.* See comments on Matthew 13:31–32.

17:22–23 *When they came together in Galilee, he said to them, "The Son of Man is going to be delivered into the hands of men. They will kill him, and on the third day he will be raised to life." And the disciples were filled with grief.* This statement is Jesus' second prediction of his suffering, death, and resurrection. See comments on Matthew 16:21. For "Son of Man," see comments on Matthew 8:20.

What the Structure Means: Three Predictions of Jesus' Passion

Before the fateful events that result in Jesus' execution, Matthew tells us that the Messiah predicted his suffering, death, and resurrection three times (see Table 17.1). Each of these predictions stands in relation to a key event in the gospel.

Despite the clarity of Jesus' statements, the disciples appear not to "get it." After the first prediction, Peter rebukes Jesus for saying such a thing. After the second, the disciples are deeply distressed. After the third, the mother of James and John advocates for honorable positions for her sons when Jesus enters into his kingdom.

The number three is not coincidental (see "What the Structure Means: Matthew's Numbers" at Mt 16:21). It holds a special place in Jewish numerology, signifying completeness or perfection. Job, for instance, prior to the tragedies that wracked his life, is described as having an ideal life with seven sons and three daughters (Job 1:2). After God restored his fortunes, he once again had seven sons and three daughters (Job 42:13). Three times the prophet Elijah stretched himself out on the widow's son and pled for God to restore the life of her son (1 Ki 17:21), a practice followed by Jesus in the Garden of Gethsemane (Mt 26:36–46). Jesus' inner circle is made up of three disciples: Peter, James, and John. Paul indicated that he prayed three times that he might be not suffer his thorn in the flesh (2 Co 12:8).

The three predictions of Jesus' suffering, death, and resurrection offer his disciples, then and now, a more complete picture of who he is and what he came to do as Messiah, Beloved Son, and King. Is there more to know about Jesus? Of course. Throughout the gospel the character and identity of Jesus is on display through his words and deeds. But his upcoming sacrifice and vindication through his resurrection validate all the extraordinary claims he makes about himself and his mission.

Table 17.1. Predictions by Jesus of His Suffering and Death

Three Predictions	Three Misunderstandings	Key Related Event	Significance of Related Event
First prediction (Mt 16:21)	Peter rebukes Jesus (Mt 16:22–23)	After Peter confesses Jesus as Christ/Messiah (Mt 16:13–20)	Jesus as Messiah
Second prediction (Mt 17:22–23)	Disciples distressed (Mt 17:23)	After Peter, James, & John witness the transfiguration (Mt 17:1–13)	Jesus as Beloved Son
Third prediction (Mt 20:17–19)	Request for positions of honor (Mt 20:20–28)	Before Jesus' triumphal entry into Jerusalem (Mt 21:1–11)	Jesus as King

17:24–27 *After Jesus and his disciples arrived in Capernaum, the collectors of the two-drachma temple tax came to Peter and asked, "Doesn't your teacher pay the temple tax?"* Jesus' teachings about the arrival of the kingdom of heaven may have caused some to wonder whether he could be counted on to pay the requisite temple tax. If Jesus ever had confidence in the temple, it seemed to be waning. Another tax question will come up later (Mt 22:15–22).

Rather than approaching Jesus, they came to Peter and posed the question. Peter did not hesitate to say that Jesus and his followers did pay. This particular tax was based on Exodus 30:11–16 (cf. Ne 10:32). The Lord directed Moses to create a system for the financial support of the sanctuary (Ex 30:16, "for the service of the tent of meeting," NRSV). Everyone over the age of twenty was required to pay two drachma (= half shekel) annually as a ransom/atonement for their lives to avoid the kind of disaster other registrations had caused (2 Sa 24). Rich and poor paid the same amount. No one paid more. No one paid less. In rabbinic sources debates ensued over who should pay the tax. Essentially, the tax—whether paid by someone in the land or away from it—established a sense of solidarity with the Jewish people and the temple itself. Not to pay the tax was tantamount to announcing your intention to abandon your people, calling, and central shrine. Jesus arranged to pay his and Peter's tax using a Tyrian stater obtained miraculously.

MATTHEW 18

What the Structure Means:
Jesus and the Books of Moses (Mt 18:1–19:1)

Matthew 18 contains "sermon" number four of the five great discourses Jesus preached in Matthew's account. (See "What the Structure Means: Five Sermons [Mt 5–25]" at Mt 7:28 and Table 0.1.) The number five is significant because it corresponds to the five books of Moses and appears as Matthew's intentional, structural nod to the Messiah as a new Moses. It contains a variety of parables and discipleship sayings that are influenced by the Hebrew Scripture but not laced completely with Scripture through and through. The sermon proper is complete in 19:1 when Matthew says "when Jesus had finished saying these things . . .". However, as Jesus moves nearer to the cross, he continues to teach and correct any who want to misappropriate the teaching of Moses for their own ends.

The gist of this fourth sermon has to do with how Jesus' followers are to relate with one another. There are two sections to it, each ending with a parable. The first describes the kingdom citizens' relation to the lowly and the danger of causing them to stumble (18:1–9); it ends with the parable of the lost sheep (18:10–14). The second instructs disciples on how they should go about correcting one another and the extent to which the true believer offers to forgive (18:15–22); it ends with the parable of the unforgiving servant (18:23–35).

18:1–4 *He called a little child to him, and placed the child among them. And he said: "Truly I tell you, unless you change and become like little children, you will* *never enter the kingdom of heaven. Therefore, whoever takes the lowly position of this child is the greatest in the kingdom of heaven."* The disciples, impertinent question in verse 1—"Who, then, is the greatest in the kingdom of heaven?"— demonstrated how far they had to go to truly understand it. They were taking their cue from earthly kingdoms that are set up with circles of people who exercise power and seek the highest honor. They imagined Jesus' kingdom would be roughly the same, built according to the image of Rome. But who could blame them? Their imaginations had not yet been enlightened by the cross and resurrection of Jesus.

For those who know well the stories of the Pentateuch, Jesus' answer may recall the last days of the patriarch Jacob. When Jacob meets Joseph's sons, he asks for them to be brought to him so that he can speak a blessing over them before he died. Since his eyes are dark, he brings them close, embraces each one, and kisses them. The picture of innocence is complete when the writer tells us that Joseph had to peel one or more of his sons off his father's lap! Jacob blesses Joseph and his boys, asking that God have them grow into that great nation that God promised Abraham (Ge 48:8–22). The children are the future: Jacob's, Joseph's, and the family's future. They are thus the epitome of hope and greatness because they will perpetuate the names of their ancestors.

Going Deeper into Jesus and Children: Matthew 18:1–5

For Jesus the child becomes exhibit A for what his disciples are to become. They must be like children, for such is the kingdom of heaven. But what quality of children is Jesus concerned with? Well, if we consider the disciples' question—"who is the greatest . . . ?"—and his statement about humility—"the lowly position of this child"—we have a glimpse at the answer. While children have a unique capacity to act badly, they also lack pretensions to power and status. They occupy a lower status (in Jesus' world and in our own) and seem to be perfectly okay with it. It is the adult of our species who strives for status, thirsts for power, and demands recognition. When we find that we are expecting to be thanked, recognized, or honored, we can stop ourselves and find ways to give that notice, thanks, recognition, and honor to others.

Jesus closely identifies with the lowly and the child: to welcome children, to show them care and hospitality, is to do the same for Jesus. Care for children is at the heart of the gospel and in the heart of God. The home is the best place to care for them, but what happens when a home becomes dangerous and destructive? What do we do when a quality education is not available? And what about access to food, healthcare, and a safe environment? Our modern issues are new but not new. Jesus followers must step in the gap and assist struggling families and at-risk children. Sharon Betsworth makes the case that the Lord's teaching underscores the vulnerability of children and their absolute dependence on God, both characteristics embodied in the life of Jesus.[1] Mother Teresa of Calcutta once said, "Let us touch the dying, the poor, the lonely and the unwanted according to the graces we have received, and let us not be ashamed or slow to do humble work" for "each one of them is Jesus in disguise."[2]

Jesus' attitude toward children is consistent with Psalm 127: "Children are a heritage from the LORD, offspring a reward from him" (v. 3).

In the next chapter Jesus offers his own blessing for the children brought to him (Mt 19:13–15). These two passages together—the recognition and blessing of the children—recall Jacob's actions (Ge 48).

18:8–9 *If your hand or your foot causes you to stumble, cut it off and throw it away. It is better for you to enter life maimed or crippled than to have two hands or two feet and be thrown into eternal fire. And if your eye causes you to stumble, gouge it out and throw it away. It is better for you to enter life with one eye than to have two eyes and be thrown into the fire of hell.* For gouging out eyes, etc., see comments at Matthew 5:29–30. For "eternal fire" and "fire of hell," see comments at Matthew 5:21–22.

18:10 *See that you do not despise one of these little ones. For I tell you that their angels in heaven always see the face of my Father in heaven.* Many have grown up with the adage "Children should be seen and not heard." Apparently, parents did not like all the noise, but they wanted to know where the kids were. So it was with children of Jesus' era too; adults had a tendency to regard children as a bit of a bother. But Jesus warns us that the little ones have angels that always look on the face of the Father. They are angels of "the presence" (literally, "the face") of God.

According to one Jewish tradition, these angels of "the face" were Michael, Raphael, Gabriel, and Phanuel (*1 Enoch* 40). But the Old Testament is not that specific and never names them. In various parts of Scripture, we read how angels protect some who have a special calling by God. Jacob, in blessing the children of Joseph, describes an angel who stayed with him and redeemed him from all harm (Ge 48:16). Elihu relates how God appears to use angels to speak to and for some people through dreams and in seasons of pain (Job 33:14–19). Right before one's death, Elihu says, an angel comes, declares to them what is right, and intercedes for their souls (Job 33:23). The ransomed becomes the confessor who celebrates God's deliverance. The little ones, Jesus says, do not just have "an angel"; they have the angels who always have access to the face and presence of the heavenly Father.

18:12–13 *What do you think? If a man owns a hundred sheep, and one of them wanders away, will he not leave the ninety-nine on the hills and go to look for the one that wandered off? And if he finds it, truly I tell you, he is happier about that one sheep than about the ninety-nine that did not wander off.* Sheep and shepherds make up key aspects of the Scriptures' imagery for the people and their leaders (e.g., 1 Ki 22:17; Jer 10:21; Zec 11). When Jesus told his story about a man who went after the lost sheep, the prophet Ezekiel may well have been in his mind and in his hearers'. Ezekiel 34 contains an oracle against false shepherds who had consistently neglected the sheep even as they were seeing after their own needs and wants. Sheep did then what they do now. As the shepherds became fat and contented, the sheep wandered away and became lost. They were scattered over the mountains and the face of the earth. They became food for the predators because the shepherds of Israel were corrupt. The images in Ezekiel are so inflated that nothing other than the exile must have been in view.

God, however, answers. After all he is ultimately the shepherd of Israel. All the other so-called shepherds are posers and pretenders. Their judgment is sure. Yet YHWH will go in search for his sheep and rescue them no matter how far he must go. He is going to bring them back to the land where pastures are green and water is in good supply. Thus, God himself is the good shepherd, as Ezekiel makes clear (34:16): "I [YHWH] will search for the lost and bring back the strays. I will bind up the injured and strengthen the weak, but the sleek and the strong I will destroy. I will shepherd the flock with justice." God's people will return from exile and become subjects of the one shepherd described as *my servant David* (a faithful and righteous son of David). There appears a co-regency of sorts in this new era, with YHWH himself as their God and the Davidic prince serving with him (Eze 34:24). The expectation of a good shepherd who goes in search for the lost sheep is deeply embedded in Ezekiel's inspired speech. (See also comments at Mt 2:3–8 and "Going Deeper into Micah's Bad Shepherds: Matthew 2:5–6.")

18:15–17 *If your brother or sister sins, go and point out their fault, just between the two of you. If they listen to you, you have won them over. But if they will not listen, take one or two others along, so that "every matter may be established by the testimony of two or three witnesses."*

While the word *church* is not mentioned here, it is implied in the language of brother and sister. The best approach for the sinner is to have a single brother or sister go and help to correct and reconcile them. But if the sinner refuses, then Jesus suggests taking one or two others. He cites a well-known passage from Deuteronomy that had become a standard principle: two or three witnesses are required to establish any matter (Dt 17:6–7). The original statement was a protection against anyone charged with a capital crime. A person could not be condemned on the testimony of only one person; it took at least two or three witnesses. Even for a noncapital crime, it took two or three witnesses to sustain a charge (Dt 19:15). Combined with Leviticus 19:17–18, we see how this comes together in Jesus' teaching. While YHWH establishes the ordinance, "love your neighbor as yourself," he condemns hatred of family (including covenant family) and commands his people to reprove their neighbors or they will incur guilt upon themselves. Grudge-bearing is not an option. Jesus' instruction on how to deal with sin in the congregation is derived from the Old Testament. Unfortunately, the Master knows that even two or three could be rebuffed and sent on their way, so Jesus provides further instruction: taking the matter to the congregation.

18:18 *Truly I tell you, whatever you bind on earth will be bound in heaven, and whatever you loose on earth will be loosed in heaven.* On the language of binding and loosing, see Matthew 16:19.

18:19–20 *Again, truly I tell you that if two of you on earth agree about anything they ask for, it will be done for them by my Father in heaven. For where two or three gather in my name, there am I with them.* The context here must not be forgotten; it is about church discipline and actions taken to restore sinners to a peaceful place in the community. It is not about asking and getting anything you want. The two- and three-ness of Matthew 18:15–16 should govern what we read here. When two witnesses agree before God about a matter of church discipline and restoration, the heavenly Father will hear and act. Church discipline must be bathed in prayer, and leaders must not fall into the patterns of "bad shepherds" who may be either negligent or harsh (see "Going Deeper into Micah's Bad Shepherds: Matthew 2:5–6"). The hope of restoration should be shared horizontally with the community and vertically with heaven. Likewise, whenever two or three gather in Jesus' name, he promises to be with them. We hear in this passage a strong echo of Jesus' prophetic name, Immanuel; he is God-with-us. It anticipates Jesus' promise to be with the disciples who go into all the world with the gospel (Mt 28:19–20).

18:21–22 *Then Peter came to Jesus and asked, "Lord, how many times shall I forgive my brother or sister who sins against me? Up to seven times?" Jesus answered, "I tell you, not seven times, but seventy-seven times."* Jesus' teaching about reconciliation naturally led to Peter's question: "What if someone keeps sinning against me? What's my obligation?" Rabbinic sources indicate that the adjudicators of the law required that a person forgive another three times (b. Yoma 86b-87a). So Peter's offer to forgive seven times appears excessive. But Jesus ups the ante on Peter's question and says, "no, seventy-seven times." His wording recalls Genesis 4:23–24:

Lamech said to his wives,

"Adah and Zillah, listen to me;
    wives of Lamech, hear my words.
I have killed a man for wounding me,
    a young man for injuring me.
If Cain is avenged seven times,
    then Lamech seventy-seven times."

Lamech is part of Cain's family. You will recall that Cain killed his brother Abel and is subsequently punished by God (Ge 4). Yet God promises that anyone who kills Cain will suffer sevenfold vengeance. That theme is picked up here in a great boast made by Lamech, a son of Cain, whose bloodlust seems to know no bounds. His overreaction—killing a man who had hit him—violates what becomes the law of retaliation (Ex 21:25). Although he fathered three sons who went on to do great things, disaster awaits his family because Lamech appears so depraved. Jesus' counsel to Peter to forgive someone seventy-seven times unravels the boast of Lamech and points to the radicality of Christian forgiveness.

18:23–34 *Since he was not able to pay, the master ordered that he and his wife and his children and all that he had be sold to repay the debt.* The parable of the unforgiving servant is unique to Matthew. From the way Jesus introduces it, the story is clearly a parable of the kingdom. Given the context and the final verse (v. 35), the term "debt" is best taken as a metaphor for "sin." So, this parable extends and expands Peter's earlier question. The enormity of the debt parallels the radical nature of forgiveness (seventy-seven times).

As the king is settling his accounts, he comes across a man who owed him ten thousand talents. One talent equaled the total amount a common laborer would make in twenty years. It's impossible to imagine how any human being could accrue such a debt. As we have stated before, Jesus was a master at hyperbole. Because the servant could not repay this debt—who could?—the king ordered his servants to sell him, his wife, his children, and his possessions. Debt-slavery was a common feature in both the biblical and the Roman world (Ex 22:2–3; Lev 25:39–43, 47; 1 Sa 22:2; 2 Ki 4:1; Isa 50:1; Am 2:6).

The condemned man fell on his knees and begged for patience with the absurd promise that he would pay him back everything. The master pitied him and canceled his debt. But the forgiven man refused to extend the same mercy to a fellow traveler who owed him far less than he had the king. He violently choked the man and had him thrown in prison until the debt was paid. When the king heard of the matter, he reversed himself, called in the man he had forgiven, and chastised him for not showing mercy. The master handed him over to the jailers who tortured him until he paid back the impossible debt.

18:35 *This is how my heavenly Father will treat each of you unless you forgive your brother or sister from your heart.* For God as the heavenly Father, see comments on Matthew 6:9.

The picture here is one of final judgment, not an interim punishment. The language of "brother or sister" indicates Jesus' deep concern that forgiveness characterize the community he founded and will soon leave behind. For the relationship of the disciples' forgiveness to God's, see comments on Matthew 6:12, 14–15.

MATTHEW 19

19:3 *Some Pharisees came to him to test him. They asked, "Is it lawful for a man to divorce his wife for any and every reason?"* When the Pharisees ask Jesus whether it is "lawful," they are approaching him as if he were a rabbi who could issue a ruling from God's law. So "law" here refers to God's Law or the first five books of Moses. The Pharisees' question is based upon a teaching found in Deuteronomy 24:1–4. It is case law having to do with a woman who is divorced, remarried, then divorced again. Jesus will return to this text, but first, he wants to point out something crucial from the first book of Moses.

On the earlier discussion of the topic of divorce, see comments on Matthew 5:31–32.

19:4–6 *"Haven't you read," he replied, "that at the beginning the Creator 'made them male and female,' and said, 'For this reason a man will leave his father and mother and be united to his wife, and the two will become one flesh'? So they are no longer two, but one flesh. Therefore what God has joined together, let no one separate."* Jesus, when asked a scriptural question, often gave a scriptural answer. On this occasion, he answered the question with a question: "Haven't you read . . . ?" Of course, they had, but they had missed something crucial. The phrase "at the beginning" takes us to the book of Genesis, whose Hebrew name is "in the beginning." The teaching about divorce as Moses allowed it (Dt 24) must be read over against God's ideal plan established at creation. In a way, Genesis is prior to and takes precedence over Deuteronomy.

So what does Genesis say? First, that on the sixth day the Creator made humanity in his image and likeness, and that he made them male and female (Ge 1:26–27). Second, Jesus links the complementarity of the two sexes with another Genesis passage (2:23–24, esp. 24) that describes what happens when a true marriage takes place. The man leaves his parents, unites with his wife, and they become one flesh.

Going Deeper into the Ideal of Marriage: Matthew 19:1–9

There is a great deal we could say about these passages: What does it mean that human beings are made in God's image and likeness?[1] And given all the discussions today about gender, why only two genders/sexes here? And what does it mean that the two become "one flesh"? What seems clear is that Jesus accepted the Genesis account of creation as true and that it supplies the ideal of what marriage can and should be. There are four elements to this ideal in Genesis that is affirmed by Jesus:

- One man
- One woman
- One flesh relationship
- For life

This is how things are supposed to be. Any deviation from this pattern, any additions or subtractions, violates the ideal and breaks down the shalom (peace). This is one reason why adultery is wrong, because it adds another person into the equation as an intimate partner. Likewise, polygamy is not ideal—though it has been widely practiced. Divorce is an infringement of the "for life" part of the equation: one man and one woman until you find someone better—often a cause of divorce—violates the ideal. Likewise, the ideal is violated when one man and one woman continue in a "marriage" that is not one flesh.

This does not mean that everyone should be married. The disciples wrongly suppose that given Jesus' teaching it would be best not to marry (Mt 19:10–12). Jesus responds that not everyone can accept this teaching, only those to whom it is given, that is, only those who have the gift of celibacy (cf. 1 Co 7:25–40). Some commit themselves to be "eunuchs" for the kingdom of heaven, but it is not expected of everyone. For if marriage was somehow required, Jesus himself would have been in violation of the teaching.

Any legal ruling about divorce or marriage must take Genesis into account. Jesus appears to draw a hard line: the husband and wife are one flesh. When God joins two together, no one should separate them. That could have, perhaps should have, been the end of it. But Jesus' answer leads to another law-based question.

19:7 *"Why then," they asked, "did Moses command that a man give his wife a certificate of divorce and send her away?"* Jesus' answer to their initial question leads to a second question. "If what you say is true, then why did Moses issue a command that gives a husband the right to divorce his wife?" The question from the Pharisees relates to Deuteronomy 24:1: "If a man marries a woman who becomes displeasing to him because he finds something indecent about her, and he writes her a certificate of divorce, gives it to her and sends her from his house . . . ". The passage as quoted is incomplete because the situation becomes more complicated when the woman remarries another man who eventually divorces her. Then the first husband is not allowed to remarry her (Dt 24:2–4). The Pharisees' point seems to be that there is an allowance of divorce particularly in one direction; that is, the man has the right to divorce his wife if he finds "something indecent about her." The open question is: What is "something indecent about her"? English translations will differ on how best to render this phrase. The rabbis debated the provision and came up with radically different answers. Jesus' ruling on the matter had a lot in common with the House of Shammai who said that a man may divorce his wife if she has engaged in illicit sexual relations. Other rabbis were more liberal in their assessment. Rabbi Hillel, for example, ruled that a man may divorce his wife if she burns the food or oversalts a dish. Rabbi Akiba decided that a man may divorce his wife if he finds another woman more attractive and wants to marry her (*b. Gittin* 90a). It all turned around the meaning of the phrase "something indecent." But what did Jesus say in response? Again, he returns to Genesis.

19:8–9 *Jesus replied, "Moses permitted you to divorce your wives because your hearts were hard. But it was not this way from the beginning. I tell you that anyone who divorces his wife, except for sexual immorality, and marries another woman commits adultery."* Jesus says that whatever permission (not "command" as the Pharisees say) God gave through Moses to the children of Israel was not the way it is supposed to be "from the beginning," that is, from Genesis. The beginning sets the stage for the ideal of marriage (Ge 1:27; 2:24): one man, one woman, in a one-flesh relationship, for life. Jesus' final ruling on the matter allows for divorce only when there has been a clear case of sexual immorality. Note that Jesus appears to level the playing field by indicating that the man who divorces for any other cause and marries another is guilty of adultery. Unfortunately, women at the time had the most to lose in cases of adultery (e.g., Jn 7:53–8:11).[2] But this was true throughout the ancient Near East. Yet, Jesus places the burden on men to deal fairly with their wives.

What the Structure Means: Questions and Answers

You have probably seen a pattern to this pericope. Table 19.1 lays it out simply.

Table 19.1. Questions About Divorce

Question from Scripture (19:3, regarding divorce)
Answer from Scripture (19:4–5, quoting Ge 1–2)
   Commentary on Scripture (19:6)

Question from Scripture (19:7, quoting Dt 24)
Answer from Scripture (19:8, alluding to Ge 1–2)
   Commentary on Scripture (19:8)

Final ruling (19:9)

Patterns like this and others are repeated in the New Testament Gospels. See for example "What the Structure Means: Chiasm (Mt 1:1–16)." The patterns themselves provide a kind of "form" that could be and was used to aid in memorization and transmission. Look for others when disciples and opponents come inquiring of Jesus. Most questions have a scriptural base, as do Jesus' answers.

19:13–15 *Then people brought little children to Jesus for him to place his hands on them and pray for them. But the disciples rebuked them. Jesus said, "Let the little children come to me, and do not hinder them, for the kingdom of heaven belongs to such as these." When he had placed his hands on them, he went on from there.* In Matthew 18:1–5 we discussed an Old Testament allusion behind Jesus taking a child and giving his disciples an object lesson about the kingdom of heaven. That allusion sits carefully behind this passage too. Like Joseph brought his children to be blessed by his father (Ge 48:8–22), various friends or family members bring their children to be blessed by Jesus. The disciples' response indicates how quickly they had forgotten the previous lesson: never hinder children from coming to Jesus, because the kingdom of heaven belongs to them.

The laying-on of hands is a practice testified to in the Old Testament. Again, Jacob placed his hands on at least some of Joseph's children as part of the blessing (Ge 48:8–22). Likewise, prior to his death Moses laid his hands on Joshua, passing along the mantle of leadership to one who had faithfully served him and God for his entire adult life (Dt 34:9).

19:16 *Just then a man came up to Jesus and asked, "Teacher, what good thing must I do to get eternal life?"* An unnamed man approaches Jesus and calls him "Teacher." That may reflect the general opinion about Jesus among those who were not his close disciples. Still, Jesus was a teacher in the best sense of the word. We've not seen the phrase "eternal life" before in Matthew's gospel, but it abounds in John's. Still, as Jesus' teaching implies, it is synonymous with "the kingdom of heaven." We could restate the question as, "Teacher, what good thing must I do to enter the kingdom of heaven?" The answer, as he would expect, involves some aspect of the law.

19:17 *"Why do you ask me about what is good?" Jesus replied. "There is only One who is good. If you want to enter life, keep the commandments."* Jesus found this to be a teachable moment and directed the man to his choice of words. He responds to the question with a question about the nature of the good. Only One is good, and that is God. Whatever question you have, the answer is God. God is good. But Jesus did take his original question seriously and drove the man back to Scripture. If you want to have eternal life, then keep the commandments. According to the rabbis, there are 613 commandments in the Torah, but not all pertain to every person. Only priests need to keep laws pertaining to the priests. Only women need to be concerned about laws dealing with them. But the man pressed Jesus, "Which commandment or commandments are you talking about?"

19:18–19 *"Which ones?" he inquired. Jesus replied, "'You shall not murder, you shall not commit adultery, you shall not steal, you shall not give false testimony, honor your father and mother,' and 'love your neighbor as yourself.'"* Jesus responded to this question by naming specific laws which come from the Ten Commandments (Ex 20:12–16; Dt 5:16–20). These are laws dealing with how we treat other human beings. But the order of commandments he gives is different from how we read them in the Decalogue. In addition, Jesus adds one additional commandment that is not part of the Ten: "Love your neighbor as yourself." This commandment comes from Leviticus 19:18, which becomes part of Jesus' teaching on the great commandment (Mt 22:36–40). We will return to this later.

19:20–22 *"All these I have kept," the young man said. "What do I still lack?"* For the first time Matthew refers to the questioner as a "young man" as he makes the assertion, "I've kept all these commandments," and then asks one final question: "What am I missing?"

Jesus replies, "If you want to be perfect, go, sell your possessions and give to the poor, and you will have treasure in heaven. Then come, follow me." The answer Jesus gives to sell possessions and give to the poor has no direct Old Testament counterpart. Nonetheless, the Scriptures are clear that caring for the poor and needy is a sign of righteousness (Job 29:12–16; 31:16–22; Ps 41:1; Pr 14:21; 29:7; Zec 7:9–10). Matthew's Jesus has mentioned perfection before (Mt 5:48), but as we saw then, moral perfection is not in view nor is it possible. The word has to do more with maturity and integrity. The young man needs to move toward maturity. As he does, he will become whole and complete; that is, his obedience to God will be undivided.[3]

To reach maturity, he needs to sell his possessions, give to the poor, and follow Jesus. The problem with possessions is that they can possess us. We become fixated on them and cannot part from them. When Jesus said give to the poor, he did not say give everything to the poor. The rabbis were quick to say in giving alms to the poor you do not give to the point of destitution, lest you become dependent on the generosity of others. But the young man is to give to the poor and give substantially, thus making it possible for him to follow Jesus and enter into eternal life. That could mean becoming an itinerant teacher as Jesus is. The ministry Jesus modeled included absolute trust in God to provide. Itinerancy is not possible if you have a lot of "stuff" holding you back. While we should be careful about universalizing Jesus' command, the passage clearly demonstrates how possessions have a gravity of their own. The point of possessions possessing their owners is made evident when the young man chooses not to follow Jesus because he had many possessions (Mt 19:22).

19:23–26 *Jesus looked at them and said, "With man this is impossible, but with God all things are possible."* The young man illustrates how difficult it is for the rich to enter the kingdom of heaven. In fact, "it is easier for a camel to go through the eye of a needle than for someone who is rich to enter the kingdom of God" (19:24). A person's riches form a formidable, but not insurmountable, barrier. Still, the disciples are astonished at Jesus' teaching and ask him, "Who then can be saved?" (19:25). The disciples may be astonished because riches can be seen as a sign of God's blessing (Pr 3:16; 8:18). The rich also had leisure time to pray and read the Scriptures, as well as the means to make sacrifices and give generously to the temple, which were much harder for ordinary people to do. So if even the rich who have all these advantages can't be saved, who can?

Jesus answers that with God all things are possible. The statement may be inspired by the miracle God performed when Sarah and Abraham learn they are going to have a son (Ge 18:13–14). When Sarah heard the news, she laughed; but when pressed, she denied laughing. The Lord himself reassured

Abraham that she would bear a child: "Is anything too hard for the LORD? I will return to you at the appointed time next year, and Sarah will have a son" (Ge 18:14).

The obvious answer is no. Nothing is too hard for God. A similar sentiment is expressed in Jeremiah when the prophet purchases property on the eve of the destruction of Jerusalem and its sister cities. After giving the deed of purchase to Baruch, his secretary, for safekeeping, he prays, "Ah, Sovereign LORD, you have made the heavens and the earth by your great power and outstretched arm. Nothing is too hard for you" (Jer 32:17). The prayer continues as Jeremiah rehearses God's loyal love to his people and the people's disobedience to God through time. Despite the calamities coming upon Judah and Jerusalem as a result of the Babylonians' attack, Jeremiah's prophetic act shows an expectation of an outcome favorable for those who remain of God's people, Israel.

19:28 *Jesus said to them, "Truly I tell you, at the renewal of all things, when the Son of Man sits on his glorious throne, you who have followed me will also sit on twelve thrones, judging the twelve tribes of Israel."* On "Son of Man," see comments on Matthew 8:20.

Once again we are drawn back to the prophet Isaiah who talked about "the renewal of all things." YHWH, the oracle declares, is about to create new heavens and a new earth. Former things will be forgotten. Jerusalem will be recreated and become a joy to all its inhabitants. In this renewal, everyone lives to a ripe old age and no children will succumb to disease. The citizens will build houses and live in them. They will plant gardens and vineyards and enjoy their fruit. God's blessing will include the animals, both wild and domestic (Isa 65:17–25). Furthermore, in this renewed creation, the offspring of God's people thrive, and the good name of Israel lives on. Indeed, all flesh comes before YHWH to worship him (Isa 66:22–23). Yet the prophecy ends on a sobering note (Isa 66:24): "And they will go out and look on the dead bodies of those who rebelled against me [YHWH]; the worms that eat them will not die, the fire that burns them will not be quenched, and they will be loathsome to all mankind." The renewal of all things is accompanied with fierce and final judgment.

Daniel 7 likely inspired Jesus' teaching on the Son of Man and his self-use of the term. The vision begins with Daniel describing multiple thrones being set in place as the Ancient of Days takes his seat on the throne. Nothing more is said of the other thrones in the vision. Jesus appears to envision twelves thrones in this vision, and his Twelve seated on those thrones in the future. (See also comments at Mt 10:1.)

MATTHEW 20

20:1–7 *For the kingdom of heaven is like a landowner who went out early in the morning to hire workers for his vineyard.* On "the kingdom of heaven," see comments on Matthew 3:1–2 and 4:17.

The parable of the workers in the vineyard describes key aspects of the kingdom for Jesus and his followers. Each parable needs to be read in its entirety to understand the teaching.

Since the time of the prophet Isaiah, the vineyard has been used to symbolize Israel (e.g., Isa 5), with God serving as the farmer who plants the vines and waits for a good crop. The workers then would be God's people. The vineyard image likely stands behind Jesus' parable here; the landowner likewise would be the farmer with a not-so-subtle reference to God (cf. Jer 12:1–13).

20:8–12 *When evening came, the owner of the vineyard said to his foreman, "Call the workers and pay them their wages, beginning with the last ones hired and going on to the first."* The parable of the workers in the vineyard demonstrates what the practice of the law looks like in an agricultural economy. The landowner was law-bound to make sure that workers were paid daily for their labors. There were likely many reasons for this provision in the law. The landowner's actions follow closely the teaching of Leviticus 19:13: "Do not defraud or rob your neighbor. Do not hold back the wages of a hired worker overnight." The same teaching is repeated in Deuteronomy 24:14–15: "Do not take advantage of a hired worker who is poor and needy, whether that worker is a fellow Israelite or a foreigner residing in one of your towns. Pay them their wages each day before sunset, because they are poor and are counting on it. Otherwise, they may cry to the LORD against you, and you will be guilty of sin." The assumption is that most agricultural workers were poor, and they had to work daily (except on Shabbat) to take care of their and their families' needs. Daily pay guaranteed them a regular source of income during the planting and harvesting seasons. But in this parable, those who worked a full day resented that they were paid the same as those who only worked part of a day. So the landowner responded.

20:13-15 *Don't I have the right to do what I want with my own money? Or are you envious because I am generous?* Many who heard the parable would be reminded of the final scene of the book of Jonah (ch. 4). The prophet had been reluctant to go and preach in Nineveh for good reason, because YHWH was gracious and merciful. Jonah preached of God's coming wrath on the city of Nineveh, but God decided not to bring calamity on them because the city repented (ch. 3). The story ends with the prophet throwing a fit that God did not punish Israel's enemy and praying to die, and when he did not die, he left the city, climbed a hill to its east, built a booth for himself, and waited (secretly hoping) for the destruction of the city. In the end God reproved the prophet for having more concern over a bush than he did the people and children of Nineveh. Jonah was so jealous and angry he wanted to die because God was merciful to Nineveh. In Jesus' parable those who worked the full day and received the agreed-upon wage were, like Jonah, jealous that the landowner showed the late-comers luxuriant generosity for their labors.

What the Structure Means:
The Parable of the Workers (Mt 19:30–20:16)

This is one of those places in Scripture where the chapters and the verses (added centuries after the Bible was written) get in the way. The last verse of Matthew 19 ("But many who are first will be last, and many who are last will be first," v. 30) is parallel to Matthew 20:16 ("So the last will be first, and the first will be last.") So the last verse of Matthew 19 belongs with the parable of chapter 20.

This pair of sayings forms a frame around the parable of the workers in the vineyard and sets the tone for how it ought to be interpreted. Everyone is dealt with justly, but not everyone is dealt with the same. With the kingdom of heaven comes a great reversal in our expectations. We are wired economically and spiritually to talk about what people deserve, what is "fair," equal treatment, and so on. But the kingdom turns that around with a big dose of "undeserved generosity." This is the theme of other parables. Consider the luxuriant treatment the prodigal son receives (Lk 15:20–24) and the fatherly rebuke of his older brother (Lk 15:25–32).[1]

20:17-19 *The Son of Man will be delivered over to the chief priests and the teachers of the law.* For "Son of Man," see comments on Matthew 8:20. For Jesus' prediction of his arrest, death, and resurrection, see comments on Matthew 16:21. See also "What the Structure Means: Three Predictions of Jesus' Passion" at Matthew 17:22-23.

20:20-22 *"You don't know what you are asking," Jesus said to them. "Can you drink the cup I am going to drink?" "We can," they answered.* Not long (apparently) after Jesus predicted for the third time that he would suffer at the hands of Gentiles, be crucified by them, and be raised on the third day (see Mt 16:21-23; 17:22-23), the mother of the sons of thunder made the impertinent request that Jesus grant her sons high positions in the kingdom. It was not just the mother, however. Probably James and John wanted to know too—as suggested by their answer to Jesus' question ("We can"). In fact, they may have put her up to it. Like any good mother, she wished her sons would do well and be well in the future; in this case, she accepted Jesus' kingship and wanted her sons to have a prominent place in his reign. The right and left hand were places of honor. Ironically, as the story plays out, those on the right and left hand were thieves crucified with Jesus (Mt 27).

20:23 *Jesus said to them, "You will indeed drink from my cup, but to sit at my right or left is not for me to grant. These places belong to those for whom they have been prepared by my Father."* The cup Jesus referred to is the cup of suffering. The image is prominent enough in the Old Testament to have been familiar to the disciples. Jeremiah describes the cup of the Lord's wrath against the nations (Jer 25:15-29). One of the most lurid prophetic examples comes in the allegory of Oholah (= Samaria) and Oholibah (= Jerusalem), two sisters guilty of whoredom and whose destinies are to drink a cup of divine wrath (Eze 23:31-34):

> You [Jerusalem] have gone the way of your sister [Samaria]; so I will put her cup into your hand.

This is what the Sovereign Lord says:

> "You will drink your sister's cup,
>   a cup large and deep;
> it will bring scorn and derision,
>   for it holds so much.
> You will be filled with drunkenness and sorrow,
>   the cup of ruin and desolation,

> the cup of your sister Samaria.
> You will drink it and drain it dry
>   and chew on its pieces—
> and you will tear your breasts."

The cup of wrath is not just sipped; it is drained to the bottom. In each case, the cups represent God's judgment and anger for various sins, including idolatry and violence (Isa 19:14; 51:17; Hab 2:15–16; Ps 75:8). Jesus had just predicted his destiny of suffering at the hands of his enemies, so the cup certainly extends that prophecy. John and James, eagerly it seems, say they can drink the cup and Jesus agrees; they will suffer a martyr's death in years to come. Their deaths, however, will not be the same; they will not die as a ransom for many (Mt 20:28).

20:25 *Jesus called them together and said, "You know that the rulers of the Gentiles lord it over them, and their high officials exercise authority over them."* The question of honor and who will be seated in places of honor led Jesus to call all the disciples together for a bit of a lesson about authority and power. That lesson draws significantly from Psalms 9 and 10.

The Greek text of Psalm 9 is a good deal longer than the Hebrew and actually combines the Hebrew Psalms 9 and 10.[2] The two psalms together form one acrostic psalm (cf. Pss 25; 34) and should be read together. Whether the Jewish Christians who first heard Matthew's gospel knew these verses is not clear but is certainly possible. Psalm 9:26, 31 (LXX) uses much of the same verbiage Jesus employs to talk about how Gentiles lord over God's people.

The psalm speaks of how the Lord has become a refuge for the needy, the afflicted, the orphan, the innocent, and the poor. These words stand in parallel and might well symbolize the covenant people of God who were frequently attacked and temporarily, at least, defeated and rendered helpless:

> His [the wicked man's] ways are defiled at every turn,
>   Your [God's] judgments are erased from before him,
> Over all his enemies he will exercise dominion
> (Ps 9:26, LXX = Heb Ps 10:5)

> In his trap he will humble him,
>   He will bend over and fall
> As he exercises dominion over the needy
> (Ps 9:31, LXX = Heb Ps 10:9–10).

The psalm ends as the writer asks God to crush the hand of sinners and evildoers. He declares confidently that the Lord is king forever, and that the

Lord will listen to the cry of the needy and bring justice to the orphans (Ps 9:36–39, LXX = Heb Ps 10:16–18).

The nations exercise power and authority in one way, arrogantly ignoring God while treating the weak with contempt and violence. The disciples are to take an upside-down approach to power. But the upside-down approach is actually right side up; it is Jesus' way.

20:26–28 *Not so with you. Instead, whoever wants to become great among you must be your servant, and whoever wants to be first must be your slave—just as the Son of Man did not come to be served, but to serve, and to give his life as a ransom for many.* The path to greatness Jesus taught is through service, not through usurping power in this world and lording over others. Jesus will point to his own example of service and ultimately giving his life (in the crucifixion) "as a ransom for many."

On the title "Son of Man," see comments on Matthew 8:20. It is the title Jesus used most often of himself, a kind of self-awareness by title. In whatever way Jesus understood his exalted status, he did not reckon it as demanding the service of others; instead, he takes up a servant's role and takes it up ultimately.

The term *ransom* (*lutron*) is suggestive on several levels. It is a Greek word used in a variety of contexts, both secular and sacred. One use has to do with actions taken to liberate a slave. Another relates to the release of prisoners of war. Typically these are not self-achieved, but liberation depends on the actions of another on behalf of the enslaved/imprisoned. As such, the disciples were likely primed to see Jesus' pronouncement here as his life given to liberate the oppressed, whether oppressed by others or by their own devices (cf. Mt 1:21).

Ransom has deep Old Testament roots, so that many would have perceived a variety of Old Testament texts behind the events Jesus says lie ahead. Perhaps the most obvious connection is seen in God's assurances to Moses that he will deliver Israel from Egyptian power and oppression (Ex 6:6): "Therefore, say to the Israelites: 'I am the LORD, and I will bring you out from under the yoke of the Egyptians. I will free you from being slaves to them, and I will redeem [or ransom] you with an outstretched arm and with mighty acts of judgment." Three times God says: "I will bring you out . . . I will free you . . . I will redeem you." In this case, God is the one who acts unilaterally, but rather than paying a price demanded by the Egyptians, God is the one who exacts a price from them in the process of freeing the Hebrew slaves. In the Septuagint the word translated "redeem" has the same root as the word Jesus used for "ransom."

A similar case in point is made in Isaiah 43:1–4, an oracle of restoration for Jacob and Israel after the exile. The prophet declares that YHWH, their creator, will redeem/ransom them, for he knows those who are his. He will give Egypt as a ransom; Ethiopia and Seba in exchange for them. Since his people are precious in his eyes and deeply loved, God promises to give other peoples in return for them and other nations in exchange for their lives. The parallelisms in this oracle are clear. Ultimately, those exiled and scattered among the nations will be brought home as God exacts a price from the "Gentiles." God will give their people in exchange for Israel.

In another Isaianic oracle, sins and transgressions are the culprit. The Lord calls upon Israel to remember the covenant, for God has not forgotten them (Isa 44:22):

> I have swept away your offenses like a cloud,
>   your sins like the morning mist.
> Return to me,
>   for I have redeemed [ransomed] you.

Again, God is the actor who sweeps away their sins and redeems them, so Israel is summoned to return to their God.

In each of these cases, the oppressors—the Egyptians, the nations, or their sins—are dealt with decisively by God, Israel's redeemer. For some, it is clear a price has been (or will be) paid. In others, God appears to act independently of any price. In the Greek translation of the Hebrew Scriptures, the connection between these texts and Jesus' pronouncement is more obvious because the Greek translators utilized a verb form for the word *ransom* (*lutron*) to describe God's redemptive actions. Now, with these words on Jesus' lips, we see God again poised to act through the ransom of Jesus' life on the cross.

Matthew 20:28 Through Old Testament Eyes: Isaiah 53

One of the biblical passages most often related to Jesus' statement in Matthew 20:28 is Isaiah 53. Isaiah in general and Isaiah 53 in particular were important for Matthew's telling of Jesus' life.

As we saw earlier, Matthew related Jesus' healing of Peter's mother-in-law and many who were demonized as fulfilling the words of the prophet, "He took our infirmities and bore our diseases" (Mt 8:14–17, quoting Isa 53:4). We may well detect the influence of Isaiah 53 behind Jesus' pronouncement in Matthew 20:28 as well. There is no word-for-word correlation or claim of fulfillment, but Jesus certainly expresses the gist of Isaiah's servant poem (Isa 53:10–12) in his pronouncement:

> Yet it was the Lord's will to crush him and cause him to suffer,
>   and though *the* Lord makes *his life an offering for sin,*
> he will see his offspring and prolong his days,
>   and the will of the Lord will prosper in his hand.
> After he has suffered,
>   he will see the light of life and be satisfied;
>   *by his knowledge my righteous servant will justify many,*
>   *and he will bear their iniquities.*
> Therefore I will give him a portion among the great,
>   and he will divide the spoils with the strong,
> because *he poured out his life unto death,*
>   *and was numbered with the transgressors.*
> For *he bore the sin of many,*
>   *and made intercession for the transgressors.* (italics added)

The italicized lines from the oracle are the most relevant here. The Lord God makes the life of his servant an offering for sin. As such, the servant makes right/justifies "the many" who are wrong before God because of their sins. He does so by bearing in himself the iniquities of the people. Since the servant willingly pours out his life until death, he bears the sins of "many." There is a rich and often complicated history of interpretation to these verses, but Matthew and many early Christians saw the life, death, and resurrection of Jesus foreshadowed in them.

As John Nolland notes, Matthew does not cleverly propose any theory of atonement from Jesus' claims. He simply reports what Jesus has said. To borrow and redeploy Nolland's phrase, the evangelist does appear to make Jesus "the lightning rod" of ransom texts like these.[3] God's ransom—past, present, and future—is concentrated in Jesus' life and his death on the cross. Matthew does not work out the implications of how and why Jesus' death is a ransom for many. His claim lies prior to any atonement theories that church fathers and theologians of later eras might propose.

20:30-31 *Two blind men . . . shouted, "Lord, Son of David, have mercy on us!" The crowd rebuked them and told them to be quiet, but they shouted all the louder, "Lord, Son of David, have mercy on us!"* As Jesus and his disciples were leaving Jericho traveling west to Jerusalem, they could not get away from the crowd. Two blind men shouted twice, "Lord, Son of David, have mercy on us." On several other occasions, others in need of Jesus' healing power called out to him with the same plea (Mt 9:27; 15:22; 17:15). For the title "Son of David," see comments on Matthew 1:1.

But the inclusion of "Lord" here addressed to Jesus clearly links the Son of David with a number of Old Testament passages that plead with the Lord, "Have mercy!" (cf. Ex 33:19; Pss 6:2; 41:4, 10; 86:3). In most cases the plea involves a personal lament, but Psalm 123:3 is part of a communal lament: "Have mercy on us, LORD, have mercy on us, for we have endured no end of contempt." Ironically, Psalm 123 repeats the word *eyes* over and over again: "On you [LORD] we fix our eyes . . . as the eyes of servants focus on the hand of their master . . . as the eyes of a maidservant focus on the hand of her mistress, so our eyes fix on the LORD our God until he has shown us mercy" (author's translation). What the two blind men lacked were eyes that could see. They had endured a great deal of hardship and ridicule because of their disability. In this instance they are shushed by crowds who likely had little regard for them. What they needed, however, were eyes to see. Moved with compassion, Jesus opened their eyes, and they followed him. In Psalm 123, the writer pleads with the LORD to have mercy; the word *LORD* is a rendering of the unspeakable name of God. In Matthew, the blind men employ the same plea but with Jesus addressed as "Lord." The close association of Jesus with God's unique, not-to-be-spoken name implies that he is more than a man; in Matthew's parlance, it suggests he is Immanuel, "God with us."

MATTHEW 21

21:1 *As they approached Jerusalem and came to Bethphage on the Mount of Olives, Jesus sent two disciples.* Jesus and his disciples made the long hard climb up from the Jericho to Jerusalem. They stopped at Bethphage—a village archaeologists have yet to identify. Standing on the Mount of Olives east of Jerusalem, Jesus sent out two disciples on an important errand. Since the time of Ezekiel, the Mount of Olives has been the center of Jewish imagination regarding messianic fulfillment. The judgment prophesied in the book (Eze 1–10) finally gives way to various hints that God was not finished with his people, but would restore them (Eze 11:14–21). When the glory of YHWH leaves the city, moving east to join the exiles, the glory stops for a time on the mountain east of the city, the Mount of Olives (Eze 11:23). Later, Ezekiel has a vision of the glory's return from exile, and it comes from the east, right over the Mount of Olives (Eze 43:1–12).

Perhaps the most memorable mention of the Mount of Olives is found at the end of the book of Zechariah (chapter 14). The final battle is ready to be waged, and YHWH himself gathers all the nations against Jerusalem to battle. But when it seems the battle is lost, the Lord arrives and fights against those nations:

> On that day his [YHWH's] feet will stand on the Mount of Olives, east of Jerusalem, and the Mount of Olives will be split in two from east to west, forming a great valley, with half of the mountain moving north and half moving south. You will flee by my mountain valley, for it will extend to Azel. You will flee as you fled from the earthquake in the days of Uzziah king of Judah. Then the LORD my God will come, and all the holy ones with him. (Zec 14:4–5)

The image of YHWH as divine warrior is common in the Hebrew Scriptures (see comments at Mt 11:9–10) but is pronounced especially in this passage. YHWH positions himself strategically on the Mount of Olives because Jerusalem has been taken by its enemies. In fact, the Mount of Olives is higher than any part of Jerusalem, which provides additional strategic advantage.[1] It is not coincidental that Jesus stops and looks down upon the temple and the winding road that leads down the mount as he sends two disciples for an important task.

21:2–5 *"Go to the village ahead of you, and at once you will find a donkey tied there, with her colt by her . . . ." This took place to fulfill what was spoken through the prophet: "Say to Daughter Zion, 'See, your king comes to you, gentle and riding on a donkey.'"* Jesus sends two disciples to retrieve two donkeys a mother, and her foal. Zechariah, it seems, is weighing heavily on Jesus' mind. Matthew's account has the disciples retrieving two animals. This represents Matthew's fondness for doubling (cf. Mt 8:28; 9:27; 20:30) and the reality that the colt would have been unruly and upset apart from its mother. Those who deal with animals know this to be true. David Garland makes the case that the two represent two sides of Jesus' identity. On the one hand, he enters Jerusalem as the royal son of David; on the other, he rides "on the son of a pack animal, he comes as the meek, suffering servant who will take away our weaknesses and bear our diseases."[2]

Matthew sees Jesus' action of riding a foal and its mother down into Jerusalem as the fulfillment of prophecy. In fact, he brings together two prophecies. The first line—"Say to Daughter Zion"—comes from an oracle of restoration (Isa 62). See Table 21.1.

Table 21.1. Two Prophecies in Matthew 21:5

Isaiah 62:11	Zechariah 9:9	Matthew 21:5
Say to Daughter Zion,	Rejoice greatly, Daughter Zion! Shout, Daughter Jerusalem!	Say to Daughter Zion,
"See, your Savior comes! See, his reward is with him, and his recompense accompanies him."	See, your king comes to you, righteous and victorious, lowly and riding on a donkey, on a colt, the foal of a donkey.	"See, your king comes to you, gentle and riding on a donkey, and on a colt, the foal of a donkey."

The prophecy says that Jerusalem will be vindicated and all the nations will see her redemption (Isa 62:1–10). Her Savior is coming with reward and judgment in hand. God will restore the city to her former glory and beyond. The people will be given new names: "the Holy People" and "the Redeemed of the LORD," and Jerusalem will be called "Sought After, the City No Longer Deserted" (Isa 62:12). Matthew relates this oracle of salvation with another which comes from Zechariah. The common thread is the city itself, "Daughter Zion" (Zec 9:9; see Table 21.1).

The oracle summons the Daughter Zion and Daughter Jerusalem to a celebration of joy for the highly anticipated arrival of her king. A similar formula occurs in Zechariah 2:10 as YHWH himself promises to come to Daughter Zion and dwell in her midst. But the king's arrival in Zechariah 9 is not in a chariot or on a finely bred warhorse. He comes on a beast of burden, a poor person's mount. No one had heard or seen a king come into his city in such an unconventional way, but Jesus was no conventional king. His left-handed power subverts all worldly authority and demonstrates to the world true greatness. Jesus arrives not on his own mount, but on a borrowed donkey and her foal. The Lord had need of it, but only temporarily. Zechariah's oracle continues proclaiming that when YHWH presents his king to Zion, he will put an end to war and command peace to the nations. His dominion will be from sea to sea (Zec 9:10).

21:8 *A very large crowd spread their cloaks on the road, while others cut branches from the trees and spread them on the road.* This was not the first time a crowd spread their cloaks before an anointed king. When Jehu's fellow officers declare him their sovereign, they do exactly as the crowd that welcomes Jesus into the holy city does. Earlier, Elisha the prophet sent one of his disciples to anoint Jehu, an Israelite commander, to be king (2 Ki 9:1–4). The wickedness of Ahab's dynasty was intolerable, so the prophet acted definitively in a time of great danger. After some convincing, the officers accepted the prophecy and quickly spread their cloaks before him; they blew the trumpet and proclaimed him king (2 Ki 9:13).

A large crowd assembled to welcome Jesus into Jerusalem the same way Jehu's officers welcomed him. They spread their cloaks on the road, cut branches and spread them before Jesus' procession.[3] Only John's gospel tells us that some were palms (Jn 12:13).

21:9 *The crowds that went ahead of him and those that followed shouted, "Hosanna to the Son of David!" "Blessed is he who comes in the name of the Lord!" "Hosanna in the highest heaven!"* As the crowd moves ahead of Jesus, they shout and chant. We should probably see these as three separate chants inspired by the Scriptures them-selves. Effectively, the people who join the procession into Jerusalem and the temple are accepting the claim that Jesus is the Messiah, the Son of David. At the heart of this procession is Psalm 118, a psalm of thanksgiving and victory, that describes a procession of the people and their leader to the temple and the altar. They are to place their branches on the altar (Ps 118:27; cf. Lev 23:40), which may explain why branches are cut and placed before the king as he enters the city. The crowd probably expects to move into the temple beyond the precincts and have their petitions to God made there.

The chant—"Hosanna"—translates a Hebrew word that means "Save us now, Lord." It implores the highest heavens to move now and redeem the city and its people. The scriptural inspiration for these chants comes, again, from Psalm 118:25–26:

> Lord, save us!
>> Lord, grant us success!
>
> Blessed is he who comes in the name of the Lord.
>> From the house of the Lord we bless you.

Psalm 118 reenacts a royal drama when the king enters the city and comes to its holy center, the temple, to sacrifice. Here, the people in the crowd accept the claim, audacious as it seems, that this son of David, Jesus, is their rightful king.[4] But the city, Matthew tells us, is in turmoil when this happens. The majority of its citizens and visitors have been caught off guard.

The chant "Blessed is he who comes in the name of the Lord" was associated with the Passover tradition, a feast that was only a few days away. The Hallel psalms (Pss 113–118)[5] were sung or chanted as part of the festival.

21:12–13 *Jesus entered the temple courts and drove out all who were buying and selling there. He overturned the tables of the money changers and the benches of those selling doves. "It is written," he said to them, "'My house will be called a house of prayer,' but you are making it 'a den of robbers.'"* Old Testament prophecies were often enacted. Among many examples, Ahijah tore a cloak into pieces to show Solomon how his kingdom would be divided (1 Ki 11:29–36); Isaiah walked naked and barefoot for three years to demonstrate the shame awaiting the Egyptians and Ethiopians in exile (Isa 20); and Jeremiah wore yokes to show that only by submitting to Babylon could Israel remain in the land (Jer 27–28).

Acting as such a prophet, Jesus of Nazareth (Mt 21:11) enters into the temple and does what prophets do. He engages in a bold, public act to dramatize his message. Ironically, the one essential task of the temple was animal sacrifices. Jesus acted to cut off the source of the sacrifices. No animals = no sacrifices. Some have called this action the "cleansing" of the temple. Others say that Jesus is announcing and enacting the first moments of divine judgment on the temple and its leadership. The episode with the fig tree (21:18–19) appears to confirm that. Forty years later when the temple is destroyed by the Romans (AD 70), temple sacrifices do cease. Eventually, prayer is understood as a form of temple sacrifice (Ps 141:2).

The doves mentioned were for the poor, who were prescribed two turtle-doves or pigeons for the sacrifice: one for the sin offering, the other for the burnt offering (Lev 5:7).

When Jesus quoted the Scripture ("it is written"), he combines two passages:[6] the first from Isaiah 56:7, the second from Jeremiah 7:11. Isaiah describes a time when outsiders join themselves to the Lord, love his name, keep the Sabbath, and become part of the covenant. Then he says (Isa 56:7, italics added):

> These [the foreigners who convert] I will bring to my holy mountain
>   and give them joy in my house of prayer.
> Their burnt offerings and sacrifices
>   will be accepted on my altar;
> *for my house will be called*
>   *a house of prayer for all nations.*

The foreigners appear to become fully enfranchised members of Israel through their devotion to the covenant. The temple is to gain the reputation as a house of prayer for all nations. This suggests the moneychangers and sellers of sacrificial animals were set up to do business in the precincts of the temple where Gentiles were to worship. With animals comes what animals do: defecate and urinate. They introduce all manner of uncleanness into the temple precincts. Jesus acts to put a stop to the uncleanness in the area where Gentiles gathered to worship.

The second half of the quotation echoes Jeremiah's temple sermon, one of his most famous (Jer 7:1–15). The gist of the sermon is that the standing, functioning temple is no guarantee of Jerusalem's safety and welfare. The presence of the Lord depends in large measure on the depth of justice practiced by worshipers and their willingness to repent when they have missed the mark. Because they did not trust in him, YHWH determined to do in Jerusalem what had already happened at Shiloh (1 Sa 3–5). There is a cast of finality to this oracle and to Jesus' actions. The lines quoted by Jesus are Jeremiah 7:11: "Has this house, which bears my Name, become a den of robbers to you? But I have been watching! declares the LORD." Jesus does not ask the question; he makes the accusation that the temple leadership had allowed the temple to become "a den of robbers," that is, a place where the criminal element of God's people feel free to do as they wish. Whatever sanctity remained was compromised by their actions.

21:14 *The blind and the lame came to him at the temple, and he healed them.* Matthew records that the blind and the lame come to Jesus "at the temple" for a miracle. Jewish law prohibited the disabled from entering the temple and participating fully in its activities. At the head of the list of those with a "blemish" are the blind and the lame (Lev 21:16–20). Jesus acts to reverse their situation, healing them and making them fit for the temple.

21:15 *But when the chief priests and the teachers of the law saw the wonderful things he did and the children shouting in the temple courts, "Hosanna to the Son of David," they were indignant.* On "Hosanna," see comments on Matthew 21:9.

Jesus' authority and the children's chants were too much for the temple leadership in Jerusalem. They became angry and called him to account. But once again Jesus responded with Scripture.

21:16 *From the lips of children and infants you, Lord, have called forth your praise.* This prophetic moment reminded Jesus of Psalm 8. This psalm became a favorite in the early church (e.g., 1 Co 15:27–28; Heb 2:6–8), perhaps on the memory of Jesus' use of it. The praise which Jesus is hearing and apparently receiving resounds with the words of Psalm 8:1–2 (italics added):

> Lord, our Lord,
>   how majestic is your name in all the earth!
>
> You have set your glory
>   in the heavens.
> *Through the praise of children and infants*
>   *you have established a stronghold against your enemies,*
>   *to silence the foe and the avenger.*

After a series of laments (Pss 3; 4; 6), Psalm 8 is the first poem dedicated to praise, acknowledging God's glory over all the earth. But it also celebrates humanity's place amidst God's creation. For some reason, God has special care for humanity, who are charged with having dominion over and thus caring for the welfare of all creation. Ultimately, Jesus takes on a special role as both the ideal human and the Lord who is sovereign.

Children and infants may know something and show something that the so-called wise are unable or unwilling to grasp. In this case, Matthew is referring to the welcome Jesus receives among children and the *hoi polloi* (the people of the land) in the triumphal entry compared to the rejection he will face later that week from the powerful of Jerusalem.

21:18-19 *Early in the morning, as Jesus was on his way back to the city, he was hungry. Seeing a fig tree by the road, he went up to it but found nothing on it except leaves. Then he said to it, "May you never bear fruit again!" Immediately the tree withered.* To understand the episode of the withering of the fig tree, we have to consider that Jesus is still in the mode of a prophet who acts (see comments at Mt 21:12–13). Though he's hungry, his action and words here are not because of hunger or disappointment; they are the occasion of it. The fig tree is a symbol.

There are a variety of prophetic oracles that describe the nations or God's people as a fig tree in peril of judgment. The prophet Isaiah utters an oracle against the nations, describing how God's wrath is sure to come against them. The starry host, he says, will fall like withered leaves of a grape vine, like a fig tree with shriveled fruit (Isa 34:4). Joel describes the arrival of the day of the Lord as a day of judgment when the fig tree withers, food is cut off, and the crops fail; seeds shrivel in the ground and the animals moan from hunger, wandering and looking for any morsel of food (Joel 1:12–17). Hosea 2:12 prophesies that God will lay waste the vines and fig trees because they were the pay given to the faithless by her lovers. Jeremiah has an entire oracle dedicated to the destiny of good figs (those in exile in Babylon) and bad figs (those who remained in the land or fled to Egypt, Jer 24:1–10). But it is probably Jeremiah 8 that informs this gospel episode most significantly (8:13, italics added):

> I will take away their harvest,
> > declares the LORD.
> > *There will be no grapes on the vine.*
> *There will be no figs on the tree,*
> > *and their leaves will wither.*
> What I have given them
> > will be taken from them.

The judgment forecast earlier by John the Baptist is underway. As the next episodes demonstrate, John is on Jesus' mind (Mt 21:23–27 and 21:28–32). Perhaps it is because John has already faced execution, a fate that awaits Jesus this week as well. Lack of repentance, corrupt leaders in Jerusalem, and compromised faith are initiating the woes that will befall God's people (Mt 23) who reject the Son of the vineyard owner (21:33–46). For those with Old Testament eyes, a fig tree without figs is a portent of things to come. According to Jeremiah, the Lord himself acts to take away the harvest; this is not simply bad luck or the roll of the dice. With a powerful word from Jesus, the leaves wither as the prophet said they were destined to do. Together the clearing of the temple and the withering of the fig tree foreshadow things to come.

21:23-27 *John's baptism—where did it come from? Was it from heaven, or of human origin?* Regarding John's baptism, see comments on Matthew 3:1–11.

What the Structure Means: Three Parables (Mt 21:28–22:14)

Not long after the temple incident, Jesus returned to the temple to face its leaders, the chief priests and elders of the people. They wanted to know who gave Jesus the authority to clear out the temple merchants and their animals. Jesus evaded their question by posing to them another question about John the Baptist, a question they refused to answer (Mt 21:23–27).

The next three parables in Matthew stand as an answer to the question and further elaboration on the authority of John the Baptist and Jesus.

21:28–32	parable of the two sons
21:33–44	parable of the wicked tenants
22:1–14	parable of the wedding banquet

In the parable of the two sons, Jesus announces that the tax collectors and prostitutes will enter the kingdom of God ahead of the Jerusalem leaders. This had to do with how these "sinners" responded to John compared to those who presumed they were righteous. The parable of the wicked tenants ends with Jesus pronouncing that the kingdom of God will be taken from the chief priests and Pharisees and given to those who will produce the fruit of the kingdom. As we will see, the parable of the wedding banquet portrays the kingdom as a royal wedding which the busy and otherwise disposed mock and are unwilling to attend; they have better things to do— or so they think—and some even attack the king's slaves, mistreat, and kill them. So the king orders the murderers to be seized and executed and their city burned (perhaps a picture of what would happen to Jerusalem in AD 70). Together the three parables form a complete response, demonstrating Jesus' complete rejection by the Jerusalem power brokers and the future demise of their authority in the temple's destruction.

21:28 *There was a man who had two sons.* The motif of two sons (one obedient/ favored, one not) is found in the stories of Cain and Abel (Ge 4:1–16), of Ishmael and Isaac (Ge 16, 21), of Esau and Jacob (Ge 25, 27–28), of Joseph's sons Manasseh and Ephraim (Ge 48) and others. In these cases, the younger son is often blessed, which would be culturally unexpected. Likewise, Jesus reverses conventional thinking by saying that sinners are blessed more than religious leaders.

Go and work today in the vineyard. Israel is referred to in various places in Scripture as the vineyard and the vine (e.g., Ps 80:8–16; Isa 1:8; Hos 10:1). Jesus uses the image elsewhere in Matthew (e.g., 7:16–20; 20:1–7 and 21:33–44).

21:32 *John came to you to show you the way of righteousness.* Regarding John and righteousness, see comments on Matthew 3:13–15. On righteousness, see also comments on Matthew 5:6, 10, 20; 6:1, and "What the Structure Means: Greater Righteousness (Mt 5)."

21:33 *There was a landowner who planted a vineyard. He put a wall around it, dug a winepress in it and built a watchtower. Then he rented the vineyard to some farmers and moved to another place.* The parable of the wicked tenants, as it is commonly known, is based loosely on the "Song of the Vineyard" (cf. Mt 20:1–16) from Isaiah 5:1–2, 7. The prophet's oracle is itself a parable and would have been recognized by Jesus' inquisitors that day (Mt 21:45). In the original parable, "the beloved" had a vineyard on a fertile hill. He cleared it of stones, planted it with the best vines, built a watchtower, and dug out a wine press, the exact actions of the landowner in Jesus' parable. Instead of yielding good grapes, the vineyard only yielded bad grapes (Isa 5:2–4). Judgment follows in the actions of the owner who removes the hedge, breaks down the wall, neglects the care of the vines, and—because the owner signifies God— commands the rains not to water it. In the end, the prophet reveals the true identity of the owner, namely, the Lord; and of the vineyard, that is, the house of Israel and the people of Judah (Isa 5:7). Jesus will rework the details of the parable, but the identity of the landowner and the proceeds of the vineyard remain the same.

21:34–36 *When the harvest time approached, he sent his servants to the tenants to collect his fruit. The tenants seized his servants; they beat one, killed another, and stoned a third. Then he sent other servants to them, more than the first time, and the tenants treated them the same way.* In Jesus' retelling of the parable, the landowner leaves for another country and leases the vineyard to tenants who are supposed to pay him for the use of the land and its produce. When the landowner's servants arrive, however, they are beaten, killed, and stoned. In Jesus' parable, the servants signify the prophets whom God has sent over and again to his people to call them back to fidelity to the covenant. As Israel's history demonstrates, the prophets are ignored (2 Ch 24:19), beaten, and put in stocks (Jer 20:1–2), and hunted down and killed (Jer 26:20–23).

Going Deeper into the Fate of the Prophets

The writer of Hebrews offers these sobering words about the faithful prophets from the past (Heb 11:32–38):

> And what more shall I say? I do not have time to tell about Gideon, Barak, Samson and Jephthah, about David and Samuel and the prophets, who through faith conquered kingdoms, administered justice, and gained what was promised; who shut the mouths of lions, quenched the fury of the flames, and escaped the edge of the sword; whose weakness was turned to strength; and who became powerful in battle and routed foreign armies. Women received back their dead, raised to life again. There were others who were tortured, refusing to be released so that they might gain an even better resurrection. Some faced jeers and flogging, and even chains and imprisonment. They were put to death by stoning; they were sawed in two; they were killed by the sword. They went about in sheepskins and goatskins, destitute, persecuted and mistreated—the world was not worthy of them. They wandered in deserts and mountains, living in caves and in holes in the ground.

Though not all these events are recorded in the Old Testament, the writer of Hebrews testifies to traditions circulating at the time about the fate of the prophets and other exemplars of faith.

It is strange that Christians today complain when they are ignored, canceled, or mistreated in some way by an overtly secular culture. God followers have lived in and through hostile environments for millennia. Did not Jesus say this is how it would be for those who follow him? If Christians follow him only when their lives are easy or pleasant, does that not ignore the history of the prophets who were maligned, maimed, and murdered for God's sake? Throughout much of the world—where Christians are not in the majority—to be a Christ follower is to be targeted. Do not be surprised when persecution comes your way.

21:42 *Jesus said to them, "Have you never read in the Scriptures: 'The stone the builders rejected has become the cornerstone; the Lord has done this, and it is marvelous in our eyes'"?* The frequency with which Psalm 118:22–23 is quoted or alluded to by early Christians (see Ac 4:11; 1 Pe 2:7) indicates that it is a favorite among those attempting to testify to Jesus' significance. The backhanded way Jesus introduces his verbatim quotation—"Have you never read in the Scriptures"—appears to discredit any who fail to see how it applies to the goings-on in Jerusalem that fateful week.

The rejected stone of the quotation echoes the "rejected" son of the landowner in Jesus' parable. The quotation comes from one of the Hallel psalms (Ps 113–118) and, as we indicated earlier (21: 9), describes a procession of those giving thanks on the way to God's house. Jesus takes this passage as prophetic of what is about to take place in Jerusalem. An outline of Jesus' quotation is found in Table 21.2.

Table 21.2. The Rejected Stone of Matthew 21:42

Rejected stone	= Jesus
The builders	= the chief priests, Pharisees, and other powerful people
The act of rejection	= the crucifixion
The cornerstone	= Jesus
The Lord's doing	= the resurrection

Interestingly, the next verse of Psalm 118 (v. 24 NRSV) is this: "This is the day that the LORD has made: let us rejoice and be glad in it." In the context of the psalm as Jesus quoted it, the day the rejected stone is made the cornerstone—that is, resurrection day (Easter)—God's people are to rejoice and be glad. And if the rejected stone is made the cornerstone, we might ask: The cornerstone of what? Again, in the context of the Hallel psalm, the people are moving in a procession to the temple. Thus, we might say that Jesus is made the cornerstone of a new temple. That is certainly how the author of 1 Peter understood it (1 Pe 2:4–8). Peter also interpreted Psalm 118:22 Christologically in Acts 4:8–11.[7]

Jesus' final pronouncement of the parable puts the chief priests and Pharisees on notice that the kingdom will be taken from them and given to another people (the followers of Jesus) who will render to God what is his (Mt 21:43, 45)

21:44 *Anyone who falls on this stone will be broken to pieces; anyone on whom it falls will be crushed."*[8] From the way Jesus interprets this parable, there may be more "stone" references that relate to this passage. It was common for rabbis

of the time to link together various scriptural passages using a particular
keyword: in this case *stone*.[9] The rejected stone becomes the cornerstone,
which is also a stumbling stone and a crushing stone. We might consider
Isaiah 28:16:

> So this is what the Sovereign LORD says:
>
> > "See, I lay a stone in Zion, a tested stone,
> >   a precious cornerstone for a sure foundation;
> > the one who relies on it
> >   will never be stricken with panic."

Earlier, Isaiah writes (Isa 8:13–15, italics added):

> The LORD Almighty is the one you are to regard as holy,
>   he is the one you are to fear,
>   he is the one you are to dread.
> He will be a holy place;
>   for both Israel and Judah he will be
> *a stone that causes people to stumble*
>   *and a rock that makes them fall.*
> And for the people of Jerusalem he will be
>   a trap and a snare.
> Many of them will stumble;
>   they will fall and be broken,
>   they will be snared and captured.

In the first passage, the Lord himself is laying in Zion/Jerusalem a precious cornerstone. And the one who depends on it/him will not have to fear.
In the second, the Lord is the holy place (the temple), and is the rock that
makes some among Israel and Judah stumble, fall, and be broken.

Likewise, Daniel revealed and interpreted aspects of King
Nebuchadnezzar's dream in accordance with a mighty stone (Da 2). In that
dream, the king saw an immense statue of extraordinary brilliance. The upper
part of the statue was made of gold, silver, and bronze. Its legs were iron, and
its feet were mixed iron and clay. As he looked on, a stone was cut, not by human hands, and it smashed the legs and feet of the statue, and the entire figure
shattered, becoming like chaff carried away by the wind. The stone that struck
the statue became a great mountain and filled the earth (Da 2:35). Daniel
interpreted the statue as a series of kingdoms that rise and fall. And in the end,
there would be another kingdom (Da 2:44–45, italics added):

In the time of those kings, the God of heaven will set up a kingdom that will never be destroyed, nor will it be left to another people. *It will crush all those kingdoms* and bring them to an end, but it will itself endure forever. *This is the meaning of the vision of the rock cut out of a mountain, but not by human hands—a rock that broke the iron, the bronze, the clay, the silver and the gold to pieces.*

The great God has shown the king what will take place in the future. The dream is true and its interpretation is trustworthy.

Although Jesus does not introduce this as a parable of the kingdom, the reference to Psalm 118 and the many "stone" references in the Old Testament ultimately link it to the apocalyptic certainty of Jesus' death, resurrection, and the kingdom he is establishing. Early Christians understood Psalm 118:22 that way. Peter, whose nickname means "rock," appears to be fond of it. In Acts 4:11 he uses it to confront the religious leaders: they were "the builders" who rejected the stone by having Jesus crucified. Likewise, the author of 1 Peter links together a variety of stone passages—including Psalm 118:22—in a passage rich in Christological and ecclesial themes (1 Pe 2:4–8).

MATTHEW 22

22:2–6 *The kingdom of heaven is like a king who prepared a wedding banquet for his son. He sent his servants to those who had been invited to the banquet to tell them to come, but they refused to come.* The parable of the wedding banquet (Mt 22:1–14) describes a key aspect of the kingdom of heaven. Among Jesus' last teachings, it describes how those invited initially to a wedding feast hosted by the king refused to come and enjoy the king's table. In fact, they belittled and humiliated the host by the way they mistreated his servants. The parable appears to be inspired loosely upon another invitation issued by Lady Wisdom in Proverbs 9:1–6 (italics added):

> Wisdom has built her house;
>   she has set up its seven pillars.
> *She has prepared her meat and mixed her wine;*
>   *she has also set her table.*
> *She has sent out her servants, and she calls*
>   *from the highest point of the city,*
>   *"Let all who are simple come to my house!"*
> To those who have no sense she says,
>   *"Come, eat my food*
>   *and drink the wine I have mixed.*
> *Leave your simple ways and you will live;*
>   *walk in the way of insight."*

In this pericope, it is Lady Wisdom who has readied her house, prepared the meal, and sent her servants into the city to invite "the simple" to come eat her food, drink her wine, and walk in her ways. The simple are those who lack wisdom and know it. They are, to use Matthew's language, "the poor in spirit" and those who "hunger and thirst for righteousness" (Mt 5), but the story of whether the simple come to the feast is not told. Lady Wisdom's invitation hangs, as it were, in the air.

Lady Wisdom holds a unique position in Proverbs;[1] she is personified and described as the Lord's first creation, his daily delight and coworker in establishing heaven and earth (Pr 8:22–31). In a way, Wisdom parallels Jesus himself who, as he nears the cross, finishes the story, because many of those invited refused to come and did horrible things to God's servants. As in the parable of the wicked tenants (Mt 21:33–46), the servants represent the prophets whom God sent to warn his people and invite them to turn back to their God.

22:7 *The king was enraged. He sent his army and destroyed those murderers and burned their city.* This image recollects the destruction of Jerusalem and the first temple (586 BC), an event predicted by Israel's prophets. Isaiah, for example, predicts the invasion of a foreign army because God's people had rejected his instruction and despised his word. So God's anger is kindled and he summons an army. They come quickly, ready for war, and like a lion seize their prey. God's people are beyond rescue, and their land knows only darkness and distress (Isa 5:24–30).

Likewise, Jeremiah prophesies the destruction of Jerusalem and Judah from a foe who comes from the north, Babylon and her confederates. Those who are in villages should seek refuge in the fortified cities because God, in his anger, will bring evil and destruction upon them. In time the land will be laid waste and the cities ruined; they will sit uninhabited because the fierce anger of the Lord has not turned away. Indeed, Judah is overrun by enemies and her leading citizens are taken into captivity (2 Ki 24–25). This is the beginning of the exile, one of the most traumatic experiences in Israel's storied history, an event so violent and stricken with grief that an entire book of the Bible is given to it (Lamentations). Careful readers will recall that the exile serves as part of the framework of Matthew's genealogy (Mt 1).

22:8–14 *But when the king came in to see the guests, he noticed a man there who was not wearing wedding clothes. He asked, "How did you get in here without wedding clothes, friend?" The man was speechless. Then the king told the attendants, "Tie him hand and foot, and throw him outside, into the darkness, where there will be weeping and gnashing of teeth." For many are invited, but few are chosen.* While those initially invited are rejected and judged by the king as unworthy, the wedding feast is scheduled to begin soon. So the king sends his slaves into the streets and neighborhoods to invite any and all who will come to fill his house. The feast is in full swing when the king notices a man not wearing a wedding robe; so he questions him, has him seized, and thrown into darkness. For the phrase "weeping and gnashing of teeth," see comments on Matthew 8:11–12. This guest is rejected not because he refused the invitation but because he did not understand the gravity of his decision to attend. He arrived in his everyday clothes, not his best. We might hear a subtle echo of Isaiah 61:10 in its description of how God clothes the righteous with "garments of salvation" and "a robe of righteousness." The prophet likens those garments to weddings adornments of a bridegroom and bride. The rejection of the guest appears to reflect the same tragedy of those who called Jesus "Lord," performed acts in his name, but in fact never knew him (Mt 7:21–23).

Jesus' pronouncement at the end of the parable is often quoted, but not well understood. The invitation to enter the feast and thus the kingdom of heaven is offered to all, but ultimately God choses "the few" who say "yes" to the call. We are thus brought to the threshold of the mystery of God's sovereignty and human free will.

22:15–16 *They [the Pharisees] sent their disciples to him along with the Herodians. "Teacher," they said, "we know that you are a man of integrity and that you teach the way of God in accordance with the truth. You aren't swayed by others, because you pay no attention to who they are.* Tension builds for Jesus as he moves inexorably to the cross. A series of public challenges by foes disguised as friends interrupts his teaching. Pharisees (at odds with Roman rule) and Herodians (accommodating to Roman rule) were an odd group to collaborate. Apparently they both see Jesus as a serious threat, so together they put him to the test, but not before buttering him up.

Their compliments echo various texts of Scripture. For example, Abraham is described as chosen by God; his task is to charge his children to walk in the ways of God by doing what is right and just. God's promise, it seems, rests upon whether or not God's people walk in integrity and truth (Ge 18:19). Similarly, the Lord God is described as good and upright; he instructs sinners in his ways and teaches the humble to do what is right (Ps 25:8–9). When Samuel stood ready to anoint a king, the Lord instructs him not to be swayed by good looks, height, or other externals, for the Lord does not see or value what mortals do; he looks at the heart (1 Sa 16:7). Jesus, it appears, is put in the same category as these scriptural models; for his inquisitors describe him as a teacher of integrity who instructs in the ways of God truthfully; he cannot be swayed to bow to the kinds of interests the rest of us find so fascinating.

22:17–22 *"Show me the coin used for paying the tax." They brought him a denarius, and he asked them, "Whose image is this? And whose inscription?"* When Jesus is asked whether he thought paying taxes to Caesar was lawful or not, he knew the question was anything but innocent. His questioners were not true seekers, so they would not get a straight answer. Jesus asked for a coin most likely because neither he nor his followers had one. But his opponents did. They had no misgivings about having a coin with a graven image of the emperor on it. The coin, a (silver) denarius, had the head of Tiberius on it and an inscription declaring him Caesar and divine.[2] Jewish tradition views human images on coins as blasphemous and a violation of the statute against "graven images" (Ex 20:4): "You shall not make for yourself an image in the form of anything in heaven above or on the earth beneath or in the waters below." By the time of the New Testament, not only do Jews not mint such coins, neither do the faithful carry them or use them for exchange. Thus, Jesus catches his interrogators in their hypocrisy.

22:23–28 *"Teacher," they said, "Moses told us that if a man dies without having children, his brother must marry the widow and raise up offspring for him."* The Sadducees join in trying to entrap Jesus publicly. They approach him with the flattering address of "teacher," and ask him a question rooted in the Torah. Moses had given to the children of Israel God's laws: in this case, the law of levirate marriage (Dt 25:5–10; cf. Ge 38:8). The law assumes two brothers are living on the same property or in close proximity. If one brother dies without fathering a son, then his brother is required to marry his widow to produce a son who will carry forward the name of the deceased (Ge 38:6–26). If he refuses to marry her, for whatever reason, he is to be brought before the elders of the city to be reminded of his responsibility. If he persists, then he is to be publicly shamed.

The situation described by the Sadducees is far-fetched and carried to an extreme most likely to try and make the idea of resurrection life look absurd. Their question only required the woman to be married to more than one brother: "At the resurrection, whose wife will she be?" (Mt 22:28).[3]

22:29–32 *Have you not read what God said to you, "I am the God of Abraham, the God of Isaac, and the God of Jacob"? He is not the God of the dead but of the living.* Jesus answered their question by first rebuffing them. They are wrong: first because they deny the resurrection; second, because they fail to understand the nature of resurrection life. Apparently, the Sadducees imagined that those who believed in the world to come held that social relationships would continue as they had in this life. Jesus corrects the two errors in reverse order. In both cases they failed to understand the Scriptures and God's power. Note that Jesus does not say people become angels, only that in heaven they are like angels in the matter of not marrying.

The truth of the resurrection, according to Jesus, is implied by God himself to Moses at the foot of Mt. Sinai. As Moses approached the bush that burned but was not consumed, God called to him and told him to remove his sandals because he was standing on holy ground. God identified himself: "I am the God of your father, the God of Abraham, the God of Isaac and the God of Jacob" (Ex 3:6). Now Abraham, Isaac, and Jacob had died hundreds of years earlier, but God says, "I am the God of . . . ," not "I was the God of . . ." This implies that the dead still live. After all, God is not God of the dead but of the living. Jesus' interpretation of Exodus strikes those schooled in modern methods of exegesis as a bit odd, but not to his first hearers who stood amazed at his teaching.[4]

22:34-36 *Hearing that Jesus had silenced the Sadducees, the Pharisees got together. One of them, an expert in the law, tested him with this question: "Teacher, which is the greatest commandment in the Law?"* According to Jewish tradition, the Torah contains 613 commandments (*b. Makkot* 23b); so, which is the greatest? It is not clear what they hoped to accomplish with this question.[5]

22:37-40 *Jesus replied: "'Love the Lord your God with all your heart and with all your soul and with all your mind.' This is the first and greatest commandment. And the second is like it: 'Love your neighbor as yourself.' All the Law and the Prophets hang on these two commandments."* (See also "Going Deeper into Fulfilling the Law and the Prophets: Matthew 5:17.")

Rather than throwing the question back to the expert in the law, Jesus answered it with words familiar to anyone remotely acquainted with the Shema (Dt 6:5): love the Lord your God with all your heart, soul, and mind. The Shema was then and continues to be the basic affirmation of Jewish faith. It assumes a community of like-minded believers all committed to this one God with complete abandon (heart, soul, mind). Jesus declares this the first and greatest commandment, but he links it to another he calls "the second": "Love your neighbor as yourself" (Lev 19:18). Jesus had given similar instruction to the young man with many possessions (see Mt 19:16-22). If the first commandment has to do with a person's vertical relationship to God, then the second has to do with horizontal relationships in this world. On what may have been another occasion, Jesus defined who one's neighbor is (Lk 10:25-37).

When Jesus claimed that all the Law and Prophets hang on these two commandments, he is clearly privileging those two above all others. He said much the same about the Golden Rule, which has to do more with horizontal relationships (see comments on Mt 7:12).

22:41-42 *While the Pharisees were gathered together, Jesus asked them, "What do you think about the Messiah? Whose son is he?" "The son of David," they replied.* Jesus now returns the favor and asks the Pharisees a question. This put an end to their attempts to trap Jesus and shame him publicly. Perhaps they were tired of being bested in the debates. He asked them their learned opinion about the Messiah: Whose son will he be? On the one hand, it was a simple question. But Jesus was setting them up for another question that would riddle them senseless.

Their answer, of course, is correct. The Messiah will be a son of David, an affirmation made in the opening lines of Matthew's gospel. But Jesus connects it now with another title, the title "Lord."

On "son of David" and its relationship to 2 Samuel 7:12–16, see comments on Matthew 1:1.

22:43–46 *He said to them, "How is it then that David, speaking by the Spirit, calls him 'Lord'? For he says, 'The Lord said to my Lord: "Sit at my right hand until I put your enemies under your feet."' If then David calls him 'Lord,' how can he be his son?" No one could say a word in reply, and from that day on no one dared to ask him any more questions.* Jesus offered the Pharisees a riddle based on Psalm 110. Its superscription calls it a psalm of David, a notion Jesus accepts and exploits. In this psalm, Jesus points out that David himself is not speaking; he is speaking "by the Spirit," that is, he is acting as a prophet. Jesus turns it into a riddle about the Messiah. If the Messiah is the son of David, how does David call him "Lord"? For in this prophetic verse, "the Lord" (YHWH) said to "my Lord," the king, David's son, "Sit at my right until I [God] put your enemies under your feet." The psalm goes on to say more about this "Lord" Messiah. Not only will he vanquish his foes, but he will rule a loyal people and act as a priest according to the order of Melchizedek. David's son will be greater than David himself; therefore, it is fitting for father David to call his son "Lord."

This turns convention on its head. Fathers never addressed sons in such a way; the older is always deemed greater by virtue of ancestry. Even Moses showed respect to and took advice from his father-in-law Jethro (Ex 4:18; 18:7, 14–24). But the particular son David has in mind is no ordinary "son of David." He is exalted, seated at the right hand of YHWH. So by "Lord," David must have meant something more, and that something more is expressed throughout the gospel.[6] Both in Greek and in Hebrew, the second word translated "Lord" is capable of several meanings. The Hebrew *adon* can refer to a person in authority—like a king—or it can be used of the Lord God. Likewise, the Greek *kyrios* is capable of a similar range of meanings.[7] On the one hand, nothing more has to be said about Psalm 110:1 than YHWH is speaking to the Davidic king, but Jesus exploits the ambiguity of the word *kyrios* to suggest that David's son has a transcendent significance that even the good king David recognized in his day.[8]

Matthew 22:43–46 Through Old Testament Eyes: Psalm 110

Psalm 110 expressed a vision of an ideal king who reigns not merely on earth but from God's right hand (110:1, 5). It stands among other Old Testament royal psalms such as Psalms 2, 20, 45, and 72. Jesus followers reckoned that this ideal is fulfilled in Jesus of Nazareth, who had Davidic credentials, and transcended father David (and father Abraham) in every way. There may also be a subtle hint of Psalm 8 that declares an ideal vision of humanity grounded in Genesis 1–2. God made humans a little lower than himself and crowned them with glory and honor, gave them dominion, and put all things under their feet (Ps 8:5–8). It is no wonder that New Testament writers quoted or alluded to Psalm 110 more than any other Old Testament passage. Not only does it link Jesus with a truly remarkable messianic text, but it also credits to him a priestly role according to the order of Melchizedek (see Heb 7). But there was more, as Jesus implied.

The Pharisees had no answer to Jesus' riddle. Indeed, how could anyone answer it prior to the cross and resurrection? Such insights could only be gained as early Christians looked back on the life, teaching, and ministry of Jesus. Moving outside of Matthew's account, it is Luke that tells us that the disciples of Jesus could not understand anything that had happened to their teacher apart from the resurrected Jesus opening their minds to the Scriptures (Lk 24:13–48). Early Christian writers returned again and again to the image of the risen Jesus seated at God's right hand to express various aspects of his significance (e.g., Mt 26:64; Ac 2:33–36; 1 Co 15:24–25; Eph 1:20; Heb 8:1; Rev 3:21).[9]

MATTHEW 23

This entire chapter is an extended critique of the Pharisees.
People have often speculated why Jesus singled them out and was "so hard on them." It may have had to do with how influential they were with the people compared to other ascetic or politically oriented groups.

On the one hand, Jesus commends them for their knowledge of the Torah. On the other, he tells his disciples not to follow them because they do not practice what they teach (Mt 23:3). Unlike the ideal disciples who do "righteousness" in secret, for God's eyes alone, the Pharisees and their scribes love public adulation (Mt 6:1–18).

23:2 *The teachers of the law and the Pharisees sit in Moses' seat.* There is no clear evidence that synagogues at the time of Jesus had a chair called "Moses' seat,"[1] so the language is figurative and ironic. It was customary for teachers to sit at the time, even as Jesus did (Mt 5:1; 24:1–3; 26:55). But there was no actual "chair," just as esteemed scholars today who have a "chair" in a university faculty do not have a literal chair they sit in. It is a symbol of status and accomplishment. The issue for Jesus is that these teachers of the law and Pharisees teach as if they have the authority of Moses, the lawgiver. As the chapter unfolds, it is clear that Jesus denies them such status.

23:5 *Everything they do is done for people to see: They make their phylacteries wide and the tassels on their garments long.* When it is time to pray, the Pharisees adorn themselves with phylacteries. These are small boxes, usually made of leather, containing key verses of Scripture (e.g., Ex 13; Dt 6:4–9; 11:13–21). They are tied to the forehead and forearm during times of prayer, often in public. Wide phylacteries would gain more attention. Though they did not shine, they would have had a certain "bling" in some circles.

Jesus wore tassels or fringes on his garments in obedience to the law (see Mt 9:20). All the Israelites are commanded to make fringes and put them on the corners of their garment. Each corner would have a fringe with a blue cord. When the people look down or, presumably, when they get dressed and undressed, they would be reminded of the commandments (Nu 15:37–41; Dt 22:12). When Israelites remember and act in accord with these commandments, they demonstrate that they are holy to God. Jesus criticizes the scribes and Pharisees for having fringes that were extra-long and extra-wide. Larger tassels would not mean more devotion, but more attention.

Going Deeper into Prayer: Matthew 23:5

Jesus is not criticizing public prayer. (See comments at Mt 6:5–6.) Prayer is often a "communal" act.[2] The Lord's Prayer begins, "*Our* Father," indicating more than one person is praying. Even when we are alone, we do not pray in isolation. We have learned to pray from people who have modeled prayer for us. We pray in concert with thousands and millions of others.[3] The challenge is when public prayer becomes a spectacle that ceases to address God and starts to draw attention to the person. This is especially the temptation for "professional" Christians, people who are paid pastors, preachers, ministers, worship leaders. Unfortunately, some do their most and best praying in public when others are watching. Public prayer is not itself the problem, but the approach of the person who prays. Thus, private prayer is often to be preferred, as Jesus makes clear (Mt 6:5–14).

23:8 *But you are not to be called "Rabbi," for you have one Teacher, and you are all brothers.* Those with large phylacteries and long fringes, according to Jesus, like to call attention to themselves. They love the honor that comes with having the best seats in the synagogue and at public banquets. They enjoy the respect that comes with their office and the address "rabbi." This may be why Jesus wants his disciples to distance themselves from the title. The term literally means "my great one," but as Jesus indicated, it was associated with those who teach the Torah. Over the centuries the office of rabbi has come to refer to a person who adjudicates Jewish law. Thus, when a question arises that has to do with life and law, one goes to a rabbi. There is nothing wrong with the title itself unless it is used to lord over others.

The prophet Jeremiah said that a day is coming when God will make a new covenant with Israel and Judah. It will not be a covenant as they had known before. In the new covenant God writes his law on the hearts of the people and they will share a reciprocal relationship. When that day comes, the prophet will not need to teach any longer because everyone will know the Lord, who forgives and removes their iniquities (Jer 31:31–34). Jesus appears to be picking up on this passage in his saying. In the new age inaugurated by Jesus, there is one teacher, God, and every other connection is as siblings.

23:9 *And do not call anyone on earth "father," for you have one Father, and he is in heaven.* On the fatherhood of God, see comments on Matthew 6:9.

We see here again a tendency of Jesus toward hyperbole. As such, his saying does not violate the fifth commandment (Ex 20:12). He is not advocating the denial of one's parents in a way that dishonors them; instead we should see here an order of priority set for kingdom citizens. The heavenly Father is Father of all those who enter the kingdom.

23:10 *Nor are you to be called instructors, for you have one Instructor, the Messiah.* In what is traditionally known as the third Servant's Song, God gives to the servant of YHWH the task of teaching (Isa 50:4–11); regular instruction of the disciples is assumed ("morning after morning"), but eventually the teacher will face the scourge and insults. The "teacher" is so attuned to God that he awakens every day to instruction from God that he passes on to those he teaches. The word *Messiah* does not occur in Isaiah 50, but early Christians had already seen Jesus' role as Messiah linked to the Servant Songs, and thus view Jesus as a master teacher. Just as the disciples are not to seek the title "rabbi," neither are they to seek the title "instructor." The Messiah is their instructor. Implied here again among one another is humility and brother-/sisterhood.

23:11–12 *The greatest among you will be your servant. For those who exalt themselves will be humbled, and those who humble themselves will be exalted.* The gospel naturally turns the world on its head. Allen Verhey called it "the Great Reversal."[4] It is built into creation's wisdom. When personal pride is pursued, humiliation will be the sure result. Likewise, "the poor in spirit" (Mt 5:3)—to borrow Matthew's earlier phrase—are quick to find honor (Pr 29:23). Similarly, the insight of Job (Job 22:29) asserts that when people are humiliated, it is because of pride, but God turns his saving grace to the humble. According to Isaiah 5:15–16, YHWH requires justice. So he judges injustice and brings low the proud. Likewise, in an oracle against King Zedekiah the prophet declares (Eze 21:26), "This is what the Sovereign Lord says: Take off the turban, remove the crown. It will not be as it was: The lowly will be exalted and the exalted will be brought low." This pattern and these values are built into creation and the new creation. Kingdom citizens are to pursue humility and recognize that the servant of all is the greatest.

23:15 *You make them twice as much a child of hell as you are.* Regarding hell, see comments on Matthew 5:21–22.

23:16–26 *You, blind guides. . . . You blind fools . . . You blind men! . . . You blind guides! . . . Blind Pharisee!* See "Going Deeper into Spiritual Blindness: Matthew 9:2–31."

23:23 *Woe to you, teachers of the law and Pharisees, you hypocrites!* Woe-formulae punctuate prophetic poetry.[5] There are often three parts to the formula:

(a) the pronouncement of "woe!" against a place or people

(b) the charge(s) leveled against them, such as
  • violence (Hab 2:12)
  • idolatry (Hab 2:19)
  • shedding blood (Na 3:1)
  • plotting evil (Mic 2:1)
  • abominations, adulteries, impurities (Jer 13:27)
  • false prophecy, misleading people (Eze 13:3)

(c) the calamity that will befall them, such as
  • God will be against them (Eze 13:8–10)
  • exile (Jer 13:15–27)
  • God will devise disaster against them (Mic 2:1–5)
  • Nineveh will be sieged and destroyed (Na 3)

In like manner, Jesus utters a series of seven woes against the Pharisees and scribes (Mt 23:13, 15, 16, 23, 25, 27, 29). He names their various faults including hypocrisy, being blind guides, and violations of God's teaching. Though he does not always name the calamity that comes upon them, he does so occasionally.

You give a tenth of your spices—mint, dill and cumin. But you have neglect-ed the more important matters of the law—justice, mercy and faithfulness. You should have practiced the latter, without neglecting the former. The law of the tithe is laid out in various places in the Torah (e.g., Lev 27:30–33, Nu 18:8–32; Dt 14:22–29). Because the Israelites were an agrarian people, agricultural produce—wheat, wine, and flocks—is the currency described. Everything tithed from the land is the Lord's and is holy to him. For various reasons, people could "redeem" the tithe, but one-fifth of the value must be added (Lev 27:30–33). The Lord gives Aaron and his priests charge over the offerings, holy gifts, and tithes. God gives it to them because the priests have no land to farm or raise livestock. They work to bear the weight of priestly duties before the Lord on behalf of the people.

The most sacred of the holy items had to be consumed by the priests in the temple precincts, but less holy offerings could be taken home and shared with their families. This was the way God provided for those who had no land. To the Levites the Lord gave every tithe because of the services they perform in the tent of meeting (Nu 18:8–32). Finally, Deuteronomy 14:22–29 recognizes that some Israelites may live and farm too far from the place where God had put his name. In that case, they can turn their gifts into money and travel to Israel with money in hand. Once they get to the sanctuary they can purchase another sacrifice, whatever they wish, and offer that to God and eat in his presence.

The Pharisees and teachers of the law took these laws seriously. Their tithes included spices from their gardens. Now the law does mention tithing from the land, specifically seed from the ground and fruit from the tree (Lev 27:30). Spices from the garden are not expressly mentioned but could be included among "a tithe of everything from the land." For Jesus the problem was this: picking some leaves from mint, dill, and cumin became more important to the Pharisees than the weightier matters of the law: justice, mercy, and faithfulness.

This triad of virtues and actions represent a variety of Old Testament texts. When the word of the Lord of Hosts came to Zechariah, he instructed the people to render true judgments (justice) and to show kindness and mercy. Examples included (a) not oppressing the poor, the widow, the orphan, and the outsider; and (b) not plotting evil against one another (Zec 7:9–10). Overlapping the spirit of that prophecy is Isaiah's opening oracle (Isa 1:16–17, italics added):

> Wash and make yourselves clean.
>   Take your evil deeds out of my sight;
>   *stop doing wrong.*
> *Learn to do right; seek justice.*
>   *Defend the oppressed.*
> *Take up the cause of the fatherless;*
>   *plead the case of the widow.*

Perhaps one of the most memorable oracles on the priority of justice, mercy, and faith comes from the prophecy of Micah (6:8, italics added; cf. Hos 6:6).

> He has shown you, O mortal, what is good.
>   And what does the LORD require of you?
> *To act justly and to love mercy*
>   *and to walk humbly with your God.*

In general, the prophets spoke with one voice regarding these weightier matters of the law. They eschewed religious rituals and festivals apart from a heart devoted to God and practices consistent with his Torah (teaching/instruction). Pursuing justice, showing mercy, and acting in faithfulness were more important than tithing garden spices. This is not only the prophets' message, it is Jesus' also, yet Jesus did say not to neglect the tithe.

Going Deeper into Justice

Wisdom and discipleship demand an ordering of priorities. We all have a tendency to focus the easier commands, the low-hanging fruit, the things we can control, than to press hard on justice, mercy, and faithfulness. These are elusive and demand more of us; in fact, *they demand our all* as the legacy hymn "I Surrender All" declares. They are weightier in God's eyes and must become so in our own.

As we do the human thing and model ourselves on others, we must be careful to model ourselves after the right people, those doing the right thing (justice) for the right reason (a heart devoted to God). Today, much is made of different kinds of justice: social justice, environmental justice, racial justice, economic justice, etc. But if we pursue justice—as the Scripture declares—we can and will right our relationships with one another, God's creation, and God himself. To right some relationships will require offering forgiveness and mercy to those who have wronged us. Likewise, it will mean confessing our faults one to another and seeking their forgiveness and mercy (Jas 5:16). This too is justice. To live in faithfulness to God fosters faithfulness to one another, for God has been faithful to us, even when we have been faithless.

23:24 *You blind guides! You strain out a gnat but swallow a camel.* The phrase "strain out the gnat" refers to those little insects that fall into someone's cup or soup as they are drinking or eating. Today we would take a spoon and scoop them off the surface. The people in Jesus' day did much the same thing. But with the Pharisaic interest in purity, the statement probes deeper and becomes all the more pointed.

Jewish law forbade the faithful from eating camel. It is named along with the hare and the pig as not kosher (Lev 11:2–8). The image Jesus creates is extreme and humorous. But the fact that the camel is regarded as unclean exaggerates the charge even more.

23:27–28 *You are like whitewashed tombs, which look beautiful on the outside but on the inside are full of the bones of the dead and everything unclean.* Contact with graves and dead bodies makes one ritually unclean and requires the passage of time and ritual to remedy (Nu 19:16; 31:19).

23:29–32 *And you say, "If we had lived in the days of our ancestors, we would not have taken part with them in shedding the blood of the prophets." So you testify against yourselves that you are the descendants of those who murdered the prophets.* Regarding "shedding the blood of the prophets," see comments on Matthew 21:34–36 and "Going Deeper into the Fate of the Prophets" also found there.

23:34–35 *Therefore I am sending you prophets and sages and teachers. Some of them you will kill and crucify; others you will flog in your synagogues and pursue from town to town. And so upon you will come all the righteous blood that has been shed on earth, from the blood of righteous Abel to the blood of Zechariah son of Berekiah, whom you murdered between the temple and the altar.* Throughout the Old Testament, God sends prophets to his people. For example, the Lord sent the prophet Nathan to King David after the king had murdered Uriah to cover up his affair with Bathsheba (2 Sa 12:1–14). He directed Amos to warn the northern kingdom of the inevitable devastation coming upon them. He brought Elijah before King Ahab to announce an extended drought that led to the showdown on Mt. Carmel (1 Ki 18). Other nations, too, benefited from the word of the prophets. Jonah, for example, the reluctant prophet, eventually preached to the great city of Nineveh and they repented (Jnh 1:2; 3:1–10). Jeremiah summarizes it well (7:25–26): "From the time your ancestors left Egypt until now, day after day, again and again I sent you my servants the prophets. But they did not listen to me or pay attention. They were stiff-necked and did more evil than their ancestors." While some of the prophets appeared to succeed in their missions, others faced persecution and death.

Jesus expected the coming days to be much the same as the former. But now it is Jesus who sends prophets, sages, and teachers among his people. As Immanuel, God-with-us, Jesus exercises the authority by which God has been known. The Pharisees and scribes will be complicit in rejecting their messages, persecuting and even killing some. But the shedding of innocent blood has always been abhorrent to the Lord; it is one of the things he is said to hate (Pr 6:17). Abel is murdered by Cain (Ge 4:8–10), who then lied to God when he said he did not know where Abel was, nor was he his "brother's keeper." The earth itself is said to revolt from Cain's actions by not yielding a crop for him. As for Zechariah son of Jehoiada, the Spirit of the Lord took possession of him, and he said to powerful people that God had forsaken them because they had forsaken God. Subsequently, the king and others conspired against him and stoned him to death in the court of God's house. The temple itself was desecrated by the blood of an innocent and righteous prophet (2 Ch 24:20–21).

23:37 *Jerusalem, Jerusalem, you who kill the prophets and stone those sent to you, how often I have longed to gather your children together, as a hen gathers her chicks under her wings, and you were not willing.* Jesus' lament over Jerusalem contains a beautiful image for those with agrarian sensibilities, a hen gathering her chicks and hiding them beneath her wings. Not everyone today had seen such a sight, but it was commonplace in Jesus' day. The Master likens himself to a hen that by instinct reaches out to protect the most vulnerable from some danger. The Old Testament contains similar language about God. In Psalm 17 the author prays for deliverance from enemies and bids God to guard him as the apple of his eye and hide him in the shadow of his wings (Ps 17:8). Likewise, another psalmist speaks with assurance of God's protection as his refuge, his fortress, and most intimately, under his wings (Ps 91:4).

In a remarkable appropriation of divine intimacy, Jesus situates himself once again in God's place. He who is Immanuel, God-with-us, recognizes the violent reactions of "Jerusalem" against his appointed prophets. Nevertheless, he wishes to gather her children in the shadow of his wings. The irony of the passage lies in Jesus' self-description, sheltering the children of Jerusalem beneath his wings: Jerusalem, the killer of prophets; Jerusalem, the torturer of God's servants. Yet, even as he addresses Jerusalem in tender images, Jesus knows she will not allow such intimacy between them, since they consider him so unworthy a prophet.

23:38 *Look, your house is left to you desolate.* Jesus could not lament over Jerusalem without also lamenting the temple as it currently stands and will in the future be destroyed. His teaching in the next chapters (Mt 24–25) continues this theme in painful and dramatic detail. Those who heard it probably scratched their heads. The temple was not desolate or forsaken. It had never been so glorious and buzzing with activity. But Jesus was seeing what truly was and is to come.

After Solomon built and consecrated God's (first) house (about 950 BC), the Lord appeared to him and promised to be with him, bless him, and further his reign if Solomon walked in God's ways. Yet there was also another possibility; if he turned away from the commandments, God said that he would cut Israel off from the land and cast away the temple from his sight (1 Ki 9:6–9). Isaiah foresaw a day when the city of Zion would become a wilderness and Jerusalem desolate (e.g., Isa 1:5–9; 64:10). He pled with God to reveal himself and his power as he had in days past (Isa 63–64). Perhaps it is Jeremiah's complaint that most succinctly sums up what happened to the temple in his day (Jer 12:7):

> I [God] will forsake my house,
>> abandon my inheritance;
> I will give the one I love
>> into the hands of her enemies.

Again, the destruction of the temple and exile into Babylon returns to the consciousness of those who knew the history and the prophets. Jesus is intimating that what happened in Jeremiah's day will happen again in the lifetimes of many who heard Jesus' lament.

23:39 *For I tell you, you will not see me again until you say, "Blessed is he who comes in the name of the Lord."* On Jesus' quotation of Psalm 118:26, see comments on Matthew 21:9.

MATTHEW 24

What the Structure Means:
The Apocalyptic Discourse (Mt 24–25)

Matthew 24 and 25 contain what is commonly known as the apocalyptic discourse. It is the fifth of five extended sermons Jesus gives in Matthew's gospel. (See "What the Structure Means: Five Sermons [Mt. 5–25]" at Mt 7:28 and Table 0.1.) The sermon is prompted by a pair of remarks (one by the disciples and one by Jesus) followed by two questions the disciples ask Jesus in private (see Table 24.1). By the way that Jesus answers, the questions appear related but not the same.

Table 24.1. The Apocalyptic Discourse (Mt 24–25)

Two Comments
    The Disciples Remark on the Buildings (Mt 24:1)
    Jesus Predicts Their Destruction (Mt 24:2)

Two Questions
    Question 1: When will the temple be destroyed? (Mt 24:3)
    Question 2: What will be the sign of your coming? (Mt 24:3)

Two Answers
    Answer to Question 1 (Mt 24:4–28)
    Answer to Question 2 (Mt 24:29–44)

Three Parables
    The Faithful and Wicked Servants (Mt 24:45–51)
    Parable of the Ten Virgins (Mt 25:1–13)
    Parable of the Talents (Mt 25:14–30)

One Final Judgment
    The Sheep and the Goats (Mt 25:31–46)

The two comments and two questions match Matthew's fondness for pairs. The questions are distinct, but the answers Jesus gives implies that the two events are related. The first seems focused on the plight of Judeans, Jerusalem, and the temple. The second has cosmic, therefore universal, significance. So what should be the posture of the disciple in light of both these events? This is explained and illustrated in the three parables. Again, three is likely significant given Matthew's propensity for numbers. Disciples are to keep watch, be prepared, remain faithful, and work diligently for the Master, knowing that *he will return*. And when he does return, he returns to separate the sheep from the goats and to fix eternal destinies.

24:1-2 *Jesus left the temple and was walking away when his disciples came up to him to call his attention to its buildings. "Do you see all these things?" he asked. "Truly I tell you, not one stone here will be left on another; every one will be thrown down."* Jesus now fills out his earlier prediction of Jerusalem's desolation (Mt 23:37–38); the temple is at the heart of it. A person who knows well the prophet Jeremiah will be inclined to remember Jeremiah's temple sermon and how God promised to do to his house in Jerusalem what he did at the shrine of Shiloh (Jer 7:14). We are not privy to the details of how Shiloh fell, but it is possible that Jesus and his disciples had heard the story. What they knew beyond a shadow of a doubt was that the shrine and the city it served were gone, long gone. What happened at Shiloh and Jerusalem in Jeremiah's day would happen again according to Jesus, although the time is not clear (cf. Jer 26:4–6).

This perspective of Jerusalem and the temple is shared by other prophets. While Micah knew that Jerusalem still stood, he foresaw a day when Zion would be plowed like a field and Jerusalem would become a heap of ruins. On that day the house of God itself would fall despite those contemporary Zionists who felt that God's presence would keep it safe (Mic 3:9–12). The fact is, God had planned to absent himself from the holy mountain because the rulers were corrupt. They had taken bribes, abhorred justice, and distorted his law. These earlier, prophetic predictions of the first temple's destruction (586 BC) may have seemed remote, but Jesus knew it would happen again and for many of the same reasons.

24:4-6 *Jesus answered: "Watch out that no one deceives you. For many will come in my name, claiming, 'I am the Messiah,' and will deceive many. You will hear of wars and rumors of wars."* From Jesus' vantage point on the Mount of Olives (Mt 24:3), he and his disciples could see the temple which had been "under construction" their entire lives. The disciples asked for a sign and Jesus gave them a vision of the future, a future that looked eerily similar to their past. Many deceivers would come and claim to be the Messiah. Josephus named a few of those deceivers in his books. These "charlatans" (Josephus, *JW* 6.288) convinced many followers to join them, but in most cases the deceived were slaughtered by the Romans. In particular, one Samaritan organized an army to climb Mt. Gerizim with the promise that they would see sacred vessels. The governor, Pilate, responded by sending his own army to slaughter them. It was this act that led Rome to recall him as governor of Judea (Josephus, *Ant* 18.85–87). The future, Jesus said, would be punctuated by false prophets and false messiahs (see comments on Mt 7:15, 21–23; 24:24; and see Ac 5:36).

24:6–7 *But see to it that you are not alarmed. Such things must happen, but the end is still to come. Nation will rise against nation, and kingdom against kingdom. There will be famines and earthquakes in various places.* As to wars and rumors of wars, is there really anything new under the sun? Isaiah (19:1–4) uttered an oracle against Egypt in which YHWH is described as behind the scenes stirring things up ahead of Egypt's fall to Assyria. Before any Assyrian ever set foot on Egyptian soil, they fought one another: Egyptians against Egyptians; neighbors against neighbors; cities against cities. In addition to the coming war, Isaiah prophesied a great drought would fall upon Egypt. The Nile would dry up and all its canals would run foul. Crops sown would wither into dust. All who gained their livelihood by the river would groan and moan (Isa 19:5–10).

For Joel, the army that threatens Israel is not human; it is an army of locusts that marches on the land and creates an ecological and economic disaster (Joel 1:1–4). Such destruction and suffering are understood as divine judgment so urgent that it compels people to their knees in repentance and prayer. The plague has cosmic consequences; the earth quakes before them, and the celestial lights dim during their invasion (Joel 2:10–11). Jerusalem may well have been the epicenter of the invasion (2:1).

Going Deeper into Matthew 24:6–8:
Wars and Rumors of Wars

In the closing chapters of Jeremiah, the weeping prophet foresees a day when Babylon is destroyed, but he says to the faithful still living in exile (Jer 51:45–46):

> Come out of her, my people!
> Run for your lives!
> Run from the fierce anger of the LORD.

> Do not lose heart or be afraid
> > when rumors are heard in the land;
> one rumor comes this year, another the next,
> > rumors of violence in the land
> > and of ruler against ruler.

Rumors of war and violence often came to nothing in the years following the end of the Babylonian exile. Jesus said it would be the same in the years before the temple's fall (AD 70).

Perhaps no prophecy of war was more disturbing and yet hopeful than Zechariah's (chapter 14). He foretold of a day when YHWH would gather the nations to come and battle against Jerusalem. Plunder will be taken. Women raped. Half the population will be thrown into exile. But then the tide turns, and the Lord takes the fight to the nations who brought such destruction onto Jerusalem. The prophet paints a beautiful picture of God's salvation and the new world that is to follow. But prior to that, the Mount of Olives breaks in two from east to west to form a new, wide valley. On that day, YHWH becomes king over all the earth (Zec 14:9). Whatever war Zechariah had in mind appears to be the last war in history.

We should not be surprised nor think the world is coming to an end if we hear about wars and rumors of wars. We should not pull out our calendars and begin predicting how long we have left. The point is that this has been happening since human beings settled the first village and built the first city. Regrettably, human beings are accustomed to raids, incursions, escalations of violence, and military operations. More than anything, these do not predict anything, but they reveal the darkness within.

War, drought, famine, and earthquakes have been the instruments of God's judgment in Israel's storied past (see Am 4:6–13; *4 Ezra* 13:31–32). These wars and rumors of wars, these skirmishes and self-inflicted wounds that are to come are not the end, Jesus says. They are only the beginning.

24:8 *All these are the beginning of birth pains.* Isaiah of Jerusalem tells of a song that will one day be sung over a restored Israel (Isa 26). It is a song of trust and joy, a celebration of shalom. Once God's judgment is spent, he will restore the fortunes of his people. But even as they wallow in their divinely ordained distress, the people pour out their prayers. Here, the singer introduces the familiar image of birth pains. Every household knew it, heard it, and agonized through it with their kin. In this case, a woman is with child; she writhes and cries in pain. Her labor, it seems, is producing nothing. When all appears lost, triumph is heard in the land (Isa 26:19):

> But your dead will live, Lord;
>   their bodies will rise—
> let those who dwell in the dust
>   wake up and shout for joy—
> your dew is like the dew of the morning;
>   the earth will give birth to her dead.

This passage is one of the earliest and clearest calls for the resurrection of the dead. Some take it more as the promise that the nation will rise from the dust; others interpret it as a God-revealed hope that dead bodies will one day wake from death and live (cf. Da 12:2; Eze 37:1–14). Clearly, later Jewish tradition and early Christians took it as the latter.

The first pains of birth are not like the last. Initial contractions are a run-up to something more; still they produce only slight pain compared to the latter stages of labor. Jesus may have had Isaiah in mind when he said that false messiahs, wars, famines, and earthquakes were just the beginning of birth pains. More suffering lay ahead, just around the corner. But the fact is that birth pains lead to the creation of new life.

In that day—as in ours—birth is a tricky business. Many women died in childbirth; the pregnant woman who survived had to go through a near-death experience to bring forth life. For the apocalyptic mindset, birth pains represent the suffering that must take place before the dawning of the age to come or, in Jesus' teachings, the kingdom of heaven.

24:10 *At that time many will turn away from the faith and will betray and hate each other.* Jesus returns to a caution he expressed in the mission of the Twelve (see comments at Mt 10:21).

24:11 *Many false prophets will appear and deceive many people.* See comments at Matthew 7:15, 21–23, and 24:24.

24:13 *But the one who stands firm to the end will be saved.* As we will see, much of what Jesus says next owes its substance to the book of Daniel. This notion of perseverance of God's elect people is expressed at the close of the book (Da 12:12–13): "Blessed is the one who waits for and reaches the end of the 1,335 days. As for you, go your way till the end. You will rest, and then at the end of the days you will rise to receive your allotted inheritance." The period of

1,335 days is a figurative number representing a period of tribulation (cf. Rev 11:3). It is equivalent (roughly) to three and one half years. Here we find an implicit promise that those who persevere, wait in hope, and come through the tribulation will "rest" and rise. The "end" here refers to the goal of history as we know it, not its complete collapse. A new history will follow, a history of God's kingdom come on earth as it is in heaven. Together with Daniel 12:1–2, we likely have a strong appeal to the final, general resurrection of the dead initiated in the middle of time by the resurrection of Jesus.

24:15–20 *So when you see standing in the holy place "the abomination that causes desolation," spoken of through the prophet Daniel—let the reader understand—then let those who are in Judea flee to the mountains.* As Jesus describes the next level of "tribulation," his thoughts center on the prophecies of Daniel. For him Daniel is indeed a prophet, a prophet who had foreseen the desecration of the temple that took place in 167 BC when the forces of Syria under Antiochus IV erected an "abomination that causes desolation" on the altar in the temple (Da 9:27; 1 Maccabees 1:54–61). Daniel's prophecy of the seventy weeks is itself a kind of intertextual reflection on Jeremiah's prophecy of the seventy years of captivity in Babylon (Jer 25). He describes a prince who is to come (likely Antiochus IV) to destroy the city and the temple. Others can do the math and suggest the meaning of the numbers, but it is likely the weeks and their relevance are both predictive and figurative. What is important for Jesus in his prophetic role is that the climax of this strife comes to a head when another Antiochus IV—the Roman general Titus—erects his own desolating sacrilege in the temple (Josephus, *JW* 6.259–64, 288). We must remember the initial question that triggered Jesus' apocalyptic discourse: When will the temple be destroyed?

Eventually the Syrian forces were repelled and the temple cleansed (164 BC) under the Maccabees. But the temple still stood, and the city was still occupied. Daniel's prophecy had yet another trajectory. There had to be another war, another attack that led to the temple's complete destruction and left Jerusalem in ruins and hostile to the covenant people. That attack would come in AD 70 when the forces of Rome, led by Titus, laid siege to the city and destroyed the temple.

This is why Jesus' imperatives are so Judean-centered (Mt 24:17–22). Those in Judea must flee to the mountains. Don't pack. Leave all your stuff behind. Alas, for the poor women who have small children and nurse during that time. It is hard to flee in terror with crying infants clutching your breasts. Pray that it is not in the winter—winter cold will bite and sting and make the journey that much harder. Pray that it not be on the Sabbath, because many Jews interpreted Sabbath law to limit travel and thus keep them in jeopardy.

The event Jesus describes did take place during the Jewish revolt (AD 66–70). When Rome attacked with overwhelming power to torch the city, Jews fled in all directions (Eusebius, *Church History* 3.5.3). Zechariah's apocalyptic vision (14:5) describes the faithful fleeing by the valley of the Lord's mountain, recalling the way they fled during an earthquake in the days of King Uzziah (783–742 BC). The people who fled were those who were saved.

24:21 *For then there will be great distress, unequaled from the beginning of the world until now—and never to be equaled again.* When Jesus described the great tribulation and anguish that was coming, he may as well have been channeling Daniel (12:1): "At that time Michael, the great prince who protects your people, will arise. There will be a time of distress such as has not happened from the beginning of nations until then. But at that time your people—everyone whose name is found written in the book—will be delivered." Michael is the chief angel whom God appointed to watch and protect Israel.[1] For Daniel as well as Jesus, the battles being waged on earth have their counterparts in the heavens. Michael has fought on behalf of God's people and prevailed. Ultimately, some of the people will be saved, those whose names are written in the book. But first they must endure a period of unprecedented distress.

Jesus' language is noticeably similar to Daniel's, informed by the prophet's apocalyptic manner. Thus, in good apocalyptic style Jesus ramps up the unprecedented distress that awaits the followers of Messiah even higher. Yet implicit with the teaching is the confidence that some will be delivered from the onslaught.

24:22 *If those days had not been cut short, no one would survive, but for the sake of the elect those days will be shortened.* The term *the elect* and concepts like it have strong biblical resonances. When the Israelites reach Mt. Sinai, Moses ascends the mountain to speak with God and the Lord tells him to address the house of Jacob and the people of Israel. He says that if they heed his voice and keep his commandments, they will be God's treasured possession out of all the peoples of the earth. He ordains them as his priestly kingdom and holy nation, set apart from all the rest (Ex 19:1–6).

Before Moses leaves the people in the care of Joshua and sends them into the promised land, he says (Dt 7:6), "For you are a people holy to the LORD your God. The LORD your God has chosen you out of all the peoples on the face of the earth to be his people, his treasured possession" (cf. Dt 4:20; 14:2; 26:18). Consistently, Moses reminds the people that God has set them apart and made them different from all the rest of the people groups in the world. This idea of "the chosen people" permeates Israel's memory of God's actions and interactions with them. It is no wonder that Isaiah's vision includes God's direct actions to bring his scattered people home (Isa 11:11–16). Now, however, it is only a remnant of the people, the survivors, who will join the highway God builds from Assyria to home. There will be a kind of new exodus from exile (Isa 43:1–21; 51:9–11). Ezekiel, too, narrates the history of the chosen people. God displayed his glory among the nations in two ways: first, by sending the house of Israel into captivity in Babylon because of their iniquity; second, by restoring their fortunes, having mercy on them, and bringing them back from exile to their own land (Eze 39:21–29). The peoples of the world will see and learn just how great Israel's God really is.

The events Jesus describes will be a defining moment for "the elect," "the chosen." It is hard for us to understand what the destruction of Jerusalem and its temple would mean to the faithful at that time. Those who lived through the nightmare of September 11, 2001, and its aftermath had a sip of what it might taste like, but the full cup of the temple's destruction was more bitter. For Matthew, Jesus' life, death, and resurrection are a defining moment for the elect as well. The elect are now identified in, through, and by Jesus and the kingdom he preaches. "Seek first his kingdom," Jesus said (Mt 6:33). ""First to the Jew, then to the Gentile," the apostle said (Ro 1:16–17). God's design for his people, the elect, has always had the nations in view.

24:24 *For false messiahs and false prophets will appear and perform great signs and wonders to deceive, if possible, even the elect.* Long before Jesus instructed his disciples on the hardships ahead, Moses instructed the house of Israel on the plains of Moab. He warned them that in the future false prophets would come and try to deceive them (Dt 13). The problem came when they made predictions that came true or performed signs in the names of other gods and urged Israel to follow and worship them. Their falsity came in their allegiance to other gods, not in what appeared to be supernatural ability. The true prophet of Israel points only to the one God of Israel. Moses had to teach this because false prophets were a clear and present danger to the people as they entered the land. Likewise, Jesus knows that history present and future would witness its fair share of charlatans. Unfortunately, the elect might be chosen, but they can be naïve and easily deceived. (See also comments on Mt 7:15, 21–23.)

24:27 *For as lightning that comes from the east is visible even in the west, so will be the coming of the Son of Man.* On the coming of the Son of Man, see 24:30–31. For "Son of Man," see comments on Matthew 8:20.

24:28 *Wherever there is a carcass, there the vultures will gather.* The prophets and sages of Israel were adept in describing reality with an economy of words. That, in part, is what made them poets. Job, for example, describes the wisdom of God. By it soars the hawk, he writes. With God's command the eagle nests on high. From lofty heights the birds spot their prey, and wherever the slain of battle lay silent, the vultures gather (Job 39:26–30). Similarly, Habakkuk portrays the ferocity and violence coming against Judah through appeals to animals and their God-given powers. He warns that the Babylonians' horses are as swift as leopards and as menacing as wolves when night settles in. Their riders fly like eagles ready to devour (Hab 1:8). As Jesus contemplates the horrors to come, we can hear echoes of these and perhaps other Scriptures. Powerful armies will leave no one and nothing standing. No one remains to bury the dead, so scavengers feast on the bodies of the losers.

24:29 *Immediately after the distress of those days "the sun will be darkened, and the moon will not give its light; the stars will fall from the sky, and the heavenly bodies will be shaken."* Thus far, Jesus has been describing what the world will be like prior to the destruction of Jerusalem and its temple. Now, he turns his poetry and prose to answer the second question: What will be the sign of your coming and end of the age?

To answer that, Jesus turns immediately to Isaiah and other prophets, for they have seen God working in their days and knew some of what lay ahead. The correspondence between them is telling. All refer to cosmic signs that take place when the day of the Lord draws near. Jesus' statement has much in common with the oracle against Babylon uttered by Isaiah of Jerusalem (Isa 13:10):

> The stars of heaven and their constellations
> > will not show their light.
> The rising sun will be darkened
> > and the moon will not give its light.

The day of the Lord would draw near, the prophet said, accompanied by celestial reversals. Those heavenly bodies—the stars, the sun, and the moon—ordained to shine since the day they were created (Ge 1) will not give off their light and will be turned to darkness. With similar effect, the prophet Joel saw that when the day of the Lord arrives, the earth quakes, the heavens tremble, and the celestial lights darken (Joel 2:10). Amos describes "that day" as a day like no other, when the sun sets at noon and spreads darkness over the earth (Am 8:9). Ezekiel utters a lament over the king of Egypt and recollects the plague of darkness that fell upon Egypt before the slaves were set free (Eze 32:7). He describes the day of the Lord as a time when God covers the heavens, darkening the stars, hiding the sun behind a cloud, and turning the moon to darkness. While Isaiah and Ezekiel prophesy against Babylon, Zephaniah sets his word against Judah and its inhabitants. For them the day of the Lord would be a day of judgment for their idolatry, violence, fraud, and adoption of foreign customs (Zep 1, esp. v. 15). Those who thought Baal was the storm god will see quickly that YHWH is God over the storm when the day of the Lord issues in darkness, gloom, clouds, and thick darkness.

A steady chorus of doom and celestial reversals characterizes the prophets' messages about the day of the Lord that presages the end. In a way the disciples should know this if they know the Scriptures. For this is not new. The end of the present age (Gal 1:3–4) and the birth of the new age or new creation (2 Co 5:17) will be ushered in as the lights that ruled the day and night are dimmed. This is theatrics on a cosmic scale.

Apocalyptic language steels the readers and hearers to understand the world-shattering nature of God's coming in judgment. The figural nature of these descriptions underscores the darkness and gloom that settles in as the light beats a hasty retreat. Darkness is often a sign of God's displeasure and judgment (Job 5:14; Isa 5:30; 8:22; 59:9–10; Jer 4:23; 13:16; 15:9; Eze 32:7; Joel 2:2; Amos 5:18; Mic 3:6; Zec 14:7). These cosmic images serve to magnify the dramatic consequences of God's coming wrath.

24:30 *Then will appear the sign of the Son of Man in heaven. And then all the peoples of the earth will mourn when they see the Son of Man coming on the clouds of heaven, with power and great glory.* The glorious appearance of the Son of Man invades the gloom and darkness. For "Son of Man," see comments on Matthew 8:20. All people will see him and all the tribes on earth will mourn. Whatever kind of event this is, it is cosmic and universal. All will see him, not just a select few. A little earlier in this "sermon," Jesus compared the Parousia ("arrival") of the Son of Man as lightning in the east which illumines even the western skies (Mt 24:27). He describes this coming in the language of Daniel 7:13: "In my vision at night I looked, and there before me was *one like a son of man, coming with the clouds of heaven*" (italics added). Daniel goes on to say that a son of man was presented before the Ancient One, who gave him an everlasting kingdom and lordship over all the nations.

Jesus' arrival elicits "mourning" from "all the peoples of the earth." This season of mourning may well correlate to the prophecy of Zechariah, who utters an oracle that begins with Judah reeling but ends with her victory. These burdensome[2] words have their genesis in a vision of a great battle against Jerusalem and Judah, a battle initiated by "all the nations of the earth" (Zec 12:1–5). But God joins the battle and brings victory to Judah. The Lord will shield the people so that the feeblest among them will be like David. In that day God will destroy all the nations that come against Jerusalem. But then the unexpected happens: "And I will pour out on the house of David and the inhabitants of Jerusalem a spirit of grace and supplication. They will look on me, the one they have pierced, and they will mourn for him as one mourns for an only child, and grieve bitterly for him as one grieves for a firstborn son" (Zec 12:10).

Who is this pierced one?[3] Zechariah does not say, and interpreters have offered various readings. The most natural is to say that they (the people of Jerusalem) pierced "me," that is, God. The language is bold and a bit hard to wrap our heads around, but it is not out of bounds for the prophet. How do humans pierce God? Well, in this regard, we should probably see it as a bold metaphor for grieving God. The list of Judah's offenses against God—her Maker and Covenant Partner—is long. Other interpreters estimate the pierced one may refer to King Josiah. Still others do a bit of engineering of the grammar to come up with other readings. The gospel of John identifies the pierced one with Jesus (Jn 19:37).

If Jesus is reading Zechariah the same way, realizing the death that awaits him, then the mourning that comes after his Parousia makes sense. Jesus is pierced, run through on the cross. But the difference is this: what had been a national mourning in Zechariah (for Judah) becomes universal mourning for Jesus. In other words, the nations, not just a nation, have pierced Jesus; thus, they mourn.

24:31 *And he will send his angels with a loud trumpet call, and they will gather his elect from the four winds, from one end of the heavens to the other.* At the Son of Man's command, angels go out from heaven to gather the elect from the four corners of the earth. The number "four" corresponds to the four points on a compass; it means from every corner of the earth. For "elect," see comments on Matthew 24:22.

Isaiah offers a series of apocalyptic oracles that conclude in Isaiah 27:12–13. The final two oracles begin with the phrase "in that day," signaling their eschatological focus. In that day, the prophet writes, the Lord himself comes to harvest his people and gather the survivors from Egypt and Assyria. In that day, a great trumpet will be blown (not stated by whom) and the scattered will be gathered to Jerusalem to worship. The blowing of the shofar (Lev 25:9) appears to relate to the fiftieth year of Jubilee and announces the day of atonement (Yom Kippur).

Zechariah, too, describes a great harvest that takes place among God's people (Zec 9, particularly 9:14):

> Then the LORD will appear over them;
>> his arrow will flash like lightning.
> The Sovereign LORD will sound the trumpet;
>> he will march in the storms of the south.

With this visionary oracle, the word of the Lord announces the defeat of several of Israel's enemies—Damascus, Tyre, Sidon, Ashkelon, Gaza, Ekron—and celebrates the arrival of a humble, righteous king (Zec 9:1–13).[4] Joy-filled acclamation spreads among the people, who are assured their covenant partner is arriving to restore them. The Lord appears and his arrow goes forth like lightning. Note the correlation to the coming of the Son of Man like lightning (Mt 24:27). The Lord himself sounds the trumpet and proceeds to trample over their enemies. "On that day" YHWH their God saves them, and they become like the jewels of a crown.

Those who know well the prophets detect in Jesus' teaching a remarkable connection between Jesus as the Son of Man with the predicted, saving actions of the Lord. He has the authority to send "his angels" to gather the elect.

24:32–35 *Now learn this lesson from the fig tree. . . . This generation will certainly not pass away until all these things have happened.* While the enacted parable of Matthew 21:18–21 (see comments there) concerned an unhealthy fig tree, this time he speaks of a healthy tree. In both cases the topic is that of coming judgment. Regarding "this generation" and those who are alive at the time seeing the fulfillment of the Son of Man coming, see comments on Matthew 16:28.

24:36–37 *But about that day and hour no one knows, not even the angels in heaven, nor the Son, but only the Father. As it was in the days of Noah, so it will be at the coming of the Son of Man.* (For "Son of Man," see comments on Mt 8:20. For "coming of the Son," see comments at Mt 24:30.) God the Father alone knows the exact time when the Son of Man will come. Although "the Son" is the one who will come and is associated with the eschatological actions of God, he is not privy to the timetable. Yet Jesus likens the period prior to the coming to be like the days of Noah. The Scripture indicates that Noah's time was filled with wickedness, corruption, and violence (Ge 6:5–12) even as people went their way doing ordinary things: eating, drinking, marrying. All that changed when God shut Noah and his family inside the ark and the rains came. The takeaway from this may well be the sobering expectation that the interim period will be one of wickedness and violence in the world interwoven with people appearing to carry on as "normal."

24:39–41 *They knew nothing about what would happen until the flood came and took them all away. That is how it will be at the coming of the Son of Man. Two men will be in the field; one will be taken and the other left. Two women will be grinding with a hand mill; one will be taken and the other left.* In Noah's day people were blissfully unaware of the destruction that was coming (Ge

7:6–24). When the floods came, those outside the ark were swept away. The only ones "saved" were Noah and the other seven in the ark. They alone were left to begin what amounts to a new creation.

Likewise, most people will be caught off guard when the Son of Man comes. (For "Son of Man," see comments on Mt 8:20.) Judgment will sweep through suddenly and without warning. People will be going about their lives sleeping, working in the fields, grinding meal. One will be taken away—to employ the flood image—one will be swept away in judgment, and the one left remains for life in the kingdom.[5] Therefore, Jesus urges his followers to stay awake, be vigilant, and be ready because the Son of Man will come when they do not expect him.

24:42–44 *Therefore keep watch, because you do not know on what day your Lord will come. . . . So you also must be ready, because the Son of Man will come at an hour when you do not expect him.* For "Son of Man," see comments on Matthew 8:20. For "the Son of Man will come," see comments on Matthew 24:30.

24:45–51 *Who then is the faithful and wise servant . . . ? But suppose that servant is wicked.* The parable of the faithful servant punctuates the correct behavior of a disciple (servant) in the interim period, when the Master is away and is yet awaited. The servants do not know the time of his arrival (cf. Mt 24:36), but in the meantime they are to nourish the community and care for it. The wicked servant stands in contrast to the faithful. Leaders who take advantage of the flock and put themselves first are profligate and squander their opportunity to please the Master.

24:50 *The master of that servant will come on a day when he does not expect him and at an hour he is not aware of.* See comments on Matthew 24:36–37.

24:51 *There will be weeping and gnashing of teeth.* See comments at Matthew 8:11–12.

MATTHEW 25

Jesus follows his teaching on the unexpected coming of the Son of Man with a series of parables: (a) the faithful and wicked servant, 24:45–51; (b) the ten virgins, 25:1–13; and (c) the talents, 25:14–30. (See "What the Structure Means: The Apocalyptic Discourse [Mt 24–25]" and Table 24.1.) Each parable urges Jesus' followers to be faithful, prepared, awake, and righteous in action. Since the end is approaching, the disciples must be vigilant. Despite this, as events unfold, they all appear to fall away.

25:1 *The kingdom of heaven will be like ten virgins who took their lamps and went out to meet the bridegroom.* Regarding the kingdom of heaven, see comments on Matthew 3:2.

The "bridegroom" in the parable stands in for the "Son of Man" and his unexpected appearance discussed in Matthew 24:26–41. In the Old Testament, a bridegroom can signify God. In a psalm celebrating the glory and goodness of creation, the writer poetically describes the sun like a bridegroom leaving his chamber, and then running its course across the sky (Ps 19:5). While it is common for God to be portrayed as the husband of Israel (e.g., Jer 31:32; Hos 2:16–20), Isaiah in particular says that God rejoices over his people in the same way a bridegroom rejoices over his bride (Isa 62:5).

25:2–12 *The foolish ones said to the wise, "Give us some of your oil; our lamps are going out." "No," they replied, "there may not be enough for both us and you. Instead, go to those who sell oil and buy some for yourselves."* The "virgins" (bridesmaids) in the parable have a particular job, that is, they are to accompany the groom as he goes about meeting his bride and escorting her to the wedding. Five virgins are described as foolish, five as wise. Categories of wise and foolish have roots deep in the wisdom tradition, particularly, in Proverbs, a book of practical wisdom. The wise are those who prepared and brought extra oil for their lamps in case they run out. The foolish are not prepared because they did not bring any extra. Lamp, light, and oil are strong metaphors in the wisdom tradition for righteousness (Pr 13:9), living by God's commandments (Pr 6:23), and the Word of God itself (Ps 119:105). Conversely, the extinguishing of the light is connected to wickedness and, in the case of the foolish virgins, not being ready to escort the groom to the wedding. When the parable ends, they are shut out of the wedding and its festivities and unrecognized by the host. They are the foolish. Jesus urges his followers to be prepared like the wise bridesmaids.

25:13 *Therefore keep watch, because you do not know the day or the hour.* See comments on Matthew 24:36–37.

25:14–15, 19 *Again, it will be like a man going on a journey, who called his servants and entrusted his wealth to them. To one he gave five bags of gold, to another two bags, and to another one bag, each according to his ability. Then he went on his journey. . . . After a long time the master of those servants returned and settled accounts with them.* Jesus often tells parables that illustrate some aspect of Scripture (e.g., Mt 21:33–46; perhaps Mt 13:1–23; 19:16–30; Lk 10:25–37). Others, like the parable of the talents—its traditional title—do not directly explicate any particular passage. Rather their characters, actions, and results draw from the deep wisdom found in the pages of the Old Testament.

This story reflects a well-known theme from the Old Testament: the promise and threat of the Lord's return after a time of absence. The exile from the land and the temple was seen as a period of separation from the Master and his presence, but the Lord's return is a steady promise found throughout the prophets. For some his return would be a time of joy and celebration (Isa 35:4–6, 9–10; 42:18; 65:17–25). For others when YHWH returns to Zion, it will be a time of fearful judgment (Isa 66:3–11; Mal 3:1–2). Isaiah, for example, describes God's glory as arriving with vengeance and dreadful consequences; but it also comes with miracles, healings, and extravagant joy. In the end, those ransomed by God will return to Zion singing and overflowing with joy (Isa 35:4–6).

Some prophets refer to this as "the day of the Lord" (e.g., Zep 1:14–18); it is both a day of wrath, distress, and anguish and a day when the Divine Warrior is in their midst giving them victory over their oppressors (Zep 3:14–20). In Micah 1:2–7, the Lord God comes out from his temple and treads upon the high places that melt beneath his step. When he arrives, Samaria is brought to ruin because of her idolatry. Through the prophet God both denounces the evils that afflict Judah and promises that "in the last days" he will (re)establish Jerusalem and make it the center of the world (Mic 4:1–2). Moreover, he will assemble the disabled and gather the marginalized into a strong nation where YHWH himself reigns over them from Mt. Zion (Mic 4:6–10). The absent landowner, the man on a journey, is coming home.

Those with Old Testament eyes heard in Jesus' parable an echo of the one who promises to return to Zion to judge and to save.

25:20–21 *The man who had received five bags of gold brought the other five. "Master," he said, "you entrusted me with five bags of gold. See, I have gained five more." His master replied, "Well done, good and faithful servant! You have been faithful with a few things; I will put you in charge of many things. Come and share your master's happiness!"* The man who received the five bags of gold and doubled his master's wealth is hailed as a faithful servant. And his reward does not come (chiefly) monetarily; it comes in honor. The faithful fellow is given higher status and greater responsibility. He shares increasingly in the happiness of his Master. Faithfulness to God's charge is celebrated and rewarded throughout the Old Testament. It is a central feature of the Deuteronomic theme: obedience to God brings blessing and prosperity; disobedience results in curses and adversity (Dt 30:11–20).

The Psalter opens with a wisdom psalm that celebrates the one who avoids the wicked and instead meditates on and delights in the law of the Lord. He will be like a tree planted firmly by streams, lush with leaves, yielding it fruit and prospering throughout life (Ps 1:1–3).

25:22–23 *The man with two bags of gold also came.* The man with two bags of gold enjoys the same destiny as the man who started with five.

25:24–26 *Then the man who had received one bag of gold came. "Master," he said, "I knew that you are a hard man, harvesting where you have not sown and gathering where you have not scattered seed. So I was afraid and went out and hid your gold in the ground. See, here is what belongs to you." His master replied, "You wicked, lazy servant!"* Motivated by fear rather than faithfulness, the third man appears to illustrate the point of the parable. He hid the bag of gold and could offer the Master only what he was given in the first place. The Master describes him as a wicked and lazy servant. These characteristics place him as the opposite of the faithful servant.[1]

The Jewish wisdom tradition has a good deal to say about wickedness, laziness, and folly. Notice the close connection between the wicked and lazy hands (Pr 10:3–4):

> The LORD does not let the righteous go hungry,
>   but he thwarts the craving of the wicked.

Lazy hands make for poverty,
   but diligent hands bring wealth.

Sluggards spend their time in bed (Pr 26:14) and refuse to work (Pr 21:25). They bring aggravation to any who depend on them (Pr 10:26).

Likewise, consider the wicked. The Lord's curse is upon them, even as he blesses the house of the righteous (Pr 3:33). The wicked plot evil but find themselves caught in their own snare (Pr 5:22).

Psalm 1, referenced above in Matthew 25:20–21, offers a stark contrast between the wise and wicked. The wise are symbolized by the tree firmly planted by the river, while the wicked are like chaff, flakes of dust, which a breeze can drive away. Nothing the wicked does lasts; his way perishes (Ps 1:4–6).[2]

25:30 *And throw that worthless servant outside, into the darkness, where there will be weeping and gnashing of teeth.* For the realm of darkness and "weeping and gnashing of teeth," see Matthew 8:12.

25:31 *When the Son of Man comes in his glory, and all the angels with him, he will sit on his glorious throne.* Jesus now describes a scene of judgment. Some regard this as a parable, others as "a word picture of the last judgment."[3] Beare considers it "an apocalyptic vision of the Last Judgment" akin to the throne scene in Revelation (20:11–15).[4]

On the "Son of Man," see comments on Matthew 8:20. The Son of Man is described as "the king" (25:34), which is consistent with the image of Son of Man receiving a kingdom (Da 7:13–14). There are other Jewish texts from that era that depict an agent of God on the throne judging the nations ("the Anointed One," 2 Baruch 72.2–6; "the Elect One," *1 Enoch* 61.8; "Melchizedek," *11QMelch* 2.13), but there are no Old Testament texts that clearly portray someone other than God executing judgment in this way.

The phrase "all the angels with him" echoes Zechariah 14:4–5 which states that "on that day" YHWH will come and "all the holy ones with him." The holy ones are angels in heaven. Zechariah's eschatological vision depicts a final battle waged by the nations for/against Jerusalem. When YHWH joins the battle, momentum shifts, and an angelic retinue joins him in the fight. In Jesus' teaching, the coming of YHWH is now redirected to the coming of the Son of Man who exercises judgment in God's stead. The theme of God judging and avenging his people and liberating them from their enemies recurs over and over again, beginning with the exodus from Egypt. Before the Israelites enter the promised land, there is a song calling upon God's people and the heavenly council to praise God who avenges his people on their

enemies (Dt 32:43). A few verses later, Moses blesses the Israelites beginning with the good news that the Lord has come from Sinai and with him
are myriads of angels (Dt 33:2).

There is a different yet overlapping eschatological scene in Micah 4:1–2.
In "the last days" the prophet says the house of YHWH is established as the
highest mountain and people from the nations stream to the mountain of the
Lord to learn his ways and walk in his paths. Micah 4:3–4 continues,

> He will judge between many peoples
>   and will settle disputes for strong nations far and wide.
> They will beat their swords into plowshares
>   and their spears into pruning hooks.
> Nation will not take up sword against nation,
>   nor will they train for war anymore.
> Everyone will sit under their own vine
>   and under their own fig tree,
> and no one will make them afraid,
>   for the LORD Almighty has spoken.

God himself judges between "many peoples," settling disputes and
ultimately putting an end to war. From now on, "wars and rumors of war"
become things of the past. And the world enters an ideal age where fear and
poverty, too, come to an end. This "age to come" is not explicitly detailed in
Jesus' depiction of this (final?) judgment, but it may well be implied. What is
remarkable, however, is that Jesus describes the Son of Man, not God, exer-
cising judgment. Other Jewish literature from the period may describe God
as working through intermediary figures—principal angels, the Messiah, and
other divine agents—but what we hear in Jesus' words and actions transcends
the role assigned to any other figure.[5] Jesus said and did the kind of things that
only God says and does.

Going Deeper into Jesus as God's Equal

To review, Jesus forgives sins (Mt 9:1–8), teaches with authority equal to the
Law and Scripture (Mt 5:17–48), proclaims and establishes the kingdom
of heaven in his miracles (e.g., Mt 12:28; see also "What the Structure
Means: The Galilean Ministry" at Mt 4:25), and exercises eschatological
judgment (Mt 25:31–33). In the words of Sigurd Grindheim, Jesus regards
himself in some sense as "God's equal."[6] Were it not true, this would be
blasphemy. If it is, then Jesus demands our ultimate loyalty. This after all
is what faith is about. Faith is not mental assent to something as true, as

in "I believe the law of physics are applicable everywhere in the universe." Biblical faith is a declaration of absolute dependence on and loyalty to God and his Son; it is a pledge of allegiance to one who has earned our trust and fealty. The unique aspect of Christianity lies in its focus on Jesus as God-with-us. It is a central claim made by the followers of Jesus, a claim which cannot be set aside.[7]

25:32 *All the nations will be gathered before him, and he will separate the people one from another as a shepherd separates the sheep from the goats.* Ezekiel describes a scene of God seeking out and gathering "my sheep" from the places they had been scattered. He will bring them back to their own land, feed them with good pasture, and care for them as a shepherd. But the passage turns when God says he will bring back the strays, bind up the injured, strengthen the weak, but destroy the fat and the strong (Eze 34:11–16). God says to "my flock": "I will judge between one sheep and another, and between rams and goats" (Eze 34:17). The "fat sheep" have abused the weak and wrecked the good pasture; so, they will be judged. The Sovereign Lord says that he will set up over his flock one shepherd, his servant David, who will feed and care for them, and YHWH will be their God. The prospect of God rescuing his flock and judging between the sheep may well have played into Jesus' own thoughts and his role regarding the eschatological judgment.

25:33 *He will put the sheep on his right and the goats on his left.* The "right hand" is a place of safety and a portent of blessings to come; the left augurs danger and disaster for the goats. For the significance of "the right hand," we note that the Lord seats the messianic king on his right hand to rule over his enemies and reign over the world (Ps 110:1). In an earlier psalm (45)—that might best be described as a wedding psalm—the poet praises the king who is seated on David's throne, to his right hand stands the queen decked out in the gold of Ophir (Ps 45:9). The "right hand" represents the favored hand, a place of dignity and honor.

25:34–40 *Then the King will say to those on his right, "Come, you who are blessed by my Father; take your inheritance, the kingdom prepared for you since the creation of the world. For I was hungry and you gave me something to eat, I was thirsty and you gave me something to drink, I was a stranger and you invited me in, I needed clothes and you clothed me, I was sick and you looked after me, I was in prison and you came to visit me."* The criteria of judgment have to do with how the righteous cared for the poor, the sick, the imprisoned, and the least among them. These echo the concerns of the prophets for the poor and the neglected. Amos, for example, condemns those who trample on the poor and push the needy aside at the city gate (Am 5:10-13 NRSV). Through Zechariah, the Lord of hosts has both a positive and negative word: (positive) render justice, show kindness and mercy to one another; (negative) do not oppress the poor, the foreigner, the orphan, or the widow (Zec 7:9-10). These reflect God's concern for the marginalized in the Torah.

In a song of praise to God, Isaiah acknowledges him as a refuge for the poor, a shelter for the needy, and a harbor for those in distress (Isa 25:4-5). So the righteous are to extend mercy and goodness in God's name; it is up to them to join God in making good on his promises. We should also consider the force of Isaiah 58:6-7, a passage that urges the faithful to positive moral action. The fast God chooses, according to Isaiah, is to break the chains of injustice, to free the oppressed, to feed the hungry, to clothe the naked, and to bring the homeless into their houses. Rather than religious ritual, God asks his people to bring dignity and justice into the world. Similar needs and actions are reflected in Jesus' vision of judgment.

Perhaps Isaiah 61:1-2 has the greatest resonance with Jesus' vision of judgment:

> The Spirit of the Sovereign LORD is on me,
>   because the LORD has anointed me
>   to proclaim good news to the poor.
> He has sent me to bind up the brokenhearted,
>   to proclaim freedom for the captives
>   and release from darkness for the prisoners,
> to proclaim the year of the LORD's favor
>   and the day of vengeance of our God,
>   to comfort all who mourn.

Jesus apparently identifies with this oracle from Isaiah (Lk 4:16-30). He is the Anointed upon whom the Spirit of the Lord has come. He is the one to minister to the poor, the brokenhearted, the captives, and the prisoners. And yet, in this eschatological scene, Jesus turns it around and identifies with the hungry, thirsty, foreigner, naked, sick, and imprisoned. When the righteous do for the poor—"the least of these brothers and sisters of mine" (Mt 25:40)—they have, unbeknownst to them, done it for the King. Thus, the righteous join Jesus in inaugurating the kingdom. The expectation is that "the sheep" are to be an instrument of feeding, visiting, helping, and welcoming in God's name.

Matthew 25:40 Through Old Testament Eyes: Jesus and the Poor

What may be surprising is how closely Jesus identifies with the poor, the sick, and the needy.[8] But Proverbs says something similar (Pr 19:17): "Whoever is kind to the poor lends to the LORD, and he will reward them for what they have done." Kind action directed to the poor amounts to lending to the Lord. The word LORD here refers to the divine name. If this bit of wisdom is in Jesus' mind, then Jesus is identifying himself with YHWH in a remarkable way. Jesus does not say when you have done this to this least of these my brothers and sisters, you have done it to God or the Lord. In this Proverbs verse, YHWH is the recipient of charity; in Jesus' vision, he is the ultimate recipient of those who feed, clothe, and shelter the poor. The promise that the righteous will be rewarded is reflected also in the eschatological vision in two ways: (a) the sheep have been placed on the right hand of the king and (b) they are invited to enter into "eternal life" (25:46).

25:41–43 *Then he will say to those on his left, "Depart from me, you who are cursed, into the eternal fire prepared for the devil and his angels. For I was hungry and you gave me nothing to eat. . . . "* The destiny of those on the left hand is revealed. They are cursed and sent to the eternal fire. The criteria that mark them as cursed refer to their lack of action, therefore their lack of compassion and mercy. In Eliphaz's third speech, he accuses Job of wickedness because of his action and inaction. In particular he charges that Job gave no water to the weary. He withheld bread from the hungry. He sent the widow away empty-handed (Job 22:5–9). As a result, calamity fell upon Job and his family, poetically described as snares, sudden terror, darkness, and flood waters. Job's friend urges him to repent and reconcile with God.

Job's response is to complain that he cannot present his case before God, the righteous. He is sure he will be acquitted of all charges. But God, he grumbles, is nowhere to be found (Job 23). Later he answers these specific charges (Job 29:11–17). In Jesus' current vision, the king's charge against the goats on the left parallels the charges Eliphaz uttered against Job. They have no time for rebuttal, no chance to make their case that they are not guilty. They are sent away. The righteous judge has spoken.

25:46 *Then they [the cursed] will go away to eternal punishment, but the righteous to eternal life.* In judgment the destiny of the wicked and the righteous is set by the king, who is the Son of Man. We see here an echo of the

Deuteronomic theme. On the plains of Moab, Moses set before the people two ways. One is the way of life and prosperity, the other death and adversity (Dt 30:15). The first involves obedience to YHWH's commands and walking in his ways. The second avenue means turning away from YHWH and pursuing other gods. This theme is reflected throughout Israel's history (in the former prophets)[9] and particularly in the wisdom tradition. To be wise is to know YHWH and his commandments, and to walk in his way. To be foolish is to know God's teaching, reject it, and walk on one's own path. In Jesus' Sermon on the Mount the destiny is signified by those who enter the broad gate as opposed to the narrow way, and those who build their houses on the sand instead of on the rock. Destruction is their end regardless of the metaphor.

Likewise, Daniel 12:2 appears in the background of this, saying: "Multitudes who sleep in the dust of the earth will awake: some to everlasting life, others to shame and everlasting contempt." The appeal in Daniel is to a final resurrection. Death is signified as sleeping in the dust. Both righteous and unrighteous awake. Afterward, final destinies are set. One group awakes to everlasting or eternal life; the other to shame, anger, and everlasting condemnation. Jesus' closing words mirror those of Daniel: the destiny of the righteous is "eternal life;" the destiny of the wicked is "eternal punishment." Jesus' vision of things to come is "according to the Scripture," that is, in full agreement with what Israel's sacred texts have said before.

MATTHEW 26

26:1–2 *When Jesus had finished saying all these things, he said to his disciples, "As you know, the Passover is two days away—and the Son of Man will be handed over to be crucified."* Matthew brings to a close the fifth and final "sermon" of Jesus in his gospel with a familiar statement. The evangelist structures much of his story around five sermons Jesus gives, and he concludes each with a formula like this: "When Jesus had finished saying all these things . . ." (Mt 7:28; 11:1: 13:53; 19:1; 26:1; see "What the Structure Means: Five Sermons [Mt 5–25]" at Matthew 7:28 and Table 0.1). The number five recalls the five books of Moses, the Pentateuch, and links Jesus directly with Moses himself, who addresses the people of Israel one more time before they enter the promised land: "And Moses finished saying all these words to all the sons of Israel . . ." (Dt 31:1, LXX; author's translation).

Passover is a spring festival that commemorates God's actions to spare the firstborn of Israel, judge their oppressors, and liberate the Hebrew slaves from the Egyptian masters. On the fourteenth day of Nisan they are to slaughter a lamb at twilight and spread some of its blood on the doorposts and lintels of their houses. The entire nation is given instructions on how to observe it in Egypt with an eye to the future (Ex 12). The Passover continues into the feast of unleavened bread (Ex 12:14–20). When Moses offered instruction about the appointed festivals (Lev 23), he mentioned the Passover offering first (in the first month, the fourteenth day) followed by the feast of unleavened bread on the fifteenth.

The Passover may be the best known of the Jewish festivals to Christians because early believers associated it closely with the death of Jesus (e.g., 1 Co 5:7–8). The link may well go back to Jesus himself, who connects the Passover with the Son of Man being handed over to be crucified. Before the Master approaches that fateful day, he wants to spend one more Passover with his disciples. It is but two days away and preparations must be made.

26:6–10 *A woman came to him with an alabaster jar of very expensive perfume, which she poured on his head as he was reclining at the table.* A person's selection as king was confirmed by the anointing by a prophet (1 Sa 16:12–13; Ps 2:2; 45:7). Priests were also anointed to signify their special role (Ex 29:4–9). The word *messiah* comes from a Hebrew root meaning "anointed" and carried strong political associations (e.g., Isa 45; *Psalms of Solomon* 17–18). This unnamed woman "anoints" Jesus with perfume, not fully understanding what her role might be in this drama.

26:11 *The poor you will always have with you, but you will not always have me.* The setting for Jesus' statement is the house of Simon the (former) leper.[1] An unnamed woman approached Jesus with an alabaster jar and anointed his head with an expensive ointment. Some of the disciples—likely because of their own sacrifices—criticized the act as excessive and thought the money would have been better spent on the poor (Mt 26:9).

Jesus' statement about the poor reaffirms what is written in the Pentateuch when God is instructing his people on liberality and generosity (Dt 15:11): "There will always be poor people in the land. Therefore I command you to be openhanded toward your fellow Israelites who are poor and needy in your land." On the one hand, the disciples got it right; they should be concerned about those in need and not tight-fisted. What they did not fully realize—if they realized it at all—is that Jesus would not be with them much longer. He will be taken away and crucified. The veil that kept them from being fully aware would soon be lifted, but only when it was too late.

Jesus interpreted the anonymous woman's actions for them, if they had ears to hear; she was preparing his body for burial. The proper care and burial of the dead is one of the most important "good works" that someone could perform (*b. Sukka* 49b), and the woman's good work would be a story that will endure.[2] (See also "Going Deeper into Giving to the Needy: Matthew 6:2.)

26:13 *Truly I tell you, wherever this gospel is preached throughout the world, what she has done will also be told, in memory of her.* Jesus fully expects that his disciples will succeed in their mission despite serious opposition. They are the planted mustard seed that grows into a tree where the birds of the air find shelter. They are the yeast in the dough that permeates the whole lump and feeds a multitude. They will take the message of Jesus, the gospel, throughout the world. The Master anticipates the Great Commission (Mt 28:18–20) here: "the gospel . . . throughout the world." And all of this fulfills what we read in the gospel's opening when Jesus is announced as the son of Abraham (see comments on Mt 1:1). The people of Abraham have a key role in salvation history. By God's promise they will be a people in whom all the families of the world will discover blessing (Ge 12:1–3).

26:14–15 *Then one of the Twelve—the one called Judas Iscariot—went to the chief priests and asked, "What are you willing to give me if I deliver him over to you?" So they counted out for him thirty pieces of silver.* From Simon's house Matthew takes us behind the scenes to see what is happening in the halls of power. One of the Twelve, Judas Iscariot, was thinking of betraying Jesus to the chief priests in Jerusalem. Already Matthew had informed us that chief priests and elders had gathered to figure out how to rid themselves of this meddlesome Galilean (Mt 26:3–5). Exactly why Judas betrayed Jesus is never clearly said.[3] Perhaps he was motivated by the money, but then why does he give it back and hang himself? Yet Judas's stealthy approach and offer gave the chief priests exactly what they were looking for; access to and identification of Jesus of Nazareth in a crowd. So they gave him thirty pieces of silver. The amount was no coincidence.

In a symbolic act and oracle of judgment, the prophet hears God say to him to become a shepherd to a flock that is doomed to slaughter (Zec 11:4–17).[4] The people of the land had suffered a parade of worthless leaders (shepherds) who enriched themselves at their expense. So the prophet obeys and becomes a shepherd. He carries two staffs: Favor and Unity. First, he breaks his staff Favor, symbolizing the end of the covenant God made "with all the nations."[5] Then the prophet says to them, "if it seems right to you, pay me my wages, but if not, keep them." And they weighed out thirty shekels of silver (Zec 11:12).

What happens next is difficult to say; God instructs him to throw it in the temple ("the house of the Lord"). The Hebrew says "throw it to the potter," but the Greek reads, "cast it into the furnace" (in order to see if the metal is good and not worthless like the leaders themselves). However, what seems clear is that the temple is the place where the money is thrown. Then, the prophet breaks his second staff, Unity, to signify the break between Judah and Israel. The oracle ends with the arrival of a new shepherd, another worthless shepherd, who will not care for the poor of the flock but will satisfy himself with their fat and flesh. In the end, that shepherd is maimed and blind.

The worthless shepherds of the prophecy mirror the chief leaders in Jerusalem who are plotting Jesus' death. The nation will continue to suffer under their foul rule until Rome responds with overwhelming power to the first Jewish revolt (AD 66). These "shepherds" pay thirty pieces of silver to Judas Iscariot which happens to be the price paid by the owner of an ox who gores (and probably kills) a slave of another (Ex 21:32).[6] The reference to this as a "handsome price" (Zec 11:13) is ironic because it was effectively the price of a slave. How could a king be so devalued? The Messiah sold for the price of a slave.[7]

Later, when Judas sees what precisely the money bought, he throws the coins back in the temple (Mt 27:3–10).

26:17–18 *On the first day of the Festival of Unleavened Bread, the disciples came to Jesus and asked, "Where do you want us to make preparations for you to eat the Passover?"* In practice the Passover and Festival of Unleavened Bread belong together and could relate like two sides of a coin. Though described as "separate" feasts in Scripture, one led right to the other. In terms of preparation, the Passover comes first, which for Jesus and his disciples was only a couple of days away. They needed a place to gather in Jerusalem. They needed the meal. The disciples were unaware that Jesus had already made preparations with an unnamed disciple in the city.

For the Passover, see comments on Matthew 26:1–2.

26:21–25 *While they were eating, he said, "Truly I tell you, one of you will betray me."* Jesus and his disciples gather that evening at a prearranged place. As they eat together, his followers do not realize what the hearers and readers of Matthew know: it will be their last supper with Jesus. During the meal he reveals to them that a betrayer is in their midst. In distress they each turn to the other and deny it. But Judas's denial is curious. Middle Eastern culture values loyalty and condemns those who turn against their friends (Job 19:19; Ps 55:20). Since table fellowship especially signified a strong bond, to betray someone you had eaten with was even more appalling (Ps 41:9).

26:26–28 *This is my blood of the covenant, which is poured out for many for the forgiveness of sins.* As they were eating, Jesus took bread, blessed God for it[8] and gave it to his disciples with these words, "Take and eat: this is my body" (Mt 26:26; see also comments on Mt 14:19 and "Going Deeper into Blessing God for Food: Matthew 14:19"). Then, after giving thanks for the cup of wine, he says: "Drink from it, all of you. This is my blood of the covenant, which is poured out for many for the forgiveness of sins" (Mt 26:27–28). Jesus wanted all of them to drink, perhaps even the betrayer himself. With these words Jesus instituted the Lord's Supper, the Eucharist, Holy Communion. Though called by various names and interpreted differently in different denominations, this practice and these words have defined Christian worship like no other. It is the last sentence that concerns us here. The wine Jesus shares becomes or represents for the followers of Jesus his "blood of the covenant," poured out for the forgiveness of sins. Each of these phrases is deeply embedded in the Old Testament story.

When Moses and the children of Israel gathered before God at Mt. Sinai, they held an official ceremony sealing the covenant. Moses told all the people the words of the Lord and his ordinances, and the people answered with one voice, "Everything the LORD has said we will do" (Ex 24:1–4). Moses then wrote down all the words[9] and set up an altar on twelve pillars for the twelve tribes of Israel. After commissioning young men to offer burnt offerings and peace offerings before the Lord, Moses took half the blood and dashed it against the altar and the other half he sprinkled on the people with these words: "This is the blood of the covenant that the LORD has made with you in accordance with all these words" (Ex 24:8). Jesus echoes these words to link his last meal, especially his words and actions, with that critical Sinai moment. Whether they realized it or not, the disciples have been whisked back to the time and place when God's covenant with Israel at Sinai was first established. Jesus' last meal and his words of institution created a new covenant moment.

In his day, Zechariah's oracle urges Jerusalem and Zion to shout for joy because "your king comes"; he will be triumphant and victorious and—with an act filled with irony—he comes humbly riding on a donkey (Zec 9:9). He returns to Zion victorious because the Lord, the divine warrior, has won the peace (Zec 9:1–8; see comments at Mt 21:1). Ultimately, war is to become a thing of the past, and the king will command peace to all the nations. His dominion will be from sea to sea and to the ends of the earth. Then the Lord says (Zec 9:11), "As for you, because of the blood of my covenant with you, I will free your prisoners from the waterless pit." The "you" in this passage refers to Jerusalem and Zion. The reference to "the blood of my covenant with you" (see Ex 24:8) is meant to take Israel back to Mt. Sinai and remind them that YHWH has been faithful all along. He has and will make good on his promises to his people. Yes, he had sent them into exile—because Israel had been faithless—but now in this new moment he will liberate and rescue the exiles (prisoners from the waterless pit; cf. Ge 37:24). For Zechariah the covenant God made with Israel was still in force. And not only should Israel expect a great king to bring peace, but they should also expect all those lost in exile to make their way home.

Going Deeper into the New Covenant: Matthew 26:28

It was the prophet Jeremiah who more than any other set the table for what becomes the "new covenant" hope. In fact, there is a textual variant in Jesus' words that include the word *new* before covenant. If original, then the saying would read, "This is *my blood of the new covenant*, which is poured out for many for the forgiveness of sins" (italics added). Though it is unlikely that the variant is original, the sentiment certainly seems to conform to what Jeremiah of Jerusalem had said in his famous oracle (Jer 31:31–34, italics added).

"The days are coming," declares the LORD,
    "when *I will make a new covenant*
with the people of Israel
    and with the people of Judah.
It will not be like the covenant
    I made with their ancestors
when I took them by the hand
    to lead them out of Egypt,
because they broke my covenant,
    though I was a husband to them,"
        declares the LORD.
"This is the covenant I will make with the people of Israel
    after that time," declares the LORD.
"I will put my law in their minds
    and write it on their hearts.
I will be their God,
    and they will be my people.
No longer will they teach their neighbor,
    or say to one another, 'Know the LORD,'
because they will all know me,
    from the least of them to the greatest,"
        declares the LORD.
"For *I will forgive their wickedness*
    and will remember their sins no more."

There is more here than we have need and time to comment on. Of special significance, however, is the link between the new covenant and how YHWH intends to restore Israel. In coming days, the new covenant does not need to be taught for it is already on the people's hearts and in their minds. Great and small alike will have access to and knowledge of God, for they will be forgiven of all their treacheries by the One who remembers their sins no more. Since chapter 1, the forgiveness of sins has been an important part of Matthew's story (Mt 1:21). So now these words of institution reinforce that the forgiveness of sins is integral to the new covenant.

We should not neglect a final phrase in the saying that would have resonated with those who knew well the prophecies of Isaiah. Jesus says, "This is my blood of the covenant, which is *poured out for many* for the forgiveness of sins." When Jesus says his lifeblood will be poured out for many, our attention immediately is drawn to the last verse of the "Suffering Servant" oracle (Isa 53:12, italics added):

> Therefore I will give him a portion among the great,
> and he will divide the spoils with the strong,
> because *he poured out his life unto death,*
> and was numbered with the transgressors.
> For *he bore the sin of many,*
> and made intercession for the transgressors.

Again, there is so much here. On the one hand, the entire poem (Isa 52:11–53:12) brings together aspects of the earlier Servant Songs (e.g., Isa 42:1–9; 49:1–7; 50:4–11). But it also intensifies and clarifies the suffering role of the servant. He bears our infirmities (53:4). He is wounded for our transgressions and crushed for our iniquities (53:5). Like a lamb led to the slaughter, he is cut off from the land of the living, a likely reference to a violent death (53:7–8). But none of this catches God off guard, for it was his will for the servant to make an offering for sin (53:10). The righteous one will make many righteous (53:11). This is clearly a substitutionary sacrifice: the one for "the many." This one has poured out his life/his blood unto death and he has borne the sin of many. Jesus' words of institution owe much of their substance to this Servant Song.

26:30 *When they had sung a hymn, they went out to the Mount of Olives.* We do not know for certain which hymn Jesus and his followers sang that night before they departed, but it was tradition to sing one or more of the Hallel psalms around the Jewish festivals: Psalms 113–118.

26:31-35 *Then Jesus told them, "This very night you will all fall away on account of me, for it is written: 'I will strike the shepherd, and the sheep of the flock will be scattered.'"* The desertion of Jesus' disciples over what is about to take place could well be anticipated if we knew the prophecies of Zechariah. Zechariah foresees the arrival and rejection of a good shepherd (Zec 11:4–14), who is also pierced by the inhabitants of Jerusalem and the house of David (Zec 12:10). John certainly associates this prophecy with Jesus (Jn 19:37), so it is likely Matthew's circle did as well. But it is another oracle that Jesus lays hold of to warn his disciples of what would be coming before the night was over (Zec 13:7).

> "Awake, sword, against my shepherd,
> against the man who is close to me!"
> declares the Lord Almighty.

"Strike the shepherd,
    and the sheep will be scattered,
    and I will turn my hand against the little ones."

The shepherd in this passage refers to the good shepherd, one who is close to YHWH. When the sword is raised and strikes the shepherd, the sheep—his flock—will be scattered. The flock of Jesus would not last the night. Peter, despite pledges of allegiance to Jesus (Mt 26:33–35), would deny him three times before the cock crows (Mt 26:69–75). When the arrest came, the disciples deserted him and fled (Mt 26:56), fulfilling the Scriptures.

26:38 *Then he said to them, "My soul is overwhelmed with sorrow to the point of death. Stay here and keep watch with me."* The overwhelmed soul is a regular feature of many psalms. Deep distress and lament pour out to God as the desperate plead their cases before him. On the one hand, they hope and remember God's saving actions of yesterday, but then it seems, in the same breath, they express the depths of despair: "My soul is downcast within me . . ." (Ps 42:6; cf. 42:11; 43:5; Jnh 4:9, LXX). Such despair seems absurd when a person knows the God of creation and the exodus, yet it is so real that it cuts through hope and shatters noble souls. The noble soul of Jesus is shattered that night; sorrow can be so deep that death seems imminent just from the sorrow itself. Jesus knew the psalms. He prayed the psalms and mourned their gallant verse.

26:39 *Going a little farther, he fell with his face to the ground and prayed, "My Father, if it is possible, may this cup be taken from me. Yet not as I will, but as you will."* Jesus appears to have prayed the same prayer three times (26:42, 44, "saying the same thing"). Exactly what Jesus has in mind by "this cup" may be enlightened by reference to Ezekiel's allegory of Olohah and Oholibah, two women who signify Samaria and Jerusalem and who will experience "the cup of ruin" (Eze 23, especially 23:33; and see comments on Mt 20:23).[10]

In similar fashion, Isaiah's oracle (51:17–23) urges Jerusalem to arise. She has drunk deeply of the cup of God's wrath, drunk it to the dregs, and she has staggered. Her fate has been devastation, famine, and the sword, but there is coming a day that YHWH will take the cup from her hand and place it in the hand of her tormentors.

Jesus' prayer to the Father for relief from this cup likely takes its tone from these Old Testament passages. The torture and execution of Jesus is less than a day away. The wrath of God on the sin and faithlessness of all humanity will be poured out on him as he pours out his blood for many. People cannot bear the weight of their own sins, much less the sins of the world. But he had to drink that cup. He had to drain it to the last drop.

What the Structure Means: The Gethsemane Prayer (Mt 26:39–44)

We should note that Jesus' prayer at Gethsemane hearkens back to the prayer he gave his disciples in his first sermon (Mt 6:9–13). See Table 26.1.

Jesus prays what he preaches, and Matthew understands.[11] The episode itself recapitulates the essentials of the Lord's Prayer.

Table 26.1. The Gethsemane Prayer

Matthew 6:9–13	Matthew 26:39	Matthew 26:41	Matthew 26:42
Our Father	My Father		My Father
Your will be done	As you will		May your will be done
Lead us not into temptation		Watch and pray so that you will not fall into temptation.	

26:40–45 *He . . . found them sleeping. . . . He again found them sleeping . . . and went away. . . . Then he returned to the disciples and said to them, "Are you still sleeping . . .?"* Just before this episode, Matthew records three parables on the importance of keeping watch, being alert and awake (Mt. 24:45–25:30). Now we see the disciples fail three times to do just that.

26:47–49 *Now the betrayer had arranged a signal with them: "The one I kiss is the man; arrest him." Going at once to Jesus, Judas said, "Greetings, Rabbi!" and kissed him.* Judas's plan was to lead a large company from the Jerusalem power brokers, armed with clubs and swords, to Jesus and identify him with kiss. Judas was not the first to betray with a greeting and a kiss. As King David is consolidating his power, he has to deal with a variety of revolts and subversive elements. David's general, Joab, sets about to deal with Amasa, a person whom David trusted but who soon failed the king. Joab finds Amasa in Gideon, goes up to kiss him with his right hand, but with the left hand plunges a sword into his belly and leaves Amasa to die (2 Sa 20:1–10; Pr 27:6). Judas's treachery will be just as lethal.

At Jesus' arrest, Judas addresses him as "Rabbi," the title used throughout the gospel by unbelievers. In Matthew's gospel, believers—even those with "little faith"—address him as "Lord" (*kyrie*). Earlier that evening, at the Last Supper, Jesus predicted that one of their company would betray him. They said to one another "Surely you don't mean me, Lord?" (Mt 26:21–22). When it came Judas's turn, he said, "Surely, you don't mean me, Rabbi?" To which Jesus said, "You have said so" (Mt 26:25).

26:54–56 *"But how then would the Scriptures be fulfilled that say it must happen in this way?" In that hour Jesus said to the crowd, "Am I leading a rebellion, that you have come out with swords and clubs to capture me? Every day I sat in the temple courts teaching, and you did not arrest me. But this has all taken place that the writings of the prophets might be fulfilled." Then all the disciples deserted him and fled.* Neither Jesus nor Matthew refers explicitly to a passage or passages that "predict" the Messiah's arrest. So the reader is left to fill in the gaps. We should likely see these two passages as referring to the same reality: that is, the self-sacrifice of Jesus (Mt 26:28), not the details of his seizure by his enemies. Rather than looking for a quick way out of his bind—by calling down legions of angels (a possibility suggested by 2 Ki 6:17 and Da 7:9–10)— Jesus stays the course of his destiny. Matthew unambiguously references "the prophets" who often appear in Matthew's fulfillment quotations. We might think specifically of Matthew 2:23 where our narrator adds that Jesus settles in Nazareth to fulfill the word of the prophets (likely Isa 11:1).[12] In fact, as the reader/hearer approaches the pinnacle of Jesus' story, Matthew wants us to see how the fulfillment of Scripture has been his constant companion and must be so until the end.

26:59–61 *The chief priests and the whole Sanhedrin were looking for false evidence against Jesus so that they could put him to death. But they did not find any, though many false witnesses came forward. Finally two came forward and declared, "This fellow said, 'I am able to destroy the temple of God and rebuild it in three days.'"* According to Jewish law, two witnesses (better three) are required to confirm a charge to pass judgment that might lead to the death penalty (Dt 17:6–7; 19:15; *b. Sanh* 8). In fact, for any crime a single witness would not do. So the chief priests and elders cast about for witnesses. Any evidence, whether it was true or not, was in play. Finally, two witnesses stepped forward with a charge they thought they could make stick: they claimed that Jesus spoke of destroying the temple. Indeed, Jesus had spoken of the temple's destruction, not by his hand but by others (Mt 24:1–28). According to John's testimony, when Jesus cleared the temple, he said, "Destroy this temple, and I will raise it again in three days" (Jn 2:19). But Jesus was referring to his body in the resurrection, not the temple standing in Jerusalem. So the false witnesses were false because they twisted Jesus' words to mean something he never meant. Neither he nor his disciples had threatened the temple, but that became a credible charge (cf. Ac 6:14).

26:62–65 *But Jesus remained silent.* Jesus' silence before the high priest is reminiscent of the silence of the lamb that is sheared of its wool before it is led to the slaughter (Isa 53:6–7). The Nazarene had nothing to say to the false charge that claimed he threatened to destroy and rebuild the temple. But his silence spoke volumes.

26:63–66 *The high priest said to him, "I charge you under oath by the living God: Tell us if you are the Messiah, the Son of God." "You have said so," Jesus replied. "But I say to all of you: From now on you will see the Son of Man sitting at the right hand of the Mighty One and coming on the clouds of heaven."* Placing him under oath, the high priest asks Jesus directly: Are you the Messiah, the Son of God? For "Messiah, the Son of God," see comments on Matthew 1:1 and 16:15–16. False witnesses were not needed if Jesus incriminated himself before such an august body. Ironically, it was not a crime to claim to be the Messiah. The interrogation would have had to go deeper. Jesus' answer—"You have said so"—sounds evasive to our ears, but it was an affirmation "perhaps with a certain reserve."[13] But it was what Jesus said next that sealed his fate. He claimed to be the Son of Man, and one day those who sit in judgment of him would see him, Jesus, sitting at the right hand of God and coming with the clouds of heaven. Whatever "Messiah" meant to the Jerusalem elite would be trumped by Jesus' stark declaration. His response is a combination of two scriptural passages we have seen before that would have been well known to his inquisitors:

The LORD says to my lord:

"*Sit at my right hand*
   until I make your enemies
   a footstool for your feet." (Ps 110:1, italics added; see Mt 22:44)

and

In my vision at night I looked, and there before me was *one like a son of man, coming with the clouds of heaven.* He approached the Ancient of Days and was led into his presence. (Da 7:13, italics added; see Mt 24:30).

While it was not a capital crime to claim to be the Messiah, the declaration that Jesus was the Son of Man who would sit at the right hand of YHWH and come on the clouds was, to their ears, blasphemy. And it would have been, were it not true. Jesus never left any doubt. He had given the council what they needed to condemn him. His prosecutors were too inept to come up with a credible charge on their own, so Jesus helped them. His own testimony condemned him.

26:69–75 *He denied it again, with an oath. . . . Then he began to call down curses.* In the Old Testament, we see the formula "May God deal with me, be it ever so severely, if . . ." one doesn't keep a promise, or if one is lying, or the like (Ru 1:17; 1 Sa 14:44; 2 Sa 19:13; 1 Ki 2:23; 19:2; 20:10). This may be the kind of curse Peter was invoking on himself. In any case, his threefold failure fulfills Jesus' prediction in Matthew 26:34 and pairs with the three times the disciples fell asleep (Mt 26:36–46).

MATTHEW 27

As the evangelist draws the story closer to Jesus' crucifixion, he leaves behind more traces of the Old Testament. In particular, Psalm 22 will play a leading role in describing Jesus' (mis)treatment by Roman soldiers and onlookers. Finally, right before his death, Jesus seizes upon the opening verse of Psalm 22 to express his pain, agony, and sense of abandonment. Latent in that cry may lie the hope of something more.

27:3–8 *When Judas, who had betrayed him, saw that Jesus was condemned, he was seized with remorse and returned the thirty pieces of silver to the chief priests and the elders. "I have sinned," he said, "for I have betrayed innocent blood."* For the biblical reference to thirty pieces of silver, see comments on Matthew 26:14–15. Judas apparently did not anticipate the possibility that Jesus might be condemned by the chief priests and elders of the city.[1] Perhaps he expected his actions to foment an insurrection against the rulers and powers that be.

Judas recognizes too late that he has violated one of the curses uttered by the Levites on Mt. Ebal. Six sons of Israel stood on the mount of blessing (Mt. Gerizim) and six stood on the mount of cursing (Mt. Ebal). The Levites called out with a loud voice to all the Israelites the curses involved in violating God's covenant (Dt 27:11–26), twelve in all. Curse eleven is this: "Cursed is anyone who accepts a bribe to kill an innocent person" (Dt 27:25). And the people responded with an "Amen." With one accord they accepted the curse on anyone of their number (present and future) complicit in shedding innocent blood. Judas fell afoul of that curse.

The prophet Jeremiah engaged in a variety of prophetic actions to accentuate his message. On one occasion, the Lord instructed him to purchase a clay pot, gather key leaders and take them to the Valley of Hinnom at the Potsherd Gate. There Jeremiah proclaimed to the kings of Judah and inhabitants of

Jerusalem that disaster would rain down on the city. Then he listed the scope of their transgressions: (a) forsaking YHWH and offering sacrifices to other gods; (b) *shedding innocent blood*; and (c) child sacrifices to Baal. In days to come, Jeremiah warned, the valley of Hinnom would be known as the Valley of Slaughter. Jeremiah held the pot aloft and shattered it so all who were present could see, and he said that God would shatter the people and the city and that these breaks could not be mended (Jer 19:1–15).

Such passages illustrate the gravity of the sin of shedding innocent blood, as Judas has done. No doubt he and Matthew's audience knew the Scriptures; curse and disaster would be coming his way.

27:9–10 *Then what was spoken by Jeremiah the prophet was fulfilled: "They took the thirty pieces of silver, the price set on him by the people of Israel, and they used them to buy the potter's field, as the Lord commanded me."* This is the final fulfillment quotation in Matthew's gospel. And like other quotations it is a mixture of prophetic insights and warnings. We see here not only the foretelling of Jeremiah but also of Zechariah. Let's begin with Zechariah, the prophet who figures prominently in Matthew 26:15. There's no reason to repeat what we said there, but there is every reason to see how that prophecy influences what Judas does next; he takes the thirty pieces of silver back into the temple (Zec 11:12–13). But it was Jeremiah's message that caught Matthew's attention particularly, as it involved the potter and the potter's field.

In Jeremiah 18, the prophet is instructed by the Lord to go down to the potter's house and wait for the Lord to speak. What he saw there was instruction enough. He saw the potter working at his wheel. When a particular clay vessel became misshapen, the artisan smashed the clay to the wheel and began to remake it. The potter's action was God's message to Israel. God's people had become misshapen, and God, the potter, would smash her and then rebuild her from the wheel up. This was Jeremiah's basic message: "to uproot and to tear down, to build and to plant" (Jer 1:10).

Elsewhere in Jeremiah's prophecy, Matthew recalls how the prophet does the oddest thing; he purchases a field from a relative just as the siege of Babylon is underway. In the prophet's message, the purchase is a downpayment on the future. Jeremiah knew he would never see the land again. The Lord of Hosts is declaring that in the future—after the exile—houses, lands, and vineyards will once again be bought and owned by God's people in the land of promise (Jer 32:6–15). All these passages coalesce around the events that take place in and around Jesus' crucifixion. Matthew signals that the exile is (finally) coming to an end, and there is a future and a hope.

The land purchased with Judas's blood money provided a place for foreigners and outsiders to be buried when they died in the land of promise. This beneficence reflects Jesus' offer that the gospel must be preached to the nations (Mt 28:18–20). But its presence in Matthew's fulfillment quotation also wraps in the promise that when the exile is complete, property and vineyards will once again be bought and sold in the land.

27:12-14 *But Jesus made no reply, not even to a single charge—to the great amazement of the governor.* On Jesus' silence before interrogation, see comments on Matthew 26:62–65.

27:15-23 *"Why? What crime has he committed?" asked Pilate.* In the story of Barabbas, we can see similarities between Jesus and the Suffering Servant: he was despised and rejected (Isa 53:3; Mt 27:22–23); he did not open his mouth (Isa 53:7; Mt 27:12–14); he had done no violence nor had he lied (Isa 53:9; Mt 27:23); he was numbered with the transgressors (Isa 53:12; Mt 27:15–17).

27:24-26 *When Pilate saw that he was getting nowhere, but that instead an uproar was starting, he took water and washed his hands in front of the crowd. "I am innocent of this man's blood," he said. "It is your responsibility!" All the people answered, "His blood is on us and on our children!"* As Pilate washes his hands of Jesus' death, he imitates something of God's instruction to Israel when a dead body is found in open country (Dt 21:1–9). The elders of the town nearest the victim were to wash their hands and ask God to hold them "not guilty" of innocent blood. Pilate wants to declare himself innocent of Jesus' death, pressured by others into doing something even the cruel governor found unpleasant. Jeremiah may have had this same teaching in view when he warned the officials and people of Jerusalem that if they put him (Jeremiah) to death, they were bringing innocent blood against themselves. The city and the inhabitants not complicit in his death would be caught up in judgment (Jer 26:15).

Despite Pontius Pilate's claim of innocence, the historic creeds of the church have laid blame for the death of Jesus squarely at his feet. The Apostle's Creed, recited by millions weekly for nearly two thousand years, confesses, "He [Jesus] suffered under Pontius Pilate, was crucified, died, and was buried." Likewise, the Nicene creed—also a regular part of liturgical worship—declares, "He [Jesus] was crucified for us under Pontius Pilate; he suffered and was buried."

Although Pilate wanted to distance himself from Jesus' death, he is ultimately the one history charged with it because he alone had the authority to make it happen. Pilate tried to transfer the guilt to the crowds in Jerusalem, and they apparently were willing to accept it.[2] Unfortunately, the cry of the people, "His blood is on us and on our children!" has often been used by Christians through the centuries as proof of the guilt of all Jews for the death of Jesus—with disastrous results. In no case can this declaration justify the persecution and murder of members of a whole race of people. However, it is possible that those who first heard this gospel read aloud understood it as the condemnation that led to Jerusalem's fall (AD 70). R. T. France remarks that the addition of "our children" implies that for Matthew it would be a new generation who would likely bear "the brunt of the Roman onslaught on Jerusalem in AD 70."[3] Thus, those taking the responsibility for Jesus' death were men and women who spoke collectively as the city of Jerusalem. Only a few days earlier, Jesus explained that Jerusalem was the city that kills the prophets (Mt 23:37–39).[4] Accordingly, it was also a city destined to be destroyed (Mt 24:1–28).[5]

There is another way, however, of taking this curious account from Matthew. The Passover celebration is the cultural and religious background for the Last Supper and the death of Jesus (Mt 26:1–2). At the first Passover, every Jew knew that the blood of a lamb was smeared on the doorposts of a house so that the angel of the Lord would pass over Israelite homes and not kill the firstborn inside (Ex 11–12). Likewise, is it not possible that being covered in Jesus' blood is the means by which all, Jews and Gentiles, are to be saved (Mt 1:21)? Under this view, the people may be uttering an unintentional prophecy of how they will be redeemed.[6]

27:27–31 *Then the governor's soldiers took Jesus into the Praetorium and gathered the whole company of soldiers around him. They stripped him and put a scarlet robe on him, and then twisted together a crown of thorns and set it on his head. They put a staff in his right hand. Then they knelt in front of him and mocked him. "Hail, king of the Jews!" they said. They spit on him, and took the staff and struck him on the head again and again. After they had mocked him, they took off the robe and put his own clothes on him. Then they led him away to crucify him.* In what is known as the third Servant Song, the servant is granted special access to YHWH as his teacher, and he eagerly listens. Yet, because of his intimate connection with God, his destiny lies down the way of suffering. The servant says (Isa 50:6):

> I offered my back to those who beat me,
>   my cheeks to those who pulled out my beard;
> I did not hide my face
>   from mocking and spitting.

Matthew and his audience would have heard in these words a direct link to what happened to Jesus on the day tradition has dubbed "Good Friday." The insults he experienced echoed loudly the words of the servant, but before the poem gives way to another oracle, the servant confesses that the Lord God will come to help him (Isa 50:7–9).

Psalm 22 may well have been on Matthew's and his hearers' minds as the evangelist relates all that happens to Jesus on that fateful day. It is a psalm of lament, pleading with God to deliver the righteous sufferer from his hostile enemies. In particular, Psalm 22:6–7 describes the attitudes and deeds of his enemies who regard him as a worm, not a human. They scorn him, despise him, mock him and wag their heads in disgust. The gospel writer sees the insults and injuries of Jesus in the hours leading up to his crucifixion in line with Psalm 22.[7] In a sense, the psalm is both (1) a lament borne when a righteous person faces hostile actors, and (2) a prophecy of what will take place when the Messiah suffers on behalf of the righteous. Through his suffering, the Messiah identifies completely with innocent sufferers who, through the ages, have felt abandoned by God to their enemies.

27:34–35 *When they had crucified him, they divided up his clothes by casting lots.* Matthew's description of Jesus' crucifixion continues to track through Psalm 22, a psalm that vacillates between cries for help and praise for God's safekeeping (compare, e.g., Ps 22:1–2 with 22:3–5). In the midst of the psalm, it seems certain that death is imminent (Ps 22:14–18):

> I am poured out like water,
>   and all my bones are out of joint.
> My heart has turned to wax;
>   it has melted within me.
> My mouth is dried up like a potsherd,
>   and my tongue sticks to the roof of my mouth;
>   you lay me in the dust of death.
>
> Dogs surround me,
>   a pack of villains encircles me;
>   they pierce my hands and my feet.
> All my bones are on display;
>   people stare and gloat over me.
> They divide my clothes among them
>   and cast lots for my garment.

It is this last verse that Matthew picks up on as did his gospel-predecessor (Mk 15:24). It turns out that this central section of Psalm 22 fits well the scenario of a Roman crucifixion: encompassed by "a pack of villains;" all one's bones visible through the skin and out of joint; a mouth as dry as a potsherd; a heart melting like wax; people staring, gloating; and the villains dividing what is left of the victim's meager belongings. Less certain is the third line of verse sixteen, rendered in the NIV "they pierce my hands and my feet." The Hebrew of the line is too uncertain to offer such a precise reading. What is clear is that it does address the victim's hands and feet. Without saying it in so many words, Matthew's hearers would have interpreted Jesus' death through the words of this prophetic psalm.

27:39-44 *Those who passed by hurled insults at him, shaking their heads. . . . In the same way the chief priests, the teachers of the law and the elders mocked him.* On insults hurled at Jesus by passersby see comments on Matthew 27:27-31. Consider also Psalm 109:25. The public shame poured out through the centuries on God's people is concentrated on Jesus.

27:46-47 *About three in the afternoon Jesus cried out in a loud voice, "Eli, Eli, lema sabachthani?" (which means "My God, my God, why have you forsaken me?").* We have seen how Psalm 22 sits beneath the surface of the torture, humiliation, and crucifixion of Jesus. Now it surfaces as Jesus cries out the opening words of that psalm. The cry is often referred to as the cry of dereliction: "My God, my God, why have you forsaken me?" (Mk 15:34). If the echoes to Psalm 22 had been faint before, now they ring clear as a bell. It is deeply ironic that the one who is called Immanuel, "God with us" (Mt 1:22-23), descends to such depths of despair that it feels as though God is no longer "with" him. But Jesus' complete identity "with us" demands the deepest levels of despair, especially with the innocent sufferers.

If you read through Psalm 22 you realize that even though it begins with this cry, it ends with the confident affirmation that God is faithful and will come through in the end. As Brian Wintle points out, "If Jesus had the entire psalm in mind, then he would be voicing despair and confident hope in the same breath."[8] Thus, when Jesus quoted the psalm's initial verse, he had in mind not just the cry of dereliction but the end of the psalm where the writer knows God will step in to rescue him.[9] Even though Psalm 22 appears to have a strong, individual strain, France thinks it may have been used as a national lament. If so, the psalm demonstrates that Jesus serves as an inclusive representative of the people, that is, true Israel, a nation despised and rejected but ultimately vindicated by God. This is the Messiah's role: to represent and embody his people before God.[10]

Apparently those standing nearby misheard what Jesus said, thinking he was calling on Elijah. They may have had in mind what the prophet Malachi wrote—that Elijah would return before the end of the age (Mal 4:5-6). See comments at Matthew 11:2-3 and 9-10.

27:48 *Immediately one of them ran and got a sponge. He filled it with wine vinegar, put it on a staff, and offered it to Jesus to drink.* Psalm 69 is a personal lament by someone who calls himself God's "servant" (Ps 69:17). The situation he faces is dire; death is all but certain by unnamed haters and haranguers. He cries and calls out to God for help and grows weary in the waiting (Ps 69:1–3). It is this psalm that says of the servant that "zeal for your house consumes me" and "the insults of those who insult you fall on me" (Ps 69:9), which link back to the temple incident (Mt 21:12–17). As with other lament psalms, the writer shifts back and forth between cries for help and declarations of confidence in God. But as he complains to God, he utters the words that echo in Matthew's account: "They put gall in my food and gave me vinegar for my thirst" (Ps 69:21). With an eye to a hope-filled future, the psalm ends with a call for the heavens and the earth to praise God because he will save Zion and rebuild her cities. His "servants"—now plural—will live there and possess it once again and "the children of his servants" will inherit it (Ps 69:34–36).

27:51–53 *At that moment the curtain of the temple was torn in two from top to bottom. The earth shook, the rocks split and the tombs broke open. The bodies of many holy people who had died were raised to life. They came out of the tombs after Jesus' resurrection and went into the holy city and appeared to many people.* God gave to the children of Israel a description of the curtain that was to separate the holy place from the most holy (Ex 26:31–35). Crafted of fine linen and blue, purple, and crimson yarns, the curtain was to have images of cherubim skillfully worked into it. The veil of the temple and the screen are intended to delineate gradations of holiness, the holiest place being behind the curtain where the ark of the covenant and the mercy seat were situated. It is the one place on earth where YHWH is said to dwell. Miraculously, the temple veil is torn from top to bottom.

Some speculate that Matthew's point may be that through Jesus' atoning death people now have access to God (cf. Heb 4:16; 9:1–15).[11] And this may provide a partial answer, for the curtain separated God from his people. The death of Jesus clearly opens access to God in a way not formerly experienced. Yet the seemingly natural and supernatural events surrounding Christ's death and resurrection may also suggest another answer, if we consider several Old Testament theophanies.

A theophany is an appearance of God, a visitation of God, and these were not without powerful manifestations. In Judges 5, for instance, the Song of Deborah describes the Lord *going out* from Seir and defeating Sisera and his army with a powerful thunderstorm (vv. 4–5). The poetic retelling depicts *the earth trembling*, the heavens pouring, and *mountains quaking* before the Lord God of Sinai. Similarly, Isaiah of Jerusalem portrays a powerful theophany when the earth is visited by the Lord of hosts with thunder, *earthquake*, tempest, and storm (Isa 29:6).

We might also consider Psalm 18, a royal psalm of David (cf. 2 Sa 22). The psalm begins with the psalmist expressing confidence that God is able to save the king from his enemies; then it describes how, when all seems lost and the situation grave, the king calls to God, and *from the temple* God hears his voice. As God comes down in anger to devour the king's foes, *the earth reels and rocks, the foundations quiver and quake.* The divine warrior thunders from the heavens, with darkness beneath his feet and all around him (see comments at Mt 11:9–10). These images suggest that the ripping of the curtain of the temple from top to bottom accompanied by the earthquake represents the powerful arrival of God through the veil to be present and mighty for his people.

If we consider the earlier chapters of Matthew, we will recall how, at the baptism of Jesus, the heavens open and the Spirit of God comes down from heaven like a dove and "lands" on Jesus (Mt 3:16–17). The gentle descent of the dove stands in stark contrast to the ripping of the rocks and the grumbling of the earth, perhaps as a hint of how angry God is over the death of Jesus, the one in whom he was pleased. Nahum (1:2–6) describes YHWH as a jealous and avenging God.[12] While slow to anger, when his anger is kindled, he stirs up the storms and clouds. He dries up seas and rivers and causes mountains to quake and hills to melt; the earth trembles at his presence. The prophet asks (Nah 1:6):

> Who can withstand his indignation?
> Who can endure his fierce anger?
> His wrath is poured out like fire;
> the rocks are shattered before him.

Theologians may wrangle over the true meaning of these events at the death of Jesus, but in the biblical record the echoes remind us that God sometimes comes in anger, and when he does, the earth trembles.

Some of the rock-hewn tombs around Jerusalem also split open. Thus, Matthew tells of the resurrection of the saints ("holy people"), perhaps the mightiest example of divine power and presence. We should probably understand the opening of the tombs and the resurrection of the saints as taking place "after his [Jesus'] resurrection," not before (Mt 27:53). The gospel writers view the cross and resurrection together, as a continuous narrative of God's saving activity, as a single, world-changing event.

Some Jewish literature in that era discussed the hope of the resurrection of the dead (2 Baruch 21:19–26; Rev 20:13; *Apoc Pet* 4.3–4). *First Enoch*, for example, describes the day when Sheol returns all the deposits it had received, and hell gives up all that it owes (51:1). Likewise, *4 Ezra* describes that day, employing the analogy of birth. As a pregnant woman reaches her nine months and can no longer contain the child, so Hades reaches the time when it must give back those who were committed there from the beginning (4:40–43).

The resurrection of the dead is attested in several places in the Old Testament. Perhaps the earliest is Isaiah 26:19, as part of a song of restoration for Judah:

> But your dead will live, LORD;
>   their bodies will rise—
> let those who dwell in the dust
>   wake up and shout for joy—
> your dew is like the dew of the morning;
>   the earth will give birth to her dead.

Ezekiel experiences in his third vision[13] a type of resurrection in the valley of dry bones (Eze 37:1–14), although scholars are divided over its interpretation. Later generations of Jews, however, did see in this vision, symbolically portrayed, the hope of resurrection when the Lord says to the dry bones that he will cause breath to enter into them and they will live. Perhaps the most relevant statement is this (Eze 37:12): "Therefore prophesy and say to them: 'This is what the Sovereign LORD says: My people, I am going to open your graves and bring you up from them; I will bring you back to the land of Israel." The opening of the graves and bringing people up from them closely parallels Matthew's statement of what happens in association with Jesus' death and resurrection.

The last and clearest of these resurrection passages comes from Daniel 12. Following a time of tribulation, God's people are going to be delivered. They are described as those whose names are written in the book of life. Death is depicted as "sleep," an image picked up by Paul as a euphemism for death (1 Th 4:13, 15; 5:7). Those who sleep in the dust, as the prophecy goes, will awake: some will enter everlasting life; others, shame and everlasting contempt (Da 12:2). Assumed in these words is a final judgment, a prelude to eternal destinies set for the faithful and the faithless.

Together these passages (and others: Job 19:26; Hos 6:2) set the stage for the New Testament hope in the resurrection of the saints ("the holy ones"). While this was to take place as the consummation of God's work to forgive his people and heal their land, Christians learned that the resurrection of the dead happens in the middle of time, not at the end. At first glance, it may seem as if the opening of the tombs takes place at Jesus' death, but Matthew makes sure his audiences understands that the saints came out and appeared after Jesus' resurrection (Mt 27:53). Thus, Jesus' death and resurrection happen first, followed by the resurrection of the saints who enter the city and appear to its populace. These events mark a turning point in history and signal that a new era of God's grace has begun which makes the resurrection possible (1 Co 15:20–23).[14]

27:54 *When the centurion and those with him who were guarding Jesus saw the earthquake and all that had happened, they were terrified, and exclaimed, "Surely he was the Son of God!"* For Jesus as "the Son of God," see comments on Matthew 3:17. The centurion and the guards witnessed the earthquake at Jesus' death and made an accurate confession, even if they did not know it. This, too, is in keeping with Psalm 22's poetic claim that one day all the earth will remember and turn to YHWH, and all the families of the nations will worship and serve him (Ps 22:27–28). We have no reason to imagine that the centurion and the guards are anything other than Gentiles. The makeup of the Roman army represented many people groups. What is witnessed and confessed here on a small scale—and without complete understanding—will be taken to the nations as the Great Commission takes the disciples of Jesus to the four corners of the earth (Mt 28:18–20).

27:57–58 *As evening approached, there came a rich man from Arimathea, named Joseph, who had himself become a disciple of Jesus. Going to Pilate, he asked for Jesus' body, and Pilate ordered that it be given to him.* Without saying it outright, Matthew gives a nod to Isaiah 53:9 when he relates that Jesus is buried in the tomb of a rich man. Those who know Isaiah could immediately grasp the connection.

Joseph of Arimathea, following the law's prescription, knows that the bodies of the executed must be buried the same day; the corpse is not to hang all night (Dt 21:22–23). So he asks Pilate for permission to take custody of the body of Jesus and perform his religious duty. The book of Tobit demonstrates the lengths to which faithful Jews would go to care for the corpses of their executed countrymen. They would steal them, if they had to, to give members of their tribe a proper burial (Tobit 1:16–20). As a result of Tobit's keeping the commandments, a death warrant was issued for him, his property was confiscated, and he became a fugitive. Joseph of Arimathea, however, had access to Pilate—perhaps his money opened the door!—and he made a modest request, to bury the body of his Master and Teacher. Pilate agreed.

27:62–66 *"Sir," they said, "we remember that while he was still alive that deceiver said, 'After three days I will rise again.'"* Jesus had said to his disciples that three days after his execution he would arise. As noted in the comments on Matthew 16:21, "the three days" motif may have arisen from Hosea 6:2. But a close reading of Hosea demonstrates that the prophet has in mind a national restoration; Israel's resurrection from the death of exile is summarily transferred to Jesus,[15] a framework which likely originated with the Messiah himself.

Reports of this promise had made it to the chief priests and Pharisees in Jerusalem. They wanted another display of Roman power, so they asked Pilate to assign soldiers to guard the tomb. Without the guard, the disciples of Jesus could steal his body and claim some sort of miracle had happened. The Romans were there to make sure that would not happen (see Mt 28:11–15).

Matthew 27 Through Old Testament Eyes

Despite the physical agony of the crucifixion, Matthew wants his audience to focus on the meaning of Jesus' death. That is best done through the holy books of Israel. As Daniel Harrington notes, Matthew "grounds Jesus' death in Jewish tradition by appealing especially to biblical phrases and themes. His concern is to show that Jesus' death occurred according to the Scriptures." [16]

Throughout this chapter we have shown how important Psalm 22 was to Matthew's account of Jesus' arrest and crucifixion. If we wanted to know the full force of this connection, we would need to stop and read Psalm 22 from beginning to end and compare it with Matthew 27. Below, the psalm is summarized and paraphrased. Note the vacillation between cries for help (in italics) and confident words of praise.

22:1–2	*My God, my God, why have you forsaken me?* *I cry out, but you do not answer*
22:3–4	But you are enthroned as the Holy One Our ancestors trusted in you, and you delivered them
22:6–8	*But I am a worm, scorned, despised, mocked, insulted* *They scoff, "Let the LORD rescue him, since God delights in him"* (cf. Mt 3:16–17)
22:9–10	But you brought me from the womb From my mother's womb you have been my God
22:11–15	*Enemies surround me like a pride of lions* *I am poured out like water, bones out of joint, Heart melted like wax, mouth is dried up, laid in the dust*

22:16–18	*Dogs surround me, villains pierce my hands and feet* *My bones on display, people gawk at me* *Divide my clothes, cast lots for my garment*
22:19–21	Be not far from me, you are my strength Deliver me from the sword/power of dogs Save me from the mouth of the lions
22:22–24	I will declare your name, praise you in the assembly Jacob and Israel, praise and honor YHWH For he has not hidden his face from the suffering one
22:25–26	I will fulfill my vows to you The poor will eat and be satisfied Seekers will praise him
22:27–28	All the ends/peoples of the earth will turn to YHWH Families of the earth will bow before him Dominion belongs to YHWH and he rules the nations
22:29–31	All the rich of the earth will feast and worship All the dead will kneel before him Future generations will hear of the Lord

The psalm begins with a cry of dereliction yet ends with the nations turning to YHWH. For Jesus and the early church, this psalm expressed both agony and ecstasy, balanced precariously on this precipice we know as life. Matthew's account of Jesus' crucifixion tracks through the psalm, not in every detail, of course, but enough to show how the psalm as a whole shapes the Master's final hours and Matthew's view of it. These include:

- Jesus' cry of forsakenness (Ps 22:1; Mt 27:46)
- The mocking enemies (Ps 22:6–8; Mt 27:28–31, 39–44)
- The casting of lots for garments (Ps 22:18; Mt 27:35)

A Jewish audience, those with Old Testament ears, are able to hear the echoes.

MATTHEW 28

28:1 *After the Sabbath, at the dawn on the first day of the week, Mary Magdalene and the other Mary went to look at the tomb.* Followers of Jesus were observant Jews, which meant that they rested on the Sabbath. They did not come and check on the body of Jesus on the day we call Saturday, most likely because travel was restricted to short distances. Furthermore, as the other gospels relate, there was work to do to prepare the spices to prepare Jesus' body for burial (Mk 16:1; Lk 24:1). Travel and work had to wait until the Sabbath was over. So it was the first day of the week, the day we call Sunday, where everything changed.

What the Structure Means: New Creation (Mt 1:1 and 28:1)

The final chapter of Matthew's gospel describes the ultimate vindication of Jesus from his death on the cross. Everything he did and said, even the outlandish claim that he would rise from the dead, came true and is true. The day of his vindication was the day after the Sabbath, the first day of the week—our Sunday—the day associated with day one of creation (Ge 1).

Jesus' resurrection marks the beginning of the new creation (cf. 2 Co 5:17; Gal 6:15). This is one of the reasons why Christians gather on Sunday to read Scripture, take communion, and worship. It marks the beginning of new creation and recalls the day that Jesus rose from the dead. In a way, every Sunday is a little Easter because during that week everything changed.

Isaiah prophesied that God would bring about a new creation (Isa 65:17–25). He did so when every political and social wind was contrary. But he heard God say and he voiced for God (Isa 65:17): "See, I will create new heavens and a new earth. The former things will not be remembered, nor will they come to mind." The things that have been will be forgotten. Joy and delight will be the moods of the age. Jerusalem is destined for re-creation. God will delight and be with his people. The sorrows of the past will be no more.

The oracle ends with a backward glance at Eden. The wolf and the lamb eating side by side. The lion eating straw like an ox. And the serpent confined to the ground eating dust! This new harmony in nature, this peaceable kingdom, extends all the way up the holy mountain of God.[1]

Likewise, by alluding here in 28:1 to the original creation on the first day of the week (Ge 1:3–5), Matthew takes us back to the beginning of his own gospel. As mentioned regarding Matthew 1:18, the word *birth* (*genesis*) found there echoes Matthew 1:1—the genealogy [*genesis*] of Jesus the Messiah. In this way, Matthew bookends his gospel, suggesting that the whole story of Jesus is the account of a new creation, a starting-over story in the history of the world.

28:2–5 *There was a violent earthquake, for an angel of the Lord came down from heaven and, going to the tomb, rolled back the stone and sat on it. His appearance was like lightning, and his clothes were white as snow. The guards were so afraid of him that they shook and became like dead men. The angel said to the women, "Do not be afraid, for I know that you are looking for Jesus, who was crucified."* This may have been the earthquake that cracked open the tombs and released the dead from their slumber (see comments on Mt 27:51–53). Matthew seeks the cause of the earthquake in the arrival of "an angel of the Lord" from heaven. No further identification is given regarding the angel, but this messenger from the Lord approaches the tomb and rolls back the stone to reveal to the women that it is empty. Is this the same angel who appeared to Joseph in a dream to instruct him prior to the birth of Jesus?

This "angel" is portrayed here in apocalyptic language similar to that of the book of Daniel. Daniel had received a vision of an angel while he stood on the edge of the great Tigris River.[2] The visitor he saw had *a face like lightning*, eyes like flaming torches, and arms and legs that gleamed like polished bronze (Da 10:6). On his way to talk with Daniel, the angel had contended with the prince of the kingdom of Persia. He had come to help Daniel understand what would be happening to the Jewish people at the end of days. The angel is also described as having the likeness of humanity (Da 10:16, 18).

Matthew's further description of the angel at Jesus' tomb resembles Daniel's vision of the Ancient of Days (Da 7:9, italics added):

As I looked,
    thrones were set in place,
        and the Ancient of Days took his seat.
    His clothing was as white as snow;
        the hair of his head was white like wool.
    His throne was flaming with fire,
        and its wheels were all ablaze.

Matthew's description of the angel appears to combine elements of two visions in Daniel: one of the angelic visitor, the other of the Ancient of Days. If anything, it underscores that this is no ordinary messenger. This one comes with the power and authority of heaven.

The phrase "do not fear/do not be afraid" is a standard feature of apocalyptic literature. Frequently, in apocalyptic scenarios, humans are granted revelations through an angelic guide. But angelophanies—appearances of an angel—stir fear in the stoutest heart. So the heavenly visitors often say to the seer, "Do not fear." We see this same feature in the context of Daniel 10 when the angel tries to comfort Daniel (Da 10:12, 19).

28:8 *So the women hurried away from the tomb, afraid yet filled with joy.* While being afraid and joyful at the same time may on the surface seem odd, we have a similar combination in Psalm 2:11: "Serve the LORD with fear and celebrate his rule with trembling." As mentioned regarding Matthew 3:17, this psalm is clearly messianic.

28:9 *They came to him, clasped his feet and worshiped him.* The women grab the feet of the risen Jesus. This was a sign of deep respect and humility. In 2 Kings 4 we have a story with similar elements. The Shunammite woman grasps Elisha's feet to implore him to bring her son back to life. And he does. In response "she came in, fell at his feet and bowed to the ground" (2 Ki 4:18–37).

28:10 *Then Jesus said to them, "Do not be afraid. Go and tell my brothers to go to Galilee; there they will see me."* See comments on Matthew 28:2–5 regarding "Do not be afraid." When Jesus foretold at the Last Supper that "the flock will be scattered," he also said, "But after I have risen, I will go ahead of you into Galilee" (Mt 26:31–32). Now Jesus reminds them of this promise. Once again the sheep will be gathered, gathered for a particular purpose.

Earlier, Matthew had noted that when Jesus began his public ministry in Galilee, it fulfilled what the prophet said in Isaiah 9:1–2 (see comments on Mt 4:14). The ancestral lands of Zebulun and Naphtali, the area known as Galilee, had become home to many non-Jews. The Jews and the Gentiles living there would both see a great light. Thus we come full circle—the ministry of Jesus began in Galilee and it concludes in Galilee. In doing so, we are also pointed to the concluding verses of the gospel, which tell us that the disciples are to continue Jesus' ministry to all nations.

28:11–15 *You are to say, "His disciples came during the night and stole him away while we were asleep."* See comments at Matthew 27:62–66. Already the powerful in Jerusalem are making plans on how to cover up the news that the body of Jesus is missing. Blaming his disciples seemed good at the time.

28:16 *Then the eleven disciples went to Galilee, to the mountain where Jesus had told them to go.* Regarding Galilee, see comments at Matthew 4:12, 14 and 17, and at Matthew 28:10. See also "Matthew 4:8 Through Old Testament Eyes: Mountains."

28:18–20 *Then Jesus came to them and said, "All authority in heaven and on earth has been given to me. Therefore go and make disciples of all nations, baptizing them in the name of the Father and of the Son and of the Holy Spirit, and teaching them to obey everything I have commanded you. And surely I am with you always, to the very end of the age."* Once again, we recognize the gravity of the moment because the eleven are on a mountain in Galilee. As we saw earlier, key moments in Jesus' life happened on a mountain (see "Matthew 4:8 Through Old Testament Eyes: Mountains"). "The Twelve" had become the "the eleven," due to the treachery and death of Judas Iscariot.[3]

While the title "Son of Man" does not occur in this verse, what the risen Jesus says about being invested with all heavenly and earthly authority fits Daniel's "Son of Man" prophecy and vision (Da 7:13–14, italics added).

> In my vision at night I looked, and there before me was one like a son of man, coming with the clouds of heaven. He approached the Ancient of Days and was led into his presence. *He was given authority, glory and sovereign power; all nations and peoples of every language worshiped him. His dominion is an everlasting dominion that will not pass away, and his kingdom is one that will never be destroyed.*

As we have seen throughout Matthew's account, Jesus has spoken about himself in cryptic ways as the Son of Man, making audacious claims about his significance and authority and taking his cue from Daniel's vision (see Mt 8:20). The resurrection of Jesus confirms and authenticates those bold claims. The ultimate authority of Jesus and an everlasting kingdom is given to him by the Ancient of Days. The language of "coming with the clouds" accords with earlier claims regarding Jesus' work and worth (e.g., Mt 24:30; 26:64). Even though some of the eleven are doubting and reluctant to worship him (Mt 28:17), in days to come all nations and all creatures will bend the knee before him (Php 2:9–11).

What the Structure Means: Bookends in Matthew

As we have seen, several times Matthew introduces a theme at the beginning of his gospel and returns to that theme at the end (see Table 28.1). The purpose is to highlight how his story of Jesus is thoroughly saturated with each particular emphasis, and that the entire gospel should be read within those frames.

Table 28.1. Bookends in Matthew

Opening Bookend	Closing Bookend	Significance
The genealogy (*genesis*) and birth (*genesis*) of Jesus (Mt 1:1, 18)	The resurrection on the first day of the week echoing the first day of creation in Genesis 1:3 (Mt 28:1)	Jesus brings a new creation, a starting-over story in the history of the world.
Three Gentile women in Jesus' genealogy (Mt 1:3–5)	"Make disciples of all nations" (Mt 28:19)	Jesus' ministry is not just for the house of Israel but to bless all nations, fulfilling the promise to Abraham (Ge 12:1–3).
"God with us" (Mt 1:23)	"I am with you" (Mt 28:20)	Jesus is more than a prophet and reminder of God's presence; he is the God-with-us One, and his abiding presence rests with the church to the end of the age.
Jesus is baptized Father, Son and Spirit present (Mt 3) and continually teaches (Mt 4–27)	"Make disciples of all nations, baptizing them in the name of the Father and of the Son and of the Holy Spirit, and teaching them to obey everything I have commanded you" (Mt 28:19–20)	Jesus taught by precept and example. His disciples are to act similarly.
Jesus' public ministry begins in the Jewish and Gentile region of Galilee (Mt 4:12–16)	Jesus' public ministry ends in the Jewish and Gentile region of Galilee (Mt 28:10, 16)	Through his disciples, Jesus' disciple-making ministry extends to "all nations" (Mt 28:19–20).

Neither Matthew nor his initial audience could have missed the significance of Jesus' words on this occasion as he now commissions the eleven to make disciples of all people groups (that is, nations) by baptizing them into the name of the triune God and teaching them to observe all that Jesus taught them. In a way, this statement recapitulates the entire gospel as it begins with Jesus' baptism (Mt 3) and continually presents his teaching (Mt 4–27). Jesus taught not only when he stood before a group of people to instruct them; he also taught by the way he healed, conducted himself, prayed, engaged in private conversation, and kept the law. In a word, he taught through *example*, thus becoming the standard for the lives of his followers. They are to walk as he walked, live as he lived, love as he loved, forgive as he forgave.

Jesus' last words to his disciples form a fitting bookend to what is said before his birth about his unique name (Mt 1:23): "'The virgin will conceive and give birth to a son, and they will call him Immanuel' (which means 'God with us')." Matthew tells the entire story of Jesus in the consciousness that he is the God-with-us One. And now, at story's end, the evangelist underscores how the God-with-us One promises to continue to be with his disciples to the end of the age.

A similar sentiment was expressed in Haggai 1:13: "Then Haggai, the LORD's messenger, gave this message of the LORD to the people: 'I am with you,' declares the LORD." The king, the high priest, and the remnant of Israel had obeyed God's message as voiced by the prophet Haggai to rebuild the temple. When they made that commitment, YHWH promised to be with them ("I am with you"). The temple, once completed, would be God's house, his special indwelling-place in the land. In 520 BC, the work began.

For Matthew, Jesus now inhabits that same promise by saying to his eleven, his church, his remnant: "I am with you always." He is their sacred space, God-with-us, the new temple.

ACKNOWLEDGMENTS

I am grateful to a number of people for their help in completing the manuscript of this book. I realize, however, that there will be others who continue to edit, proofread, promote, and design the volume. To these unnamed and, in some cases, unknown skilled people, let me begin by saying, "Thank you."

I am deeply grateful to Andy Le Peau, who invited me to be part of this series. Andy has been and remains one of the best editors in the publishing business. His talent as a creator, designer, writer, and editor is hardly matched in the industry. In my case, he had to exercise patience and pastoral care as well when our middle son, Daniel, was diagnosed with a rare and aggressive cancer at the age of thirty-six. The battle was intense and, in the end, despite countless procedures, treatments, prayers, and pleadings, he died in August 2019. As my friend John Lennox said, to lose a child is a punch in the gut. I had already begun to research and write this project by the time we became aware of Daniel's illness, but for more than two years I was unable to make any progress on it. With time and encouragement, I continued researching and writing and to bring it to submission. I am and continue to be grateful to Andy for his care and professionalism through this.

Although most of my research and writing up to this point had dealt with Paul, his theology, and Christology, Andy Le Peau knew of my interest in the gospel of Matthew. We both share a fascination with how the earliest Christians were reading their Bible, that is, the Old Testament, on their own spiritual journeys to make sense out of the remarkable events that happened among them. Andy's first book in the series, *Mark Through Old Testament Eyes,* served as a good model for how the commentary might contribute to our understanding of the earliest gospel's re-reading of Scripture. My hope is that the series will help teachers, students, pastors, and serious Bible students read the text more fully.

To those colleagues and friends who asked me, "What are you working on these days?" I am grateful. Whether they realized it or not, they stirred me to think about the book and to "hit" the library for another source, reference, or idea. Speaking of libraries, I want to acknowledge the staff of the Lanier Theological Library in Houston, Texas: Jennie Enright, Sharon Cofran, Kathy Fisher, Mary Alice Fields, Zoila Dilma Valladares, Vickie Reynolds, Nancy Ambrose, Monica Colson, Krista Liller, and Dan Enright. In one way or another, each helped to pave the road so that I could access resources I needed or carve out the time necessary to bring this book to completion. The staff at the library consistently supports the thousands of patrons who have used the library since it opened in 2010. They are ensuring that the Lanier Theological Library will become a world-class resource for church and academy.

I want to also thank Becky and Mark Lanier for their care for my wife and me through the most painful ordeal of our lives. They have given us the space we need to grieve and find some sense of faith and purpose in sorrow's wake. My work at the library, first as Senior Research Fellow and now as Director of the Library, has contributed to our lives in enormous ways. Despite COVID and a growing list of duties, Mark has offered me time to work on my scholarship and writing projects. We are so grateful for Mark and Becky Lanier's friendship, vision, and hospitality. This is why the book is dedicated to them.

I am grateful to those who have read the manuscript and made recommendations for changes that needed to be made. Their encouragement, challenges, and additions have made this a better book. In this era when publications abound, there is always more to read, more to know, and more to add to any endeavor. Any errors or omissions you find herein are mine and mine alone.

Finally, I am fortunate to have the company of a wonderful wife, Cathy, who has carved out space in our home for some of my books and my often messy desk. She frequently encourages and helps me in my work and research, and complains little about the time they take away from family. We have traveled a long way together, and perhaps, by God's grace, we will finish the course.

—David Capes
Lanier Theological Library
Lent 2023

LIST OF TABLES

LIST OF WHAT THE STRUCTURE MEANS

LIST OF THROUGH OLD TESTAMENT EYES

LIST OF GOING DEEPER

ABBREVIATIONS

1QM	*Mihamah* or *War Scroll,* from Qumran Cave 1
1QpHab	*Pesher (Commentary) on Habakkuk*, from Qumran Cave 1
1QS	*Serekh ha-Yahad* or "Community Rule," from Qumran Cave 1
4Q521	*Messianic Apocalypse*, from Qumran Cave 4
4Q525	*Beatitudes*, from Qumran Cave 4
4QFlor	*Florilegium (4Q174)*, from Qumran Cave 4
4QTestimonia	*The Testimonia*, from Qumran Cave 4
11QMelch	*Melchizedek*, from Qumran Cave 11
11QPsa	*The Great Psalms Scroll*, from Qumran Cave 11
ABD	*Anchor Bible Dictionary*
Ant	*The Antiquities of the Jews,* Josephus
Apoc Pet	*Apocalypse of Peter*
ASV	American Standard Version
b. Berakhot	Babylonian Talmud, Tractate Berakhhot
b. Gittin	Babylonian Talmud, Tractate Gittin
b. Makkot	Babylonian Talmud, Tractate Makkot
b. Qidd	Babylonian Talmud, Tractate Qiddishin
b. Sanh	Babylonian Talmud, Tractate Sanhedrin

b. Shabb	Babylonian Talmud, Tractate Shabbat
b. Sukka	Babylonian Talmud, Tractate Sukka
b. Yoma	Babylonian Talmud, Tractate Yoma
BAGD	*Bauer's Lexicon*
Barnabas	*Epistle of Barnabas*
CBQ	*Catholic Biblical Quarterly*
CD	*Cairo Damascus Document*, Qumran
CEB	Common English Bible
De Spec Leg	*De Specialibus Legibus (The Special Laws)*, Philo
Did	*Didache*
ESV	English Standard Version
Hist	*Histories*, Tacitus
Hyp	*Hypothetica*, Philo
JSOT	*Journal for the Study of the Old Testament*
JSOTSup	*Journal for the Study of the Old Testament Supplement*
JTS	*The Journal of Theological Studies*
Jubilees	*Book of Jubilees*
JW	*Jewish Wars*, Josephus
LNTS	Library of New Testament Studies
LXX	Septuagint
m. Abot	Mishnah, Tractate Abot
m. Avot	Mishnah, Tractate Avot
m. Meg	Mishnah, Tractate Megillah
m. Qidd	Mishnah, Tractate Qiddushin
m. Shabb	Mishnah, Tractate Shabbat
m. Sot	Mishnah, Tractate Sotah
NAC	The New American Commentary
NASB	New American Standard Bible

NCV	New Century Version
NET	New English Translation
NICNT	New International Commentary on the New Testament
NICOT	New International Commentary on the Old Testament
NIGTC	New International Greek Testament Commentary
NIV	New International Version
NLV	New Living Version
NRSV	New Revised Standard Version Updated Edition
NSBT	New Studies in Biblical Theology
Pss Sol	*Psalms of Solomon*
Recogn	*The Recognitions,* Pseudo-Clementines
RSV	Revised Standard Version
SBL	Society of Biblical Literature
SNTSMS	Society for New Testament Studies Monograph Series
T. Levi	*Testament of Levi*
TOTE	Through Old Testament Eyes, New Testament Commentary Series
VOICE	The Voice Bible
WBC	Word Biblical Commentary
WUNT	Wissenshaftliche Untersuchungen zum Neuen Testament

SELECT BIBLIOGRAPHY

Aune, David Edward. *The New Testament in Its Literary Environment*. Philadelphia: Westminster, 1987.

Averbeck, Richard. "Reading the Ritual Law in Leviticus Theologically." In *Interpreting the Old Testament Theologically: Essays in Honor of Willem A. VanGemeren*, edited by Andrew Abernethy, 135–49. Grand Rapids: Zondervan, 2018.

Balabanski, Vicky. *Eschatology in the Making: Mark, Matthew and the Didache*. Cambridge: Cambridge University Press, 2005.

Barton, Stephen C. *Discipleship and Family Ties in Mark and Matthew*. New York: Cambridge University Press, 2005.

Beare, F. W. *The Gospel According to Matthew: Translations, Introduction and Commentary*. San Francisco: Harper & Row, 1981.

Beasley-Murray, G. R. *Jesus and the Kingdom of God*. Grand Rapids: Eerdmans, 1986.

Beaton, Richard. *Isaiah's Christ in Matthew's Gospel*. Cambridge: Cambridge University Press, 2007.

Blomberg, Craig L. *Matthew*. New American Commentary. Nashville: Broadman, 1992.

_____. *A New Testament Theology*. Waco, TX: Baylor University Press, 2018.

Bock, Darrell L. "Son of Man." In *Dictionary of Jesus and the Gospels*, 894–900. 2nd ed. Downers Grove, IL: IVP Academic, 2013.

Boda, Mark. *The Book of Zechariah*. NICOT. Grand Rapids: Eerdmans, 2016.

_____. *Haggai, Zechariah*. The NIV Application Commentary. Grand Rapids: Zondervan, 2004.

Bond, Helen. "Herodian Dynasty." In *Dictionary of Jesus and the Gospels*, 381–82. 2nd ed. Downers Grove: InterVarsity Press, 2013.

Brown, Jeannine K. *Matthew*. Teach the Text Commentary. Grand Rapids: Baker Books, 2015.

Bruner, Frederick Dale. *Matthew: A Commentary*. Grand Rapids: Eerdmans, 2007.

Capes, David B. *The Divine Christ: Paul, the Lord Jesus, and the Scriptures of Israel*. Grand Rapids: Baker Academic, 2018.

_____. "Intertextual Echoes in the Matthean Baptismal Narrative." *Bulletin of Biblical Research* 9 (1999): 37–49.

_____. *Old Testament Yahweh Texts in Paul's Christology*, WUNT 2/47. Tubingen: J. C. B Mohr, 1992; repr., Waco, TX: Baylor University Press, 2017.

Capes, David B., Rodney Reeves, and E. Randolph Richards. *Rediscovering Jesus: An Introduction to Biblical, Religious and Cultural Perspectives on Christ*. Downers Grove, IL: InterVarsity, 2015.

Childs, Brevard. *The Book of Exodus: A Critical, Theological Commentary*. Old Testament Library. Louisville: Westminster, 1974.

Collins, John J. *The Scepter and the Star: Messianism in Light of the Dead Sea Scrolls*. 2nd ed. Grand Rapids: Eerdmans, 2010.

Comfort, Philip Wesley, David W. Baker, Dale A. Brueggemann, and Eugene H. Merrill. *Cornerstone Biblical Commentary*. Carol Stream, IL: Tyndale House, 2008.

Conyers, A. J. *The End: What Jesus Really Said About the Last Things*. Downers Grove, IL: InterVarsity Press, 1995.

Craigie, Peter C. *Psalms 1–50*. WBC. Waco, TX: Word, 1983.

Daube, David. *New Testament and Rabbinic Judaism*. New York: Athlone, 1956.

Davies, W. D., and Dale C. Allison. *Matthew: A Shorter Commentary*. London: T&T Clark, 2004.

Dunn, James. *Jesus and the Spirit: A Study of the Religious and Charismatic Experience of Jesus and the First Christians as Reflected in the New Testament*. Philadelphia: Westminster, 1975.

_____. "Son of God." In *Encyclopedia of the Historical Jesus*, edited by Craig A. Evans, 587–92. New York: Routledge, 2008.

Evans, Craig A. *Matthew*. Cambridge: Cambridge University Press, 2012.

_____. *To See and Not Perceive: Isaiah 6:9–10 in Early Jewish and Christian Interpretation*. JSOTSup 64. Sheffield: JSOT, 1989.

France, R. T. *Matthew: Evangelist and Teacher*. Downers Grove, IL: InterVarsity Press, 1987.

Garland, David. *Reading Matthew: A Literary and Theological Commentary on the First Gospel*. New York: Crossroad, 1993.

Gathercole, Simon J. *The Pre-Existent Son: Recovering the Christologies of Matthew, Mark, and Luke*. Grand Rapids: Eerdmans, 2006.

Grindheim, Sigurd. *God's Equal: What Can We Know about Jesus' Self-Understanding?* LNTS 446. London: T&T Clark, 2011.

Gundry, Robert. *Matthew: A Commentary on His Handbook for a Mixed Church under Persecution.* 2nd ed. Grand Rapids: Eerdmans, 1994.

Gurtner, Daniel M. *The Torn Veil: Matthew's Exposition of the Death of Jesus.* Cambridge: Cambridge University Press, 2010.

Hagner, Donald. *Matthew 1–13.* WBC. Nashville: Thomas Nelson, 1993.

Hare, Douglas R. *The Theme of Jewish Persecution of Christians in the Gospel According to St. Matthew.* Cambridge: Cambridge University Press, 1967.

Harrington, Daniel J. *The Gospel of Matthew.* Sacra Pagina. Collegeville, MN: The Liturgical Press, 1991.

Hays, Richard B. *Echoes of Scripture in the Gospels.* Waco, TX: Baylor University Press, 2016.

_____. *Reading Backwards: Figural Christology and the Fourfold Gospel Witness.* Waco, TX: Baylor University Press, 2016.

Heiser, Michael. *The Unseen Realm: Recovering the Supernatural Worldview of the Bible.* Bellingham, WA: Lexham, 2015.

Hurtado, Larry W. *Lord Jesus Christ: Devotion to Jesus in Earliest Christianity.* Grand Rapids: Eerdmans, 2003.

_____. *One God, One Lord: Early Christian Devotion and Ancient Jewish Monotheism.* 3rd ed. London: T&T Clark, 2015.

Imes, Carmen Joy. *Being God's Image: Why Creation Still Matters.* Downers Grove, IL: InterVarsity Press, 2023.

_____. *Bearing God's Name: Why Sinai Still Matters.* Downers Grove, IL: InterVarsity Press, 2019.

Kapolyo, Joe. *A Commentary on the Gospel of Matthew.* Grand Rapids: Eerdmans, 1999.

_____. *And Marries Another: Divorce and Remarriage in the Teaching of the New Testament.* Peabody, MA: Hendrickson, 1991.

_____. *Matthew.* Downers Grove, IL: IVP Academic, 2011.

_____. "Matthew." In *Africa Bible Commentary*, edited by Tokunboh Adeyemo, 1151–52. Grand Rapids: Zondervan, 2006.

Kreitzer, Larry. *Jesus and God in Paul's Eschatology.* Sheffield: JSOT Press, 1987.

Kupp, David D. *Matthew's Emmanuel: Divine Presence and God's People in the First Gospel.* Cambridge: Cambridge University Press, 1997.

Lane, William. *Hebrews 9–13.* WBC. Dallas: Word, 1991.

Le Peau, Andrew T. *Mark Through Old Testament Eyes.* TOTE. Grand Rapids: Kregel Academic, 2017.

Luz, Ulrich. *Matthew 8–20.* Translated by James E. Crouch. Hermeneia. Minneapolis: Fortress, 2001.

_____. *The Theology of the Gospel of Matthew*. Translated by J. Bradford Robinson. Cambridge: Cambridge University Press, 1995.

Middleton, J. Richard. *A New Heaven and a Near Earth: Reclaiming Biblical Eschatology*. Grand Rapids: Baker Academic, 2014.

Milgrom, Jacob. *Leviticus: A Book of Ritual and Ethics*. Minneapolis: Fortress, 2004.

Murphy, Roland. *Proverbs*. WBC. Nashville: Thomas Nelson, 1998.

Nolland, John. *The Gospel of Matthew: A Commentary on the Greek Text*. NIGTC. Grand Rapids: Eerdmans, 2005.

Peeler, Amy. *Women and the Gender of God*. Grand Rapids: Eerdmans, 2022.

Pennington, Jonathan T. *The Sermon on the Mount and Human Flourishing: A Theological Commentary*. Grand Rapids: Baker Academic, 2018.

Perrin, Nicholas. *The Kingdom of God: A Biblical Theology*. Grand Rapids: Zondervan, 2019.

Przybylski, Benno. *Righteousness in Matthew and His World of Thought*. Cambridge: Cambridge University Press, 1980.

Reeves, Rodney. *Matthew*. The Story of God Bible Commentary. Grand Rapids: Zondervan, 2017.

Rowland, Christopher. *The Open Heaven: A Study of Apocalyptic in Judaism and Early Christianity*. New York: Crossroad, 1982.

Sanders, James A. "A New Testament Hermeneutic Fabric: Psalm 118 in the Entrance Narrative." In *Early Jewish and Christian Exegesis: Studies in Memory of William Hugh Brownlee,* edited by C. A. Evans and W. F. Stinespring, 180–90. Atlanta: Scholars Press, 1987.

Schnackenburg, Rudolf. *The Gospel of Matthew*. Translated by Robert Barr. Grand Rapids: Eerdmans, 2002.

Schreiner, Patrick. *Matthew, Disciple and Scribe: The First Gospel and Its Portrait of Jesus*. Grand Rapids: Baker Academic.

Sim, David C. *Apocalyptic Eschatology in the Gospel of Matthew*. Cambridge: Cambridge University Press, 2005.

Smith, Ralph L. *Micah–Malachi*. WBC. Waco, TX: Word, 1984.

Stewart, Steve. *The Beatitudes for a Time of Crisis*. Rio Rancho, NM: Impact Nations, 2020.

Talbert, Charles. *Matthew*. Paidea Commentaries on the New Testament. Grand Rapids: Baker Academic, 2010.

Ter Ern Loke, Andrew. *The Origin of Divine Christology*, SNTSMS 169. Cambridge: University Press, 2017.

Verhey, Allen. *The Great Reversal: Ethics and the New Testament*. Grand Rapids: Eerdmans, 1984.

Walton, John W. "Genealogies." In *Dictionary of the Old Testament: Historical Books*, edited by Bill T. Arnold and H. G. M. Williamson, 309–16. Downers Grove, IL: InterVarsity Press, 2005.

Watson, Duane F. "Michael." In *Anchor Bible Dictionary*, vol. 4. New Haven, CT: Anchor Yale, 1992.

Wintle, Brian. "Matthew." In *South Asia Bible Commentary*, edited by Brian Wintle, 1259–60. Rajasthan: Open Door, 2015.

Witherington, Ben III. *The Christology of Jesus*. Minneapolis: Fortress, 1990.

———. *Matthew*. Macon, GA: Smyth & Helwys, 2006.

Wolters, Al. *Zechariah*. Historical Commentary on the Old Testament. Leuven: Peeters, 2014.

Wright, N. T. *Matthew for Everyone*. 2 vols. London: SPCK, 2004.

———. *Paul and the Faithfulness of God*. Minneapolis: Fortress, 2013.

Yilpet, Yoilah. "Zechariah." In *Africa Bible Commentary*, edited by Tokunboh Adeyemo, 1088. Grand Rapids: Zondervan, 2006.

INTRODUCTION

1. Alan Culpepper, *Baylor Annotated Study Bible* (Waco, TX: Baylor University Press, 2019), 1197.

2. Bruce M. Metzger, *The Canon of the New Testament: Its Origin, Development, and Significance* (Oxford: Clarendon, 1987), 194–95.

3. The Center for the Study of New Testament Manuscripts (www.csntm.org) provides scholars and other interested parties with images of many of the oldest and best manuscripts. The majority of early available manuscripts are on papyrus and fragmentary. Of the four New Testament Gospels, the gospels of Matthew and John are the best attested. The earliest papyrus manuscript with all four Gospels is from the third century and is known as P45. Matthew is attested in the following manuscripts (note, the Roman numerals in parentheses refer to the centuries in which experts believe the manuscript was copied): P39 (III); P53 (III); P37 (III-IV); P64 (III); P45 (III); P64 (III); P1 (III); P101 (III); P104 (II); P102 (III-IV); P70 (III); P77 (II-III); P103 (II-III).

4. Thanks to Ed Stetzer for allowing me to use him in this example.

5. "Apostolic Fathers," in *The Oxford Dictionary of the Christian Church*, 3rd ed., eds. F. L. (also, keep F. L. on one line) Cross and E. A. Livingstone (Oxford: Oxford University Press, 2005), 91. See Michael W. Holmes, *The Apostolic Fathers: Greek Texts and English Translations*, 3rd ed. (Grand Rapids: Baker Academic, 2007). David Lincicum, "The Paratextual Invention of the Term, 'Apostolic Fathers,'" *Journal of Theological Studies* 66, no. 1 (2015): 139–48, makes the case that the well-known title "The Apostolic Fathers" derives from a "paratextual" shortening of Cotelier's longer title, *Patrum qui temporibus Apostolicis floruerunt opera.*

6. *Barnabas* 4.14 = Mt 22:14; *Barnabas* 5:9 = Mt 9:13; *Barnabas* 5.12 = Mt 26:31; *Barnabas* 12.11 = Mt 22:45. Otherwise, see James Carleton Paget, "The *Epistle of Barnabas* and the Writings that Later Formed the New Testament," in *The Reception of the New Testament in the Apostolic Fathers*, eds. Andrew Gregory and Christopher Tuckett, 229–49 (Oxford: Oxford University Press, 2005), 248–49, who takes a minimalist view and his investigation reveals that the author of *Barnabas* does not know any book that later became part of the New Testament. He does say he comes the closest to quoting Matthew (22:14 in *Barnabas* 4.14).

7. *Did* 7.1 = Mt 28:9; *Did* 8:2–3 = Mt 6:9–13; *Did* 9.5 = Mt 7:6; *Did* 10.5 = Mt 24:31; *Did*
   12.1–2 = Mt 21:9; *Did* 13.2 = Mt 10:10; *Did* 16.1 = Mt 25:13; *Did* 16.3 = Mt 24:11–14;
   Did 16.4 = Mt 24:10; *Did* 16.5 = Mt 24:13; *Did* 16.6 = Mt 24:30; *Did* 16.7 = Mt 24:30.
   Any parallel passages with Matthew or the so-called "Q" material could be accounted
   for by its placement in Matthew.
8. Christopher Tuckett, "The Didache and the Writings That Later Former the New Testament," in Gregory and Tuckett, *Reception of the New Testament*, 126, thinks it likely
   that the author of *Didache* knew the gospel of Matthew, not just Matthean traditions.
9. There is a version of the Lord's Prayer in Luke (Lk 11:2–4), but it has not been the
   preferred version through the centuries.
10. Gershom Scholem, "gematria," in *Encyclopaedia Judaica* (Jerusalem: Keter, 1971),
    7:369–74. The earliest known examples of *gematria* are reliably dated to the eighth
    century BC.
11. For a thorough investigation of the theme of divine presence in reference to the Im-
    manuel in Matthew's gospel see David D. Kupp, *Matthew's Emmanuel: Divine Pres-
    ence and God's People in the First Gospel*, SNTSMS 90 (Cambridge: Cambridge Uni-
    versity Press, 1997). According to Kupp the presence motif includes but goes beyond
    the three verses typically cited (Mt 1:23; 18:20; 28:19–20).
12. David Gooding, *The Riches of Divine Wisdom: The New Testament's Use of the Old
    Testament* (Coleraine: Myrtlefield Trust, 2012), 102–18.
13. John P. Meier, "Matthew, gospel of," *ABD*, 4:622–25.
14. Simon Gathercole, "The Alleged Anonymity of the Canonical Gospels," *Journal of
    Theological Studies* 69, no. 2 (2018): 447–76. Josephus includes his name in *Jewish
    War* (1.3) but not in *Antiquities*.
15. Gathercole, "Alleged Anonymity," 447–76.
16. Eusebius, *Ecclesiastical History*, Loeb Classical Library 153, trans. Kirsopp Lake
    (Cambridge: Harvard University Press, 1926), 297.
17. For a discussion of why Mark's account might seem to have been disordered, see
    Francis Watson, *Gospel Writing: A Canonical Perspective* (Grand Rapids: Eerdmans,
    2013), 123–29.
18. Dale Allison, *Constructing Jesus: Memory, Imagination, and History* (Grand Rapids:
    Baker Academic, 2010), 455–58, begins his study by examining memory and ac-
    knowledging that people may not remember exact details but do remember the "gist"
    of an event that happened. He concludes his study by acknowledging the gospel writ-
    ers believe that they were telling a true story.
19. Richard Bauckham, *Jesus and the Eyewitnesses: The Gospels as Eyewitness Testimony*
    (Grand Rapids: Eerdmans, 2006), 5–11.
20. Bauckham, *Jesus and the Eyewitnesses*, 508.
21. Krister Stendahl, *The School of St. Matthew and Its Use of the Old Testament* (Philadel-
    phia: Fortress, 1968).
22. The designations "BC" and "AD" themselves are confessional. Today, it is common to
    see these designations replaced by "BCE" (before the common era, for BC) and "CE"
    (common era, for AD). The reason is the recognition that we share this world with
    people of other faiths and confessions. In this book, where appropriate, I will continue
    to use the traditional dating scheme. Those who gave us the calendar we use today
    configured AD 1 as the year of Jesus' birth. They likely missed it by a few years; as a
    result, scholars today think Jesus was born 6–4 BC.
23. See Jens Schröter, "How Close Were Jesus and the Pharisees?" in *The Pharisees*, eds.
    Joseph Sievers and Amy-Jill Levine (Grand Rapids: Eerdmans, 2021), 220–39. Schröter
    understands some of tension between Jesus and the Pharisees as arising from competi-
    tion to gain and retain influence. Regarding purity issues, Jesus advocated a kind of
    "contagious purity" compared to the Pharisees' aversions to impurity (238).

24. For a good analysis, see Steve Mason, "Josephus's Pharisees," in Sievers and Levine, *The Pharisees*, 80–111.
25. Amy-Jill Levine, "Preaching and Teaching the Pharisees," in Sievers and Levine, *The Pharisees*, 403–27, demonstrates how Jesus' criticisms of Pharisees becomes the demonization of all Jews.

MATTHEW 1

1. Consider the following examples: the generations from Adam to Noah's sons (Ge 5:3–32); the generations of Noah (Ge 10:1–32); the children of Abraham (Ge 25:1–4); the sons of Levi (Ex 6:14–25).
2. John W. Walon, "Genealogies," in *Dictionary of the Old Testament: Historical Books*, eds. Bill T. Arnold and H. G. M. Williamson (Downers Grove, IL: InterVarsity, 2005), 309–16.
3. Matthew Novenson, *Christ among the Messiahs: Christ Language in Paul and Messiah Language in Ancient Judaism* (Oxford: Oxford University Press, 2015).
4. Much of this is explored and hashed out in Jewish texts we know today as the pseudepigrapha, apocrypha, and the Dead Sea Scrolls.
5. Andrew Le Peau, in personal correspondence, says correctly that Jesus came close to claiming he was Messiah (Mk 14:61–62; Mt 26:63–64).
6. Chris Bruno, Jared Compton, and Kevin McFadden, *Biblical Theology According to the Apostles: How the Earliest Christians Told the Story of Israel* (Downers Grove, IL: IVP Academic, 2020), 15–16.
7. For chiasms in Mark, see Andrew T. Le Peau, *Mark Through Old Testament Eyes*, TOTE (Grand Rapids: Kregel Academic, 2017), 20. Le Peau describes these as literary "sandwiches."
8. Whether their sexual encounter was "consensual" or a matter of sexual assault is hotly debated among scholars. A close reading of 2 Samuel 11:1–4 does not answer all our questions: "Then David sent messengers to get her. She came to him, and he slept with her. (Now she was purifying herself from her monthly uncleanness.)" How can an ordinary woman refuse the king? What status did she have or resources would she have drawn on to walk away from the king's advances? Matthew characterizes it as: David fathered Solomon by the wife of Uriah. David took the wife of another man. He violated not only Bathsheba, but also the dignity and ultimately life of the Hittite.
9. The practice of skipping a name or a generation was acceptable in constructing genealogies. See Nancy Dawson, *All the Genealogies of the Bible* (Grand Rapids: Zondervan Academic, 2023).
10. Samuel Emadi, *From Prisoner to Prince: The Joseph Story in Biblical Theology*, NSBT (Downers Grove, IL: IVP Academic, 2022), 140n49.
11. See the excellent treatment by Amy Peeler, *Women and the Gender of God* (Grand Rapids: Eerdmans, 2022).
12. Hays prefers the term "figural reading." See David B. Capes, "Typology," in *Encyclopedia of the Historical Jesus*, ed. Craig A. Evans (London: Routledge, 2008). Also see Leonhard Goppelt, *Typos: The Typological Interpretation of the Old Testament in the New*, trans. D. H. Madvig (Grand Rapids: Eerdmans, 1982), published originally in 1939 in German. Goppelt makes the case that a typological interpretation of Scripture is the main strategy by which New Testament writers read the Old Testament and thought out their theologies. And many post-New Testament writers continued the practice.
13. Richard Hays, *Reading Backwards: Figural Christology and the Fourfold Gospel Witness* (Waco, TX: Baylor University Press, 2014), 162.
14. Erich Auerbach, *Mimesis* (Princeton, NJ: Princeton University Press, 1968), 73.
15. Hays, *Reading Backwards*, 2–3.

MATTHEW 2

1. As I was working on this book, I became aware of an important new book: Eric Van-den Eykel, *The Magi: Who They Were, How They've Been Remembered, and Why They Still Fascinate* (Minneapolis: Fortress, 2022).

2. John J. Collins, *The Scepter and the Star: Messianism in Light of the Dead Sea Scrolls*, 2nd ed. (Grand Rapids: Eerdmans, 2010), has written the classic treatment on these themes demonstrating that Balaam's oracle was widely accepted as having messianic overtones (see especially 71–73). See CD 7:19; *4QTestimonia*; *1QM* 11.6–7.

MATTHEW 3

1. Josephus (*Ant* 18.116–119) tells how John the Baptist gained popularity among the people. He describes John as a "good man" who urged his fellow Jews to practice righteousness toward one another and piety toward God. The crowds were aroused by the eloquence of his sermons. Because Herod Antipas feared that his movement might lead to sedition, he had John arrested and brought in chains to Machaerus where he was summarily executed.

2. Jonathan Pennington, *Heaven and Earth in the Gospel of Matthew* (Grand Rapids: Baker Academic, 2009), 13–98, argues against the consensus that "heaven"—as in the phrase "kingdom of heaven"—is merely a reverential way of referring to God for a Jewish audience. Instead, he proposes the heaven and earth theme throughout Matthew has the net effect of underscoring the tension between the realm of God and the realm of humankind.

3. Hays, *Reading Backwards*, 96.

4. There is a translation issue that emerges from Isaiah 40:3. The poetry makes it ambiguous. Is the voice, the prophet, supposed to go and cry out "in the wilderness" (thus Mt 3:3 and *1QS* 8.12–14)? or is the way of the LORD to be prepared in the wilderness (thus the Masoretic/Hebrew text)? The Qumran covenanters took this as a mandate to go into the wilderness (the northwest side of the Dead Sea) and prepare the way of the LORD by studying the law of Moses in order to follow what had been revealed there (*1QS* 8.12–14). (The name of God was considered so holy it was not always written; it could be represented by four, thick dots in the middle of the line.)

5. The term *honey* could refer to either the product of bees or a syrup made from sweet fruits like grapes and dates.

6. Jesus is described as the son of a *tekton* (Mt 13:55), which has traditionally been understood as a carpenter. But the word can mean someone who builds with stone, like a mason. Since most building construction was with stone, that may be a better way to understood Jesus' pre-baptism profession.

7. James Dunn, *Jesus and the Spirit: A Study of the Religious and Charismatic Experience of Jesus and the First Christians as Reflected in the New Testament* (Philadelphia: Westminster, 1975), 62.

8. I am using the word *audition* in an atypical sense from modern dictionaries, as something heard or the act of hearing something.

9. Le Peau, *Mark Through Old Testament Eyes*, , 35–37.

10. I am assuming Markan priority here and the likelihood that Matthew used some form of Mark in composing his gospel.

11. Mark Lanier likens Matthew's special use of "behold" to Emeril Lagasse adding spice to a dish: "Bam!" And "Bam! The heavens were opened." Podcast "Emeril Lagasse, *idou*, and the gospel of Matthew," accessed December 16, 2019, https://exegetical-lyspeaking.libsyn.com/emeril-lagasse-idou-and-the-gospel-of-matthew.

12. E.g., Pss 2; 20; 21; 45; 72; 110.

13. David B. Capes, "Intertextual Echoes in the Matthean Baptismal Narrative," *Bulletin of Biblical Research* 9 (1999), 39; Ben Witherington, *The Christology of Jesus* (Minneapolis: Fortress, 1990), 148–49.

14. Christopher Rowland, *The Open Heaven: A Study of Apocalyptic in Judaism and Early Christianity* (New York: Crossroad, 1982), 358. This is not limited to Matthew. Luke records an account of Jesus having a vision of Satan falling from heaven (Lk 10:17–20). David Aune, *The New Testament in Its Literary Environment* (Philadelphia: Westminster, 1987), 226–40, offers a good summary of apocalyptic beliefs and practices during this period.

MATTHEW 4

1. Along the way there are numerous examples of God regularly putting Israel to the test, e.g., when God made the bitter waters of Marah drinkable (Ex 15:25) and when God fed them with manna six days and commanded them to collect more on day six so they could rest on the Sabbath (Ex 16:4).

2. It rained for forty days and forty nights to flood the earth in Noah's day (Ge 7:12); Jonah announced to the people of Nineveh that the city would be overthrown in forty days (Jnh 3:4); the spies sent to scout out the land of Canaan returned after forty days (Nu 13:25); after Elijah retreated to Beer-sheba and partook of God's provision, he "went in the strength of that food forty days and forty nights to Horeb the mount of God" (1 Ki 19:8 NRSV).

3. Noah Hacham, "Fasting," in *T&T Clark Encyclopedia of Second Temple Judaism,* eds. Daniel M. Gurtner and Loren T. Stuckenbruck (London: T&T Clark, 2019), 2:268–70.

4. Deuteronomy is one of the most quoted books in the New Testament and the Dead Sea Scrolls.

5. The "devil" takes him and places him on the pinnacle or highest point of the temple. What kind of experience is this exactly? Is Jesus bodily still in the wilderness? Is he having a vision? Or did the devil track him back to Jerusalem to harangue and harass him? Is it likely that these temptations followed Jesus and latched on to him as he left the wilderness behind?

6. As an example, the word *angle* has a variety of meanings in English, including "to fish."

MATTHEW 5

1. Jonathan Pennington, *The Sermon on the Mount and Human Flourishing: A Theological Commentary* (Grand Rapids: Baker Academic, 2018), makes the case that the best translation of the Greek *makarios* may be "flourishing," but it is unlikely that it means all that moderns mean when they use the term.

2. Quoted from the LXX. Albert Pietersma and Benjamin G. Wright, eds. *A New Translation of the Septuagint: And the Other Greek Translations Traditionally Included under That Title,* trans. Moisés Silva (New York: Oxford University Press, 2007). All LXX translations are taken from this source unless noted otherwise.

3. For a helpful explanation of this and other Beatitudes see Steve Stewart, *The Beatitudes for a Time of Crisis* (Rio Rancho, NM: Impact Nations, 2020).

4. See Psalm 107, a thanksgiving psalm, that describes the exiles' joy in God's provision on the way back to the land. In vv. 6–9, they are described as hungry and thirsty, and yet God satisfies them.

5. David deSilva and James Charlesworth, *Introducing the Apocrypha: Message, Context, and Significance* (Grand Rapids: Baker Academic, 2018), offers a useful introduction to the apocryphal literature and its potential importance in reflecting Jewish perspectives in the Second Temple period.

6. In the narrative of 1 Maccabees there are many examples of those who make peace (1 Maccabees 6:58; 9:70; 10:4; 13:45, 50). In describing how difficult it is for a person to be right before God, Bildad says that God makes peace in heaven (Job 25:2 NRSV). Perhaps the best example of peacemaking on earth is found in the *Proverbs of Solomon* (10.10 NRSV): "Whoever winks the eye causes trouble, but one who rebukes boldly makes peace." The winking of eyes typifies the scoundrel and the villain along with crooked speech and pointing of fingers (Pr 6:12–13). It is interesting to note that peacemaking in 10:10 is not about giving in or appeasing an opponent; it is about a bold and likely public rebuke. Isaiah 27:2–6 echoes the earlier "Song of the Vineyard" (Isa 5:1–7). A day is coming, the oracle says, when a pleasant vineyard will be planted and YHWH himself will be its keeper. And unlike the earlier song that portrays the fruit of the vines as wild and undrinkable, this apocalyptic vineyard flourishes and fills the earth with its fruit. The vineyard is urged to "make peace" with its keeper. Here it is the responsibility of God's people to make peace with him. For God as maker of peace and fashioner of evil see Isa 45:7 (LXX).

7. Harmut Beck and Colin Brown, "Peace" in *The New International Dictionary of New Testament Theology* (Grand Rapids: Zondervan, 1986), 2:776–83. Also, Gerhard von Rad, "εἰρήνη," *TDNT*, 2:402–6. For shalom as God's gift, see Psalm 85.

8. Of course, too much salt in the earth can turn good ground into a wasteland (Jdg 9:45; Ps 107:34; Jer 48:9; Zep 2:9).

9. We cannot say exactly what Jesus had in mind when he says that salt becomes μωρανθῇ. The root of the word means "folly," which stands in contrast to wisdom. There is a special kind of folly around "religion," as normally reasonable people become unreasonable or people competent in one area of life fall apart in the more vital parts. Perhaps the point here has to do with the possibility that disciples can lose whatever it is that makes them the salt of the earth and thus become useless to the kingdom.

10. Jesus claims to be "the light of the world" in the gospel of John (8:12). The claim is complementary because those who follow him have the light of life. Conformity to Christ is the goal of Christian existence (Ro 12:1–2).

11. The classic work on annihilation of the wicked is by Edward Fudge, *The Fire That Consumes: A Biblical and Historical Study of the Doctrine of Final Punishment*, 3rd ed. (Eugene, OR: Cascade, 2013).

12. Exodus prohibits coveting the neighbor's house before his wife. Deuteronomy reverses the order.

13. Jesus will return to the question of marriage and divorce later, in another context (Mt 19:1–12).

14. The passage is complex and not easily to translate. For a good survey of the interpretive possibilities see Craig Keener, *And Marries Another: Divorce and Remarriage in the Teaching of the New Testament* (Peabody, MA: Hendrickson, 1991). Also see David Instone-Brewer, *Divorce and Remarriage in the Church: Biblical Solutions for Pastoral Realities* (Downers Grove, IL: InterVarsity, 2008).

15. See Carmen Joy Imes, *Bearing God's Name: Why Sinai Still Matters* (Downers Grove, IL: IVP Academic, 2019).

16. In the laws of restitution, a person could only take a garment in pledge of a debt during the daylight hours; it had to be returned in the evening so the debtor could stave off the cold of the night (Ex 22:26–27; cf. Dt 24:12–13). In the case of Jesus, his clothes would not be returned.

17. Quoted in *The Dead Sea Scrolls Translated: The Qumran Texts in English*, trans. Florentino García Martínez (Leiden: E. J. Brill, 1994).

18. Pennington, *The Sermon on the Mount*, 204–5.

MATTHEW 6

1. David J. Downs, *Alms: Charity, Reward, and Atonement in Early Christianity* (Waco, TX: Baylor University Press, 2016), 1–26, proposes that almsgiving in the early centuries of the Christian church was regarded by many Christians as having an atoning effect. This did not replace the atoning death of Jesus, but it operated in some manner as covering or atoning for sins.
2. Psalm 113:1–2 offers praise to "the name of YHWH" and states: "blessed be the name of the Lord/YHWH from this time on and forevermore" (NRSV).
3. See the discussion in G. R. Beasley-Murray, *Jesus and the Kingdom of God* (Grand Rapids: Eerdmans, 1986), 17–25.
4. N. T. Wright, *Paul and the Faithfulness of God* (Minneapolis: Fortress, 2013), 633–45. Wright goes on to say that the return of YHWH to Zion is the origin of Christology (654).
5. Beasley-Murray, *Jesus and the Kingdom of God*, 20.
6. The King James (Authorized) Version was right to leave it untranslated: "Ye cannot serve God and mammon."
7. On the *Elohim*, see Michael S. Heiser, *The Unseen Realm: Recovering the Supernatural Worldview of the Bible* (Bellingham, WA: Lexham, 2015), 314–21.
8. The technique known as *qal vahomer* is listed among Hillel's seven exegetical principles.

MATTHEW 7

1. I quote the King James Version here primarily because it is so often quoted by others.
2. John R. W. Stott, *The Message of the Sermon on the Mount (Mt 5–7)* (Downers Grove, IL: InterVarsity, 1978), 180–83.
3. With the emphasis in this sermon on wisdom, one should consider as well what the wisdom tradition says. Proverbs 11:22 regards the beautiful woman without sense to be like a gold ring in a pig's snout. Proverbs 23:9 indicates that it is better not to speak at all in the presence of a fool who will only despise your wisdom.
4. Quoted from https://www.sefaria.org/Shabbat.31a.6?lang=bi&with=Sheets&lang2=en (accessed March 6, 2020).
5. Israel is referred to in various places in Scripture as the vineyard and the vine (e.g., Isa 1:8; Ps 80:8–16; Hos 10:1).
6. Scott Brazil, "The Significance of Old Testament YHWH-Texts Applied to Jesus in the Synoptic Gospels" (PhD diss., Southeastern Baptist Theological Seminary, 2022), 81–83.

MATTHEW 8

1. This is not the end of the story, for one of Elisha's servants pursued Naaman to receive payment for his healing, which Elisha initially refused. Prophets were not supposed to take money for their ministry. When Elisha discovered what his servant had done, the disease of Naaman infected the servant.
2. During the time people with "leprosy" are considered unclean, they must live alone outside the city and announce their presence both with an oral warning and in the way they dress.
3. Richard Averbeck, "Reading the Ritual Law in Leviticus Theologically," in *Interpreting the Old Testament Theologically: Essays in Honor of Willem A. VanGemeren*, ed. Andrew Abernethy, 135–49 (Grand Rapids: Zondervan, 2018); Jacob Milgrom, *Leviticus: A Book of Ritual and Ethics* (Minneapolis: Fortress, 2004), 168–69.
4. See, for example, Tobit 6; *1QM* 13.11–12; *Jubilees* 10.10–13.
5. Robert Gundry, *Matthew: A Commentary on His Handbook for a Mixed Church under Persecution*, 2nd ed. (Grand Rapids: Eerdmans, 1994), 150.

6. C. Hassell Bullock, *An Introduction to the Old Testament Prophetic Books* (Chicago: Moody, 1986), 240.

7. John P. Meier, "Matthew, Gospel of," *ABD,* 4:638–39.

8. Larry Hurtado, *Lord Jesus Christ: Devotion to Jesus in Earliest Christianity* (Grand Rapids: Eerdmans, 2003), 290–305; Christopher Tuckett, *Christology and the New Testament: Jesus and His Earliest Followers* (Louisville: Westminster John Knox, 2001), 112–14; Seyoon Kim, *The Son of Man as the Son of God* (Grand Rapids: Eerdmans, 1983).

9. At the end of the gospel when Jesus stands trial before the Council, the "accused" makes it clear what he means by it when he says "the Son of Man" will be seated at the right hand of the Mighty One and coming on the clouds (Mt 26:62–68).

10. Bruce Chilton, "Archaeology and Jesus," in *Encyclopedia of the Historical Jesus,* ed. Craig A. Evans (New York: Routledge, 2008), 32–34.

11. Ulrich Luz, *The Theology of the Gospel of Matthew,* trans. J. Bradford Robinson (Cambridge: Cambridge University Press, 1995), 4–5.

12. Richard Hays, *Echoes of Scripture in the Gospels* (Waco, TX: Baylor University Press, 2016), 67.

13. On the significance of Psalm 82 and the spiritual realm see Michael S. Heiser, *The Unseen Realm: Recovering the Supernatural Worldview of the Bible* (Bellingham, WA: Lexham, 2015), 23–37.

MATTHEW 9

1. Nicholas Perrin, *Jesus the Priest* (Grand Rapids: Baker Academic, 2019), demonstrates the value of understanding aspects of Jesus' ministry in priestly categories.

2. Or sexual assault.

3. Jesus' comment follows the Greek version (LXX) in its call for "mercy" (*eleos*). In the Hebrew it is *chesed,* often translated "steadfast love."

4. In addition to fasts like on the Day of Atonement, the Pharisees appeared to have fasted twice per week (*Did* 8.1; Lk 18:12; *Pss Sol* 3.8). On the textual variant, see Bruce M. Metzger, *A Textual Commentary on the Greek New Testament,* 2nd ed. (New York: United Bible Societies, 1994), 20.

5. The destruction of the first temple in Jerusalem by the Babylonians (586 BC) and the second by the Romans (AD 70) took place on the same day, the ninth day of the Jewish month Av.

6. David B. Capes, Rodney Reeves, and E. Randolph Richards, *Rediscovering Jesus: An Introduction to Biblical, Religious and Cultural Perspectives on Christ* (Downers Grove, IL: InterVarsity, 2015), 31.

7. See E. P. Sanders, *Judaism: Practice and Belief, 63 BCE–66 CE* (London: SCM, 1992).

8. Paul uses sowing and reaping in more of an ethical sense (Gal 6:7).

9. See, e.g., Larry Kreitzer, *Jesus and God in Paul's Eschatology* (Sheffield: JSOT Press, 1987).

MATTHEW 10

1. Otherwise see D. A. Carson, *Exegetical Fallacies,* 2nd ed. (Grand Rapids: Baker Academic, 1996), 28–30, who prefers to render *apostolos* as "special messenger." True enough. A messenger is sent by someone with a message. Sometimes etymology does inform word meaning.

2. Donald Hagner, *Matthew 1–13,* WBC 33a (Nashville: Thomas Nelson, 1993), 276–77.

3. BAGD, 30.

4. The poetry and prophets of the Old Testament are rich in imagery associated with doves. The name "Jonah," for example, means "dove." In the Song of Solomon, the lovers' eyes are compared to doves (Song 1:15; 4:1: 5:12). Doves are creatures who moan

mournfully, as do God's people as they wait for justice and salvation (Isa 59:11). The survivors of Judah are like doves moaning over their iniquity (Eze 7:16). The children of God return from exile in Assyria like doves (Hos 11:11). In Psalm 74, a communal lament for the exiles, the psalmist urges God not to deliver the soul of his dove to wild animals (74:19). Psalm 56, a psalm of lament, may have been chanted, sung, or performed to a melody called "The Dove on Distant Oaks" (NIV).

5. John Nolland, *The Gospel of Matthew: A Commentary on the Greek Text*, NIGTC (Grand Rapids: Eerdmans, 2005), 434–55.

6. We might also mention the Christian disposition toward traveling teachers and missionaries. See, e.g., 3 John 5–8 and Philippians 4:15–20; for a negative example, 2 John 9–11. See Joshua Jipp, *Saved by Faith and Hospitality* (Grand Rapids: Eerdmans, 2017).

MATTHEW 11

1. Simon J. Gathercole, *The Pre-Existent Son: Recovering the Christologies of Matthew, Mark, and Luke* (Grand Rapids: Eerdmans, 2006), 83–192, 253–71.

2. Quoted in John J. Collins, *The Scepter and the Star*, 131–32. Not only are the Isaiah passages above in play, but the release of the captives implies Isaiah 61.

3. Ralph L. Smith, *Micah-Malachi*, WBC 32 (Waco: Word, 1984), 327–28.

4. "Sirach" refers to the author, Jesus, son of Eleazar, son of Sirach (Sirach 50:27). The book is also known as Ecclesiasticus because of its extensive use in the church. It predates Jesus' birth by nearly two centuries. Catholics consider it inspired and part of the canon. Protestants do not accept it; they place it among the Apocrypha. Still it well reflects what pious Jews of that era thought. See David deSilva, *Introducing the Apocrypha: Message, Context, and Significance*, 2nd ed. (Grand Rapids: Baker Academic, 2018).

5. The term "Law" translates the Hebrew "Torah" which may better be translated "teaching" or "instruction," but here Jesus points out that the Law also prophesies.

6. Donald Hagner, *Matthew 1–13*, 305.

7. R. W. L. Moberly, *Old Testament Theology: Reading the Hebrew Bible as Christian Scripture* (Grand Rapids: Baker Academic, 2013), 173–75.

8. There are 430 references to "rest" in the Old Testament in thirty-five of the thirty-nine books. Many of these relate to Sabbath and God's promise of rest for his people. See Stephen Westerholm, "Sabbath," *Dictionary of Jesus and the Gospels*, 716–19 (Downers Grove, IL: InterVarsity, 1992).

9. Brevard Childs, *The Book of Exodus: A Critical, Theological Commentary*, Old Testament Library (Louisville: Westminster, 1974), 594–95.

MATTHEW 12

1. See *m. Shabb* 7.2. Other actions considered "work" on the Sabbath included, among the forty less one: sifting, spinning, weaving two threads, sewing two stitches, writing two letters, curing a hide, building, tearing down, and carrying anything from one place to another. Other Jewish groups at the time, like the community of the Dead Sea Scrolls, appear to have been as or more careful about delineating what constituted "work" (*CD* 10–11).

2. Nicholas Perrin, *Jesus the Temple* (Grand Rapids: Baker Academic, 2012); James Charlesworth, ed., *Jesus and Temple: Textual and Archaeological Explorations* (Minneapolis: Fortress, 2014), 75–94, 145–82.

3. Hays, *Echoes*, 127–28, italics original.

4. Geza Vermes, *The Dead Sea Scrolls in English*, 3rd ed. (New York: Penguin, 1987), 95. On the sectarian nature of this community, see 1–18.

5. Josephus, *Antiquities* 8.46–49, describes how he witnessed one of his own country-men, Eleazar, cast out demons in a public way, employing the smell of a root pre-scribed by Solomon and invoking Solomon's name.
6. Carmen Joy Imes, *Bearing God's Name: Why Sinai Still Matters* (Downers Grove, IL: IVP Academic, 2019).
7. I am grateful to my editor, Andy LePeau, for his insight, reminder, and suggestion.
8. Mark Lanier, *Old Testament Survey* (unpublished manuscript), 2:779. Lanier alerted me to how Paul substitutes "death" for "Sheol" as he quoted Hosea 13:14 (1 Co 15:55: "O death, where is your sting?").
9. Consider Paul's statement of the gospel (1 Co 15:3–5): "For what I received I passed on to you as of first importance: that Christ died for our sins according to the Scrip-tures, that he was buried, that he was raised on the third day according to the Scrip-tures." Paul appears confident that the Scriptures (plural) speak of the Messiah being raised on the third day. Other than Hosea 6:1–2 and Jonah, there are no other con-tenders for the resurrection on the third day.
10. Robin Jensen, *Understanding Early Christian Art* (New York: Routledge, 2000), 171–73.

MATTHEW 13

1. The number eight figures prominently in the Old Testament: (a) circumcision on the eighth day (Ge 17:12; *T. Levi* 12:3); (b) likewise, the firstborn of oxen and sheep were dedicated to God on the eighth day (Ex 22:30); (c) the tabernacle walls to the east consisted of eight frames (Ex 36:8–30); (d) a variety of sacrifices took place on the eighth day (e.g., Lev 14:10, 23; 15:29); Feast of Tabernacles, a seven-day festival, was followed by a special Sabbath on the first (or eighth) day (Lev 23:33–43). Perhaps the most significant from a New Testament perspective is the resurrection of Jesus on the first day of the week (Mt 28), which signified a new creation. In John's gospel, the declaration by Thomas of his faith in Jesus occurs on the eighth day (Jn 20:26–29). See David Capes, "The Eighth Day," A Word in Edgewise (blog), January 9, 2013, https://davidbcapes.com/articles/brief-articles/the-eighth-day/.
2. G. K. Beale, *We Become What We Worship: A Biblical Theology of Idolatry* (Downers Grove, IL: IVP Academic, 2008), 15–17, recognizes the human tendency to imitate those things that we love and admire, often unconsciously. In his study of idolatry in the Scriptures he argues: "What people revere, they resemble, either for ruin or resto-ration." Idolatry involves any claim on a person's life, the soul, that rightly belongs to God.
3. David Garland, *Reading Matthew: A Literary and Theological Commentary on the First Gospel* (New York: Crossroad, 1993), 147.
4. Craig Evans, *To See and Not Perceive: Isaiah 6:9–10 in Early Jewish and Christian In-terpretation,* JSOTSup 64 (Sheffield: JSOT Press, 1989), 110.
5. Among the champions of faith listed in Hebrews 11 are Abel, Enoch, Noah, Abraham, Sarah, Isaac, Jacob, Moses, Rahab, Samson, David, Samuel, and others.
6. Craig Keener, *A Commentary on the Gospel of Matthew* (Grand Rapids: Eerdmans, 1999), 381, italics original.
7. Some people have suggested that it would be better to brand this parable "the parable of the soils" since the sower is the same, the seed is the same, but it is the soils that are different.
8. One approach is found in Ben Witherington III, *Jesus the Sage: The Pilgrimage of Wis-dom* (Minneapolis: Fortress, 2000), 147–208, who makes the case that Jesus presents himself as Wisdom through some of the parables.
9. R. T. France, *The Gospel of Matthew,* NICNT (Grand Rapids: Eerdmans, 2007), 527, discusses a couple of cultivar possibilities for what kind of "mustard" plant this might be.

10. Susan Gillingham, "From Liturgy to Prophecy: The Use of Psalmody in Second Temple Judaism," *CBQ* 64, no. 3 (2002): 470–89, investigates the reciprocal relationship between prophecy and psalmody. The prophets, she opines, "imitated cultic forms, hymns, laments and thanksgivings, and also alluded frequently to the stereotypical language in the psalms" (470).
11. Living creatures with scales and fins are considered kosher; those without them are nonkosher (Lev 11:9–12; Dt 14:9–10).
12. See the groundbreaking book, Chris Keith, Jesus against the Scribal Elite, rev. edi (London: T&T Clark, 2020).
13. There are six laments scattered throughout the first part of the book: Jer 11:18–23; 15:10–21; 17:14–18; 18:18–23; 20:7–13; 20:14–18.
14. William Lane, *Hebrews 9–13*, vol 47b (Dallas: Word, 1991), 390. Among other examples, consider Jeremiah (Jer 20:2–8); Micaiah (1 Ki 22:26–27); Hanani (2 Ch 16:10); Isaiah (*Lives of the Prophets* 1.1).
15. To cite a few examples: (a) the "leper, Matthew 8:1–4; (b) the centurion's servant, Matthew 8:5–13; (c) the paralytic, Matthew 9:2–8; and (d) the two blind men, Matthew 9:27–30.

MATTHEW 14

1. Helen Bond, "Herodian Dynasty," *Dictionary of Jesus and the Gospels*, 2nd ed. (Downers Grove, IL: InterVarsity Press, 2013), 381–82.
2. I am grateful to John Beukema for these insights.
3. John Nolland, *The Gospel of Matthew*, 594.
4. Le Peau notes that the language of "pass by" may also suggest a theophany as found in Exodus 33:19–23; 34:6–7; and 1 Kings 19:11. Le Peau, *Mark Through Old Testament Eyes*, 124–25.
5. Richard Hays, *Echoes of Scripture in the Gospels*, 70–73, regards the Septuagint's version the most important for linking Mark 6:45–52 with Job 9:8.
6. Brazil, "Synoptic Gospels," 95–97.
7. David B. Capes, *Old Testament Yahweh Texts in Paul's Christology*, WUNT 2/47 (Tubingen: J. C. B Mohr, 1992; repr., Waco, TX: Baylor University Press, 2017), 3–5.
8. Brazil, "Synoptic Gospels," 95–97.
9. James D. G. Dunn, "Son of God," in *Encyclopedia of the Historical Jesus*, ed. Craig A. Evans (New York: Routledge, 2008), 587–92. *Fourth Ezra* 7:28–29 describes the Messiah as "my [God's] son."

MATTHEW 15

1. Daniel J. Harrington, *The Gospel of Matthew*, Sacra Pagina (Collegeville, MN: The Liturgical Press, 1991), 231–33.
2. Rodney Reeves, *Matthew*, The Story of God Bible Commentary (Grand Rapids: Zondervan, 2017), 304–5.
3. Peter C. Craigie, *Psalms 1–50*, WBC, vol. 19 (Waco, TX: Word, 1983), 212–13.
4. Ulrich Luz, *Matthew 8–20*, trans. James E. Crouch, Hermeneia (Minneapolis: Fortress, 2001), 338, thinks it is likely that "Canaanite" by Matthew's day meant a Phoenician.
5. This is seen most clearly in the Greek translation of the psalms (LXX, Ps 6:2; 30:9; 85:3).

MATTHEW 16

1. Some take this "rock" as Peter himself; therefore, Peter is the person upon whom the church is built. This becomes the basis for Peter becoming the first "pope." Others take the "rock" as Peter's confession of faith or having a faith like Peter's.
2. F. W. Beare, *The Gospel According to Matthew: Translations, Introduction and Commentary* (San Francisco: Harper & Row, 1981), 355.

3. See Le Peau, *Mark Through Old Testament Eyes,* 272–73.
4. Darrell L. Bock, "Son of Man," in *Dictionary of Jesus and the Gospels,* 2nd ed. (Downers Grove, IL: InterVarsity Press, 2013), 894–900.
5. "Holy ones" could refer to angels or to Christ followers who had fallen asleep in Jesus (1 Th 4:13–18). More often than not, the apostle Paul associated the title "Lord" with eschatological contexts: the coming of the Lord, the day of the Lord, and final judgment. See David B. Capes, *The Divine Christ: Paul, the Lord Jesus, and the Scriptures of Israel* (Grand Rapids: Baker Academic, 2018), 64–71.
6. Roland Murphy, *Proverbs,* WBC 22 (Nashville: Thomas Nelson, 1998), 18.

MATTHEW 17

1. France, *Matthew,* 648.
2. Charles Talbert, *Matthew,* Paidea Commentaries on the New Testament (Grand Rapids: Baker Academic, 2010), 206.
3. Talbert, *Matthew,* 206.
4. Jezebel did her best to kill Elijah (1 Ki 19:2, 10), but the Lord provided and protected him. He appears to have escaped death in his own day (2 Ki 2:9–12).
5. Keener, *Matthew,* 440–41.
6. Keener, *Matthew,* 440–41.

MATTHEW 18

1. Sharon Betsworth, *Children in Early Christian Narratives,* Library of New Testament Studies, ed. Chris Keith (London: T&T Clark, 2015), 92–96.
2. Brian Wintle, "Matthew," in *South Asia Bible Commentary,* ed. Brian Wintle (Rajasthan: Open Door, 2015), 1259–60.

MATTHEW 19

1. Carmen Imes, *Being God's Image,* makes a compelling case that the Hebrew preposition often translated "in" may better be rendered "as." So, rather than human beings made "in God's image," they are made "as God's image," that is, they are to represent God to one another and creation.
2. Most scholars regard this episode as a later addition to the text of John. See Bruce Metzger, ed., *A Textual Commentary on the Greek New Testament* (New York: United Bible Societies, 1975), 219–22. Still it indicates an important disparity between the sexes.
3. Ulrich Luz, *Matthew 8–20,* trans. James E. Crouch, Hermeneia (Minneapolis: Fortress, 2001), 512–13.

MATTHEW 20

1. Joe Kapolyo, "Matthew," in *Africa Bible Commentary,* ed. Tokunboh Adeyemo (Grand Rapids: Zondervan, 2006), 1151–52.
2. Psalm 9 (LXX) contains the Hebrew text of both Psalm 9 and Psalm 10.
3. Nolland, *The Gospel of Matthew,* 823–26.

MATTHEW 21

1. Mark Boda, *The Book of Zechariah,* NICOT (Grand Rapids: Eerdmans, 2016), 753–57.
2. Garland, *Reading Matthew,* 210–11. Tucker S. Ferda, "Doubling Down: Zechariah's Oracle, Judah's Blessing, and the Triumphal Entry in Matthew," *JTS* 71, no. 2 (2020), 486–518, makes an interesting case that Matthew's doubling of the animals stems from messianic exegesis of Zechariah 9:9 along with Genesis 49:10–11.

3. Leviticus 23:39–40 describes how the faithful are to take the fruit of certain trees, palm branches, and boughs of leafy trees and rejoice before the Lord with them during the Feast of Booths (Sukkot). There is no evidence that Jesus' entry took place during the fall feast.

4. James A. Sanders, "A New Testament Hermeneutic Fabric: Psalm 118 in the Entrance Narrative," in *Early Jewish and Christian Exegesis: Studies in Memory of William Hugh Brownlee*, eds. C. A. Evans and W. F. Stinespring (Atlanta: Scholars Press, 1987), 180–90, makes the case that Jesus' enactment and the crowd's actions would have been deemed blasphemous were they not making a messianic claim.

5. Psalms 113–118 were known as the Egyptian Hallel. Psalms 113–114 were chanted prior to the Passover meal, Psalms 115–118 after.

6. Jesus and the New Testament writers have a habit of connecting Scripture passages which have a similar theme or catchword. In this case, both passages deal with the temple. He brings them together in complementary fashion. Other Jewish and Christian interpreters at the time did the same thing (Ro 4:7–8 [Ge 15:6; Ps 32:1–2]; Ro 9:25–29 [Hos 2:23, 2:1; Isa 10:22, 28:22, 1:9]; 1 Pe 2:4–8 [Isa 28:16; Ps 117:22, LXX; Isa 8:14]; *4QTestimonia*). Donald Juel, *Messianic Exegesis: Christological Interpretation of the Old Testament in Early Christianity* (Philadelphia: Fortress, 1988), 40–42. Steve Moyise, *Paul and Scripture: Studying the New Testament Use of the Old Testament* (Grand Rapids: Baker Academic, 2010), 37.

7. C. H. Dodd, *According to the Scriptures: The Substructure of New Testament Theology* (London: Nisbet, 1952), 35–36, described the threefold witness to this passage as a *testimonium*.

8. Some manuscripts of Matthew do not have 21:44; thus, some translations skip from v. 43 to v. 45. However, the presence of this saying in many early and reliable manuscripts make it likely that it is original. See Metzger, *Textual Commentary*, 58.

9. For a classic treatment of how early Christians read and interpreted their Bible, see Richard N. Longenecker, *Biblical Exegesis in the Apostolic Period*, 2nd ed. (Grand Rapids: Eerdmans, 1999). On the principles and practice of Jewish midrashic interpretation, see especially 18–24.

MATTHEW 22

1. Lady Wisdom stands in contrast to the "strange" or "loose" woman (Pr 5–7) who invites those lacking wisdom into sexual indulgence; such liaisons lead to great pain, embarrassment, and loss.

2. W. D. Davies and Dale C. Allison, *Matthew: A Shorter Commentary* (London: T&T Clark, 2004), 374–75.

3. Craig Blomberg, *Matthew*, NAC, vol. 22 (Nashville: Broadman, 1992), 332–33.

4. Forth Maccabees 7 contains a eulogy of praise for a holy man named Eleazar. He endured a season of torture and ridicule and kept his emotions in check. Reason guided him. Those who attend to religion with their whole heart are able to control their passions for they know that "they, like our patriarchs, Abraham and Isaac and Jacob, do not die to God, but live to God" (7:16–19).

5. Andrew Le Peau offered me the following observation: "A partial answer may be the trajectory of questions, which appear to lessen in intensity from the question about authority (21:23) to taxes (22:17) to resurrection (22:28) to what becomes an easier question on the law (22:36) to Jesus actually throwing a question back at them. Matthew may thus show Jesus' superiority/victory over his opponents."

6. Davies and Allison, *Matthew*, 384–85.

7. David B. Capes, *The Divine Christ: Paul, the Lord Jesus, and the Scriptures of Israel* (Grand Rapids: Baker Academic, 2018), 2–12.

8. Hays, *Echoes of Scripture*, 53–57. Jesus' riddle requires a "redefinition" of the "Son of David" title.

9. David M. Hay in *Glory at the Right Hand: Psalm 110 in Early Christianity*, SBL Monograph Series, no. 18 (Nashville: Abingdon, 1973), provides a classic investigation into the Jewish background and early Christian use of Psalm 110. The practice begins in the New Testament and continues into the post-apostolic period (e.g., *1 Clement* 36:5–6; *Barnabas* 12:10–11).

MATTHEW 23

1. Lee I. Levine, *The Ancient Synagogue: The First Thousand Years* (New Haven, CT: Yale University Press, 2000), 322–27.
2. Regarding the phenomena of prayer in the Second Temple period, see Jeremy Penner, *Patterns of Daily Prayer in Second Temple Period Judaism,* Studies on the Texts of the Desert of Judah (Leiden: Brill, 2012).
3. On Jewish prayer practices at the time, see Paul Bradshaw, *The Search for the Origins of Christian Worship* (Oxford: Oxford University Press, 1992), 1–29. The Mishnah requires a minyan, a quorum comprised of ten Jewish men, for certain prayers to be made (*m. Meg* 4.3).
4. Allen Verhey, *The Great Reversal: Ethics and the New Testament* (Grand Rapids: Eerdmans, 1984).
5. "Woe" is pronounced in Numbers (21:29, against Moab), Job (10:15, against Job), Psalms (32:10, against the wicked), and Proverbs (23:29, against drunkards).

MATTHEW 24

1. Duane F. Watson, "Michael," *ABD*, 4:811.
2. The word *oracle* itself has at its root a "burden."
3. Al Wolters, *Zechariah,* Historical Commentary on the Old Testament (Leuven: Peeters, 2014), 413–25.
4. Note the correlation of this passage with Jesus' entry into Jerusalem on the back of a beast of burden (Mt 21:1–10).
5. This seems to be the import of Jesus' analogy. Those taken are taken in judgment. Those left are the rescued from peril. This becomes increasingly clear in Luke's version of this teaching which goes into more detail (Lk 17:22–37). After Jesus teaches his disciples about the days of Noah and the days of Lot and its similarity to the arrival of the Son of Man, the disciples inquire, "Where, Lord?" The natural meaning is "Where are they taken, Lord?" not "Where are they left"? Jesus responds, "Where the corpse is, there the vultures will gather."

MATTHEW 25

1. Brian Wintle, "Matthew," *South Asia Bible Commentary* (Grand Rapids: Zondervan, 2015), 1276, makes an interesting point that the last servant tries to cover up his laziness by presenting a false view of the Master.
2. Notice the close connection between folly and wickedness in Ecclesiastes 7:25; 10:13.
3. Talbert, *Matthew,* 274–75.
4. Beare, *The Gospel According to Matthew,* 492.
5. For example, Enoch (Ge 5:24) is described as a chief agent of God in Jewish literature. He seems to be associated with the "Son of man" in *1 Enoch* 37–71. In later Jewish literature, he is glorified and takes on angelic aspect (*3 Enoch*). See Larry Hurtado, *One God, One Lord: Early Christian Devotion and Ancient Jewish Monotheism,* 3rd ed. (London: T&T Clark, 2015), 17–96.
6. Sigurd Grindheim, *God's Equal: What Can We Know about Jesus' Self-Understanding?* LNTS 446 (London: T&T Clark, 2011), 220; Andrew Ter Ern Loke, *The Origin of Divine Christology,* SNTSMS 169 (Cambridge: University Press, 2017), 173.

7. See Matthew W. Bates, *Salvation by Allegiance Alone: Rethinking Faith, Works, and the Gospel of Jesus the King* (Grand Rapids: Baker Academic, 2017). Bates advocates the power of the gospel is diminished when Jesus followers do not understand the nature of faith. He proposes "allegiance" as an appropriate response to the gospel since Jesus is in fact the King (Messiah).

8. Another possible interpretation of this passage is that the nations are gathered and judged for how they dealt with Jesus' followers in the period from Jesus' execution to his Parousia. If this is the case, Jesus is identifying with those who have become his disciples, not necessarily all the poor and imprisoned.

9. Among the former prophets of the Hebrew Bible are books often classified as "history": Joshua, Judges, 1–2 Samuel, 1–2 Kings.

MATTHEW 26

1. Simon had been healed earlier but still carried the epithet "the leper." See Robert Mounce, *Matthew*, New International Biblical Commentary (Peabody, MA: Hendrickson, 1991), 239.

2. David Daube, *New Testament and Rabbinic Judaism* (New York: Athlone, 1956), 315.

3. Luke 22:3 indicates that Satan entered Judas.

4. Mark Boda, *Haggai, Zechariah*, The NIV Application Commentary (Grand Rapids: Zondervan, 2004), 461, describes this as a "prophetic sign-act" that consists of three parts: (a) exhortation, (b) execution, (c) explanation.

5. Boda, *Haggai, Zechariah*, 463. The referent is unclear. To what covenant does the prophet refer?

6. Even if the slave is not killed, he/she is likely injured so badly that the slaveowner must care for him/her for the rest of their lives. So the price paid, while handsome, is in reparation for value lost.

7. Yoilah Yilpet, "Zechariah," in *Africa Bible Commentary*, ed. Tokunboh Adeyemo (Grand Rapids: Zondervan, 2006), 1088.

8. In Judaism "food" is not "blessed." The faithful bless and thank God for the food. The food is already a blessing. One of earliest blessings recorded is the *Birkat HaMazon*: "Blessed are you, O LORD, Our God, King of the World, who brings forth bread from the earth."

9. This establishes the tradition that Moses wrote some or perhaps all of the Torah. That is why Genesis, Exodus, Leviticus, Numbers, and Deuteronomy are referred to as "the Books of Moses."

10. Their political alliances are cast in language stout with explicit sexual acts and violent responses from their "lovers." These disturbing images demonstrate the depths of their infidelity to YHWH and foreshadow the coming wrath of God toward his unfaithful people. This wrath is described again in explicit language as a cup of wrath. Oholibah (Jerusalem) is to drink her sister's cup (Oholah/Samaria). She will be scorned and mocked, filled with drunkenness and sorrow; Jerusalem will drain "the cup of ruin and desolation, the cup of your sister Samaria" (Eze 23:33).

11. John P. Meier, "Matthew, Gospel of," *ABD*, 4:635.

12. Robert Gundry, *Matthew: A Commentary on His Handbook for a Mixed Church under Persecution,* 2nd ed. (Grand Rapids: Eerdmans, 1994), 539–40.

13. Rudolf Schnackenburg, *The Gospel of Matthew*, trans. Robert Barr (Grand Rapids: Eerdmans, 2002), 277.

MATTHEW 27

1. Joe Kapolyo, "Matthew," in *Africa Bible Commentary*, ed. Tokunboh Adeyemo (Grand Rapids: Zondervan, 2006), 1167, draws attention to Matthew's contrast between Peter and Judas. Peter wept bitterly, but made no attempt to undo what he did. Judas, on the

other hand, felt great remorse, tried to reverse course, and committed suicide. Rather than trying to work oneself back into God's favor, we ought instead to rely on God and his mercy when we sin, even when we sin gravely.

2. See the blood-guilt language inherent in passages like Leviticus 20:9; Deuteronomy 19:10; 2 Samuel 1:16; and Ezekiel 33:4–6.

3. France, *Matthew*, 1056–59.

4. Ross Shepard Kraemer, *The Mediterranean Diaspora in Late Antiquity: What Christianity Cost the Jews* (Oxford: Oxford University Press, 2020), investigates the actions powerful Christians took against the Jews and their results on diminishing Jewish culture in the centuries following the ascendency of Christianity in the Roman Empire.

5. The fact that Jesus dies as an innocent sufferer only magnifies the offense.

6. Jennifer M. Rosner, *Finding Messiah: A Journey into the Jewishness of the Gospel* (Downers Grove, IL: IVP, 2022), 139–41, makes an artful case for this ironic reading of the crowd's statement.

7. Rodney Reeves, *Matthew*, The Story of God Bible Commentary (Grand Rapids: Zondervan Academic, 2017), 547, thinks that all the details are on display in Psalm 22 for an event like a crucifixion. This may be why Jesus' mind goes to Psalm 22 as he quotes its opening verse. Jesus "connected the dots, watching Scripture be fulfilled before his eyes." Enemies might have concluded that God had abandoned Jesus, but Jesus saw it differently.

8. Brian Wintle, *South Asia Bible Commentary: A One-Volume Commentary on the Whole Bible,* ed. Brian Wintle (Rajasthan: Open Door, 2015), 1282.

9. Reeves, *Matthew*, 547.

10. R. T. France, *Matthew: Evangelist and Teacher* (Downers Grove, IL: InterVarsity, 1987), 209.

11. Craig Blomberg, *Matthew*, New American Commentary, vol. 22 (Nashville: Broadman, 1992), 420–21.

12. Suggested by Mark Lanier, "Chapter 17—Snapshots of Jesus as Seen through the Gospels; Gospel of Matthew," May 9, 2022, https://www.youtube.com/watch?v=9RIqyunh4mw&t=160s. God's reasons for tearing the temple veil from top to bottom, shaking the earth, and splitting the rocks at the death of Jesus are likely complex.

13. The first vision is recorded in Ezekiel 1:4–28; the second in 8:1–11:25; the third in 37:1–14; and the fourth in 40:1–48:35.

14. Harrington, *Matthew*, 401–2.

15. France, *Matthew*, 209.

16. Harrington, *Matthew*, 403.

MATTHEW 28

1. J. Richard Middleton, *A New Heaven and a Near Earth: Reclaiming Biblical Eschatology* (Grand Rapids: Baker Academic, 2014), 105–7.

2. It is unclear whether this was the Tigris or the Euphrates River.

3. In the sequel to Luke's gospel, one of the first things the followers of Jesus did was to add Matthias to (re)constitute "the Twelve" (Ac 1:12–26). If Matthew had written a sequel, would he have included the same thing?

SCRIPTURE INDEX

Note: All Scripture references are indexed except for those in Matthew.